The Purpose of Playing

THEATER: THEORY/TEXT/PERFORMANCE

Series Editors: David Krasner and Rebecca Schneider
Founding Editor: Enoch Brater

Recent Titles:

THE PURPOSE OF PLAYING

Modern Acting Theories in Perspective

By Robert Gordon

The University of Michigan Press
Ann Arbor

2009   2008   2007   2006   4   3   2   1

A CIP catalog record for this book is available from the British Library.

Library of Congress Cataloging-in-Publication Data

Gordon, Robert, 1951–
    The purpose of playing : modern acting theories in perspective /
Robert Gordon.
    p.   cm.
    Includes bibliographical references and index.
    ISBN-13: 978-0-472-09887-3 (cloth : alk. paper)
    ISBN-10: 0-472-09887-X (cloth : alk. paper)
    ISBN-13: 978-0-472-06887-6 (pbk. : alk. paper)
    ISBN-10: 0-472-06887-3 (pbk. : alk. paper)
    1. Acting.   2. Acting—History.   I. Title.
PN2061.G66   2006
792.02'8—dc22   2006011677

For Susan and Janet

Acknowledgments

For permission to reprint extracts from John Willett, ed. and trans., *Brecht on Theatre* I grate-fully acknowledge Methuen. Extracts from Susan Sontag, ed., *Artaud: Selected Writings,* trans. Helen Weaver are reprinted by kind permission of Farrar, Straus and Giroux, New York. I want to thank Enoch Brater and the editorial staff of the University of Michigan Press for their encouragement and support of this project; Anna Lobbenberg for picture research; Olaf Jubin, Peter Lobbenberg, and Sam Aaron for their kind assistance in proofreading the draft type-script; and Brian Pearce for his comments on a number of draft chapters. My gratitude is due to Naomi and Peter Lobbenberg and to Olaf Jubin for their unstintingly generous support of my work on this book in all sorts of ways.

Contents

Introduction

Acting is a human activity that seems so natural it can at times be difficult to recognize as art. Role-play is inherent in the notion of society. In the process of becoming a human individual the baby learns to play a role, using an instinct for mimicry to define its own identity in relation to its mother and father, and developing a consciousness of self in a process that involves the rehearsal and enactment of a primal family drama. Consciousness of the distinction between self and other is concomitant with an awareness that it is possible to pretend. As the child learns to perform deliberate actions, it learns to *play*.

Some kind of theater-making activity is common to most cultures; however, the verb *to act* has two different meanings. These meanings are complementary and in some respects overlap. In one sense, acting signifies *doing* (i.e., action in the real world); in a secondary sense it signifies *pretending to do* (i.e., symbolic action), usually through the assumption of a role that may be indicated by the wearing of a mask or costume. In virtually all societies, acting in the sense of symbolic action has an important function, not only as theater but also in the rituals and ceremonies, both religious and secular, through which the society defines and advertises its identity. Every individual plays more than one social role. Social role-playing is a spontaneous human activity. Children learn to act in this sense by playing games. The instinctive aptitude for such role-playing provides the foundation for the development of acting as an art. Acting in the sense of *doing* is thus intimately connected with the sense of acting as *pretending*. Although doing and pretending (purposive action and playacting) may often seem indistinguishable, the child already possesses a subtle ability to separate one kind of acting from another.

For the student and teacher of acting, the apparent "naturalness" of acting as a human function is both a blessing and a problem. Most amateurs assume that because they have some intuitive talent as mimics, they can act. Although in some sense this is true, acting as an art requires the performer to make a break with the spontaneous activity of mimetic role-play in order to cultivate its craft as a conscious form of representation. To be artistically effective, acting must be removed from the context of lived experience and viewed as a part of the artistic process of theater-making, even while it may employ much of the behavioral repertoire of social role-playing. The subject of this book is acting as an aspect of theater art.

All theatrical performance starts from the assumption that a performer is using her body to represent a virtual body. The actor's creation of a virtual body transforms an actual place demarcated as a playing space into a virtual place. Real time is transformed into virtual time for the duration of the performance. For the actor, the central paradox of acting is always the way in which her real body is used to represent a virtual body. No matter what aesthetic forms are employed, or how abstract the conception of the performing body is, the actor's body must always be cultivated as an instrument capable of varied and subtle expressive forms. All theories of acting start from this point, but each proposes a different solution according to *what* each aims to represent, and *for what purpose* the representation is being made.

Methodologies and Myths

Perhaps because acting is a practice at the core of all cultural expression, articulating social values "invisibly" as well as being overtly the medium in which dramatic writing is communicated, the question of what acting is and what constitutes "good acting" is hotly debated. Battles between rival schools of thought and practice on the subject of actor training are common today, as indeed they have been at various times throughout history. The actor's body and voice may themselves become the subject of argument.[1]

Most handbooks on acting aim to persuade the student actor that there is *one* correct approach to acting—that a particular set of techniques and attitudes will produce good acting, whereas others are unhelpful or even harmful to the student. Discourse is commonly framed in such a way that one is led to assume that the word *acting* signifies a coherent body of practice—that at its best there is one thing that acting *is*. Teachers will often point out a famous actor as exemplar of "great acting" without making the necessary observation that he demonstrates the values of a particular tradition of performance. Each acting tradition consists of the peculiar possibilities and limitations formed by an ideology constitutive of a particular culture.

Today's actor should understand the relationship between the techniques being acquired in rehearsal and training and the meanings they are designed to express. Acting technique is never devoid of social or political significance. *What* is expressed is a product of *how* it is being expressed. In surveying the relationship between twentieth-century ideas about acting and its techniques, this book aims to comprehend the different possibilities offered to the practitioner and the spectator by the major aesthetic traditions that constitute Western theatrical performance in the new millennium.

To talk about acting in a theatrical context today, one may need to consider such diverse kinds of performance as the delivery of an aria in a grand opera, the real behavior of a group of people at a street event, a clown act in a circus, and a completely "lifelike" portrayal of a fictional character in a television drama. At one level, each of these is a distinct mode of performance, entailing a particular methodology of training and a unique technique of presentation. Most actors today are trained according to the one method favored by their particular teacher or school. Most often the specific approach is not taught in a conscious or critical process, but is absorbed *experientially* by the student as a unique set of practices. During the course of their training, students are transformed into competent expressive instruments, able to actualize the performance aesthetic that they have unconsciously absorbed, and to function effectively as a particular kind of performer. Problems occur when, during the course of their professional careers, actors are asked to create performances utilizing techniques and stage conventions other than the ones in which they were schooled. These problems arise not merely because actors are unfamiliar with the alien conventions and techniques, but also because their performing identity has already been formed by the aesthetic they have unself-consciously absorbed in training. Asking a Strasberg-trained actor to perform in a Brechtian style is a bit like asking an American football player to adapt his particular physical skills to the demands of a game of tennis.

In order to be able to utilize the wide range of performance vocabularies that are current in contemporary theater, an actor needs to be aware of the variety of aesthetic traditions that coexist in opposition or parallel, or that cross-fertilize to produce new traditions. Few actors can or wish to encompass all the different aesthetic modes available at any given historical moment, but as we become increasingly aware that we live in a culturally diverse world, it is more important than ever for actors to be conscious of the limitations of the tradition within which their initial training has located them, in order to be free to learn and adopt new methodologies of performance if necessary.

Recurrent debates among practitioners and critics in Britain and the United States are often formulated in terms of the following questions:

- Are there universal acting problems that can be addressed in forms of "preexpressive" training, innocent of cultural or ideological bias?[2]
- More specifically, does the notion of training the voice and body carry with it inherent values that ultimately ensure that the actor's identity is tailored to fit a stereotype of "normality"?[3]
- Should the actor work from the "outside in" (commonly associated with the traditional British acting practice of characterization through techniques of voice and movement) or from the "inside out" (somewhat misleadingly assumed to be a Stanislavskian approach)?[4]
- Does Stanislavski's system involve an exclusively naturalistic approach to acting and production, or can it be used as a training and rehearsal method for other kinds of theater?[5]
- Is Lee Strasberg's influential "Method" a faithful version of Stanislavski's system?
- Is the actor an interpreter who must remain "faithful" to the text or a creator who reinvents the play in performance?[6]
- If the former, how is it possible for her to ensure fidelity to the text?
- Should the actor work "intuitively" in rehearsal (as is common in the British theater) or follow a systematic approach to the rehearsal process (as is more often the case in the United States and eastern Europe)?
- Should the actor be conscious of style in acting?[7]
- What is the status of Brecht's performance theories? Should his plays be performed in accordance with his acting theories?
- Is the actor preeminent in the theater-making process, or is she merely an instrument manipulated by the director to produce signs with no more status than stage props or lighting?[8]

An exploration of these questions reveals that in most cases no general answer can be given. Although very commonly raised by Western practitioners and critics, each would be differently answered by practitioners in accordance with the viewpoint represented by the acting tradition in which they were situated. As generally expressed, each question conceals assumptions and problems that reflect the particular perspective and set of prejudices of the questioner. This is because when theatrical innovators propound their ideas or theorize their practices, they do not usually explain what they do in wholly rational terms. Like most artists, they have recourse to rhetorics aiming to persuade us (and themselves) that their approach is the "true" way to creativity. Each of these rhetorics becomes a kind of shorthand by means of which they can indicate the particular attitudes and methods of their craft, but at the same time each rhetoric constructs an aesthetic vocabulary that aims to validate the artistic process it ostensibly describes. These rhetorics function as myths, *justifying* the principles they express. As with any discourse of culture, these "myths" are themselves the product of ideology. Therefore, when we try to make sense of the ideas and working methods of various theater practitioners, it is important to identify the "myths" or systems of belief (with their concomitant ideological inscriptions) that generate their rhetorics.

The Purpose of Playing is an attempt to introduce conceptual clarity into discussions of twentieth-century Western acting by identifying the ideas that underlie the major alternative traditions as manifested in the rhetorics and practices of rehearsal and training. My analysis of key practitioners and theorists in their historical contexts is intended to suggest the outline of a conceptual framework. The taxonomy of categories I have produced is intended to enable the reader to grasp the dialectical relationship between major traditions of performance, arguments over which are obfuscated by the lack of an agreed terminology.

This is not a technical handbook of current theater practice, although I believe it will stand as a guide to contemporary practice. It is rather an attempt to relate theory and practice in an effort to locate the theorized practice (praxis) that manifests itself in the various modes of acting current in the new millennium. All of these modes have their origins in traditions formed during the twentieth century. To do this successfully, I must at times demystify and demythologize areas of practice. Discussions of acting have, on the one hand, long been dominated by artists, teachers, and "gurus" who have tended to produce highly personal books describing their own working methods in the form of manifestoes. On the other hand, performance has been analyzed by scholars of performance studies, with its various critical methodologies derived from anthropology, semiology, sociology or cultural studies. This book attempts to bridge the gap that exists between these two modes of discourse, to provide practitioners with a conceptual vocabulary and knowledge that will permit them to contextualize their own practice within the wider field of performance, and conversely to encourage theorists and scholars to be more sensitive to the material realities of artistic practice.

My choice of exemplary practitioners is not intended to privilege either mainstream or avant-garde, but to examine the work of those practitioners without whose contribution the contemporary traditions of Western acting could not be properly understood. By identifying the tensions between mainstream and alternative theatrical practice I intend to map the points at which actual changes have occurred in the practice and conceptualization of theatrical performance, as well as those where alternatives might promote change within the mainstream.

Six Major Approaches

Six major approaches to acting can be identified in twentieth-century Western theater, each valorized by its own "myth" or explanation through which each asserts its value (chapters in which the approach is discussed are listed):

1. Realistic approaches to characterization: acting as psychological truth (chap. 2)
2. The actor as scenographic instrument: performance as artifice (chap. 3)
3. Improvisation and games: theater-making as play (chaps. 4–7)
4. Performance as political praxis: acting as rehearsal for change (chaps. 8–9)
5. Exploration of the self and the other: acting as personal encounter (chaps. 10–11)
6. Performance as cultural exchange: playing one's otherness (chaps. 12–13).

The terms of modern acting were established between Stanislavski's foundation of the First Studio in 1909 and the start of World War II. Six practitioners—Craig and Meyerhold (who independently elaborated consonant conceptions of the actor), Stanislavski, Copeau, Artaud, and Brecht—replaced the paradigms of nineteenth-century acting with new models appropriate to modernist notions of theater. From the matrix of their ideas developed the first five traditions listed above, the first phase in the history of modern Western acting. A wide range of recent and contemporary practices take one of these traditions as a starting point, although more recent practitioners often try to synthesize specific ideas and practices from opposed or parallel traditions in attempts to establish new performance aesthetics with new techniques and training methods. At this moment, the sixth category demands recognition as a tradition distinct from the others: performance as cultural exchange. This derives from the idea of performance as personal encounter, but by the late 1970s had differentiated itself from the earlier tradition sufficiently to constitute a distinct category. The new idea is that personal encounters with alien performance traditions provide a necessary technique of alienation from the performer's own inherited culture, allowing her to discover a unique performing identity through an intercultural exchange with a foreign tradition.

In the twenty-first century the six traditions I have identified continue to underpin and motivate the development of theater performance, both mainstream and avant-garde, even though the practices themselves may draw as much on techniques and models from other art forms (visual art, music, and dance) as they do from models of theater performance. The first and third categories have in common a conception of acting as an organic process. Both approaches emphasize the immediate empathic connection between the actor, the character, and the spectator. Opposed to this organic notion is a semiotic view of acting as merely one of the signifying systems within the whole ensemble of theatrical signs that in performance can be identified as mise-en-scène. Associated with a conception of theater-making as an artificial process, this notion of acting is variously exemplified in the work of Craig, Reinhardt, Meyerhold, Piscator, Brecht, the Futurists, the Dadaists, Merce Cunningham, Robert Wilson, and Pina Bausch. The second and the fourth categories share a conception of theater-making as a synthetic process in which the actor merely animates a number of the signifying systems in the process of generating meaning. The fifth and sixth approaches, while insisting on the organic process of the *actor,* regard the principle of montage as the *director's* structural device. The director thus mixes the artifice of a semiotic approach to scenic composition with the actor's organic process, permitting the human presence of the actor to remain the definitive component of performance. In an increasingly globalized world, this postmodern tendency to "mix and match" forms and techniques of performance from around the world may well herald the start of a new epoch in the history of performance.

1. Nineteenth-Century Acting

In order to recognize and describe modern acting, we need to know something about the types and traditions of performance from which it emerged and against which it defined itself as new. Whatever claims about the realism of nineteenth-century acting were made in its own time, the performance of a nineteenth-century actor—even in a naturalistic play—would today appear somewhat artificial or stylized. This may be partly attributed to changes in the manners and fashions of social behavior between that period and the present, and partly to the difference between nineteenth-century conventions of theatrical representation and our own.

Conventions of Performance

Pictorial Realism

One of the features of nineteenth-century theater that rendered styles of acting different from those of today was a convention of pictorialism that could be seen at its most striking in the histrionic storms of Gothic melodrama and Romantic verse drama in the first half of the century and at its most subtle in the domestic "teacup and saucer" realism of the productions of Tom Robertson's plays at the Prince of Wales Theatre between 1867 and 1885. As managers and scene painters became progressively more adept at creating two-dimensional scenic illusions of three-dimensional reality, so actors learned to exploit the staging principles of proscenium-arch trompe l'oeil as an expression of the underlying materialism that had motivated its development. The tendency toward realism in acting therefore represented both a shift from an idealist to a materialist view of human nature and a response to the changing architectonics of proscenium-arch staging. Acting was pictorial in the sense of being oriented out front to an audience who viewed it within the pictorial frame of the proscenium arch, and increasingly realistic in its representation of the material features of human behavior. Such changes were in turn motivated by Western culture's increasingly materialist conception of the physical universe.

The nineteenth-century tradition of pictorial realism in scenography can be seen to have originated four centuries earlier in Italian Renaissance theater. This in turn gave rise to Continental opera and ballet and also exerted a powerful influence on Inigo Jones's scenic elaboration of the English court masque in the first three decades of the seventeenth century. The principle of two-dimensional, changeable scenery within a picture-frame stage gradually transformed the courtyard theater of the Renaissance according to the logic of two-dimensional pictorialism that led inevitably (given the technological possibilities of moving pictures) to the cinema.

The dominance of these conventions of pictorial realism was to be observed at their most archaeologically insistent in the productions of Charles Kean at the Princess Theatre during the 1850s and at their most convincingly domestic in the realist productions of Tom Robertson's plays. The development of gas and electric lighting systems and the introduction of the box set equipped theaters with the technology that would promote the development of naturalistic staging until well into the twentieth century. Naturalistic staging principles began to emerge from the coherent historicism of the Duke of Saxe-Meiningen's ensemble productions during the last quarter of the nineteenth century and could be seen fully-fledged in the intimate productions of Antoine's Théâtre Libre in the 1880s and 1890s. Individual actors at the Théâtre Libre (including Antoine himself) were vastly superior to those employed by the Duke of Saxe-Meiningen so that the acting matched the naturalistic coherence of the mise-en-scène.

The advent of naturalistic drama, however, exposed an incipient tension between the terms *pictorialism* and *realism* that nineteenth-century conventions had masked. The orientation of the picture-frame stage toward the audience encouraged the performer to act directly *to* and *for* the audience. However realistically he may have portrayed characters in action, his aim was to move the audience to laughter or tears. In one respect, prenaturalistic acting concentrated on presenting the character's feelings or temperamental attitudes to the audience in the most direct and affecting manner. Eyewitness accounts of great actors such as Sarah Siddons, Edmund Kean, Henry Irving, Sarah Bernhardt, Eleanora Duse, Tommaso Salvini, and others testify to the powerful effect on the audience of their portrayal of intense emotions. While the savoring of intense feelings may have been peculiarly characteristic of Romantic theater, there is no doubt that the actor's ability to affect an audience through a vivid display of feeling—or humor, in comedy and farce—was a persistent feature of nineteenth-century European theater.

Mid-nineteenth-century acting in Britain, France, and Italy was realistic in the sense of developing increasingly sophisticated approaches to the accurate portrayal of symptomatic details of human behavior on stage, but it was nonetheless rhetorical in its aim of illustrating or acting out the thoughts and feelings of the characters so as to affect the spectator. This rhetorical aspect of acting could be traced back to the sixteenth century. The tradition had been successively modified as the visual dimension of theater gradually assumed preeminence over the aural, to the point in the late eighteenth century when the pictorial qualities of acting and scenic spectacle may have predominated over the vocal and rhetorical, more particularly in vast metropolitan theaters that housed audiences of above three thousand.

Goethe's "Rules for Actors" (1803), written as a summation of the principles of the Weimar Court Theatre that he directed between 1791 and 1817, represent an exceptional instance of the survival of a neoclassical theatrical aesthetic in an epoch of nineteenth-century Romantic art. The widespread adoption of Goethe's rules made their influence so pervasive in Germany that even at the end of the century, naturalistic directors such as Otto Brahm had difficulty in persuading actors to relinquish them.

Goethe's rules represented a compromise between the earlier rhetorical approach and the visual logic of the picture-frame stage. The style aimed at was a refined and elegant formalism. Speech was intended to be well modulated and varied, but never arbitrarily emotional: "The art of the actor is made up of speech and bodily movement. . . . As in music the correct, precise, and pure striking of each single tone is the foundation of all further artistic execution, so in the art of the actor the clean and perfect pronunciation of each word is the basis of all higher recitation and declamation. . . . By recitation is understood a delivery which . . . lies midway between cold, quiet speech and highly excited speech. The auditor must always feel that . . . the speech is objective."[1]

Goethe's rules for recitation and declamation were informed by an underlying principle of decorum.[2] He emphasized beauty of vocal tone, precision, standardization of dialect, slight variations of tone and tempo, moderation of feeling, and musicality, but advised against either "monotony" or "singing." His rules of visual composition strike a present-day theatergoer as equally prescriptive and even more formalistic:

First, the player must reflect that he must not only imitate Nature, but must also present her ideally, and that therefore his presentation must unite the true with the beautiful. Hence each part of the body must be completely in his control so that he can make use of each member for the desired expression, freely, harmoniously, and gracefully. Let the position of the body be erect, the chest up, the upper half of the arms to the elbows close to the body, the head turned slightly towards the person to whom one is speaking, yet so slightly that three-quarters of the face is always turned towards the audience. For the actor must constantly remember that he is on the stage for the sake of the public. Accordingly, it is mistaken for the actors to play to each other as if no third person were present; they should never play in profile, nor turn their backs to the audience. . . . The theatre is to be regarded much as a figureless tableau to which the actor adds the figures.[3]

Goethe's prescriptions constitute the most overt and extreme formulation of the pictorial principle in eighteenth- and early-nineteenth-century theater. A full consciousness of the audience was a definitive feature of such acting, which required the actor to perform with a degree of self-consciousness that seemed to preclude any spontaneous feeling. Strange though some of his neoclassical prescriptions may now appear, Goethe did have a coherent grasp of the architectural logic of the proscenium arch stage. He also rationalized clearly the terms of the actor-audience relationship that were dictated by it, in the period before the advent of gas and electric lighting permitted the complete separation of the lit stage and darkened auditorium.

Less prescriptively, a term applied by the French Romantic actor Francois-Joseph Talma—*l'optique du théâtre*—was later employed by the English critic George Henry Lewes in his accounts of nineteenth-century performances to explain the sense of proportion and decorum that guides actors in translating their nervous impulses into "symbols" that would be communicated effectively on the picture-frame stage.[4]

The Logic of Realism

Strictly speaking, the logic of realism dictates that the actor should not *act out* the character or allow the character to *act out* the narrative. The actor as impersonator should become wholly immersed in the character, ceasing to *show* him to the audience in the type of approach perfected by David Garrick, but merely *behave* as the character. The technical conventions of stage naturalism required the actor to disappear behind the character. The advent of naturalism necessitated the elaboration of a technique that would enable actors to portray stage characters without *demonstrating* their temperament to the audience.

Realism of representation was also consonant with the new materialism that motivated the development of science, from the late eighteenth to the early twentieth century. Zola's use of the term "physiological man" to describe the subject of naturalistic drama directly expressed the Darwinist biological science that became the philosophical template for early naturalist drama.[5] The new, slice-of-life drama required the actor to be both analyst and exhibitor of *behavior*. Clearly there could be no place in such a theater for acting that attempted to appeal directly to the spectator's moral judgment by means of rhetoric or to his feelings by means of a display of emotion. The terms of Zola's naturalism required the actor to perform as though completely unaware of the existence of an audience, presenting a fragment of the character's physiological existence as a series of symptoms that exposed his social and biological history.

The Influence of Diderot's *Paradoxe*

Sensibility versus Physical Technique

In *The Player's Passion,* Joseph Roach has demonstrated that the nineteenth-century discourse of acting was dominated by the perspective and terminology of the French philosopher Denis Diderot. The paradox of the actor was identified by Diderot in the opposition of sensibility and premeditated physical technique. This was analogous to the paradoxical spectatorial relationship between pictorialism, through which scenic spectacle directly affected the spectator via the senses and emotions, and realism, which was a principle of representation that determined the treatment of the subject matter of drama according to Enlightenment standards of scientific objectivity. Diderot's *Paradoxe sur le comédien* (written 1773, published 1830) brought into focus late-eighteenth-century arguments about acting to create a paradigmatic text for nineteenth-century acting theorists and practitioners. Throughout the century, French and English actors both wittingly and unwittingly restated Diderot's opposition of sensibility and technique. The French actor Constant Coquelin's *L'art et le comédien* (1880) was directly informed by Diderot. Coquelin's book in turn prompted one of the two major English studies in the period, the critic William Archer's survey of actors' views on their art, published as *Masks or Faces* (1888).[6]

Diderot was concerned to discover whether great acting was produced by the exercise of "sensibility," through which the actor feels the emotions of the role he is playing, or by the mechanical application of an external technique, by means of which the actor's intelligence exercises control over his corporeal instrument. Like David Garrick, who was commonly regarded

as the greatest European actor of the eighteenth century, most late-eigh-
teenth- and nineteenth-century actors would not commit themselves to one
side of the argument, preferring to describe acting as a combination of both
sensibility and physical technique. Diderot eventually decided that great acting was produced by the exercise of technique alone: "extreme sensibility
makes middling actors. . . . in complete absence of sensibility is the possibility of a sublime actor."[7] For Diderot, the paradigmatic example of the actor
who affected the audience through the intelligent exercise of physical technique was Garrick: "Garrick will put his head between two folding doors,
and in the course of five or six seconds his expression will change successively from wild delight to temperate pleasure, from this to tranquility, from
tranquility to surprise, from surprise to blank astonishment, from that to sorrow, from sorrow to the air of one overwhelmed, from that to fright, from
fright to horror, from horror to despair, and thence will go up again to the
point where he started. Can his soul have experienced all these feelings, and
played this kind of scale in concert with his face? I don't believe it, nor do
you."[8]

According to Roach, Diderot anticipated the ideas of nineteenth-century nerve physiology; in analyzing the technique of the eighteenth-century
actor, he observed that it was the spectator who should be moved by the
acting, and not the performer. In this respect, he not only described the
actual working methods of eighteenth-century actors, but seems also to
have anticipated the practice of the majority of actors in the next century.
His description of the actor manipulating his face, voice, and body on behalf
of the dramatist represented an early model of Edward Gordon Craig's conception of the actor as Über-marionette. His insight into the kinesthetic
effect on the spectator of the physical signs of the performance was more
than a century in advance of the biomechanical theories of Meyerhold,
Stanislavski's method of physical actions, the notion of the kinesthetic qualities of performance in the work of Laban and Michael Chekhov, and the
influential notion of the performance score adumbrated by Grotowski and
Barba:

[W]hat of those touching and sorrowful accents that are drawn from the
very depths of a mother's heart and that shake the whole being? Are these
not the result of true feeling? . . . most certainly not. The proof is that
they are all planned; that they are part of a system of declamation; that,
raised or lowered by the twentieth part of the quarter of a tone, they
would ring false . . . that to hit the right mark once, they have been practiced a hundred times; . . . the actor has listened over and over again to

his own voice. At the very moment when he touches your heart he is listening to his own voice; his talent depends, not as you think, upon feeling but upon rendering so exactly the outward signs of feeling, that you
fall into the trap. He has rehearsed to himself every note of his passion.
He has learnt before a mirror every particle of his despair. . . . The broken voice, the half-uttered words, the stifled or prolonged notes of
agony, the trembling limbs, the fainting, the bursts of fury—all this is
pure mimicry, lessons carefully learned . . . which leaves him, luckily for
the poet, the spectator and himself, a full freedom of mind.[9]

Diderot's recognition of the relationship between what the actor performed and what the spectator experienced was complemented by his theory that artistic creation produced an *illusion* of reality rather than an *imitation*. As a philosopher, he would not have considered it his task to reflect
systematically on the technical details of the actor's vocal and physical craft.
His theory of artistic creation did, however, represent in general terms an
explanation of the process by which the actor might construct a convincing
and effective aural-kinetic score guaranteed to provoke appropriate feelings
within the spectator. Diderot believed that the artist created a *modèle idéal* or
inner model of his subject based on a process in which imagination transformed details provided by observation or memory. This inner model
guided the actor in the rehearsal and execution of the physical details of gesture and speech through which the role was expressed. The creative process
was the result of "observation of nature, reflection and experiment. Observation gathers the facts, reflection combines them, experiment verifies the
result of the combination. . . . Rarely does one see these abilities in combination. And so, creative geniuses are not common."[10]
    During the process of reflection, the actor drew upon his stored memo-
ries of gestures, facial expressions, and vocal mannerisms, employing imagination to create a "collection" of passions appropriate to the type being portrayed. The phase of experimentation partly coincided with that of
reflection, involving a process of rehearsal whereby the actor discovered the
precise form of physical and vocal expression through repeated trial and
error. Once the correct form of the inner model had been realized, it
became a blueprint for all future performances. These performances were
achieved by the exercise of pure vocal and bodily technique.
    Nineteenth-century actors and critics of performance saw little need for
a systematic analysis of the relationship between *histrionic expression* and *theatrical signification*. The question of whether the audience experienced the
feelings that Diderot believed the actor to represent through physical signs,

or perceived the representation as behavior and analyzed it objectively, was subsequently addressed by the teacher of oratory Francois Delsarte, who attempted a rudimentary semiology of theatrical speech and gesture. Delsarte's idiosyncratic psychology of emotional expression was entirely speculative, and it was not until the twentieth century that systematic studies of theater semiology and the psychology of spectatorship were undertaken. The relationship between the actor's state and that of the spectator became the crux of a disagreement between Stanislavski and Meyerhold in the first decade of the twentieth century. Modern versions of the psychophysiological technique have either asserted that the physical technique stimulates the actor to feel, which in turn stimulates the reactions of the spectator, or that the physical signs produced mechanically by the actor merely provoke the audience to feel. Brecht, by contrast, insisted that the physical presentation should stimulate the audience to judge rather than to empathize.

Goethe's "Second Nature" and Talma's "Organisation of Sensibility"

Joseph Roach believes that Diderot anticipated most of the significant arguments that were manifested in nineteenth-century accounts of the art of the actor: "At root the question came down to this: Is the actor's bodily instrument to be interpreted as a spontaneously vital organism whose innate powers of feeling must somehow naturally predominate? Or is it best understood as a biological machine, structured by and reducible to so many physical and chemical processes, whose receptivity to reflex conditioning determines its behaviour?"[11]

Most theorists of acting followed Diderot in mediating between the two positions, but the contrast between Goethe's and Talma's resolutions of the apparent contradiction between vitalism and mechanism reveals the typical difference between a director's approach to the problem and an actor's. Goethe reconciled the strict neoclassical formalism of his "Rules for Actors" with a Romantic conception of the artistic process, by describing as the development of a "second nature" the rehearsal process whereby repeated application of the rules of the craft produces the appropriate speech and movements. For Goethe—as for Craig, Meyerhold, Brecht, Robert Wilson, and many other twentieth-century practitioners—acting is subordinate to the process of theatrical composition, and the actor must acquire sufficient technical discipline to control the spontaneous functioning of emotions.

Although the great French actor Talma firmly rejected Diderot's suggestion that good acting was not the product of sensibility, Roach has demonstrated that his argument employed the language and assumptions of Diderot's analysis. His attempt to demonstrate in *Reflections on the Actor's Art*

(1825) that the actor exercises the faculties of both sensibility and intelligence in deploying the physical properties of the medium was a compromise position adopted by many actors in the period.

> [It] is necessary that the actor should have received from nature an extreme sensibility and a profound intelligence. Indeed the strong impressions which actors create on the stage are the result only of the alliance of these two essential faculties. . . . I also call sensibility that faculty of exaltation which agitates an actor, takes possession of his senses, shakes even his very soul, and enables him to enter into the most tragic situations and the most terrible of the passions, as if they were his own. The intelligence which accompanies sensibility judges the impressions which the latter has made us feel; it selects, arranges them, and subjects them to calculation. If sensibility furnishes the objects, the intelligence brings them into play. It aids us to direct the employment of our physical and intellectual forces . . . and sometimes to add the shades that are wanting, or that language cannot express—to complete, in fine, their expression by action and physiognomy.[12]

For Talma, sensibility included not only the ability to be physically and emotionally affected by others and in turn to affect others, but also the "creative, active and powerful" *imagination* that enabled the actor fully to comprehend the physical, emotional, and intellectual life of historical and fictional personages. Talma believed that the actor possessed a "peculiar organisation of sensibility," a "nervous system" that was peculiarly "mobile and plastic." In 1875, this idea informed G. H. Lewes's notion of the "imaginative sympathy" that produced "vibrations" within the actor's body sufficient "to excite the nervous discharge," which Lewes pictured as the physiological aspect of emotional expression.[13] William Archer's analysis in 1888 of the actor's "mimetic emotion" further elaborated on Talma's idea, translating it into the terms of late-nineteenth-century physiology: "[It] is surely illogical to deny the 'reality' of this mimetic emotion, since all emotion, except that which arises from instant physical pleasure or pain, is due to the action of the imagination upon the nerve centres."[14]

Although apparently influenced by Diderot's analysis of the process of artistic creation and by his innovatory ideas of physiology Talma was not concerned, as was the philosopher, to formulate a physiology of human emotions. Talma's career represented the triumph of Romantic principles on the French stage. His equal ranking of the functions of sensibility and intelligence within the artistic process was consonant with Talma's revolutionary politics, and typical of the ideology of romanticism as it manifested itself in the arts early in the nineteenth century. While Diderot's scientific materialism was ahead of its time in anticipating the theories of conditioned reflexes produced by behaviorist psychologists such as Ivan Pavlov at the end of the nineteenth century, the compromise position maintained by Talma represented the predominant understanding actors had of their art throughout the century.

Physical Basis of the Actor's Art: Kean's Technique as Paradigm

Most nineteenth-century actors were at pains to point out that great performances were not the product of technique alone but demanded the engagement of the actor's feelings. On a visit to Edinburgh, Edmund Kean was not reticent in expressing his views on "the genius of Shakespeare, and on the eloquence which elucidated him":

> [Kean] maintained that Shakespeare was his own interpreter, by the intensity and wonderful genius of his language. Shakespeare, he continued, was a study, his deep and scrutinising research into human nature and his sublime and pathetic muse, were to be comprehended only by a capacity alive to his mighty purposes. He had no rhetorician's laws to expound. If a higher estimate was at any time placed upon his performances than upon those of some others . . . he thought it might be due in part to the devotion which he bestowed on the author . . . I have [said he] thought more of intonation than of gesticulation. It is the utterance of human feelings which rises superior to the rules which the professor of rhetoric enjoins. It is the sympathy of mental impression that acts. I forgot the affectation of the art, and relied upon the emotions of the soul.[15]

Kean's views constitute a typically Romantic defense of sensibility as the essential attribute of the great actor. Whatever nineteenth-century actors professed to believe, they apparently made no attempts to develop any consistent method of cultivating sensibility in practice. Kean's approach to acting was more shocking in its vivid use of histrionic and kinesthetic effects than his cautiously conservative explanation of his working method would suggest, but he seems here concerned to represent himself as possessing the spontaneity of the Romantic artist, while at the same time demonstrating respect for the genius of Shakespeare.[16] Coleridge said of him, "To see Kean, was to read Shakespeare by flashes of lightning," and Byron wrote in his diary of Kean's Richard III, "By Jove, he is a soul! Life, nature, truth without exaggeration or diminution." Both these Romantic responses to

Kean's performances perpetuated the myth of the artist as inspired genius, re-creating "nature" by imaginative participation in its organic processes.

It is somewhat paradoxical that the actor so famous for his startling immediacy and intensity of histrionic expression was at times concerned to prove that his performances were not merely the result of inspiration. In contradiction of his defense of sensibility in the acting of Shakespeare, Kean complained in a letter to Garrick's widow of the critics' obtuseness with respect to his physical technique: "These people don't understand their business; they give me credit where I don't deserve it, and pass over passages on which I have bestowed the utmost care and attention. Because my style is easy and natural they think I don't study, and talk about the 'sudden impulse of genius.' There is no such thing as impulsive acting; all is pre-meditated and studied beforehand. A man may act better or worse on a particular night, from particular circumstances; but although the execution may not be so brilliant, the conception is the same."[17] The language in which Kean expressed himself reflects a rather different conception of the actor's art as a technique—a conscious method of physically conveying histrionic effects—which, although it does not exclude the possibility that the actor would feel the passions he is presenting, does not make the actor's sensibility or intuitive capacity to experience what the character is feeling a sine qua non. Even the critics (such as Leigh Hunt and William Hazlitt) who found that his powerful histrionic effects undermined the coherence of his characterizations agreed with those like G. H. Lewes (who wholeheartedly admired Kean's virtuoso displays of emotional volatility) on the careful calculation with which the actor deployed his overtly physical technique in order to manipulate the feelings of his audience. On Kean's American tour in 1821, the reviewer "Betterton" was perspicacious in analyzing the effectiveness of the actor's technique while at the same time recognizing that his "excellencies" had a tendency to become defects when exaggerated or overused: "His studied play of physiognomy borders on grimace; his animation of manner becomes incoherent bustle. . . . He obviously relies more on mechanical resources than on his general mental preparation and powers, or his fervour of feeling and thorough possession of his part. He is called a natural player, but his style of acting is highly artificial and technical; it is uniformly elaborate, systematic, and ambitious. Nothing is left to the inspiration of the moment."[18]

Kean was very influential.[19] His style was imitated by a number of contemporaries and successors, including, at the start of his career, his younger rival, William Charles Macready. Kean's meteoric yet relatively short-lived success helped to perpetuate the image of the actor as an emotionally volatile genius, who nevertheless achieved his effects through the deployment of a virtuoso physical technique. Although able to produce vivid vocal and physical characterizations that were remarkable both for their emotional intensity and variation and for an apparent spontaneity that produced the illusion of life, Kean's portrayals were not noted for their underlying psychological consistency. At the height of the Romantic epoch, turbulence of feelings may have signified a character's sentience more powerfully than a coherent portrayal of psychological identity. Edmund Kean's art was exemplary of early-nineteenth-century English acting in the way it maintained a paradoxical tension between sensibility and technique. After his death, the image of Kean as exemplary actor was perpetuated by G. H. Lewes's appreciative analysis of his acting in *On Actors and Acting* (1875).

Expression and Signification

The manuals of acting that abounded in the eighteenth and early nineteenth centuries aimed to codify the relationship of facial and gestural signs with the emotions they were alleged to signify. The theater historian George Taylor quotes the following example from *The Thespian Preceptor* of 1810: "DESPAIR, as in a condemned criminal *(George Barnwell)* or one who has lost all hope of salvation *(Cardinal Wolsey)* bends the eye-brows downward, clouds the forehead, rolls the eyes and sometimes bites the lips and gnashes with the teeth. The heart is supposed to be too much hardened to suffer the tears to flow; yet the eye-balls will be red and inflamed. The head is hung down upon the breast; the arms are bended at the elbows, the fists clenched hard, and the whole body strained and violently agitated. Groans expressive of inward torture, accompany the words appertaining to his grief; those words are also uttered with a sullen, eager bitterness, and the tone of his voice is often loud and furious."[20]

At times the relationship between the physical sign and the feeling that it expressed was explained in terms of the pseudoscience of physiognomy, and no attempt was made at a properly scientific analysis; the relationship was assumed to be self-evident. As in the above instance, examples were often drawn, not from life, but from traditions of theatrical performance, which merely reinforced a sense of the arbitrariness of the supposed connection between a signifier (gesture or facial expression) and its signified (emotion). The *Physiognomical Bible,* written in 1772 by the Swiss Calvinist minister Johann Kaspar Lavater, aimed to reveal how the passions were expressed in the facial muscles and how the ruling passion, or personality, was reflected

in a person's physical appearance. Such assumptions about the external manifestation of feelings were based on the eighteenth-century hypostatization
of individual emotions as universal passions.

Phrenology was another pseudoscience popular in the early and middle
century that purported to analyze character by means of a person's physical
features. According to Franz Joseph Gall, the inventor of phrenology, the
shape and size of the brain determined the shape and size of the human
skull. Each mental faculty was thought to be located in a specific organ
within the brain. Gall believed that a person's character and temperament
could be assessed by "observing the unerring and wonderful Laws of Nature
in the various shapes and developments of the head."[21]

Theater historians have drawn attention to the way in which the acting
of melodrama, in particular, derived its physical and visual techniques from
various forms of spectacular art such as *tableaux vivant, poses plastique,* dumb
shows, pantomime, and specialized scenic effects such as panoramas and
dioramas. Popular forms of culture, including theater and the novel, constantly utilized such "speaking pictures" as a method of signification, so that
an ability to employ mime and gesture was assumed to be one of the essential tools of the actor's trade.[22] The assumption that emotions and thoughts
could be spontaneously externalized by actors in physical and visual form
was an automatic one. It was only during the last half of the century, however, that popular views of the connection between physiognomical features and bodily sensations, on one hand, and their significance as emotional
states, on the other, were challenged by the changing conception of human
physiology, confirmed in turn by evidence from twentieth-century anthropology.[23]

A New Paradigm: Post-Darwinian Physiology

The Romantic preference for explaining human functions in terms of the
concept of organicity rather than through the Enlightenment image of
mechanism reflected the preeminence of biology as the paradigmatic nineteenth-century science. It constituted a new model of life as *process* or
growth, transforming scientific explanations of spheres of human activity as
different as history and acting. The image of the living organism became *the*
model of process and of self-identity. History was envisaged as a process of
biological development, works of art as being organically whole, like plants.
In outline, Darwin's theory of evolution can be seen as an elaboration in
materialist terms of the biologism inherent in Romantic theories of society
and art. Mechanistic theories of the passions came gradually to be replaced

during the nineteenth century by biological explanations of the physiological organization of the nervous system, which was conceived to be the product of an individual's history as a genetically and environmentally determined psychophysiological organism.

Advances in the field of physiology prepared the way for the introduction in the 1870s of psychology as a discrete area of scientific study. Sir Charles Bell's important investigations in the field of "nerve physiology" were outlined in *The Anatomy and Philosophy of Expression as Connected with the Fine Arts* (1806), which anticipated Darwin by elaborating a comparative method for analyzing the features of emotional expression common to both man and the higher animals. Developments in theories of the structure and function of the nervous system exposed as superstition the apparent psychological insights of such pseudosciences as physiognomy and phrenology, providing materialist accounts of emotional expression based on new scientific principles. Although Bell's comparison of human and animal facial expression was somewhat reductive, he did perceive what Darwin later confirmed—that patterns of expressive behavior were inherited as a consequence of the evolutionary process. According to Darwin, the fact that the chief aspects of expressive behavior were inherited and not learned meant that the signs of powerful emotion such as blushing, pallor, and perspiration were not directly subject to the individual's control. In Darwin's view, the body was formed in a process of adaptation to the environment. Rather than being voluntarily produced by the organism, expressive movements were the product of reflex actions. However, Darwin did note that exceptional individuals possessed voluntary control over certain sets of facial muscles, which suggested that such control might be achieved by practice.

Two concepts deriving from nineteenth-century biology are particularly relevant to an understanding of the way in which ideas about acting manifested themselves in the late nineteenth century. The first was central to the development of human physiology—the idea of the psychophysical unity of the human organism *(monism)*. The other was the idea of the *unconscious* that became prominent in the 1870s as an elaboration of evolutionary theory. Instinct was perceived as an unconscious force driving the organism toward survival and self-enhancement. Speculative psychology distinguished consciousness from the unconscious aspects of bodily function. Physiologists, on the other hand, located the higher mental processes in the cerebrum, and the lower ones such as emotion—which was subconscious—in the brain stem. According to his younger contemporary William Archer, it was G. H. Lewes who first applied the word *psychology* to the art of acting. Lewes was a seminal figure in the field of acting theory, combining the talents and experience of an actor with expert knowledge of physiology and psychology. His book *The Physiology of Common Life* (1859) was widely read. Lewes's ideas made an impact on two scientific figures whose work was directly to influence Stanislavski's praxis—the French psychologist Theodule Ribot, and Pavlov, the Russian physiologist who memorized passages of Lewes that he read in a Russian translation, and whose theory of conditioned reflexes represented a development of Lewes's ideas.

Joseph Roach has pointed out that many of the principles underpinning modern acting theory were first articulated by Lewes. All modern approaches to training assume the unity of the performer's body-mind. Their disagreements reflect the different views on how, for what purpose, and from which aspect—subjective or objective—to approach the integrated mind-body complex: "As a psychologist, G.H. Lewes was an associationist in the direct line of descent from David Hartley's *Observations on Man*. . . . Abandoning Hartley's parallelism for monism, however, Lewes believed that mind and body constitute one entity, not two. Every experience presents a double aspect—objective and subjective. The body is merely the objective aspect of a subjective process called mind."[24]

The nervous system was viewed by Lewes as a single entity determining the reciprocity within the organism between mental and physical acts. Emotional expression was the result of nervous activity operating as a hierarchy of mechanisms. The primary sense datum, the *neural tremor,* was reciprocally related through *sensation* (or grouping of neural tremors) to the *image,* formed by the reproduction of sensations, and the idea or *symbol,* which was produced when the image lost its immediacy in sensation. This meant that a symbol might recall a primary tremor, while conversely a physical stimulus might recall an image. Lewes contributed to the elaboration of the concept of the *reflex,* which he believed connected all actions through the arc of the cerebrum and the spinal cord and was the consequence of a complex of physiological mechanisms, which "are sentient; even when unconscious they are therefore never purely mechanical, but always organical."[25]

For Lewes, expressiveness was the crux of the actor's art; it was produced by the human organism's "fluctuating spontaneity"—the plasticity of organization of the nervous system that ensured the fluid interdependence of body and mind, muscle and imagination. But in addition to a peculiar form of nervous organization, the actor required discipline and skill to construct symbols out of the raw material of nervous sensation: "It is not enough for the actor to feel, he must represent."[26] Equally, the calculated construction of a role by a mechanical accumulation of conventional histrionic symbols was not sufficient to animate a performance. The "fixed stare" of Charles Kean (Edmund's well-educated but less talented son) in response to the appearance of the witches in the first act of *Macbeth* was a "pantomimic convention" that failed to evoke the "fluctuating spontaneity" of Macbeth's emotions at that moment. What Charles Kean lacked, his father had possessed in abundance—the "mimetic flexibility of organisation" that might easily activate the reciprocal relationship of inner impulse and outer expression. Lewes noted with particular approbation Edmund Kean's ability to suggest the residual nervous tremors—the "subsiding emotion"—that followed a moment of intense emotional excitement. The elder Kean's success in replacing the eighteenth-century representations of fixed "passions" with the turbulent evocation of changing emotional states had created a new criterion for good acting, theorized by Lewes in the terms of post-Darwinian concepts of physiology and psychology. By the 1870s, there existed, therefore, a new physiological paradigm of acting based on the representation of continual transitions between rising and subsiding feelings.

Yet Lewes's notion of the "fluctuating spontaneity" of feelings did not imply, as had some earlier theories of sensibility in acting, that the actor relied for expressive vitality on the inspiration of the moment. Lewes noted the following "antinomy": "If the actor lose all power over his art under the disturbing influence of emotion, he also loses all power over his art in proportion to his deadness to emotion. If he really feel, he cannot act; but he cannot act unless he feel. . . . As in all art, feeling lies at the root, but the foliage and flowers though deriving their sap from emotion, derive their form and structure from the intellect. . . . It is from the memory of past feelings that he [the artist] draws the beautiful image with which he delights us. He is tremulous again under the remembered agitation, but it is a pleasant tremor, and in no way disturbs the clearness of his intellect."[27]

The actor's ability to function simultaneously on a number of conscious and unconscious levels was recognized by Lewes, who cited the extraordinary dumb-show performances on horseback of Etiénne Ducrow, the equestrian pantomime artist, as evidence of the phenomenon of double or multiple consciousness. The actor's mental state resembled that of Ducrow, whose attention when riding six horses at once would alternate from one moment to the next, some activities being performed automatically (practice having rendered the required movements involuntary), while others were at the forefront of consciousness.

Introspection was for Lewes a valid form of scientific enquiry, complementing the acquisition of knowledge by objective observation. Memory supplied access to the storehouse of past emotions, which were recalled through introspection and processed into "symbols" by the "artistic intel-lect" that was able to select and heighten ("idealize") appropriate elements of emotion on the basis of past observation and interpretation of the actor's experience of his own feelings and those of others. Lewes's monistic approach to the human organism offered actors the possibility of either acti-vating the function of the nervous system by working from an external, physical stimulus, as in the example he gave of Macready shaking a ladder backstage to provoke an appropriate feeling for his portrayal of Shylock's anger, or of acquiring through introspection an understanding of the appro-priate mental state to be expressed in characterizing a particular role. His demonstration of the continuity of psychological and physiological processes within the human being gave rise to the behaviorist theory of William James and Carl Lange, which stated that the physiological manifes-tation of the emotion *is* the emotion. The commonsense order of experi-ence, "I see the bear. I am frightened. I run," should, according to the James-Lange thesis, be altered to "I see the bear. I run. I am frightened." The idea that the perception of the emotion succeeded its expression was later to have a considerable influence on the elaboration of Meyerhold's biomechanics and Stanislavski's method of physical actions.

In 1880 Diderot's paradox was restated by Coquelin in *L'art et le comédien.* This book informed the controversy between "emotionalists" and "anti-emotionalists" as researched and analyzed by William Archer in *Masks or Faces.* While the majority of actors (the most eminent being Henry Irving) insisted that whatever technique the actor may have employed, good acting was produced not solely by physical technique but by an investment of the actor's feelings in the moment of performance, there were, by the end of the century, still no coherent accounts of how this fusion of physical tech-nique and feeling might be achieved. Coquelin's stark conclusion may not have appealed to the majority of nineteenth-century actors, but in most respects it reflected their practice: "I hold [Diderot's] paradox to be literal truth. . . .The actor is within his creation, that is all. . . . It is from within that he moves the strings which make his character express the whole gamut of human consciousness; and all these strings which are his nerves, he must hold in his hand, and play upon as best he can."[28]

Referring to Macready's account of how his own personal circumstances had affected his emotional identification with the playing of Leontes in *The Winter's Tale,* Irving attempted a rebuttal of Diderot (and Coquelin) by exploiting a notion in all probability suggested by Lewes, but which antici-pates twentieth-century concepts of the unconscious: the "mind should have, as it were, a double consciousness, in which all the emotions proper to the occasion may have full swing, while the actor is all the time on the alert for every detail of his method."[29] This perception of the simultaneous functioning of sensibility (intuitive) and technique (conscious) not only mirrored the image of the divided self so strikingly rendered in Irving's stage characterizations, but also anticipated one of the insights into human personality achieved by Freudian psychoanalysis. Ironically, Irving's complete mastery of an idiosyncratic vocal-physical technique made him Craig's ideal model of the actor as Über-marionette.

The psychological theories adumbrated in the last half of the century by Lewes, James, Lange, Ribot, Sechenev, and Pavlov were eventually to revolutionize methods of rehearsal and actor training. Although Lewes's essay provided the model of a modern conception of acting, there is no evidence to suggest that the new understanding of the structure and function of the nervous system actually affected the working practice of the nineteenth-century actor. The system of actor training remained largely unchanged until the innovations of Stanislavski and Copeau. Rehearsal methods were transformed during the last half of the century, not in response to the new views of the psychology of acting, but as a result of the growing power of the director to control the interpretation of the play through the elaboration of more complex forms of mise-en-scène.

From the Star System to the Modern Ensemble

The Star in the Stock System

Evolutionary theory offered an account of the way the human organism could modify its behavior to adapt itself to changed environmental circumstances, thus providing justification in physiological terms for Goethe's idea of rehearsal as a process of training whereby the actor might transform his natural bodily and vocal functions into the "second nature" of art. Talma believed that it required twenty years of experience in performing his repertoire of roles for the great actor to train his nervous system to execute spontaneously in performance the directives given by his intelligence in planning the portrayal. Both Talma and Goethe perceived the importance of rehearsal as a method of translating the conception of a character in a play into the physical terms of performance. More often than not, however, rehearsals in the nineteenth century were a haphazard affair, conducted by stage managers or prompters with actors mumbling their words at speed and in a low voice, and intended chiefly to establish cues and fix positions for exits and entrances and to coordinate the relative position of one actor with another (known today as *blocking*) at key moments of the play. Actors assumed their own responsibility for interpreting and learning their roles.

In practice, the actor's training involved a kind of apprenticeship in provincial productions, whereby actors acquired their craft playing small roles and making their mistakes in front of provincial audiences before appearing in large urban theaters. Apart from some instruction in specific skills such as fencing, tumbling, and dancing, apprentices learned by imitating leading actors or visiting stars who joined the company for a season. When an actor felt sufficiently confident of his own abilities, he would begin to vary the interpretation and execution of his roles, drawing attention to his innovations in order to establish his own reputation.

The stock system, which operated until the late nineteenth century, determined the working practices of most actors, reinforcing the assumption that rehearsal was merely a mechanical way of planning and fixing a performance. A theater would own a stock of conventional scenery, including a setting or two for tragedies, a few country landscape scenes, a forest, a park, a few street scenes, various domestic interiors, and so on. A single play would run for three or four nights during a season; all productions of plays in the repertoire would be furnished with scenery from the available stock. Each theater company assigned roles to actors according to a typology of well-established lines: an actor would, for example, be hired to play either "heavy" roles such as villains or romantic juveniles, comic sidekicks or aging parents. Rehearsals consisted mainly of a technical preparation for the performance that proceeded according to well-established conventions of scenic staging. There was little or no sense of rehearsal as a creative method of assisting the actor to discover and master a new approach to the role.

Although Edmund Kean was meticulous in the planning and accurate execution of his own performance (even checking to ensure that a provincial stage was large enough to accommodate the predetermined number of steps by which his character crossed the stage in a particular play), he was notoriously cavalier with respect to the integration of his performance within the whole production. He only called one rehearsal when he made his debut performance as Shylock at the Drury Lane Theatre in London in 1814. His letter to the stage manager of the Croydon Theatre before he was to act there for the first time read as follows: "I shall not require rehearsals for my plays; but be particular in your selection of Wilford. [in *The Iron Chest*]. He is all-important to me. I will run through the library scene when I come down. He must be young, mind."[30] When Kean actually met to rehearse with Stirling, the actor engaged to play Wilford, he instructed him merely to sink gradually on his right knee with his back to the audience during the library scene, and to keep his eyes fixed on Kean's when he laid his hand on Stirling's head to curse. Although this is possibly an extreme example, it does reveal the typical features of the star system and suggests how they determined the qualities of nineteenth-century acting until the long run began to change the conditions of performance in the 1850s.

Like opera and ballet (vestiges of whose nineteenth-century performance conventions are still present in a way that they are not in drama), acting was considered as the art of the virtuoso. The performance was organized on hierarchical principles, with audience attention being specifically directed toward the "points" being made by the star actors, and the other actors providing support by way of delivering an intelligible account of the fiction that provided the raw material for the stars' displays of histrionic effects. Instead of expecting a consistently compelling level of enactment, spectators might accept a somewhat cursory performance of certain sections of the drama as frames for the full excitement of the great moments. In the words of George Taylor, "the stock style emphasised individual expression rather than social interplay, and the outward expression of feeling rather than the gradual revelation of motives . . . or the exploration . . . of the characters in social context."[31] Occasionally, young or supporting actors would show so much ability that their theatrical effectiveness would challenge the position of the star. In *Othello,* theater managers actually pitted Edmund Kean against his rivals (Junius Brutus Booth, Edwin Forrest, his own son Charles) so that each performance became a kind of competition to see whether a new actor would win the laurels from Kean.

Impact of the Actor-Manager

Enlightened actor-managers such as John Phillip Kemble at Drury Lane (1788–1802) and Covent Garden (1802–17), William Charles Macready at Covent Garden (1837–39) and Drury Lane (1841–43), and Charles Kean at the Princess Theatre (1850–59) spent most of their rehearsal time blocking elaborate crowd scenes and managing the production of stage spectacle. The elevation of the director to a position of overall artistic control was anticipated in London by such innovative actor-managers as Madame Vestris, Macready, Charles Kean, and the Bancrofts, who, although they insisted on longer periods of rehearsal and paid meticulous attention to the interpretation of plays by means of fairly detailed staging plans, did not see it as the primary function of rehearsals to assist the individual actor in developing the detailed interpretation of a role. Resolving as manager "to rehearse with the same passion as I would act," Macready provoked complaints by actors, who were unpleasantly surprised by the strictness of his regime as a manager. The seriousness Macready demonstrated in spending two hours rehearsing one page of the club scene from Bulwer-Lytton's *Money* was the exception that proved the rule. An entry from his diary in 1849 reflects the usual practice: "Rehearsed *King Lear* with several characters absent and several not cast: Planché calls the Haymarket 'The Patent Self-Acting Theatre.'"[32]

Charles Kean's production of *Henry VIII* in 1855 ran for over one hundred performances, hastening the end of the stock system of theater production and promoting the idea of individually mounted productions that would run long enough to recoup production costs and ensure the management a good profit. Although the stock system survived in a few London theaters until 1880, the major companies began to avail themselves of the opportunities provided by long runs, to design scenery and costumes especially for a single play, and to spend time planning and coordinating the mise-en-scène. Rehearsal periods became longer, but concerns about approaches to the playing of individual roles (even those assigned to stars) were subordinate to the drive to achieve coherence in the external production scheme and to the promotion of fluent and subtle interaction among the various characters on stage. The introduction of the three-dimensional box set made it possible to simulate the material features of domestic reality with photographic accuracy.

The development of the ensemble approach to performance was fueled in Continental Europe by the Duke of Saxe-Meiningen's company, which pioneered the role of the "autocrat-director," shifting artistic control from the star actor to the director. Such ensemble playing was paralleled by the excellence of the realistic acting on view in some London theaters, in particular, the Prince of Wales, where from 1865 to 1885, Squire and Mrs. Bancroft (Marie Wilton) maintained a talented company of actors in order to produce new well-made plays of contemporary life that were in effect directed by the playwrights, Tom Robertson, W. S. Gilbert, A. W. Pinero, and the "stage manager," John Hare. The staging approach of the Bancrofts and that of the Meininger troupe offered models of integrated production to English actor-managers like Irving, Herbert Beerbohm Tree, and George Alexander. Criticism of the quality of the acting during the Meiningen company's appearances in London in 1881 suggests that, although the mise-en-scènes of the company—in particular its crowd scenes—were admired, its detailed realism of staging was not regarded by English critics and audiences as a fair substitute for the excellent acting and coherent staging that characterized the best of the English actor-managers' productions. London audiences may not have fully appreciated the protonaturalistic approach to the presentation of a historical or contemporary milieu that the Duke of Saxe-Meiningen and his company achieved by means of scholarly research and systematic rehearsal, and that represented an advance in the theater's capacity to portray the relationship between character and environment. The challenge to the modern theater remained that of creating ensemble companies in which there was no distinction between stars and "supers," where small roles and large roles were conceived and executed as part of an integrated process and according to the same principles.

The Actor as Personality

While a criterion of naturalness had come increasingly to determine the approach to acting since the late 1850s, the image of the star as both virtuoso and extraordinary personality persisted throughout the century. By the 1820s, Sarah Siddons and Edmund Kean had established the image of an actor as a virtuoso in the expression of emotion. Eyewitness accounts of their performances regularly emphasized the astonishing emotional impact on spectators who attended the theater with the assumption that it was the task of the actor to delineate feelings. The impersonation of character was from the Romantic period viewed as a primary function of the actor, and some actors (Edmund Kean, for example) were especially praised for the mimetic skills that enabled them to submerge their own personalities beneath the image of the character they had constructed. Actors like Sarah Siddons, George Frederick Cooke, Rachel, Edwin Forrest, Tommaso Salvini, and Sarah Bernhardt more often than not attracted commendation for the power and intensity of feeling that they conveyed, rather than for the subtleties of their characterization. Stars like Sarah Bernhardt, Ellen Terry, Irving, and Beerbohm Tree had clearly recognizable personalities that they never entirely disguised. Such personality acting, although deplored by theatrical reformers such as George Bernard Shaw, may have been promoted by the economic imperatives of the actor-manager system. To draw the public, actors needed to be identifiable through their idiosyncratic images. It was the charm or intensity with which they employed their personalities to externalize characters' attitudes and feelings that was considered most effective.

Sarah Bernhardt's extraordinary stage persona was the vehicle through which she effected a transformation of every character she played into a version of herself—a *monstre sacre,* possessed of a beautiful voice, unique personality, and volatile temperament. Irving's acting appeared mannered to his admirers and detractors alike. His walk and his halting, emphatic pattern of speech were often criticized, yet there was no denying his mesmeric power to affect an audience. His capacity to suggest the inner consciousness of the troubled or guilty echoed the growing interest of the late nineteenth century in depth psychology, which manifested itself in literary and artistic studies of the double or split personality *(Dr Jekyll and Mr Hyde, The Picture of Dorian Gray)* and of hypnotism *(Trilby)*. In some respects, one might regard Irving's approach to characterization not so much as a failure of mimetic ability but as a refusal to reduce characters to the mechanistic level of stock Victorian social or psychological types. Although typically Victorian in its melodramatic presentation of social morality, his characterization of his most famous role, Matthias in *The Bells,* involved a virtuoso demonstration by Irving of the return of repressed conscience, and was a haunting study of the psychopathology of guilt. In many ways, his idiosyncratically poetic acting style anticipated twentieth-century attempts to render the impact of the unconscious on human behavior.

Irving's popular stage partner Ellen Terry, by contrast, emblematized in visual terms the virtues of the ideal Victorian woman, her virtuous persona as a star being rather different from the reality of her Bohemian lifestyle. The reception of Terry's performances suggests that her audiences habitually confused the actress's charm, intelligence, and beauty with the qualities attributed to her characters. Terry worked under Irving's management during the most significant period of her career, and her acting style, although natural, was picturesque in a way that clearly suited Irving's painterly mise-en-scènes. In preparing a performance, she devoted a great deal of attention to her costume, so that while she may not have entirely transformed her own personality, the visual image of the character was very carefully constructed.

Natural Acting and the Technique of Byplay

The materialist theories adumbrated in the fields of biology and social history in the mid–nineteenth century were paralleled in the sphere of theatrical performance, not only by increasingly realistic scenery and historically accurate costumes, but by a tendency observable from the 1850s toward a new kind of realism in acting, based not on emotional vitality, but on the detailed depiction of social behavior through the subtle use of *byplay*.

As an actor in the full-bloodedly Romantic vein, Macready was no match for his elder contemporary Edmund Kean. In the 1830s and 1840s, however, his acting began to be recognized as different in kind from Kean's, its distinctive feature being a type of domestic realism sustained by the exploitation of small bits of stage business that would not have been amiss in the drawing-room comedies staged by Eliza Vestris and her husband,

Henry Irving in his most famous role of Matthias in *The Bells*. Courtesy of the Theatre Museum Picture Library, London.

Charles Matthews, but which were until Macready never a feature of performances in tragedy. Many critics disapproved of Macready's use of these realistic pieces of business, but gradually such byplay began to become the norm in the performance of socially realistic melodramas such as Dion Boucicault's *The Corsican Brothers,* first produced in London by Edmund's son Charles Kean in 1854. In this production, Charles Kean and Alfred Wigan introduced to the London stage a new, more natural scenic and acting style said to derive from French actors, establishing a vogue in what became known as "gentlemanly melodrama."

The French actor Charles Fechter applied the realism and emotional reticence of the new French melodrama to the playing of Hamlet, which was a great success in London in 1861. Fechter's Hamlet was much admired and imitated in Britain, and he was viewed as having effected a reformation of Shakespearean acting. Another popular actor in the new, more natural vein was the American Edwin Booth, who also played in London. The Italian Eleanora Duse, who was regarded as the greatest actress of the early modern period, was famous for her refined combination of realism with a sense of the poetic. Without overt displays of histrionic virtuosity, she was able to transform herself into a wide variety of characters.[33] Yet the ease and apparent spontaneity of her performances were clearly the result of careful contrivance: "Only an artist of the highest type could create so profound an impression with so little apparent effort or forethought, by some light and seemingly spontaneous gesture, by a sudden change of facial expression, or by some subtle inflection of the voice. The chief beauties of impersonation are to be found in its lesser and to the inexperienced eye, insignificant details. All her by-play, although it appears to be due only to the impulse of the moment, is clearly the result of the most deliberate design, and changes with every variety of mood or condition which it is meant to illustrate."[34]

By the end of the century, naturalness in acting embraced many different approaches, including the genuine ensemble naturalism of Antoine's Théâtre Libre and Otto Brahm's Freie Bühne, the polished, off-the-cuff presentation of middle-class English manners in the work of Charles Wyndham, the sensitive and subdued poetic realism of Duse and the neoromanticism of Irving and Tree. Great actors such as Irving and Duse had perfected a technique capable of expressing a wide range of nuances of thought and feeling. Although Duse's style was natural while Irving's was filtered through the prism of his unique personality, each was able to evoke a character's psychology coherently and in depth through the creation of carefully composed scores of physical activity or byplay. No matter how subtle the effects they produced, actors like Irving and Duse relied on the traditional physical techniques of the nineteenth-century actor to produce their effects.

The best actors of the late nineteenth century began to recognize the need for a detailed interpretation of each role they were assuming in relation to the play as a whole. Intelligent actors began to speak of "close study" of the dramatist's text as an essential aspect of their creative process. Adelaide Ristori, Duse's Italian predecessor, wrote a highly intelligent account of her approach to playing Lady Macbeth that illuminates the main features of the enlightened star actor's method of preparing a performance. Her account stresses the difficulties presented by the mythic image of Lady Macbeth as a "colossal conception of perfidy, of dissimulation, of hypocrisy." She was at pains to emphasize her careful study of the role, including her reading of criticism and historical accounts of great performances, and her awareness of the need to identify a coherent line of interpretation and justify it with reference to the playwright's intentions. Ristori's account consists chiefly of a description of how she employed stage business (byplay) to illustrate her interpretation of the speeches and to fill in the gaps between the lines so as to create a pattern of underlying motives and feelings that would evoke the character in terms that seemed psychologically coherent. Here is an example of her account of her working method:

> During this first scene with Macbeth I show a cold, reserved and patient demureness, not minding at all the weak denials of my husband in his endeavour not to listen to my criminal insinuations. I make it apparent that he will have to yield to my influence. I therefore imagined a counter-scene at the exit of the *personae,* in order to portray the powerful fascination that this woman exercised upon her husband. I fancy that Macbeth wished to interrogate me again and ask of me further explanations. For the purpose of preventing him, I had the thought of inducing him to pass his left arm around my waist. In that attitude I take his right hand and placing his index finger upon my lips I charge him to be silent, in the meanwhile, I am slowly pushing him behind the wings, his back turned to them. All this was executed with a mingling of sentiments and magnetizing glances, which fascinations Macbeth could not very well resist.[35]

The account is remarkable for its precise detailing of the physical business Ristori employed to illustrate each moment of interpretation. From a modern perspective, it may appear surprising that despite her completely systematic application of a physical technique in order to illustrate her intellectual conception of the role, Ristori never felt the need to outline a process that might stimulate the unconscious aspect of the imagination in creating the performance. Until Stanislavski, however, actors and theorists rather vaguely conceived of such an imaginative process as occurring spontaneously as a function of the actor's sensibility. The method of preparation and execution of a role described by Ristori was essentially the same as that employed by Irving at the Lyceum, except that as manager, he had the power to integrate his own acting with that of the whole company. Ellen Terry's account of his working methods reveals that "he studied a play in depth for some three months, read it entire to the company, analysed individual parts and character relationships, and in rehearsal explored the most minute details of interpretation, grouping and performance."[36] Even Irving, however, as sensitive as he was to the operation of sensibility, did not devise a specific method to stimulate the imaginative process of each actor in his company. The same, however, could be said today of many directors working with good actors in the West End, on Broadway, or in the major established theaters in western Europe.

It was not until Stanislavski that the individual actor's private study was integrated with the new approach to the composition of mise-en-scène. Stanislavski's system of rehearsal was designed not only to provide a working method that might guarantee a true ensemble production but at the same time to stimulate and harness the actor's unconscious imaginative process. The methods of Irving as actor-manager, of Antoine as actor and director, and the establishment of a number of European art theaters in imitation of Antoine's Théâtre Libre did, however, provide a matrix from which Stanislavski's new rehearsal system could emerge.

Naturalism and Demands of the Ensemble

Zola's call for a theater that would present "a man of flesh and bones on the stage, taken from reality, scientifically analyzed, without one lie" represented the response of an avant-garde artist in the 1870s to the revolution in thinking about human nature and history that had followed in the wake of Darwinian biology and positivist views of society.[37] According to Zola, "we are an age of method, of experimental science; our primary need is for precise analysis."[38] It was not until André Antoine's establishment in 1887 of the Théâtre Libre that the first proper attempt was made by a European theater to realize Zola's naturalistic program.

Superficially, the technique of Antoine's theatrical naturalism might have appeared to resemble the realism of the Meiningen company or the naturalness of the new style of acting championed by the Bancrofts, Charles Wyndham, George Alexander, or Gerald Du Maurier in well-made plays of middle-class English society. Naturalistic drama, however, required more than mere naturalness in acting style. In fact, the naturalism sponsored by Antoine constituted a radical break with the polished colloquialism of the English stage. Adopting the historicism and some of the rehearsal methods of the Meiningen Theater, Antoine was the first director to present naturalistic drama in genuinely naturalistic productions. He made a virtue out of the poverty of his means, using real furniture—at times transported from his mother's home—in place of conventional stage props, and playing in an intimate space that became a model for successive generations of experimental art theaters. He exploited the fact that his actors were talented amateurs who might develop their new naturalistic acting style through an ensemble approach to production, free of the artifice and mannerism that typified the approach of professional actors trained at the Conservatoire to achieve the rigid style of the Comédie Française: "We must ask ourselves if we cannot draw some conclusion from the work of these inexperienced actors, possessing only their natural gifts, their good will and their intelligence, lacking all traditional theatre training and yet for three years successfully carrying out the difficult task of interpreting the plays of widely assorted dramatists. May we not simply conclude that the traditional training they lacked is perhaps dangerous— and at the very least useless and above all badly organised? . . . The instructors at the *Conservatoire* themselves do not believe in the merits of the system; and one of them eagerly sends his pupils to the Théâtre Libre where they can learn their profession at the best and the only great school: *the audience.*"[39]

In *Le Théâtre Libre,* Antoine attacked the star system, criticizing "the profession [as] . . . the enemy of art" for the way its meretricious "tricks and cleverness" masked the conviction and sensitivity of the true artist and lamenting the way that most actors substituted their personality in place of the author's characterization.[40] Antoine was sensitive to the relationship between stage setting, props, and acting as determined by naturalism, understanding that naturalism worked through the accumulation of small details of stage activity, and the rejection of the pictorial gesture and vocal rhetoric of earlier acting styles. Naturalistic acting consisted of the representation of human behavior as dissected and analyzed by the playwright to reveal the relationship between characters and their milieu, which was in turn symptomatic of the interaction between the factors of heredity and environment identified by Darwin as operative in the evolutionary process. Naturalistic drama required the actor to embody what Zola called "physiological man." Technically, what distinguished naturalistic acting from that of the traditional forms of nineteenth-century realism was the performer's ostensible ignorance of the presence of an audience. Whereas the realistic actor was able to *demonstrate* the character's behavior to the audience, the naturalistic actor had to incarnate the forces of biological and historical causality that issued in the dramatic situation.

Since the naturalistic actor was to be skilled at *being* rather than *performing,* Antoine's actors did not need to possess the virtuosity of traditional actors. He championed the idea of the acting ensemble of "thirty actors of moderate talent, all equally gifted" as the only system of production capable of achieving the balanced and harmonious slice of life that naturalistic drama aimed to expose.[41] Unlike the productions of the Meiningen company or some of the English actor-managers, Antoine's scenic realism never functioned at the expense of dramatic significance. Above all, his acting and his productions demonstrated his sensitivity to the requirements of the texts he was interpreting, so that in each case the mise-en-scène served the play, rather than merely drawing attention to its own lifelikeness.

The Beginning of Modern Acting

Modern acting has its roots in the nineteenth century. The working methods of Irving, Ristori, and Duse were not different in principle from those employed by many accomplished actors today. A large number of experienced contemporary professionals performing conventional forms of drama on stage, film, and television would say that they do not themselves possess a prescribed system of working, but derive their stimulus and guidance from the demands of the play text—which is the gist of what Edmund Kean had claimed with respect to Shakespeare! Actors still invent pieces of physical action (byplay or stage business) to indicate their character's attitudes, thoughts, and feelings, without having to editorialize upon them in a rhetorical manner. What has changed is our conception of human psychology, which determines the way in which a spectator *reads* acting, and the form and style of the drama that represents human psychology.

By the end of the nineteenth century, the development of naturalistic drama had necessitated a new style of acting that was capable of portraying individual behavior on stage as well as carefully observed social interaction. An ensemble of trained actors rather than a star surrounded by supporting actors was a precondition for staging the new drama. Social interaction cannot be convincingly represented by star actors learning their roles and planning their performances in isolation from the other members of the company. The painstaking and regular rehearsals insisted upon by the Duke of Saxe-Meiningen, by the German director Otto Brahm, and later by Stanislavski were absolutely necessary for the proper representation of the social milieu.

The development of post-Darwinian theories of physiology had produced a new understanding of the nervous system, which rendered obsolete the earlier rhetoric of acting based on a simple use of corporeal and facial signs to express inner feelings. New notions of acting as behavior not only served the Darwinian logic of naturalistic drama appropriately, but also reflected the modern physiological conception of the body as a unified psychophysical organism. Naturalistic actors did not try to manipulate the spectator's feelings through the use of histrionic effects, but presented behavior as a symptom of the character's psychophysical condition. To achieve this new kind of naturalistic acting properly, however, a new approach to rehearsing and training the actor was required. It was Stanislavski who created it.

2. Acting as Psychological Truth: Stanislavski's Legacy

Stanislavski's ideas about training and rehearsal represent a genuine shift away from nineteenth-century notions of the function of the actor, constituting the first identifiably modern approach to the aesthetics and technique of acting.

The Significance of Stanislavski's System

Stanislavski's approach to drama was actor-centered. Whereas other practitioners and theorists might locate acting as merely one element within the complex signifying process of a theater event, Stanislavski conceives the art of the actor as the essence of dramatic performance. While always quick to acknowledge the preeminent status of the playwright as author of the written text, which Stanislavski believes it is the task of the actor faithfully to express, for him acting constitutes the apex of a hierarchy of theatrical sign systems that interact in performance. In his view, the playwright supplies a scheme of action and indications of behavior that to a large extent predetermine the actor's characterization of the agents of the drama. It is the actor's job to flesh out an author's preestablished role with a mimetic representation that is both convincing as a delineation of human behavior and expressive of its function in relation to the overall import of the play. Even though the initial conception is that of the dramatist whose words to an extent control its actualization, Stanislavski nevertheless assumes that it is primarily through the acting that a play is actualized.

While he himself was often at pains to demonstrate that his system was not limited to naturalistic plays, Stanislavski's theory and practice clearly articulated a response to the development of naturalism as a major movement in Western drama. The moment at which he began to formulate his ideas about actor training followed shortly after his experience of creating elaborate mise-en-scènes for Chekhov's *The Seagull, Uncle Vanya, The Three*

Sisters, and *The Cherry Orchard* and Gorky's *The Lower Depths.* The aim of a systematic approach to training and rehearsal is to help actors to create characters who can *live* (or at least seem to) on stage. The idea that the actor should create the illusion that she actually *is* the character inheres in the project of the naturalistic theater to transform the pictorial realism typical of nineteenth-century theater into the perfect illusion of the slice of life. In developing approaches to characterization and to training that addressed the requirements of naturalistic mise-en-scène, Stanislavski made discoveries about the nature of acting that could be useful for other forms of theater; nevertheless his approach was rooted in a notion of character derived from naturalism. Its most successful applications have been in the production of plays that are, in the widest sense, naturalistic.[1]

As early as 1903, Stanislavski was moving beyond the first phase in the historical development of the stage director's art (the writing of a production score and its execution as mise-en-scène) that the Moscow Art Theater (MAT) had perfected under the joint directorship of Stanislavski and its cofounder, Vladimir Nemirovich-Danchenko. Stanislavski's exploration of rehearsal as a process that could unlock the drama inherent in the written text was to transform both acting and directing: "For Nemirovich-Danchenko the basis of a production lay in a detailed literary analysis which was then, as it were, 'illustrated' by the staging; for Stanislavski, a production was created in the actual rehearsal period itself through the active collaboration of actor, director and designer."[2] Stanislavski is the first Western practitioner to have problematized the function and technique of the actor in creating the mise-en-scène.

Stanislavski introduced an idea wholly new to the Western tradition of performance—the idea that the actor's imagination can be developed through systematic training. Before Stanislavski, the training of European actors had more often than not been a haphazard affair. Most actors learned their craft by serving an apprenticeship as small-part players in provincial productions, gaining any insights into acting through their observation of visiting stars or leading actors in the company. Since nineteenth-century acting was itself an art of mimicry, it must have seemed logical that the training of fledgling actors should take the form of an apprenticeship that required them to study and mimic the great exemplars of the art. Stanislavski was the first Western practitioner to conceive of actor training as anything more than a physical training in vocal and bodily techniques. In many ways, he anticipated modern educational approaches to the development of the imagination.[3]

Dialectical Development of the System

Although actively engaged in adumbrating a grammar of acting from 1906 until his death in 1938, Stanislavski worked as a practitioner rather than a philosopher, and his system emerged gradually as a series of practical solutions to concrete problems encountered in the rehearsal room or in performance. He continually tested and revised his ideas, so that, while a number of key elements remained present throughout his career, they were reconceived in a dialectical process in which ideas were derived from concrete experiments, and theories tested through rehearsal and performance. This feature of his work has given rise to confusion about what is and is not authentically Stanislavskian theory, since a number of his students and associates left the MAT over the years and taught versions of the system as they had learned it at particular moments of its practice. To make sense of the major changes in his praxis, it is useful to divide Stanislavski's career into five phases, although only the last three were specifically devoted to the development of the acting system.

In *My Life in Art* (1924) Stanislavski himself analyzed the gradual emergence of his system in the form of a creative autobiography, employing a teleological notion of progress to chart the growth of his awareness of the principles of acting as an experimental process whereby genuine understanding is achieved through trial and error. It was more than ten years later that he propounded his notions of the *method of physical actions* and its associated process of *active analysis,* through which he finally achieved an integration of the practices he had developed in dialectical engagement with the problems encountered in his work. Until the 1930s, "the actor's inner work on himself" (the psycho-technique) and "the actor's outer work on his body" (physical technique) had seemed to coexist, but without any logical means of integration.

The method of physical actions was a way of synthesizing the dialectically opposed techniques of psychological and somatic training by way of a strategy of study and rehearsal whose synthesis of the two techniques involved a psychophysical approach to rehearsal. While *training* might at times require a degree of separation between the actor's physical and mental faculties, the process of *rehearsing* a role would assume the actor's psychophysical integrity as a given. To grasp the sophistication of Stanislavski's latest formulation of the system, it is useful to trace the dialectical process of its development. His identification of the fundamental problems of the modern Western actor became paradigmatic, signifying the transition from nineteenth- to twentieth-century conceptions of acting. It is probably true to say that modern attitudes to acting derive from his praxis.

Early Acting Experience

From the age of fourteen, when he took part in the first performance (1877) of the Aleseyev Circle, his family's amateur dramatic group based in a theater in their country house especially converted for them, Stanislavski was utterly serious about the craft of acting. Soon after this performance he began to keep a notebook in which he reflected upon his difficulties and progress as a fledgling actor. One of the fundamental problems, identified early in his career, was the difference between the feeling of the actor during the performance and the effect of that performance on the audience. Playing the main role in the one-act play *A Cup of Tea,* Stanislavski—in typically nineteenth-century mode—imitated the performance of one of his favorite actors:

> I knew every bit of business in it, I knew his every intonation, gesture and his full scale of mimetics. . . . When the theatre was filled with the public, I felt myself much better. . . . What excited me was not my lines, nor the meaning of what transpired. . . . I was excited by the public, by the consciousness of the crowd and of myself on show before it. . . . Words and gestures flew out . . . and my nervousness and lack of restraint were mistaken by me for true inspiration. While acting, I was certain that I held my audience in my power. Judge of my surprise when . . . we were met with rather thin applause, and when I walked back-stage I met with no praise and no enthusiasm. . . . Later it was explained to me that no one understood me, so swiftly had I moved, so low and hoarsely had I talked. No one had seen anything, for I had moved my hands in the air with unbelievable rapidity. What a difference there is between your own impressions while on the stage and the impression created in the auditorium by your acting![4]

Stanislavski had understood what modern actors call the need to "tell the story." His first systematic attempt in 1896 to develop an aesthetics of stage performance was in fact a response to this problem of communication. The first phase of his work as actor and director involved the integration of the approach to mise-en-scène elaborated by the Duke of Saxe-Meiningen with the nuanced realism of behavior characteristic of the best English acting and of Antoine's productions at the Théâtre Libre. By perfecting this external realism in performance Stanislavski inaugurated a tradition of naturalistic production in the Russian theater. Of his performance in *The Miserly Knight* (the inaugural performance of the Society of Art and Literature in 1888), he wrote: "It's strange, when you are right inside it [the role], audience reaction is not so good; when you are in control of yourself and don't let the part take you over, it is better."[5]

Having developed a rehearsal method that obliged the actor to work in detail with a director in order to "control" himself, Stanislavski began to perceive the danger that this external approach to staging restricted the actor's spontaneity and creativity in performance. Between 1906 and 1922 Stanislavski worked to create a technique designed to promote the actor's relaxation and concentration on stage in a way that would not undermine the clear communication of the action. It was only in the 1920s that Stanislavski began to devise ways of ensuring that the actor's process of identification with the role could be integrated with the discipline of physical performance.

Apart from reflecting on his own experience in rehearsal and performance (assisted in no small measure by the actor Fedotov and his ex-wife, Glikeria Fedotova), Stanislavski learned to make creative use of his observation of great actors—in 1882 Tommaso Salvini, later Eleanora Duse and then Fyodor Chaliapin and Ermolova—in developing his own approach. Whereas in his youth he had slavishly imitated the performances of others in the kinds of roles he was required to play, he later began to reflect critically on the working methods that characterized the performer of genius. Stanislavski's critique of his own approach to acting as mimicry involved a realization that the new form of naturalistic theater demanded acting that did not depend on the imitation of other actors' effects, and led him to formulate methods of inducing the "creative state" and of achieving the illusion of spontaneity on stage.

Ensemble Approach to Production

From 1891 until 1906, Stanislavski was as much concerned with the role of the director as he was with his own acting. Under the influence of the Saxe-Meiningen company, who had visited Moscow in 1890, he began to develop a consistent approach to rehearsal and production. The earlier theatrical model in which the star actor is surrounded by a supporting company was replaced by an ensemble under the control of the autocrat-director assisted by a team of designers and technicians. The director assumed responsibility for creating a detailed production score that provided the blueprint for the finished performance. The problems of the individual actor's performance were subsumed by the problems of interpreting the written text and expressing it in scenic terms. The director composed a mise-en-scène as an ensemble of scenic effects that integrated the stage business of the actors with scenery, sound effects, and lighting. Acting was largely a matter of imitating social behavior. If an actor had a problem, Stanislavski would demonstrate a solution in rehearsal that the actor could mimic. What Stanislavski perfected in this phase of his work was essentially a late-nineteenth-century technique of scenic composition. From the actor's standpoint, this involved the devising of a complex score of behavioral details or stage business as an accompaniment to the delivery of the written text. The director integrated all the individual indications of human behavior to create a production score that orchestrated the series of social interactions in order to create mood and convey the meaning of the play.

From the inception of the Moscow Art Theater in 1898, Stanislavski in collaboration with Nemirovich-Danchenko had created major successes using this approach—essentially a refinement of the working practice of the Saxe-Meiningen company. This is the model of production that still operates in parts of the commercial theater sector in the West End or on Broadway. The triumphant success of the productions of Chekhov and Gorky made the Moscow Art Theater famous throughout Europe between 1898 and 1905; nevertheless, it did nothing to reassure Stanislavski that his sense of the shortcomings in the company's approach to acting was unfounded. Even though he had, in response to the drama of Chekhov, formulated an approach to mise-en-scène that effectively exploited the scenic and histrionic possibilities of naturalistic drama, Stanislavski recognized that, from the actor's perspective, this directorially led method was problematic. There was an urgent need to address the problems of the actor in a new way

Development of the Psycho-Technique (1906–22)

The immediate impetus for Stanislavski to experiment in the creation of a grammar of acting was the crisis he experienced in 1906. The MAT's hugely successful tour to Berlin that year earned Stanislavski an international reputation that, ironically, seemed to offer him no consolation. Exhausted and in all likelihood in the throes of a nervous breakdown, he went on holiday to Finland, having lost all confidence in himself as an actor. Notwithstanding the great praise elicited by his own performances in Berlin, he felt dead on stage.

While playing Stockmann in *An Enemy of the People* in March 1906 he had experienced his own performance as completely mechanical. Having triumphed in the role only a few years earlier, he could now experience nothing of the pleasure he had derived from his intuitive creation of the

Stanislavski as Astrov and Artem as Telegin in the Moscow Art Theater's production of Chekhov's *Uncle Vanya*. Courtesy of Vera Gottlieb.

character. There was no functioning of inner impulse in the re-creation of the role on stage, merely a rote repetition of the movements, gestures, and speeches as he had originally performed them.

> Why was it that the more I repeated my roles the more I sunk backward into a stage of fossilization? . . . I came to see clearer and clearer that the inner content which was put into a role during its first creation and the inner content that was born in my soul with the passing of time were as far apart as the heaven and the earth. I remembered that when I played [Stockman] . . . at first it was easy for me to assume the viewpoint of a man with pure intentions. . . . The perceptions that I had put into the role of Stockman had been taken by me from living memories. On the stage, during the playing of the role, these living memories used to guide me, and always and invariably awoke me to creative work. But with the passing time I had forgotten the living memories, I had even forgotten

the feeling of truth which is the fundamental element . . . and the lever of the spiritual life of Stockman. . . . I had exaggerated the manner of walking, the gestures typical to the role, and the outer results of an emotion that was long dormant. I copied *naivete,* but I was not naive. . . . I had played more or less artfully, copying the outer appearances of experiencing my part and of inner action, but I had not really experienced the part or any real necessity for action. From performance to performance I had merely made a mechanical habit of going through all these technical gymnastics, and muscular memory which is so strong among actors, had powerfully fixed my bad theatrical habit.[6]

As early as 1903, his experience of playing Brutus in Nemirovich's archaeologically accurate production of *Julius Caesar* had exposed him to the limitations of the MAT's own autocratic approach that subordinated the actor's imagination to the director's. The initial question that preoccupied Stanislavski in Finland was how an actor could achieve the creative state—which great actors like Salvini, Chaliapin, and Duse seemed able to access at will. No doubt Stanislavski's recent difficulties helped him identify the normal actor's state—an unnatural one caused by the consciousness of being watched by a thousand pairs of eyes. Under the usual conditions of the stage, the actor could not be sufficiently relaxed or focused to experience the emotion that would help her to *live* the role, but could only mimic the supposed behavior of the character in a self-conscious repertoire of movements and gestures. Stanislavski noticed that the experience of the actor is typically split between an everyday consciousness of self and a body that is being forced through the behavioral motions prescribed by the play. The average nineteenth-century actor had recourse to a repertoire of stock physical and vocal signs, which conventionally evoked a range of feelings and mental attitudes. It was a more modern insight into human psychology that led Stanislavski to recognize the actor's need for an inner technique, or psycho-technique, in order to allow the subtextual drama of a character's interior life to stir the spectator's feelings. Stanislavski believed that only by being free to draw on impulses that were not fully conscious could an actor profoundly affect an audience.

Another significant if less immediate stimulus to the coherent articulation of his thoughts was the persistent criticism that the MAT aesthetic was fundamentally naturalistic.[7] Stanislavski was always sensitive to criticism that the MAT merely accumulated a battery of scenic effects and behavioral mannerisms to construct a facsimile of real life. "We have often been and still are accused of falling into a Naturalistic expression of detail in our pursuit of the Realism of life and truth in our stage actions. Whenever we have done this we were wrong. . . . Realism in art is the method which helps to select only the typical from life. If at times we are Naturalistic in our stage work, it only shows that we don't yet know enough to be able to penetrate into the historical and social essence of events and characters. We do not know how to separate the main from the secondary, and thus we bury the idea with details of the mode of life. That is my understanding of Naturalism."[8] Stanislavski's distinction between naturalism and realism is idiosyncratic. However, it clearly expresses his desire to prove that the MAT approach was not a mere technical trick to produce verisimilitude, but reflected a serious wish to realize written texts in appropriate theatrical forms. Stanislavski had transformed theater production into an art in itself. The next challenge was to articulate the laws that pertained to acting as an art form. The discovery of these would render obsolete not only the rhetorical techniques of nineteenth-century acting, but also the naturalistic behavioral mannerisms that MAT actors employed when their imaginations failed to respond intuitively to the director's overall production plan. The aim was to enable the performer to achieve the feeling of spontaneity on stage. Rather than consciously displaying the character's behavior to the audience through a series of rhetorical devices, such spontaneity would authenticate the character's existence on stage in the person of the actor.

Between 1904 and 1908 Stanislavski directed a number of symbolist plays. Although only Maeterlinck's *The Blue Bird* (1908) was accounted a success, Stanislavski was determined to demonstrate the MAT's ability to perform avant-garde drama that was neither realistic nor naturalistic. The grammar of acting on which Stanislavski was working from 1906 was to be applicable to stylized forms as well as to realism. Many of the problems encountered in attempting to stage Hamsun's *The Drama of Life* (1907) and Andreiev's *The Life of Man* (1907) informed the development of the system. The success of his production of Ostrovski's realist classic *A Month in the Country* (1909) was felt by Stanislavski to be the first complete vindication of his new ideas.

Initially, the grammar of acting was conceived simply as a new method of rehearsal. Stanislavski and his valued assistant Sulerzhitsky used MAT productions to experiment with the techniques they were evolving, their empirical method being informed by Stanislavski's reading of theatrical theorists and practitioners of the eighteenth and nineteenth centuries, such as Diderot, Coquelin, and William Archer and, perhaps more importantly, by the writings of the French psychologist Theodule Ribot. In 1912 the MAT First Studio, comprising fifteen younger members of the MAT, was instituted to provide an appropriate forum for these explorations into the nature of acting. It was the first of a series of studios that were founded as laboratories for investigating the art of acting and aimed to develop not only a rehearsal technique but also a program of training.

Relaxation, Concentration, Belief, and Imagination

The elements that Stanislavski first identified as necessary for the achievement of the "creative state of mind" were relaxation, concentration, belief, and imagination. In acquiring the ability to relax and concentrate by means of a series of classroom exercises, the actor places herself in a state of heightened awareness that minimizes the possibility of being distracted by events in the real world and enhances her sensitivity to the fictional world that it is her task to inhabit.

A key aspect of most modern programs of actor training is the cultivation of an appropriate degree of *relaxation*. Stanislavski came to understand that the self-consciousness and nervousness that the actor experienced in front of an audience caused muscular tensions that inhibited the body from being expressive and prevented the mind from functioning spontaneously. The notion Stanislavski was later to articulate explicitly—of the human being as psychophysical unity—is implicit in his earliest approach to achieving the creative state. By learning to relax, the actor removes those tensions in the body that prevent the free flow of thought and feeling. The relaxation exercises devised by Stanislavski and Sulerzhitsky involved the isolation of individual sets of muscles and the control of breathing. In order for the mind and body to remain fully absorbed in the performance, the actor must learn how to concentrate on stage. Early exercises in *concentration* required the actor to focus attention on one object, feeling, thought, or sensory impression at a time. To do this the actor had to become interested in all its aspects, learning in this way to exclude any distractions and to maintain her concentration exclusively on the world of the stage fiction. Concentration was also developed through exercises in the *circle of concentration,* that is, a sphere surrounding the actor. (It could be the space immediately around her body, extend into the middle distance, or stretch to the limits of her visual field.)

If it is the task of the actor to submerge herself in the role so completely that she appears onstage to *be,* rather than merely *present,* the character, then the difference between the actor's actual presence and the surrounding stage artifice must be effaced. "The feeling of truth" arises from the actor's capacity to make believe, to be open and childlike in the use of the imagination. The actor must learn to believe so completely in the imagined reality of the play that she can experience the situations of the drama on stage as if she were in the position of the character. However, Stanislavski took pains to distinguish the feeling of truth from naturalistic verisimilitude: "Scenic truth is not like truth in life; it is peculiar to itself."[9] Exercises in *belief* and *imagination* included a series of games in which actors would imagine objects not present in the room or create spontaneous improvisations in reaction to given stimuli, often transforming objects or the space into other objects and places. The games were enacted physically with the aim of helping actors recover the ability to make believe that Stanislavski thought was usually lost after childhood.

Implicit in all Stanislavski's techniques is the assumption that the goal of the actor is to merge completely with the role in the creation of a character. Some of the exercises involved a substitution of the character's experience for that of the actor, whereas in others the actor substituted her own analogous experiences for those of the character.

Affective Memory

An important influence on Stanislavski's thinking was the work of the French behavioral psychologist Ribot, from whose *Problemes de Psychologie Affectif* he derived the idea of *affective memory,* which he later called *emotion memory.* Affective memory became a central component of the psychotechnique and became widely known in the United States as a cornerstone of Lee Strasberg's Method (based on an early version of the system), practiced by American actors long after Stanislavski himself had ceased to find it helpful. According to Ribot, traces of past experience are recorded in the nervous system. Although not immediately accessible to the conscious mind, the memories may be triggered by a sensation (sound, smell, visual image) associated with the original experience. Exercises in affective memory ranged from remembering simple sense impressions to the recall of complex emotional experiences, aided by the precise recall of sensory impressions connected with the original memory. Complex emotions might take as long as two hours to recapture in full. Having reexperienced the exact feelings and sensations inherent in the original event, it was thought possible for an actor to project the complex of feelings onto the character's set of circumstances in the fictional world of the play.

For the production of *A Month in the Country,* Stanislavski reduced the scenery and stage business to a minimum, rejecting his earlier method of expressing the characters and atmospheres of the play through an elaborate mise-en-scène, and asking his actors instead to radiate their feelings, to communicate the subtext of inner emotions and motivations through eye contact with one another. These notions of *radiation* and *communion* of feelings were based on yoga. In order to achieve depth of characterization without external mimicry, each actor was asked to invent a "subtext" of thoughts and feelings to be sustained beneath and between the lines.

Work on the grammar of acting between 1909 and 1922 manifested two distinct tendencies. The first was a continuing search for a technique to achieve a closing of the gap between the actor's personality and the dramatist's role in order to create a character who might appear to exist on stage as a real person does in life. By means of a reciprocal process the actor progressively comes to identify herself with the character, alternately imagining the character's circumstances as if they were her own, and substituting her own experiences for the character's as appropriate to the drama. The second was the goal of discovering a key to unlocking the processes of the actor's unconscious mind.[10] If author and actor had done their creative work properly, then the creation of character might occur as a direct consequence of the actor's ability to access the unconscious. Such a process would be an organic one, as the discovery and creation of character proceeds naturally from the actions specified in the play.

Stanislavski's organicist notion of artistic creation has its origin in a biological metaphor common to Romantic and naturalistic conceptions of art—the idea that a work of art is like a biological organism, and that in creating it the artist is following a biological process by discovering its organic form in nature and revealing it as art. Whether the subject of the work is intuitively apprehended as a form in nature (romanticism) or scientifically analyzed and represented as a slice of life (naturalism), the process of creation is believed to derive from natural laws and to proceed organically. A good play is therefore viewed as a potential form of nature, the actor helping to nurture it to full life. This aesthetic motivates the later phase of Stanislavski's work concerned with the actor's method of reading the text—*the logic of action*.

Techniques of Physical Expression

Stanislavski's psycho-technique was a new and radical approach to actor training and rehearsal. Since his goal had been to replace the purely external physical approach of nineteenth-century training with a technique that addressed the problems of portraying a character's interior life, it seems inevitable that in his working practice after 1906 he would emphasize the psycho-technique at the expense of technical training and physical characterization. Even during the period between 1916 and 1922, however, when he placed special emphasis on emotion memory as a technique for the creation of characters' feelings, Stanislavski did not entirely neglect physical training.

His sense of his own failure to handle the verse expressively when playing Salieri in Pushkin's *Mozart and Salieri* (1914) led him to search for better methods of training himself and his fellow actors in the techniques of voice and speech. The failure of his ambitious production of Byron's *Cain* (1920) made him very much aware of the MAT actors' lack of physical control and plasticity and of the need for a corporeal training that would provide an adequate basis for the expression of psychological states *through* the body.

While his practical explorations and notes on the psycho-technique formed the basis of his second book, *An Actor Prepares* (1936), his thoughts on physical training constituted the core of his third projected book, which was posthumously published as *Building a Character* (1949). If this aspect of his work is not as well known as his psycho-technique and his later method of physical actions, this is due to the fact that ideas about physical and rhetorical training for the actor were not entirely new.[11] Stanislavski listed the physical techniques of expression as follows: physical characterization, bodily expressiveness, plasticity of motion, restraint and control, voice and speech, including diction, singing, intonations and pauses, and accentuation.[12] The most original aspect of his thinking about physical techniques is the notion of inner and outer *tempo-rhythm* in movement and speech. Tempo-rhythm was Stanislavski's way of recognizing the connection between the dynamic of a dramatic situation (the actor's experience of its intensity) and its rhythmical measure. By varying the tempo-rhythm of a scene, actors could vary its mood and feeling.[13]

Until the 1930s, work on the psycho-technique was undertaken in parallel with training in physical expression, but no method existed of employing the technique to produce an integration of what Stanislavski called the internal and external theatrical states. It was simply assumed that if the actor had acquired both a psycho-technique and physical skills, there would be no difficulty in utilizing physical techniques to express the thoughts and feelings of characters in appropriate scenic terms. In practice, Stanislavski discovered that this was not so. The relation between the two approaches was highly problematic. Actors used either the psycho-technique to create the inner life of their roles and were blocked when they attempted to communicate it in theatrical terms, or they proceeded on the basis of external, physical techniques and were unable to activate their imaginations to create the psychological dimension of a character's thoughts and feelings.

Toward the Method of Physical Actions

During the 1920s Stanislavski began to realize that the key to enabling an actor to function as a psychophysical whole was inherent in the analytical method he called *the logic of action*. The dialectical process of his thinking and practice led him to discover a radically new approach to rehearsal—the method of physical actions. While working on *A Month in the Country* in 1909, Stanislavski had already begun to think of ways in which a new approach to characterization might actualize the dynamic of a drama. The notion of making connections from one to another of a character's individual psychological states and to supplement the playwright's presentation of character by creating a continuous imagined life (subtext) for the character beneath and between the explicit indications in the text gradually led to the formulation of the method of analysis through *actions*. When talking to the director and cast of *The Battle of Life* (a Dickens adaptation) in 1924, he described this "work around the table" as follows:

> First everything has to be prepared so that the emotion will come: the actor's concentration and his correct state of being on stage at that particular moment, either in rehearsal or performance. For this the character's biography must be as familiar as his own. . . . Then the circumstances given him by the author and director must be understood and must be perfectly justified. Second you must define the exact feeling for each beat. . . . Third, after having defined what feeling the actor must have, we must analyse the nature of this feeling. For example, egotism is first of all pity for oneself. Fourth, after defining the nature of the feeling, the actor must search for actions which will arouse the feeling. This is the bait which the feeling will rise to. Fifth, having caught the feeling, he must learn how to control it. Remember that it is the actor who controls the feeling, not the feeling which controls the actor.[14]

As early as the production of *A Month in the Country,* Stanislavski was exercised to find a way for the actor to stimulate her imagination in respect of the emotional content of the role, at the same time enabling her to grasp the way in which the external events of the play are determined by social and historical factors and shaped by the literary style and aesthetic qualities (visual and musical) of the play as a work of art. In order to bring the actor's unconscious mind into play in rehearsal, the psycho-technique was at first applied to the process of reading the play so that the actor might invest the actions of the character with motivations and feelings derived from her own experience.

The approach to reading a play text that Stanislavski outlined in the section on Griboyedov's *Woe from Wit,* which constitutes part 1 of his unfinished work *Creating a Role,* represents his thinking between 1916 and

1920. During the 1920s the emphasis shifted away from emotion memory and the direct presentation of feelings on stage. In order to avoid the danger of repressing the actors' creativity—which had been the case when the director determined the interpretation of the play—it became the responsibility of the actor to identify the *objective* (or *problem*) that motivated each of her character's actions.[15]

If all action were motivated, there would be no separation between the psychological state and its physical manifestation. Characters' actions were a logical consequence of their objectives; in performance the action became a revelation of the characters' motives. An underlying *superobjective* gave coherence to a character's sequence of objectives. Once the actor had discovered the objectives that led to her actions in the play, she should connect all her character's individual actions as a *score* whose complete sequence formed the character's *through-action* or *through-line of action*. The idea was to conceive the play as a dynamic and causal process of action, rather than a literary artifact with every line accompanied by a demonstrative emotional gesture. This method of physical actions represented the first stage in moving away from the nineteenth-century norm of directly presenting hypostatized feelings on stage, and it had the great advantage of enabling the actor to identify and play her character as an agent of the plot.

As late as 1924 during rehearsals for *The Battle of Life,* Stanislavski was still recommending the use of physical actions as bait to stimulate actors to experience and communicate feelings on stage. Shortly after, however, he began to reconceive the function of the text analysis through which the actor identified the physical actions that Stanislavski began to comprehend as the proper medium of drama. During his work on eight productions between 1925 and 1928, he experimented with a new use of the logic of action. When Stanislavski came to direct *Woe to Wit* in 1931, what had initially been an actor's method of reading a play text was transformed into a new system of rehearsal (active analysis) that reversed the habitual order of MAT's rehearsal process. Dispensing with the lengthy period of analysis through reading and discussion, actors would from the start of rehearsals improvise their characters' physical actions in what Stanislavski termed the *given circumstances* of the play.

The given circumstances of a play are all the facts that are explicitly stated in the text or can be deduced from it. This included information about the place and period of the play, the past and future of the characters, and even the subtextual information implied in the dialogue. Characters' given circumstances define and determine their objectives in the play. Having worked out the relevant given circumstances for her character in a *unit of action,* an actor would express the character's objective in the form of a transitive verb (e.g., "I want to . . .") in order to motivate the action that occurs. A unit of action is the smallest coherent event that could be identified as a significant constituent of the plot.[16] Each unit of action comprises a number of *activities,* which are purely physical pieces of stage business such as washing, eating, smoking. In order to become an element of action an activity has to be motivated by the character's objective.

The overall outcome of a scene is a consequence of the interaction of the characters' different and often competing objectives. If a character's objective is frustrated by an obstacle in a particular unit of action, the character will be forced to make an *adaptation,* which may modify the original objective. By performing each moment of a play as an interaction of different and often opposed objectives, the actors are able to express the complexity and dynamism of human interaction. The *magic if* was a corrective to the affective memory exercises. The actor asks, "What would I do if I were placed in the same circumstances as the character?" From the start of rehearsals the actor is thus required to perform the character's actions in relation to the specific set of circumstances given by the playwright. Influenced by Evgeny Vakhtangov and Michael Chekhov (who were themselves aware of Meyerhold's experiments in biomechanics), Stanislavski stressed the psychophysical nature of all action. Inherent in the structure of the play itself was the resolution of the actor's problems in finding a form of expression for a character's inner experiences.

To give actors a better sense of the whole arc of their character's action, Stanislavski then divided the play into three or four *events,* which were longer than the units of action into which a play had been divided in the earlier work on text analysis. Through active analysis the actor would perform the logical sequences of motivated actions prescribed by the playwright, short-circuiting the process of analysis (work around the table) and beginning at once to experience the play as action. By playing her character's objectives in each unit of action with an awareness of her super-objective through the whole play, the actor would achieve a somatic identification with the character from the beginning of rehearsals; consequently the ubiquitous problem of connecting inner impulse to outer form would cease to exist. The psychophysical integrity of the performance would be assured, and there would be no gap between the process of analysis and the process of physical incarnation of the role. The new method of rehearsing a play involved identifying and enacting the sequence of physical actions (score) that embodies the causal logic of the action. The appropriateness of individual physical actions would be tested by enacting the score without words in the form of *silent études.* In this way, the actor would be able to physicalize and explore every element of action that expresses her objective in a given unit of action, playing the strategies by which purposeful action is accomplished.

By 1936, during rehearsals for *Tartuffe* (the last production he worked on before his death in 1938) Stanislavski had completely abandoned the view that it was the aim of performance to represent emotional states. "Do not speak to me about feeling," he said. "We cannot set feeling; we can only set physical action." Vasily Toporkov described Stanislavski's response when, during rehearsals for *Tartuffe,* he was asked about the exercises he had devised to help actors in the creation of characters' emotional states: "When we reminded him of his earlier methods, he naively pretended that he didn't understand what we were talking about. Once someone asked: 'What is the nature of the "emotional states" of the actors in this scene?' Constantin Sergeyevich looked surprised and said: '"Emotional states" What is that? I never heard of it.'"[17]

Although Stanislavski had not read Freud, his new directorial method of analyzing a play implied a conception of the human mind that has points in common with Freud's model of personal identity. Freud's theory of ego formation as a function of the conflict of the instinctual drives of the id with the repressive force of the superego (social reality as enacted through the authority of the father) is paralleled on the level of dramaturgy by Stanislavski's model of character as a function of the motivational needs and drives of the individual agents of the drama in the encounter with the obstacles represented by social and material reality.

The relationship between the character's overarching or underlying superobjective with her series of contributory objectives might well be conceived in the light of Freud's theories, as paralleling the contradiction and tension between the unconscious and conscious elements of the psyche: the unconscious might be pictured as determining motivation at the deepest psychic stratum; the conscious mind determining intention at the surface level of social behavior.[18] Despite its apparent lack of sophistication as a theory of the human personality, Stanislavski's new system of characterization is amenable to interpretation as a forerunner of a modern understanding of psychological characterization. His idea that the actor should convey the character's *motivation* rather than her feelings represented the decisive break with nineteenth-century conceptions of dramatic character.

Active Analysis

The third section of *Creating a Role,* dealing with *The Government Inspector,* together with some notes left by Stanislavski provides his only written account of the way active analysis was put into practice during the final years of his life. The director would first outline the plot of the play to the actors in basic terms. This would occur before the actors themselves had read the play. The actors were then required to act out the actions, based on their own given circumstances, insofar as these are implicit in the director's outline. This was followed by an exercise in which each actor improvised her character's past and future. Obviously, much of the detail of a character's history was invented by the actor as she improvised her character's life in action but the interpretation of the plot of the play had already been established by the director.

Next the director explained the plot of the play in greater detail, providing further given circumstances for the characters that the actors translated into action using the "magic if." This was followed by the director's rough outline of the character's super-objectives and the super-objective of the play. After this each actor traced her own through-line of action based on the scenario as she then perceived it. The play was then broken down into large segments of action (or events) and actors performed their characters' physical actions using the "magic if" as stimulus. While the coherent shape of the events was maintained, the physical actions were broken down so that they could be performed in smaller units. At this stage, the actors improvised without props or scenery. They then worked on shaping the physical actions through repetition until they attained coherence and believability from the actor's point of view. These events were to be given the kind of immediacy that would allow the actors to feel they could actually happen as they were playing them. Each actor should improvise the events in such a way that she experienced them as if they were happening to her, unconsciously absorbing the character's psychic biography within her own person.

Only at this point did the actors read the play. In the process of studying the text, each actor would justify her actions within the given circumstances specified by the play. The actors would then perform the play, substituting nonsense words ("Tra-lala") in place of the actual dialogue. Then there followed a stage when the actors tried to fit the real text of the play to their justified actions. While speaking the nonsense sounds, they were required to translate the characters' thoughts into their own words. Each actor communicated her internal monologue to her fellow performers. In addition, the actors were expected to visualize the scenic environment. For the first time the actors would seat themselves around the table to read the play as a group. As they did this they were required to convey their physical actions without moving. They then read the play a second time, moving only their heads and hands to suggest their physical actions. Next the actors were to read the play on stage, using rough blocking. The actors then discussed their ideas for the mise-en-scène, after which the director described the actual setting within which the actors would locate their physical actions as appropriate. Different stage plans were tested out. The social, political, and artistic meanings of the play were then discussed. At that moment the director would fill in any extrinsic information about the characters that the actors had not discovered through their own working process.

As outlined above, the active analysis offered another model of the two-way process by which the actor was simultaneously to project herself into the role and accommodate herself to it. This double movement of substituting her own experiences for the character's and enacting the character's experiences as if they were her own, directly paralleled the work undertaken during the earlier phase in which Stanislavski had formulated the notion of the psycho-technique. Active analysis was a deliberate attempt to collapse the vitiating dualisms of mind and body, actor and character, inner impulse and outward form, exploiting the psychophysical nature of human agency by beginning rehearsals with improvised action. No separation would occur between actor and character because the actor was improvising the actions of the character *in her own person* before even reading the play. Whatever questions one may have about precise details of each phase of the process as outlined (and one must remember that active analysis was implemented for the first time during the last few years of Stanislavski's life), this remains an unconventional system of rehearsal that directly addresses many persistent acting problems. The method of physical actions and active analysis anticipated much twentieth-century praxis that has concerned itself with resolving the mind-body split typically experienced by actors in the Western tradition.[19]

Stanislavski's Assumptions and Bias

Despite Stanislavski's many disavowals of the necessary connection between the acting his system was designed to enable and the naturalistic theater, there is little doubt that the aesthetic that underlies it is fundamentally naturalistic and that it is an approach to performance that is most appropriate for naturalistic drama. In essence, the system is based on the assumption that the aim of acting is the representation of the psychology of characters who function on stage as if they were real people.

Although Stanislavski had not read the work of Freud, the rationale of the system, with its recognition—admittedly somewhat simplistic—of the function of the unconscious mind in acting, anticipates and parallels aspects

of Freud's thinking about the nature of the human personality and the
process of artistic creation. The methods of tapping the unconscious that
Stanislavski elaborated are somewhat mechanistic, and he has been criticized
for introducing a new self-consciousness to the process of acting that, far
from enabling the actor to draw on the unconscious, merely creates another
set of inhibitions.[20] In his eagerness to demonstrate the efficacy of his
approach and as a consequence of his naïveté about the functioning of those
parts of the mind that do not function consciously Stanislavski may well
have overstressed the effectiveness of the psycho-technique as a way of
accessing the unconscious levels of the imagination. There is no doubt,
however, that the system has come to provide the foundation of a technique
for investigating and expressing human psychology in the terms of stage
action. Its vocabulary (subtext, motivation/objective, through-line, super-
objective, emotion memory) has become the actor's equivalent of the
pseudo-Freudian jargon of popular psychology, and its very high reputation
among actors and teachers in the United States suggests that its dissemina-
tion as an acting technique (and not merely in Strasberg's version) coincided
with the assimilation of psychoanalytic concepts by the culture at large.

For various reasons, Stanislavski did not fully succeed with Shakespeare,
either as an actor or director. Just as he was inclined to overdo the use of historical settings and spectacular effects in the staging of Shakespeare's plays, it
seemed his insistence on fleshing out each role as a living person was inim-
ical to the more elliptical and suggestive manner in which Shakespeare's
characters are presented through those particular features of personality that
are pertinent to the issues of the play. Whatever he may have said to the
contrary, Stanislavski appears at times to have been unable to resolve the
question of style because of his determination to translate all the figures in a
Shakespeare play into the detailed terms of psychological character study.

Nevertheless, the dramaturgical model provided by his method of analysis through actions, with its notion of the through-line of actions, of the
character's super-objective, and of the super-objective or governing idea of
the play, does offer a useful schematization of the way in which character
and plot are fused in the process of dramatic enactment. In *Creating a Role*
the rationale of this scheme is outlined for the actor thus: "[We] evoke a
series of physical actions interlaced with one another. Through them we try
to understand the inner reasons that give rise to them . . . the logic and consistency of feelings in the *given circumstances* of the play. When we can discover that line, we are aware of the inner meaning of our physical
actions."[21]

From a psychoanalytic perspective, Stanislavski's understanding of "the logic and consistency of feelings" appears somewhat naively to suggest that human motivation functions according to the logic of the conscious mind, revealing ignorance of the major insights that psychoanalytic theory has offered into the seemingly irrational logic of the unconscious.[22] Although highly suggestive, the scheme is, however, both inadequate and misleading as a putative account of the way in which meaning is generated in the semiotic process of theater-making. No real explanation is given of the relationship between the super-objectives of the various characters—which must, logically, be in conflict at different points in the drama. Equally, there is no explanation of the relationship between these super-objectives and the super-objective or *governing idea* of the play. The use of the term to signify both the overall project of an individual character and the dominant thematic idea of the play as a whole implies a reductive conception of the meaning of a play in performance, as though this could be conceived along the lines of an underlying train of human motivation.

This crudely teleological model of dramatic structure treats a play as a kind of organism that aspires toward a certain goal of meaning. By ignoring the role of the spectator in the construction of meaning during a performance, Stanislavski oversimplifies the hermeneutic process. The model fails to take account of the complex process of reflection on the words and actions of the various characters through which a spectator exercises judgment in comparing the behavior of one individual with another in the situations given by the playwright, and with other possibilities of human action under equivalent circumstances. Stanislavski's paradigm seems to assume a simple process of identification with the characters in which the spectator empathizes to the same degree with each character in performance, coming to understand the motives of each one without exercising critical judgment. In addition, the model apparently ignores the other typical ways in which dramatists have traditionally sought to determine and manipulate the spectator's point of view on the action of the play—rhetorical speech and argument, verbal, visual, and aural imagery, atmospheric and other devices—each of which forms a kind of metatext or commentary to be read in counterpoint to the characters' actions.

As is often the case, it is by overlooking the spectator's role in the construction of mise-en-scène that Stanislavski betrayed his Romantic assumptions about the organic process of artistic creation, assumptions that caused him to ignore the function of critical judgment and the social positioning of the spectator and the playwright within an ideologically determined field of meaning. This Romantic conception of performance, on the contrary, privileged the emotional identification of actor, character, and spectator in a process that conceived the character not as an artifact but as a living creature engendered from the artistic inspiration of both actor and playwright.

Working in opposition to Stanislavski's aesthetic, Meyerhold offered the first major corrective to this problematic conception of the process of creating mise-en-scène. He was the first in a line of theorists and practitioners to base his performance techniques on the paradoxical phenomenon that Stanislavski had noted at the age of fourteen—that what the actor feels and what the audience experiences in the moment of theatrical communication do not logically coincide, and that the spectator may indeed be affected by a moment of performance in a manner diametrically opposite to its effect on the actor.

One of the major difficulties scholars and practitioners encounter in trying to give a coherent account of the system stems from the fact that Stanislavski kept changing his working practice and modifying his ideas in the light of both difficulties his actors came up against and discoveries he made in trying to overcome them. Throughout his career, from the earliest days of MAT, when Meyerhold was the company's most daring young actor, until his death, when he was collaborating with the director Mikhail Khedrov on *Tartuffe* and with Meyerhold himself on a production of *Rigoletto*—both productions completed after his death—Stanislavski's influence on those working with him was profound. He was invariably assisted by young actors, students, and directors, some of whom published their own accounts or versions of the system before Stanislavski had even published *An Actor Prepares,* the first of what he conceived as a sequence of books intended to supplement the autobiographical *My Life in Art* in providing a complete step-by-step guide to the training and rehearsal process for both performers and directors of drama and opera.

He was greatly helped in the first phase of the development of the system after 1906 by Leopold Sulerzhitsky, who he himself paid as an assistant from his own private resources, and who contributed ideas and conducted many of the classes at the First Studio. Two brilliant students whose ideas and example contributed much to his thinking (even when they disagreed radically with their teacher) were Evgeni Vakhtangov and Michael Chekhov. In the 1920s and 1930s Stanislavski incorporated some of their modifications and developments of aspects of the system. The method of physical actions probably owed much to the thinking of Vakhtangov and Michael Chekhov. It is also likely to have been a response to Meyerhold's biomechanics, although it is characteristic of Stanislavski's way of thinking and talking about physical actions that he studiously avoided any reference to the notion of the body as a machine or to the overtly Marxist ideology of the artist as a worker that is a reflection of the constructivist aesthetic and early Soviet ethos that motivated Meyerhold's own system of physical training and performance.

Vakhtangov's Elaborations

Stanislavski invited Evgeni Vakhtangov to run the First Studio when Sulerzhitsky died in 1916. Vakhtangov, who was widely regarded as Stanislavski's most talented student, had collaborated very closely with Stanislavski and Sulerzhitsky in the formulation of the chief elements of the psycho-technique. In his first production at the studio, *The Festival of Peace* in 1913, the acting was so emotional that some members of the audience were reduced to hysterical tears. Throughout his short but brilliant career as a director, Vakhtangov's work exhibited a paradoxical tension between the heightened emotional intensity of the acting and the stylization of the mise-en-scène. This tension created a production style that came to be known as *fantastic realism*.

Although his approach to relaxation and concentration was fundamentally drawn from Stanislavski's ideas, in other respects Vakhtangov went further than his teacher in claiming that, not only did the actor employ the strategy of the "magic if" to place herself imaginatively in the character's situation in the drama, but that in representing the feelings of the character, she communicated the reality of *her own* emotions and experiences. However logical this may seem, it represented a genuine, albeit subtle, shift away from Stanislavski's view of characterization that in the 1930s made a major impact on Lee Strasberg and other proponents of Method acting in America. Eventually, Vakhtangov came to the conclusion that it did not matter how the actor motivated her behavior on stage, as long as it had the desired effect on the audience. From 1915, Vakhtangov emphasized the form and rhythm of a performance as much as its intensity of feeling. He believed that Stanislavski's system limited the actor to a style that was entirely naturalistic. Vakhtangov sought a technique that would divorce the actor's motivation from that of the character, permitting the actor to perform apparently illogical sequences of action (as in, for example, surrealist drama) with an intensity of commitment that would make it appear artistically appropriate. He called the actor's private method of motivating her actions *justification*.

In establishing a "constant faith" or "naive belief" in every individual moment of a performance, the actor should at the start of the project have asked herself about her personal motives, and have supplied an inner justification for doing so. The justification did not have to be logical or related to the circumstances of the play as long as it provided a powerful private reality as a personal stimulus to the actor. For example, she might pretend that a critic who had once played the same small role would be reviewing her performance with great enthusiasm. "Justification is the actor's secret." According to Vakhtangov, fantasy was produced by the combination of imagination and naïveté. He invented exercises to develop fantasy that allowed the actor to practice justifying every imaginary element in an improvisation.

Vakhtangov adapted Stanislavski's exercises on the circle of concentration as the *circle of attention,* which was conceived as an area surrounding the actor (like the area illuminated by an electric lightbulb). The actor created the space around her by playing with imaginary objects, first in a small area around the body, then gradually expanding to include the whole stage. Vakhtangov differed from Stanislavski in that he preferred the use of imaginary rather than real objects, being followed in this respect by Lee Strasberg. In his emphasis on rhythm and tempo, Vakhtangov remained close to the ideas elaborated by Stanislavski and Sulerzhitsky at the First Studio. His concept of the *task* was a modification of Stanislavski's notions of given circumstances, objectives, and actions. Vakhtangov wished to integrate all the aspects of motivation—analytical, psychological, and physical. It was the actor's task to understand on an intellectual level what the character's *goal* was, to feel the character's physical *desire,* and to make an *adjustment* to the circumstances of the text and the requirements of the director: "For example, the actor's goal is to quiet an hysterical person. His desire is to shake and slap the hysteric. However the actor is directed not to touch him. One truthful adjustment would be for the actor to feel pity and cry out of helplessness towards the hysterical character."[23]

The techniques so far explicated were grouped together by Vakhtangov as *preparatory work.* The second phase of the actor's work was known as the *method of work,* comprising two elements of training introduced at the First Studio—communication (involving nonverbal communication among actors) and public solitude, which became a key element of Strasberg's Method. The third phase was the *analysis of plays and roles,* and the final one was *outer characterization,* incorporating exercises in rhythm.

After the tremendous success of Vakhtangov's production of Carlo Gozzi's *Turandot* and his premature death in 1922, Stanislavski realized that many of his modifications to the system were helpful, and began to utilize them as he elaborated his own praxis. Certainly, Vakhtangov made him realize the importance of physical expressiveness, and Vakhtangov's experiments appear to have influenced Stanislavski to try the practice that became the method of physical actions.

Michael Chekhov

Variations on Stanislavski's Ideas

Michael Chekhov initially developed his approach to acting and actor training as a version of the system taught at the First Studio, where he worked with Stanislavski, Sulerzhitsky, and Vakhtangov, who was both his friend and rival. A nephew of Anton Chekhov, he was a remarkably versatile actor, whose striking and original performances in productions by Stanislavski, Sulerzhitsky, Boleslavsky, and Vakhtangov gained his acting a reputation for intensity and spontaneity. Between 1918 and 1922, Chekhov ran his own acting studio in the Arbat area of Moscow. In 1923, Stanislavski appointed him director of the Second Moscow Art Theater. In his own teaching, Chekhov had begun to diverge from Stanislavski's praxis, integrating his own more mystical ideas drawn from the "eurythmy" of Rudolf Steiner and the anthroposophists, with elements of the psycho-technique. Both he and Vakhtangov were influenced by Meyerhold's experiments in biomechanics. In exile in Berlin in 1929, Chekhov explained some of his new ideas to Stanislavski, articulating his objections to the technique of emotion memory, which he believed promoted uncontrolled hysteria in acting, and stressing the importance of imagination and a physical approach to characterization. Although Stanislavski at first disagreed, Chekhov's arguments were among those that caused him to reconsider the psycho-technique and to experiment with the method of physical actions in the mid-1930s.

Chekhov was initially motivated to reformulate some of Stanislavski's acting strategies in order to make them more appealing to actors, who he believed would find it easier to respond to artistic challenges expressed in the form of suggestive instructions than to be reminded to correct faults: to help actors relax, he would tell them to move "with a feeling of ease," rather than merely identify points of tension and instruct them to relax. He was acutely aware of the need to stimulate the imagination at the unconscious level, and he devised exercises and improvisations that anticipated the concept of play and game later used by educators and acting teachers to develop the imagination without increasing self-consciousness.[24]

At times, however, Chekhov's language was obscure and his explanations of the exercises so idiosyncratic that they confused his students.[25] Chekhov differed from Stanislavski in his emphasis on the actor's use of imagination as opposed to her past experience. Although the Stanislavski system formed the matrix of his thinking, his own approach offered a corrective in certain areas. During rehearsals for his production of *Hamlet* in 1923, he said, "If the System of K.S. is high school, then my exercises are university."[26]

Thus, whereas Stanislavski emphasized the sense experience of the actor as the source of her creative work, Chekhov started from the observation of images already shaped by art or the actor's imagination. Chekhov emphasized the *form* of the characterization as a guiding principle, stressing the primacy of the integrated psychophysical form, by contrast with Stanislavski's dualism of inner psychological impulse and outer physical form. Aspects of Chekhov's praxis parallel Stanislavski's method of physical actions, and indeed some of the exercises appeared to be concrete applications of Stanislavski's principles. However, Chekhov's exile made it impossible after 1928 for Stanislavski to collaborate directly with his former student, so the similarities and differences in their ideas can be attributed to their separate attempts to elaborate some of the implications of Stanislavski's "analysis through *actions* and *objectives*" under different circumstances and from somewhat different perspectives.

During the early phase of his teaching, Chekhov modified the exercises for relaxation and concentration that had been developed at the First Studio, framing them in vivid physical images that appealed directly to the actor's imagination, rather than as instructions for the achievement of predetermined goals. Some of Chekhov's early exercises aimed at stimulating the creative spirit seem to be forms of self-hypnosis. The Actor's March was an exercise that required actors virtually to will themselves through movement into certain imagined states: "March around the room following a leader. Think to yourself: 'I am strong, I am healthy. My hands and arms are free and beautiful, my legs are strong.' Imagine yourself divided into three parts: 1) around your head is the feeling of space and power, the power of thought; 2) around your chest, the power of feeling; and 3) around your feet, the power of will. Keep marching in a circle until these three are in perfect harmony."[27]

Cultivation of Images as Training for the Imagination

The Actor's March exercise reveals that, even in his earliest phase, Chekhov addressed the need to conceive acting as a psychophysical process. Imaging the different faculties of thinking, feeling, and physical will in three different parts of the body, while the actor supported her imaginative process by marching in a circle, represents an integrated psychophysical approach to the actor's most fundamental tasks.[28] From the outset, Chekhov appears to have been frustrated by the insistence at the First Studio on separating the "actor's inner work on himself" from physical training. Chekhov's exercises ensured the integration of the psychological and the physical by concentrating on images. Chekhov believed that there was "an objective world in which our images lead their independent life," and that by accessing this world of the imagination, the artist might avoid the danger of her work being either too personal or too intellectual.[29] Many of the improvisations and exercises designed to develop concentration and imagination utilized images from dreams and from painting, sculpture, music, dance, and fairy stories, with which the students were to play, remaking artistic compositions in fantasies that drew on the unconscious. Although he never explained it in these terms, Chekhov's thinking here is suggestive of Jung's notion of the archetypes in the collective unconscious. In Chekhov's words, "The inner life of the images, and not the personal and tiny experiential resources of the actor should be elaborated on stage and shown to the audience."[30]

The development of Chekhov's approach to acting might well have been influenced by the example of Vakhtangov's fantastic realism, with its fusion of the psychological realism of Stanislavski's method of acting and a stylized approach to scenic staging. The exercises he invented while working in Russia on atmospheres, characterization, and working with a text represent significant attempts to engage the actor's imagination in expressing the moods and meaning of a play by means of games that help the actor incarnate character and situation through the medium of the body rather than through the exclusively mental processes of affective memory and emotional recall. Chekhov conceived of an atmosphere as a physical medium, akin to water or fog, and devised simple improvisations that aimed to teach the actor to absorb and radiate the atmosphere of a scenic space to an audience. The characterization exercises were at this stage simple ways of stimulating the actor to impersonate characters in physical terms, again, an early corrective to Stanislavski's "magic if" that sought to effect characterization by asking the actor to place herself in the character's situation, functioning by empathy rather than by means of physical transformation. Some of the ideas on working with a text were surprisingly modern, anticipating games devised in the 1960s and 1970s of throwing a ball while speaking the text, and transforming the sound of a word into a movement. A number of years before Stanislavski seriously explored the method of physical actions,

Chekhov was experimenting with ways of integrating mental and physical processes in creating character and mise-en-scène.

When Chekhov was forced to leave Russia in 1927, he lost his valuable connection with the Moscow Art Theater and its studios, and spent many frustrating years in exile working to establish schools where he might teach and test his acting praxis. Between 1927 and 1934, he worked as an actor and occasional director in Vienna, Berlin, Paris, Latvia, and Lithuania, before arriving in the United States in 1934. He set up a studio in Paris in 1931, and established a new theater and studio at Dartington Hall in England that he ran from 1936 to 1939. The imminence of World War II caused him to relocate his theatrical activities to Ridgefield, Connecticut, a short distance outside New York City, in 1939, and the Chekhov Theater Studio, as it was known, moved from Connecticut to Fifty-sixth Street in New York in 1941. In 1942, the war forced Chekhov to close the Theater Studio and move to Hollywood, where he played character parts in nine films between 1943 and 1954. After the war, he resumed teaching, and a shortened version of the book on acting that he had written in 1942 was published as *To the Actor* in 1953.

The later elaboration of Chekhov's major concepts of actions and qualities, the imaginary body, and the psychological gesture were all based on the fundamental principle that creativity consists in the actor's ability to apprehend and use images. According to Chekhov, each individual possessed a *higher ego* that transcended the selfish limits of the personality. This higher ego was the source of creativity, a kind of visionary consciousness that functioned apart from the everyday realm of means and ends to enable the actor to achieve a unique perspective on the characters and events of a play, providing her with moral understanding, enabling her to achieve a proper understanding of the contemporary world, and guaranteeing "the objectivity of humour." It is the higher ego that ensures the interrelationship between the play world, the consciousness of the actor, and the world of the spectator.

The Psychophysical Process

Chekhov's conception of actions and their qualities is a variant of Stanislavski's notion of actions and objectives. Having created exercises that aimed to enable the actor's personal feelings to interact with the changing atmospheres that surround her in various environments, Chekhov addressed the vexed question of emotions in terms similar to Stanislavski, although his solution was strikingly divergent from the technique of affective memory: "How often the actor tries to force his Feelings, to order himself to become sorrowful, gay, or happy, to hate, to love. It seems that such forcing is rarely successful. . . . That is why he so often seeks refuge in his old theatrical habits and worn-out clichés. But since the actor's Feelings cannot be commanded, are there any other means of governing them at will? There are."[31]

Every action can have a number of different qualities. One can raise one's arm slowly, gently, aggressively, cautiously, and so on. Each of these qualities of action possesses a unique "psychological tint." Chekhov noticed that feelings were evoked as a by-product of acting with intention: "Our doing, our action is always in our will, but not our Feelings. Here lies the key: the feeling was called forth, provoked, attracted indirectly by our 'business,' doing, action. . . . We can combine a number of Qualities in our action, and in every case we will get the same result. We will have at our disposal Feelings—real Feelings—that will follow our movements, our actions, slipping into them easily and with sufficient strength."[32]

Provoking appropriate emotions thus became for Chekhov a matter of performing physical actions with qualities that embodied clear intentions. His idea of the qualities of action, although not as sophisticated in its elaboration, is remarkably similar to Rudolf Laban's concept of the dynamic qualities of effort actions.[33] Chekhov recognized that if the performance of physical movements was controlled by the exercise of will, feelings that were not in themselves amenable to the control of will could be stirred by physical movements. The psyche could be stimulated by the movement of the body in such a way that "the Action (and Will) shows 'what' happens, whereas the Quality (and Feelings) shows 'how' it happens."[34] Chekhov resolved the dialectical tension between the introspective idealism of Stanislavski's psycho-technique and the behavioristic materialism of Meyerhold's biomechanics. His concept of actions and qualities represented a synthesis between the antithetical positions of the two earlier approaches, overcoming the reductionism inherent in concentrating exclusively on either inner psychological sensations or on bodily responses to purely physical stimuli.

In *On the Technique of Acting,* exercise 20 implies a notion of the dynamic qualities of movement similar to that which underlies Laban's scale of effort actions, although it lacks the framework of an overall system that relates qualities of energy (effort) with spatial forms and is phrased in a suggestive manner that is easily accessible to a student actor's commonsense assumptions about intention and feeling:[35] "Train yourself to make certain gestures with the utmost expressiveness, as fully and completely as you can. These gestures might express, for instance: drawing, pulling, pressing, lifting, throwing, crumpling, coaxing, separating, tearing, penetrating, touching, brushing away, opening, closing, breaking, taking, giving, supporting, holding back, scratching. You can produce each of these gestures with different qualities: violently, quietly, surely, carefully, staccato, legato, tenderly, lovingly, coldly, angrily, cowardly, superficially, painfully, joyfully, thoughtfully, energetically."[36]

It is significant that Chekhov advised that the student should not permit the movements to "become a kind of acting" while executing the exercise. Like Laban, he perceived the psychophysical impact of movement to be created by the precise articulation of its quality of energy (which Laban named *effort*). In practicing the actions, Chekhov advised the student to make them as broad as possible, thus ensuring that the actions would be properly articulated in space and that the investment of particular qualities in the performance of each might be more easily achieved. (According to Laban, small movements are less clearly articulated in space and therefore more difficult to execute precisely.) Chekhov recommended the student repeat the actions and qualities exercises regularly in order to stimulate and enhance the body's psychophysical function. The exercises could be varied in tempo and intensity. Once perfected, the actions could be executed by different parts of the body, with the remaining parts engaged in the quality of the movement but not actually performing the action, or even "in the imagination" with the body immobile, so that the actor might become sensitive to the psychological dimension of the movements.

Chekhov's approach to actor training was entirely based on the actor's psychophysical integrity as an organism: "There are no purely physical exercises in our method . . . our primary aim is to penetrate all of the parts of the body with fine psychological vibrations. This process makes the physical body more and more sensitive in its ability to receive our inner impulses and to convey them expressively to the audience from the stage."[37] Chekhov viewed the actor's task as a training in four linked psychophysical movement skills he called *feelings*. The *feeling of ease* was Chekhov's term for relaxation and was achieved in the body by means of flowing, flying and radiating movements. The *feeling of form* constituted the actor's ability to shape movements in space in a choreographic manner, and it was "akin to *molding* movements." Chekhov's ideas of how the actor articulates the body as a form in space were derived from Steiner's eurythmy: the "aesthetic consciousness" promotes the actor's awareness of the expressive function of the head, chest, and legs-feet.

Significantly, Chekhov rejected the nineteenth-century belief that facial expressions were indexical signs of emotion that had inspired the various codifications of physiognomy and facial expression (the system of Delsarte being the most sophisticated example). "The head is expressive only as a whole . . . 'expressions' on the actor's face are nothing other than illegitimate attempts to make 'gestures' with the head."[38] The head was connected with intellectual and spiritual activity; the chest with emotional and visceral feelings; the legs and feet with the operation of the will. By developing the feeling of form, the student learned to shape the movement of the body in time (rhythm) and space in order to render the natural movements of everyday life expressive as art. The *feeling of beauty* was to be developed by acquiring sensitivity to the expressive economy of gesture or movement as psychophysical form. It was manifested as a satisfaction or pleasure in the harmony of expressive means and ends, and was to be trained by practice in simultaneously performing and observing oneself. Even horrible violence, like the blinding of Gloucester in *King Lear,* should be performed with a feeling of beauty, the observance of its aesthetic propriety within the drama ensuring that it would not be performed merely to provoke a sensationalist effect of pure horror. The *feeling of the whole* was conceived as the actor's overall sense of the relationship between the expressive movements that are component parts of dramatic action and the overall shape of that action as a complete aesthetic form.

An Innovative Approach to Characterization

The Psychological Gesture

Chekhov conceived the notion of the *psychological gesture* while teaching in the United States in the early 1940s. It was a further development of the idea of the psychophysical character of movement first articulated in his work on actions and qualities. Having noticed the tendency in idiomatic speech to express psychological states and processes in physical terms, for example, to grasp an idea, to fall into despair, to draw a conclusion, Chekhov saw the possibility of using a concentrated gesture to picture the definitive psychological attitude of a character in kinesthetic terms. A psychological gesture was not actually to be performed as part of the stage action, but was a way of imaginatively embodying in a kinesthetic image the character's fundamental psychophysical attitude. Such an imaging of character was a corrective to the tendency for the director to work with an analytical concept of character, which the actor was then obliged to translate into the physical and kinetic language of the stage. The psychological gesture would stir the actor's unconscious, guiding her in shaping the various individual psychophysical actions called for by the play.

The actor was required "to 'see' *what* the character is aiming at, *what* is his wish, his desire."[39] There are parallels between the psychological gesture and Stanislavski's notion of the character's objectives and her super-objective in the play, although Chekhov tried to translate the character's active project in the drama into kinesthetic images that would stir the imagination rather than appeal to the intellect. The actor was not to confuse the gestures executed as part of the action of the play with the character's psychological gesture—a movement that was used in preparing the characterization by representing in iconic form the essence of the gestures and qualities indicated by the text. As an example, "Hamlet's Psychological Gesture might be a large, slow, heavy movement with both arms and hands, from above downward toward the earth. You may find this Gesture right for Hamlet's dark, depressed mood at this time of his life."[40]

Having practiced the gesture in order to fix its image kinesthetically, the actor then performs the action of a scene, while visualizing the psychological gesture. By alternating the performance of the psychological gesture with acting the scene as prescribed in the play text, the actor would progressively to incorporate the meaning of the psychological gesture into her enactment: "[It] becomes evident to you [the actor] that behind each internal state or movement in acting is hidden a simple and expressive Psychological Gesture that is the essence of the acting. . . . Boastful Falstaff may have big, brave, unbridled acting gestures while the invisible Psychological Gesture that inspires the actor can be a small, cowardly, compressing one—as if he holds in his hand a small piece of paper that he crumples."[41]

Psychological gestures might be employed in animating individual sequences of stage action, or a speech or section of dialogue, as well as a character's overall role in the play's action (a notion different but complementary to that of Stanislavski's super-objective). By finding a psychological gesture that underlies a speech, the actor was to motivate the speech as a concrete psychophysical action, thus avoiding any tendency to exploit a merely rhetorical style. The psychological gesture might be practiced for as long as the actor found it necessary to stimulate her imagination, as a kind of first draft for the detailed action of the scene that was gradually built up through rehearsal. The psychological gestures, however, helped the actor to identify the kinesthetic outline of a character through a psychophysical process.

Transitions from one psychological gesture to another were to be practiced by the actor in order to help her to structure the role in psychophysical terms and to perfect the kinesthetic pattern of the performance as a whole.

The Imaginary Body as a Key to Characterization

According to Chekhov, "The actor imagines with his body."[42] Chekhov was determined to exploit the actor's highly cultivated sensibility through a process he named *incorporation:* the actor first visualized a character in terms of physique and movement before incarnating the character's psychophysical form in a series of separate phases. In order not to avoid clichéd characterizations, the actor was not to physicalize the character before having imagined her fully: "The actor should look upon the character in his imagination, seeing it moving, hearing it speaking, thus displaying its inner life before his mind's eye. He should first fix his attention on one chosen feature."[43]

In order to incorporate the one feature, the actor studied it first in the imagination until she was able to imitate it physically. Gradually, the repetition of the single feature was absorbed kinesthetically, dictating an appropriate psychophysical attitude as it became *incorporated* by the actor. Eventually all aspects of the character would reveal themselves through the method of incorporation, which involved the achievement of a psychophysical identification with the character through a physiological process.

Chekhov echoed Stanislavski in his insistence on the importance of observation of real people, rather than characters performed by great actors, as a source for characterization. His emphasis, however, on the difference between the actor's and character's physical (and therefore psychological) attitudes represented a marked divergence from Stanislavski's method of creating the character through the magic if. Whereas Stanislavski's method basically required the actor to place her person in the character's situation, leaving physical details of characterization to be added on at a final stage of rehearsal, if necessary, the principal aim of Chekhov's technique was to enable the actor to use movement in order to transform the actor's body into that of the character. "[The] actor must . . . try to imitate, to incorporate all the characteristic features he has accumulated during his observations. This valuable material will be stored in the actor's subconscious and, being forgotten, will appear of itself when needed, in a transformed, individualised way. . . . Under the training of observation, the actor's imagination will acquire more variety and his humour will also grow. Sooner or later, the actor will come to the firm conviction that there are no parts without characterisation. . . . He will cease once and for all acting himself in his appearances on the stage."[44]

Although the actor might not be able to change the physical shape of her body, Chekhov believed that she could create an *imaginary body* through movement, which would convey the illusion of another physical being. The actor was first to imagine herself as another body, located in the same place as her body. Once this invisible body had been fully imagined, she would begin to work on her movements until she was able to articulate a kinesthetic pattern and body posture that would evoke the body of the character. By combining an imitation of what Laban would call another *body shape* with careful delineation of an appropriate *movement personality* (Laban), Chekhov's imaginary body formed the psychophysical basis of a characterization that could be further elaborated by means of makeup and costume. Significantly, the imaginary body had to be conceived through an imaginative process that involved the integration of psychological and physiological processes. Mechanical means of external characterization were merely aids to the complete imaginative embodiment of character.

In creating the imaginary body, the actor would find a specific center in the body that was the initial point of motivation for the character. Faust's center, for example, might be in his head; Tartuffe's in one of his eyes; Falstaff's in his stomach. The actor was able to unify various aspects of the character's personality by employing the center as a point of focus for intentions and movements. Chekhov's suggested class exercises for characterization involved alternately starting from the creation of an imaginary body with its own center and gradually observing what kind of character emerged in the process, or choosing a character from a literary work or play and working from an image of her given psychology, arriving at her imaginary body through various phases of incorporation.

While accepting the efficacy of Stanislavski's concept of the objective as a principle that determined the actor-character's shaping of action, Chekhov was concerned that the actor should learn to imagine the character's objectives in concretely physical terms, rather than merely to attempt to illustrate what had initially been analyzed. The problem for an actor was in "transmitting the Objective from the purely mental sphere to the region of the actor's Will, where it belongs." According to Chekhov, the actor should first imagine her character in action, until she was intuitively able to identify her objective. She might also appeal directly to her will by acting out "on the sly"—without complete theatrical realization—moments or scenes that might allow her gradually to recognize an objective that could supply a coherent motivation for executing that particular sequence of action. This was a clever method of ensuring that unconscious processes would be stimulated by an imaginative investment in purely physical patterns of stage activity.[45] In Chekhov's view, "the Psychological Gesture, as the crystallised Will, is the Objective." Having identified the objective in the analytical terms represented by a transitive verb ("I wish to . . .") the actor's job was to "pour the Objective out into the body." The psychological gesture provided the form in which to achieve this.

In addition to the psychophysical exercises on characterization, Chekhov devised a number of group exercises aimed at teaching a group of actors to play as an ensemble. He also invented a number of improvisations designed to cultivate in the actor a sense of style, which he believed should arise directly from the drama as a physical expression of its aesthetic form. Chekhov's praxis was an idiosyncratic mixture of pragmatic experimentation with the problems of physical expression on stage and quasi-mystical ideas about the imagination. He did, however, possess a highly sophisticated grasp of the practical problems of integrating the psychological and physiological aspects of the actor's technique, and most of his theories were intended as concrete methods of addressing them. In this respect, they not only constituted a further elaboration of Stanislavski's method of physical actions but anticipated some of Laban's theories of effort, albeit in less systematic terms.

Stanislavski's Influence in the United States

Stanislavski's praxis had very little impact on the British theater until the 1960s. Although the MAT's productions had by the mid-1920s been seen in France, Germany, Poland, and the United States, the company never performed in London. The most notable early performances of Chekhov's plays in Britain were the English-language productions of Theodore Komisarjevsky, brother of the actress Vera Komisarjevskaya. These productions were not influenced by Stanislavski, as Komisarjevsky had not trained with the MAT but had succeeded Meyerhold as artistic director of his sister's theater in Saint Petersburg. Stanislavski was just a name to most British actors, and there was widespread misunderstanding of his theories in Britain until the 1960s.

In 1923 the Moscow Art Theater embarked on a tour of the United States that almost immediately made Stanislavski's name famous throughout the country and was to have a profound impact on the American acting tradition. During the 1920s Stanislavski's ideas were initially disseminated in the United States by Richard Boleslavsky, who had acted in the MAT's *A Month in the Country* in 1909 and was not conversant with Stanislavski's later praxis, having emigrated to the United States in 1922. Shortly after the MAT's American tour of 1923, Boleslavsky gave a series of lectures on

Stanislavski's work as he had experienced it at the First Studio; this led to his setting up of a theater school in New York. After moving to new premises in 1924, he was joined by two other alumni of the MAT, Maria Ouspenskaya, who remained in the United States after the tour, and Maria Germanova, who had emigrated some years earlier. The school they founded became the American Laboratory Theater.

In 1927 Boleslavsky began to publish sections of what became *Acting: The First Six Lessons* (1933), codifying his knowledge of Stanislavski's early teaching into a method attractive to American acting students. The book was reprinted numerous times during the next fifty years, and became a standard text for students.

It was Boleslavsky's version of Stanislavski's praxis that was absorbed by its most influential exponents in the United States, Lee Strasberg and Stella Adler. They in turn taught generations of actors and acting teachers versions of Stanislavski's system that had by the 1950s come to be known as the Method. Although in 1934 Strasberg and Adler had a fundamental disagreement over the relative importance of imagination and emotion memory, they were both regarded as disciples of Stanislavski. In America, the Method came to be viewed as indistinguishable from Stanislavski's system rather than as Strasberg's American version of Stanislavski's early psycho-technique.

Boleslavsky emphasized the importance of personal and natural emotion. According to Boleslavsky, "an actor who 'lives his part' is a creative actor; the one who simply imitates different human emotions without feeling them each time is a 'mechanical' one." The creative actor should use "a brand-new, fresh feeling each time he plays his role."[46] This unequivocal demand for both real emotion and spontaneity formed the cornerstone of Strasberg's approach, and became the chief criterion by which American audiences and critics judged acting in film, on television and in the theater. Boleslavsky's idea that "'living one's part' means complete psychological and physical self-abandon for a definite period of time" chimed perfectly with the growing interest in psychoanalysis as a way of liberating oneself of inhibitions that are supposedly a result of psychological repression, a practice valorized by the liberal myth of individualism enshrined in the American Constitution as the right to the pursuit of happiness.[47]

Boleslavsky's book was written in dialogue form as a series of six private classes given to a young woman referred to as "the creature." The lessons began with "concentration," continuing with "memory of emotion," "dramatic action," "characterisation," "observation," and "rhythm." The presentation of praxis in Boleslavsky's book was far more simple than it was in those of Stanislavski. Whereas Boleslavsky's dialogue form was merely a convenient way of correcting the student's misunderstandings with regard to good acting and how it is produced, the dialogue form of *An Actor Prepares* and *Building a Character* was intended to give a sense of the concrete problems encountered by actors under the material conditions of their practice. The discussion among Tortsov the teacher, Kostya the student actor, and other actors illustrated problem-solving in the actual conditions of training and rehearsal, something Boleslavsky did not attempt.

There appears to be a contradiction in Boleslavsky's thinking that he was unable to resolve in the book. At one point he states: "The actor who is to express to us a peculiar passion and its effects, if he would play his character with *truth,* is not only to assume the emotions which that passion would produce in the generality of mankind; but he is to give it that peculiar form under which it would appear, when exerting itself in the breast of such a person as he is giving us the portrait of."[48] This stress on the particularity of every detail of characterization has always been a key aspect of Method acting, and also reflects Stanislavski's naturalistic assumption that each character's emotions are an aspect of her own specific history and social position. However, Boleslavsky also makes an opposite claim, implying that the circumstances of the character's particular biography might be ignored or changed if they do not fit the actor's feelings about what emotions are appropriate for the role: "The emotion of a character is the only sphere where the author should pay attention to the actor's demands and adjust his writings to the actor's interpretation or, an actor is justified in adjusting the author's writing to achieve the best results for his own emotional outline of the part."[49] The latter idea initiated the tendency critics have often noted in Method performances to substitute the actor's own personality and emotions for those indicated by the playwright. Boleslavsky's attitude prefigured current practice in filmmaking, but had little in common with Stanislavski's respectful approach to the dramatist's text.

From Stanislavski to Strasberg

In 1931 the Group Theater was founded by Harold Clurman, Cheryl Crawford, and Lee Strasberg. As Clurman, Strasberg, and Stella Adler, a leading actor with the Group, had all been students of Boleslavsky and Ouspenskaya, they acquired secondhand experience of the approach to acting practiced by Stanislavski and Sulerzhitsky during the days of the First Studio. The Group Theater was to become the most prestigious and influential theater company in the United States, a breeding ground for left-wing directors, actors, and writers who constituted the first generation of recognizably

American theater and film artists, including Elia Kazan, Robert Lewis, Clifford Odets, William Saroyan, Franchot Tone, Lee J. Cobb, Luther Adler, and Frances Farmer. The disintegration of the Group in 1941 led eventually to the formation by Elia Kazan, Robert Lewis, and Cheryl Crawford of the Actors Studio in 1947. Its roster of famous students included Montgomery Clift, Julie Harris, Paul Newman, James Dean, Rod Steiger, Shelley Winters, Geraldine Page, Al Pacino, and Robert De Niro. It promoted the work of playwrights such as Tennessee Williams, Arthur Miller, William Inge, and Edward Albee, and fostered directors such as Arthur Penn.

Early in the history of the Group Theater a serious argument culminated in Lee Strasberg's decision to leave the company in 1937. Stella Adler met and worked with Stanislavski in Paris in 1934, learning his later approach directly. Adler learned the importance of building the logic of the character's actions from the given circumstances, and of Stanislavski's reconsideration of emotion memory, by now viewed as an aid to dealing with emotional inhibition during training but no longer thought of as useful in performance. Adler returned to New York to tell her colleagues about the method of physical action. "Her work with Stanislavski on her own acting problems led her to believe that 'the company had been misusing emotional memory . . . by overemphasising personal circumstances.'"[50] Adler reminded her colleagues of the importance of imagination (the "magic if") in realizing the given circumstances when creating a role.

Strasberg, who had visited Moscow in 1934 and been unimpressed with the productions of the MAT (in what was a rather uninspired phase of its work), insisted that there was no reason for the Group to follow Stanislavski's later methods uncritically. On a visit to Moscow in 1935, Harold Clurman discussed the method of physical actions with Stanislavski and confirmed Adler's view of the importance of his later work; nevertheless Strasberg refused to change his own approach. While acknowledging his debt to Stanislavski in "laying the foundations of our modern technique. . . . [which] concentrated on the inner approach to the exclusion of external theatrics,"[51] Strasberg asserted the superiority of his own system of training the actor. The Method, he claimed, was an American approach that had been developed to suit the needs of American actors.

One of the historiographical problems regarding Stanislavski's influence in the United States results from Strasberg's presenting the Method, on the one hand, as a straightforward extension of Stanislavski's system and, on the other, as a distinctively American transformation: "I feel it both theoretically wise and practically sound to talk of the work done by the Group Theater and the Actors Studio, as being an adaptation of the Stanislavski System.

'The Method' is therefore our version of the System."[52] This seems equivocal, as does his statement in the *New York Times* on September 2, 1956: "The methods of the Studio derive from the work of Stanislavski and his pupil Vakhtangov with modifications based on the work of the Group Theatre and other work since then."[53] Stella Adler and many others (such as Robert Lewis, Sanford Meisner, Elia Kazan, Herbert Berghof, Uta Hagen), remained critical of certain Method practices throughout their working lives, claiming that they and not Strasberg were perpetuating the legacy of Stanislavski.

With the establishment of the Actors Studio, the Method began to make a profound impact on the style and techniques of American acting. Since Kazan was the most prestigious young theater and film director of the time, his casting of a number of Actors Studio alumni in productions on Broadway and in Hollywood films (Marlon Brando, Eli Wallach, Julie Harris, Rod Steiger, Montgomery Clift) ensured its international standing. After Strasberg was chosen to succeed Kazan as a regular teacher there in 1951, the status of Strasberg's Method as the preeminent American version of Stanislavski's teaching was assured. Such was the personal mystique of Strasberg at the Studio that, even though he never published a coherent account of his own approach, at least three generations of young American actors were spellbound by his charisma, assuming that what the Actors Studio taught was authentic Stanislavskian praxis. The first serious challenge to the dominance of the mannered emotionalism of Method acting came in the 1960s from the radical antinaturalistic theater of avant-garde groups like the Living Theater, the Bread and Puppet Theater, and the Open Theater. Inspired by the plays of Beckett, Brecht, Genet, and Ionesco, and informed by the theories and practices of Brecht, Artaud, and Grotowski, this movement had by the 1970s stimulated a wholesale reassessment and revision of systems of rehearsal and actor training by professionals and teachers within university theater departments.

Strasberg's Approach to Acting and Actor Training

What were the fundamental principles of Strasberg's Method, and how did he teach them to student actors? Unlike other members of the Group Theatre such as Harold Clurman and Elia Kazan, Strasberg never achieved great acclaim as a professional theater director. This may explain why the Actors Studio seldom mounted productions, although a typical class session involved the presentation of rehearsed solo or duologue scenes before an audience of Studio members. These were analyzed by a moderator, who invited critical responses from the audience, before summing up at the end. Actors were expected to have undergone conventional training before being admitted to the Studio. There were group classes in which improvisations were performed, relaxation and concentration exercises taught and practiced, and attention paid to individual actors' problems; but apart from the scene study there was no timetabled production work.[54]

This schedule was designed to accommodate the fact that most members of the Studio were working actors who attended classes for two or four hours a week in order to monitor and sustain their own personal process of development as artists; such professionals could not afford to stop working to attend on a full-time basis. As a consequence of the practical limitations imposed by the commercial system of Broadway theater, the structure and aim of the teaching distinguished Strasberg's approach from that of Stanislavski, whose various studios functioned continuously as laboratories for experimenting with artistic problems that were to be resolved in actual productions, and were attended by actors who were usually appearing in MAT productions in the evenings.

Strasberg and Vakhtangov

Throughout his life Strasberg claimed to have been strongly influenced by Vakhtangov, whose diary notes "Preparing for the Role" were arranged by Boris Zakhava and available to Strasberg in an English translation by 1931.[55] Vakhtangov was more interested than Stanislavski in what they both referred to as the "subconscious," and Vakhtangov's version of Stanislavski was particularly appealing to Strasberg. Strasberg recognized that the actor is the only artist whose own body is the instrument and whose own experience the potential material of her art.[56] "The extraordinary thing about acting is that life itself is actually used to create artistic results . . . since the actor is also a human being, he does not pretend to use reality. He can literally use everything that exists. The actor uses . . . real thought . . . real sensation and real behaviour. That actual reality is the material of our craft."[57]

Echoing the thinking that led Edward Gordon Craig to demand that the actor acquire the technical control of an Über-marionette, Strasberg perceived this paradox to be the source of the actor's chief problem: "The actor's human nature not only makes possible his greatness, but also is the source of his problems. . . . The approach to this actor's problem must therefore deal first with relieving whatever difficulties are inherent in himself that negate his freedom of expression and block the capacities he possesses."[58] Although Strasberg's identification of the central problem of the actor is common to both Craig's and Copeau's ideas about the paradoxical duality of the actor as both instrument and creator, his proposed solution is based on Stanislavski's recognition of the creative mood as one free of the nervous tensions typically experienced in the moment of performance.[59]

Strasberg defined his notion of good acting in opposition to the kinds of performance that it was intended to replace. Natural acting, in other words, was presumed to be a definitively human function that Western education had tried in various ways to repress. In terms that were especially appealing to midcentury American actors, Strasberg offered his Method as a way of eradicating blocks, of destroying clichés, of liberating the actor from the deadening effect of convention and habit. Strasberg was given to comparing American Method acting with the mannered theatricality that in his view threatened to render the technically contrived British approach redundant. True to an untheorized liberal ideal, spontaneity and naturalness were regarded as positive values, convention and technique as inherently bad. Method acting was "proletarian," whereas British acting was "aristocratic."

Recordings of his comments at Actors Studio sessions indicate the personal force of his obsession with liberating the actor from clichéd responses, of freeing her from old habits, and of releasing the natural creativity trapped within her by neurotic patterns of behavior. Strasberg's ideology of spontaneous and "live" acting represents an extreme version of Stanislavski's organicist conception of acting as a natural process, although the rhetoric by which Strasberg demanded the removal of the tensions and inhibitions that modern social life has placed upon the actor has little similarity with Stanislavski's search to discover the "natural laws" of artistic creation. The language of Method actors and teachers mimicked the popular jargon of psychoanalysis as it was expressed in midcentury American culture. Whether this was a deliberate strategy on Strasberg's part cannot be conclusively determined. Although he was on occasions compared by his students to both psychoanalyst and God, Strasberg was not trained as a psychiatrist or psychoanalyst and denied that he used psychoanalytic methods. However, if an actor had a persistent creative block that seemed to be the result of a psychological problem, Strasberg would recommend psychoanalysis as a way of dealing with it.

Strasberg's concept of good acting reveals some striking similarities with that of Vakhtangov: "A theatrical school must clear the way for the creative potentialities of the student—but he must move and proceed along this road by himself; he cannot be taught. The school must remove all the conventional rubbish which prevents the spontaneous manifestation of the student's deeply hidden potentialities. . . . If the school . . . attempts to teach him creativeness itself, then it may ruin a scenic talent given by nature. . . .

It is impossible to teach anybody how to create because the creative process is a sub-conscious one, while all teaching is a form of conscious activity which can only prepare the actor for creative work."[60] Vakhtangov's view of the aim of training provides a coherent rationale for the teaching methodology that emerged at the Actors Studio. Rather than teaching any specific techniques, Strasberg and his colleagues operated in a heuristic way, provoking the actor into the genuine expression of the creative impulses inside her and goading her into shedding the defensive masks of social performance in order to reveal a core of genuine feeling that was believed to express the essential self. Vakhtangov was extremely sensitive to the creative workings of the unconscious, and expressed a more sophisticated view than that of Stanislavski of the motivational process through which the actor creates the through-line of the character's actions. Vakhtangov utilized a pseudo-Freudian terminology of volitional drives.

> An action directed towards the gratification of will is continuously accompanied by a series of spontaneous feelings, the content of which is the anticipation of the coming gratification or the fear of failure. . . . Thus feeling is a product of will and the conscious (and sometimes subconscious) actions directed towards its gratification. . . . The emotion, as well as the means of expression, is being directed subconsciously, spontaneously, in the process of executing actions directed towards the gratification of a desire. The actor must therefore come on stage not in order to feel or experience emotions, but in order to act. "Don't wait for emotions—act immediately," Stanislavski said. . . . Stanislavski did not invent anything. He teaches us to follow the road pointed out by nature itself.[61]

The Method actor's privileging of spontaneous impulses and reactions is rather different from Stanislavski's carefully planned sequence of units and objectives, whose through-line and superobjective promote consistency in the construction of character through the framework of circumstances and intentions. Where Stanislavski's approach resulted in unified characterizations that invested dramatic characters with complete coherence of motive Strasberg emphasized the incoherent behavior of people driven by unconscious complexes of desire and need, and thus typically expressing a sense of self as fractured and contradictory.

Vakhtangov emphasized to an extreme one aspect of Stanislavski's approach to characterization. Stanislavski had, perhaps uncritically, assumed that an actor is capable of imagining most human experiences through a process of empathy that enables the actor to employ the techniques of the "magic if" and emotional memory. Vakhtangov, possibly sensing a problem in relying on empathy, devoted attention to the process by which the actor justifies the character's actions, which he called "agitation from the essence":

> The actor must work during rehearsals upon whatever surrounds him in the drama, he must make this become his atmosphere, so that the problems of the part become his problems, i.e. the acting out of the character must become the actor's natural need. . . . The actor must come to realize the necessity of actions pointed out by the author—they must become organic. . . . In order that such an *agitation from the essence* arise, it is necessary to live your own temperament on the stage and not the supposed temperament of the character. You must proceed from yourself and not from a conceived image; you must place yourself in the position of the situation of the character. . . . To create and not be oneself is impossible. . . . You cannot seek the character somewhere outside yourself and then fit it on—you must make it up out of the material which you yourself possess.[62]

This is the most extreme formulation of Stanislavski's idea that the actor's aim is to place herself entirely in the fictional situation, acting as she would if *she* were in the character's circumstances. Vakhtangov transposes the psychology governing the motivation of characters to the sphere of the actor, insisting that the actor should justify every action she performs with the motivational force of her own psychological identity. The action of the play should on a psychological level stimulate the actor's mechanism of desire. To do this the actor has in some way to substitute her person for that of the character. No matter how competent the actor's imagination is in accomplishing the required substitution of actor for character, Vakhtangov is unable in theory to resolve the difference between the history and experience of the actor and the implicit biography of the character. Granted the impossibility of such a perfect overlap, Vakhtangov's words imply that the actor's reality is privileged over the fictional identity of the character. The same choice was advocated by Boleslavsky and through the influence of Strasberg seems to have been adopted by the majority of Method actors, causing generations of literary and theatrical critics to berate their "infidelity" to the playwright.[63]

Strasberg's Acting Exercises

In the absence of an organized body of theoretical reflection by Strasberg, an analysis of his class exercises must suffice to indicate his praxis. Relaxation was a fundamental principle, deriving from Stanislavski's earliest observations regarding the ability of the great actor to achieve the creative state as a precondition for successful performance. For Strasberg, as for Stanislavski and Sulerzhitsky, "tension is the actor's occupational disease. . . . in order to act, the actor must relax."[64] Before commencing any other class exercises or scene work, the actor should ensure that she is properly relaxed.

Relaxation Exercise

Strasberg believed that his basic relaxation exercise might in itself release creative impulses (energy) that had been blocked by tension. Typically, Strasberg connected physical relaxation with freedom from repression, and exercises were viewed as a kind of therapy for the actor's imagination. The relaxation exercise required the actor to find a sitting position in a straight-backed chair that would allow her to fall asleep. (The uncomfortable chair supplied an analogy for the obstacles to relaxation the actor might encounter on stage.) At that point, the actor usually believed she was fully relaxed, but by isolating separate muscle groups, she was made to recognize the different tensions of which she had not even been aware. Once the actor had become conscious of the different locations of tension, particularly those associated with mental tension, such as the bridge of the nose, the temples, the muscles of the lower jaw and the neck, she could begin to relax at will, a process that would take at least twenty minutes. On the occasions when an actor experienced any emotional disturbance during this attempt, she was asked to open her throat and emit sound from deep in the chest, thus supposedly releasing any excess emotional tension.

Concentration through the Use of Sense Memory

For Strasberg, relaxation and concentration were two sides of a coin. Concentration was achieved by using a graduated series of "object exercises" that stimulated and developed the sense memory. As the primary faculty of the actor the sense memory permits the actor's imagination to function with the precision necessary to create a convincing fictional world in performance. Strasberg insisted that the actor perform improvisations involving imaginary objects (in this respect contradicting Stanislavski's later method of rehearsing on the set with real props). Actors would perform sequences of activities such as drinking a cup of coffee, brushing teeth, washing dishes, shaving, making up, exploring sensations such as extreme cold, heat, pain, smells, sunshine, rain. The aim was not so much to mime the objects, but to visualize them so fully that the actor might achieve a physiological reaction as a result of the kinesthetic process.

"Song and Dance"

The use of sense memory was a preparation for imaginative expression. Often actors might be working freely with their imaginations yet unable to externalize their imaginative experience. In some cases, particularly where powerful emotions were involved, Strasberg perceived the actor as being prevented by conditioning from freely expressing what she might have been experiencing internally.[65] The actor was asked to make eye contact with the audience and to sound the melody of a familiar song (sometimes from the chest, if the throat was tense), experiencing the feelings evoked by the sound without using the words or *acting* their meaning. The audience invariably observed signs of tension such as involuntary movements, muscular spasms, laughter, and even tears. The performer's self-consciousness of singing in front of an audience made her aware of the conflict between her will to maintain control of her body and the spontaneous impulses and inner feelings that refuse to be controlled. Later the actor was asked to move in different ways (skipping, jumping, running, dancing in various styles) and in different tempi, changing the movement suddenly without breaking the line of the song, yet ensuring that the singing flowed from the movements, thus helping to free the actor of her vocal inhibitions by relating impulse to expression.

Private Moment

The most controversial aspects of Strasberg's teaching at the Actors Studio were his use of the private moment and affective memory exercises. The private moment was an improvisation derived from Stanislavski's idea of "public solitude," the paradoxical demand that the actor reveal the most private moments of experience in the public context of a theatrical performance. In order to learn to overcome the normal inhibitions that prevent actors from exposing intimate feelings and behavior in public, Strasberg asked them to perform for the class a private moment drawn from their own experience—not merely a situation in which they were alone, but one in which they were doing something that they would immediately cease to do if someone else entered the room. Often, those actors who were very inhibited in class were able to perform with great abandon and vivid expression during the exercise, talking out loud to imaginary friends, for example, or doing an imitation flamenco dance or lounging around the room with absolutely no anxieties about how they appeared to others. Clearly, however, the exercise could be open to abuse, and there were occasional reports of exhibitionist behavior such as actors taking their clothes off to have a shower, or performing intimate acts.

Affective Memory

The area of work in which Strasberg deliberately chose to diverge from Stanislavski's later praxis was affective memory. He asserted that Vakhtangov was the source of "the idea of affective memory as the central experience with which the actor works," stressing that "the basic idea . . . is not emotional recall but that the actor's emotion on the stage should never be really real. It should be only *remembered* emotion."[66] According to Strasberg affective memory functioned in a Proustian manner through the associations of specific sensory objects with important emotional experiences from the past. The use of sense memory provided a trigger for the actor's memory of particular emotions, allowing the actor to remember the particular form in which these feelings were manifested, as opposed to the generalized imitations produced by external mimicry of emotional behavior.

The actor therefore started by trying to recall precisely where the past event took place, re-creating in her mind the precise details of the environment, for example, the size of the room, temperature, shape, texture, colors, smells, details of furniture. The actor was asked to close her eyes and try to verbalize the sequence of sense impressions leading up to the emotional moment, for example, the sounds she heard, how she saw someone enter the room, how his voice sounded. All this was to be recalled with as much attention to particular sensory details as possible, the actor refraining from saying what she felt, but instead describing the impressions accurately. The exercise stimulated the actor to feel in the present the emotions associated with the situation in her past by exploiting the Pavlovian conditioned reflex. The affective memory exercise was to be used not only in class as a way of making the actor aware of her own repertoire of stored emotions but also in rehearsal and performance to re-create the authentic form of feelings analogous to those of the character in the fictional situations of the play. With practice, an actor could learn to recall a particular emotion in a minute. Since Stanislavski and Sulerzhitsky introduced the exercise at the First Studio there has been much criticism of it, including the logical objection that the specific terms of the drama are ignored because the actor is obliged to substitute memories of her own unique experience for the feelings of the character in the context of fictional action. Opponents of Strasberg's approach have also pointed out the potential damage that might be done by interfering in the private sphere of actors' personal experience, and critics of Method acting often blame the emphasis on affective memory for Method actors' tendency to play emotions rather than actions and motives.

Animal Exercises

Strasberg invented a number of exercises to enable the actor to rid herself of physical and psychological inhibitions. Animal exercises aimed to develop the actor's powers of observation, assisting her to physicalize her characterizations: "The animal exercises are the beginning of character work, which depends upon seeing the differences between yourself and the character. They help the actor to discover and use parts of himself."[67] Actors were required to observe a specific animal in a zoo, then to work on physically re-creating their movement behavior and finally to attempt to inhabit the animal's behavior "from within." A suitable animal could then function in place of the character to be portrayed. By playing the character's action as though she were an animal, the actor learns to observe the external features of the character's attitude and behavior as an extension of the inner life.[68]

Speaking Out

When an actor had problems in playing a scene (e.g., excessive tension, confusion over motives, physical difficulties in coordinating stage business), Strasberg employed the device of speaking out the problem. By verbalizing the difficulties as she set about performing them, the actor would admit that which was disturbing her, rather than repress it. Gradually the actor would rid herself of the anxiety surrounding the problem, which would usually disappear.

Most of these exercises were strategies for stimulating the various functions of the actor's psychophysical mechanism. Although Strasberg shared Stanislavski's assumptions concerning the integration of psyche and soma as a principle of human behavior, he believed that social conditioning and the tension of the performance situation were responsible for creating blocks and inhibitions that Method training aimed to remove. Strasberg possessed an apparently obsessive desire to liberate the spontaneous activity of the unconscious, regarding the actor's expression of intense emotion as the essential sign of a character's interior life.

Versions of the Method

Stanislavski or Strasberg?

In *The Method as Means* (1961), Charles Marowitz gave British readers a succinct explanation of what he considered to be the most useful aspect of

Method training, making no clear distinction between Stanislavski's system and the American Method:

> Playing the Objective, one of the basic tenets of the Method, ensures a particular involvement. It employs the actor; gives him something to concentrate on and something to do. Consequently, the temptation to *act in general* . . . is reduced. And there is a very real likelihood of a *particular* feeling being engendered; particular because it conveys the whys and wherefores of a specific character enmeshed in a set of specific circumstances. It is this *particularisation* in the drama which interests the spectator in the happenings on the stage. For he is not being asked to imagine *any* character in a general context *somewhat like* the one suggested on the stage, but a *particular* character in a *particular* context, acting for these *particular* reasons.[69]

This sounds much more like Stanislavski than Strasberg. In essence it represents the version of Stanislavski's thinking that Stella Adler communicated to her colleagues in the Group Theatre on her return from Paris in 1934. It is certainly the case that many American actors believe that playing actions according to their character's sequence of objectives is essentially a Method approach, being unaware of the distinction between Strasberg's Method and other American variants of Stanislavski's system.

Certainly Elia Kazan, artistically the most significant American theater and film director of the late 1940s and 1950s, employed this genuinely Stanislavskian method of establishing the actor's contribution to the creation of a scene.[70] Like Stella Adler, Kazan was highly critical of the exploitation of emotion memory and somewhat skeptical of the private moment exercise: "The emotion should really come out of what happens in the scene. To recall some personal event in your life and so to go in and play a quite different scene is not good. It's false. You see the worst misuse of emotional recall in actors who are really playing with something in themselves—not with the person in the scene. There is this glazed, unconnected look in their eyes and you know they're somewhere else."[71] Kazan was true to Stanislavski's method of physical actions in his belief that "Improvisation without objectives is useless."[72]

Robert Lewis, one of the three founding directors of the Actors Studio and an early member of the Group Theater, was also extremely critical of Strasberg's approach. Lewis emphasized the need to help the actor find forms of physical expression appropriate to the stylistic demands of different types of drama. He rejected the Method actor's "devotion to the principle that the only important thing for the actor is truthful feeling," pointing out that this approach had failed "to express in form the truth of the period or style of any given play" other than naturalistic works that were contemporaneous with the actors' cultural moment.[73]

Yet Lewis followed Stanislavski in his resolve to enable the actor to integrate inner impulse and outer form. He was very impressed by the acting of Michael Chekhov, citing his performance of Strindberg's *Eric XIV* as a demonstration of the way in which the psychological gesture enabled a powerful physical expression of a psychological attitude.[74] In some respects, Lewis's ideas about the need to teach actors how to express the form of particular plays through appropriate acting styles paralleled the praxis of Michel Saint-Denis:

> The speech and voice teachers have to get together with the acting teachers, re-examine their exercises, and involve them with simple acting problems so that they are learned as part of the movement, the inner movement of acting. . . . the body must be used in the exercise to express some inner wish so that it gets tied in with the acting process. . . . We must insist that the manner in which the acting exercises . . . are done incorporates the way in which something is spoken and moved and get away once and for all from the idea that any *pure* expression of some personal, inner feeling is the end. It is not the end, it is the beginning.[75]

However, the negative criticism of experts did little to undermine Strasberg's status as guru for generations of student actors.[76]

Stella Adler's Teaching

The argument between Stella Adler and Lee Strasberg concerning the proper use of Stanislavski's early version of the psycho-technique (and especially the function and value of emotion memory) created a rift that persisted throughout their lives, and was the major source of disagreement between rival proponents of the Method. Marlon Brando, probably the most famous actor to be associated with the Method, studied first with Stella Adler at Piscator's Dramatic Workshop. Later he joined the Actors Studio (before Strasberg began to teach there), during which time he was chosen by Elia Kazan to play Stanley in *A Streetcar Named Desire*. He was unequivocal in rejecting the suggestion that he was influenced by Strasberg, acknowledging the invaluable help he received from Adler as a teacher and friend.

Adler was a highly successful actress before the formation of the Group, and it was Adler who had actually been taught by Stanislavski. Her approach echoes Stanislavski's insistence that an actor creates character by observing the logic of action determined by the playwright: "Although the exercises may change in detail and the ideas may vary, the creative key remains the same—to experience the action in the circumstances. It is the foundation of the Stanislavski System."[77] She gave up acting in the late 1940s to concentrate on teaching at her own conservatory, and continued teaching until her death in 1992. Adler rejected emotion memory as a way of animating the character's emotional life. She followed Stanislavski in insisting on playing the action inherent in the plot of a play: "In teaching I do not require a student ever . . . to use emotion as a source. . . . I discourage the student from reaching out for any emotion, conscious or unconscious. . . . All the emotion is contained in the action. The action can be a personal or imaginative one. . . . To go back to a feeling or emotion of one's own experience I believe to be unhealthy. It tends to separate you from the play, from the action of the play, from the circumstances of the play."[78]

In teaching actors to motivate action in the play, she required they seek its objective and its explanation by asking "what, where, when, why." After being analyzed by the actor, a character's actions should be given physical form in performance in order to avoid "acting feelings." Adler named intended actions that were not fully accomplished as a result of obstacles *incomplete actions*. Adler considered that the actor could find all the emotion she needed through the use of her imagination, and that the only aspect of personal memory that could be of use was the physical act itself.

Her idea of "justifying" each of the character's actions by giving it a reason, appears to have been derived from Vakhtangov. Although Adler taught actors that the actions come first, she believed that the words come second, offering various techniques of rehearsal to help the actor translate words on the page into actions. Her "vocabulary of action" enabled actors to recognize the mode of action that determined particular forms of language as speech, for example, chatting, reminiscing, arguing, dreaming, and praying. Thus the actor was helped to identify and express different speech modes as different categories of action.[79]

Sanford Meisner's Innovations

In 1936, Sanford Meisner, a founder of the Group Theater, established the Neighborhood Playhouse as an acting school where he developed his own approach by integrating what he had learned about Stanislavski from Adler and Strasberg with his knowledge of Michael Chekhov's techniques. Although he did not reject emotional recall and justification ("substitution" in Strasberg's terminology) as preparatory exercises in developing a characterization at rehearsal, his approach emphasized *doing* and *reacting* as the key to liveness and spontaneity on stage. His famous repetition exercise represents an elaboration of Stanislavski's later ideas about objectives and obstacles, with its emphasis on relationships between actors in the attempt to realize their intentions. By requiring the actors to look at their partners onstage and repeat in words the reactions they see after they have spoken their own lines, Meisner provoked actors to notice and respond to the reactions of their fellow performers, thus ensuring a spontaneous moment-to-moment interaction in which actors were constantly having to readjust their social strategies as part of the progress of the scene. Stanislavski had referred to the process of readjustment of objectives to obstacles as adaptation; Meisner made it a key to spontaneous interaction on stage. Provided that actors observed the logic of the situation in the play, the exercise is a highly effective method of enhancing the spontaneity and realism of the interplay among characters on stage. Where Stanislavski's approach to physical actions was in danger of isolating characters by encouraging each actor to play her intention in the form of a through-line of action, and Strasberg's approach almost paralyzed the actor in a subjective state of retrospection and private reverie, Meisner offered a corrective by way of an innovative extension of Stanislavski's own thoughts about motivation and action.

Stanislavski's Influence

Whatever the limitations of Stanislavski's system, his precise formulation of all the important questions concerning naturalistic acting established the foundation upon which a large number of practitioners have elaborated new variants. Its impact on mainstream theater in Russia, the United States, and latterly in Britain has been immense. Versions of the vocabulary that Stanislavski invented have been widely adopted in the United States and Russia (indeed in the whole of the former Soviet Union). In countries where the system is not consistently used for training and rehearsal, theater practitioners are at least familiar with its vocabulary and key concepts.

A number of famous alumni of the Group Theater, including Morris Carnovsky, Sanford Meisner, and Robert Lewis, continued for many years to teach versions of Stanislavski's system derived from Boleslavsky, Strasberg, or Stella Adler. Actors who had studied at the Actors Studio such as Herbert Berghof and his wife, Uta Hagen, derived their approach as teachers from one or other version of Stanislavski. Hagen, who became famous for her great stage performances on Broadway, ran the Berghof Studio in New York until her death in 2004. The Stella Adler Conservatory still operates in New York and Los Angeles. The Actors Studio continues to operate under the leadership of Estelle Parsons, and there are Lee Strasberg Institutes in New York, Los Angeles, and London. In Britain, Stanislavskian notions of motivation and character biography have entered the actor's vocabulary and are used by actors who may not even be aware of their derivation. Many British drama schools offer some classes on Stanislavski, but only a few, such as the Drama Centre and East 15, teach Stanislavski's ideas in a systematic way.

The most widely recognized notion of acting today is probably the psychological realism propounded by Stanislavski. In most films, "truth" of characterization is now evaluated not merely in terms of its "truth to life" (verisimilitude) but also by its "aliveness." Sharon Carnicke reminds scholars that an accurate rendering of Stanislavski's word *perezhivanie* is "living through," stressing the fact that the actor's apparent spontaneity on stage signaled a virtual experiencing of the life of the character, rather than a merely accurate mimicry of the external signs of behavior.[80] Such virtual life could therefore only be "organically" created from the actor's own life experience. Stanislavski's aesthetic derives from theories of the organicity of art propounded by late-eighteenth- and early-nineteenth-century Romantic philosophers, but his attempt to help actors achieve such "aliveness" through a system of training and rehearsal was revolutionary.

Although he himself did not possess a wholly modern conception of the unconscious, his notion of actions and objectives does in an intuitive way anticipate Freudian conceptions of the influence of unconscious drives as motives of human behavior. Stanislavski's emphasis on both introspection and the psychophysical integrity of the performing instrument constituted the first identifiably modern approach to the aesthetics and technique of acting. His actor-centered approach to drama was informed by modern behaviorist models of the neurological function and anticipated twentieth-century preoccupations with psychoanalytic notions of human experience originating with Freud.[81] The Stanislavskian tradition not only determined the development of training in Russia and various countries of the former Soviet bloc, its adaptation and popularization as the Method by Lee Strasberg and others defined the terms of acting on the American stage and in Hollywood films from the late 1940s to the 1980s, determining the form and content of American drama until it began to be challenged by other traditions in the 1960s.

3. The Actor as Scenographic Instrument

Appia and Dalcroze

Directly opposed to the naturalistic conception of the actor as imitator of human behavior was the notion of the actor as an instrument. This idea animated a tradition of avant-garde performance that has offered an alternative to mainstream theater up to the present day, underpinning postmodern performance praxis. In the first two decades of the twentieth century, Adolphe Appia, Edward Gordon Craig, and Vsevolod Meyerhold each resolved that the realism of dominant nineteenth-century traditions—privileging the repertoire of gesture and facial expression representing the performer's histrionic personality—should be replaced by a mode of acting in which a more aesthetically controlled vocal and bodily expression might be fully integrated within a unified artwork.[1] Rejecting the idea that the actor's job was to create psychologically credible characters on the basis of the indications provided by the playwright, these practitioners redefined the actor's function as akin to the musician or the dancer. The actor might *indicate* character without attempting to create the illusion of *being* the character.

The Aesthetics of Symbolist Performance

This new idea of the actor as instrument was initially motivated by the symbolist conception of art. Angelo Bertocci characterizes this aesthetic in a way that suggests its implications for theater art:

> *Symbolisme,* in its most general sense . . . may be seen as the aspiration common to several families of spirit toward a thoroughgoing poetic unity conceived in terms of the metaphor of "colour" (which, as we have seen, also has its "music") in a philosophical context which permits interflow and interglow of meanings, both horizontally and vertically between areas of experience formerly maintained distinct. . . . From "line" to "color"; from plot line as the very sinew of unity, to recurrence in pat-

terned shapes of images, events, sounds, rhythms as the real inner "life" of this unity; from the "fable" or "story" developing in linear fashion and conveying "meaning" easily susceptible of paraphrase, to an "import" suddenly, if fleetingly, "coming together" in consciousness, so that the "whole story" or "what the story has to say" consists of a perception distorted if lifted out of context—it is of this development in Western art that *Symbolisme* itself is for the historian the "symbol."[2]

While naturalism was establishing itself in Paris in the 1880s through the brilliant productions of André Antoine at the Théâtre Libre, its preeminence as an avant-garde movement was challenged by the influence of the symbolists—most significantly through the success of symbolist productions of Ibsen and the increasing number of productions of plays by Maurice Maeterlinck. By the end of the 1890s, the expressionist movement in the visual arts had begun to exert a strong influence on a number of playwrights. In the plays of writers such as August Strindberg, Gerhart Hauptmann, and Frank Wedekind, the representation of action was increasingly abstract, so as to render the subjective quality of dream or nightmare. Symbolist and expressionist drama made demands on the actor that were very different from those made by realism or naturalism. Avant-garde theater movements of the 1890s had in common a rejection of the specious conjunction of materialism and scientific objectivity that characterized naturalism.

Rejecting the idea that reality can be comprehended by the presentation of photographic images of experience on stage for the spectator to observe and analyze, the symbolists sought to communicate in the theater the essence of a universe dimly perceived behind the surface appearances of everyday life. Maeterlinck expressed this antimaterialist conception of reality in *The Treasure of the Humble:*

> Indeed, it is not in the actions but in the words that are found the beauty and greatness of tragedies that are beautiful and great; and this is not solely in the words that accompany and explain the action, for there must perforce be another dialogue besides the one which is superficially necessary. . . . Side by side with the necessary dialogue will you almost always find another dialogue that seems superfluous; but . . . this is the only one that the soul can listen to profoundly, for here alone it is the soul that is being addressed. . . . these are words that conform to a deeper truth, and one that lies incomparably nearer to the invisible soul by which the poem is upheld. . . . Are not other forces, other words one cannot hear, brought into being, and do not these determine the event?

What I say often counts for so little; but my presence, the attitude of my soul, my future and my past . . . a secret thought, the stars that approve my destiny, the thousands of mysteries which surround me and float about yourself—all this it is that speaks to you at . . . [the] tragic moment.[3]

By the turn of the century Maeterlinck's plays were known throughout Europe. He was greatly admired by Anton Chekhov, who, in his last years, contemplated writing a symbolist drama.

Richard Wagner's theories of music drama (widely promulgated between 1885 and 1888 through the publication of the monthly *Révue Wagnerienne*) reinforced the development of a symbolist theatrical aesthetic. Wagner's idea of the *Gesamtkunstwerk* provided a model of music drama as a total synthesis of the arts that might be more than the sum of its constituent parts. Experiments in the staging of symbolist drama were most notably attempted by Paul Fort at his Théâtre D'Art (founded 1891) and, more successfully, by the actor Lugné-Poe at the Théâtre de L'Oeuvre (founded 1893). Often, symbolist plays were performed behind a gauze curtain, the ghostly appearance of the actors being matched by the hushed, incantatory style of vocal delivery. There were, however, no conventions by which to present such a drama and no forms of training to assist actors to acquire appropriate techniques.

Music as Organic Staging Principle

Independently, Appia and Craig had recognized the need for a new kind of acting consonant with the innovatory approaches to scenography promoted by the aesthetics of symbolism and expressionism. They agreed that in order to achieve the harmonious integration of all the elements of theatrical production, the actor had to surrender artistic control to the stage director.[4] Under the influence of his compatriot Emile-Jacques Dalcroze, Appia came to believe that training in eurhythmics would transform the actor into a suitable instrument for his *word-tone drama*. In Appia's view, "the art of staging can be an art only if it derives from music."[5] Music was the key to his concept of artistic expression, and thus constituted the unifying principle of his theater art: "The loftiest expression of the Eternal in Man can only be reborn and forever renew itself in the lap of Music. . . . In order to express the inner reality underlying all phenomena the poet renounces any attempt to reproduce their fortuitous aspects. . . . Then Wagner appeared. At the same time as his music-dramas revealed a purely expressive form of art, they also confirmed, what we had hitherto dimly sensed, the omnipotent power of music. . . . Music and music alone can coordinate all the elements of scenic presentation into a completely harmonious whole."[6]

What music was to the ear, light was to the eye, so the word-tone drama would need to be lit according to "musical" principles in order to ensure that the aural unity created by the musical patterning of sound would achieve its spatial equivalent through the creative orchestration of light: "Light is the most important plastic medium on the stage. . . . Without its unifying power our eyes would be able to perceive what objects were but not what they expressed. . . . Light and light alone, quite apart from its subsidiary importance in illuminating a dark stage, has the greatest plastic power, for it is subject to a minimum of conventions and so is able to reveal vividly in its most expressive form the eternally fluctuating appearance of a phenomenal world."[7]

For Appia, the actor was *massgebend,* the measure by which the spatial aspect of theatrical presentation was determined. For the two-dimensional pictorial illusionism of nineteenth-century proscenium arch theater he substituted a plastic approach to the volume of the stage, which would be made to appear through the agency of lighting. In this context the stage space could acquire visual unity only if every element (e.g., stage floor, scenic units, background) was scaled to the moving body of the actor. Appia's principle became the rule for modern scenographers, who start from the assumption that the stage space is a cube defined by its relationship to the movement of the actors within it. During the last fifty years stage illusion has seldom involved the trompe-l'oeil effects of nineteenth-century naturalism, but instead has emphasized the three-dimensional reality of the actor moving in a space whose volume may appear to change as it is shaped by lighting. "[The] bodies of actors, and the continuous changes in lighting . . . provide an integrated, plastic and visual equivalent to music."[8]

Appia was greatly impressed by Dalcroze's idea that rhythm connected the ability to make music with the body's capacity to move. Dalcroze devised his system of eurythmics to promote an integration of musical and bodily expression that represented the harmonious ideal of organic being. The exercises did not separate music, gymnastics, or dancing (though some observers chose to see them as one or the other of these forms) but was, according to Appia, "an attempted transfusion of musical rhythm into the organism."[9] The eight theoretical conclusions through which Dalcroze's system was articulated assumed rhythm as the key that determines the relationship between movement in space (plastic rhythm) and movement in time (musical rhythm).[10] This perceived organic relationship between music and movement led Appia to believe that in his word-tone drama music would impose a natural discipline upon the actor: "If music did not so profoundly alter the natural time durations of life, it could not force the actor to renounce his ordinary activity in order to become a means of expression."[11]

Paralleling the experiments of modern dancers such as Loie Fuller, Isadora Duncan, and Ruth St. Denis, Appia formulated a notion of the actor as instrument that profoundly influenced Copeau, although Copeau was to develop it in ways that bore little resemblance to Appia's word-tone drama. Whereas Copeau developed a method of improvisation that allowed the actor a good deal of freedom to play with the text in order to discover its form in performance, Appia's insistence that the performer be subject to the control of the author-composer reflects his more abstract conception of the actor's role as one of many instruments in the complex score of the performance: "What the actor loses in freedom will be gained by the stage designer; and the setting, in giving up all pretense at scenic illusion, becomes an atmosphere in which the actor can be totally expressive."[12]

It is a paradox that in order to become fully expressive in the new theater, the actor must surrender some of the freedom possessed by the nineteenth-century star. Although this is consonant with Craig's idea that the new art of the stage requires the actor to be subordinated to the artistic control of the stage director, Craig's view that art should be artificial differs greatly from the notion of the performer as a naturally expressive instrument—a notion shared by Appia, Dalcroze, and Copeau.[13] Whereas Appia had endorsed Dalcroze's aim "to give back to the body its good harmony, to make music vibrate in it—as to make music an integral part of the organism," Craig's preference for the artificial (in parallel to both Meyerhold and the Italian futurists) is an early manifestation of the trend in twentieth-century thinking about theater that leads to postmodern theories of performance.

Craig's Conception of Performance as Artifice

Rejection of the Organic

In 1915, Craig had written, "we find that the body of the modern theatre is composed of strangely contradictory elements; of the organic and the inorganic hopelessly clinging together."[14] Listing eight compositional elements—language (verse or prose), speech, scenery, actors' bodies, movement, light, painted faces, facial expressions—Craig drew attention to the combinations of organic, inorganic, and hybrid material from which late-nineteenth-century theater "fatuously believes it can fashion a work of art."[15] As he considered it an error to mix natural and artificial elements in creating a work of art, Craig proposed two rearrangements, each of which was logical because it was consistent in its selection of compositional materials.

The first type of theater involved the use of inorganic elements. The writer was to use verse or an "unnatural mode of speech," which would require the actor to employ "an unnatural mode of delivery." The scene would be abstract, not attempting to represent a particular location. By analogy with marionettes, the actors would be both masked and completely disguised, so that their own humanity was not apparent. Movements, like speech, would be systematized according to a coherent set of conventions. This would ensure that expression was conveyed by means of the interplay of mask and movement, controlled by the actor, rather than being a random by-product of the actor's spontaneous feelings. Lighting would be recognizably artificial to provide illumination and effect, and designed so as to avoid seeming to derive from natural sources. In this way, Craig sought to harmonize the constituent elements of theater in order to create a coherent principle of composition.

The second rearrangement was based on a combination of natural elements. The playwright would provide speech that seemed as natural as improvisation, which the actor would deliver colloquially with the accompaniment of natural movements. Scenery would imitate reality completely, by using genuinely organic elements in its composition. Actors would be cast for their suitability for a role so that no disguise and no makeup were necessary, thereby permitting facial expressions to be completely natural. The plays would be performed under the conditions of natural light, by day or at night.

Although these two proposed approaches to the composition of theater works may appear either fanciful or extreme, they illustrate the dualism inherent in Craig's view of theatrical art, suggesting that he identified the inconsistency of nineteenth-century illusionism as a consequence of its indiscriminate mixing of natural and artificial elements in the attempt to construct coherent fictions. The underlying aim of Craig's reforms was to produce theatrical conditions conducive to the creation of unified artworks—whether these were wholly designed by the director-scenographer or the result of the improvisational genius of skilled performers.

After an early career working at the Lyceum as an actor (1889–97) in the company of the great actor-manager Henry Irving, Craig embarked in 1900 on a series of productions as a director-scenographer, which culminated in the legendary Moscow Art Theater *Hamlet* in 1912. Although he lived until

1966, Craig's only other work for the theater was a production of Ibsen's *The Pretenders* in Denmark in 1926. His major impact on the theater was made through his written publications in the form of a series of books and a theater journal he edited. From the first publication of *The Art of the Theatre* in 1905, his views circulated among theater practitioners and critics in Europe, causing widespread debate and controversy, and influencing progressive directors such as Reinhardt, Meyerhold, and Granville Barker.

The Actor as Über-Marionette

Perhaps because he knew early on in his career that his revolutionary views would not earn him employment in the English theater, Craig courted controversy by expressing radical ideas in a deliberately provocative way. His ideas, particularly as expressed in the essay "The Actor and the Über-Marionette" (1907), appeared not merely as contradictory but also as a deliberate affront to the acting profession. Taken literally, the essay seems to call for the replacement of the living actor by a large puppet (this echoes some of the experiments of the symbolists with plays for marionettes). In reality, however, Craig was using the image of the marionette to evoke an acting style that is depersonalized, abstract, and subject to control by the mind of the artist (director-scenographer).

The conception of acting articulated by Craig in the essay is rather different from Appia's:

> Acting is not an art. It is therefore incorrect to speak of the actor as an artist. For accident is an enemy of the artist. . . . Art arrives only by design. Therefore in order to make any work of art it is clear we may only work in those materials with which we can calculate. Man is not one of these materials. . . . In the modern theatre, owing to the use of the bodies of men and women *as their material,* all which is presented there is of an accidental nature. The actions of the actor's body, the expression of his face, the sounds of his voice, all are at the mercy of the winds of his emotions. . . . emotion *possesses* him; it seizes upon his limbs, moving them whither it will. . . . As with his movement, so it is with the expression of his face. . . . Instantly, like lightning, and before the mind has time to cry out and protest, the hot passion has mastered the actor's expression. . . . It is the same with his voice as it is with his movements. Emotion cracks the voice of the actor. It sways his voice to join the conspiracy against his mind. . . . emotion is the cause which first of all creates, and secondly destroys. . . . That . . . which the actor gives us, is not a work of art; it is series of accidental confessions.[16]

With these words, Craig identified the tendency of realistic acting to merge the feelings of the actor with those being represented. Craig's point, though possibly exaggerated by him for perverse effect, is enormously suggestive, and was the first in a series of modernist approaches to performance (the best-known parallel views are those of Meyerhold and Brecht) that emphasized the need for the performer to maintain a certain detachment from what he was representing in order to create an effect of histrionic *defamiliarization* that would distinguish acting from everyday behavior. If the actor fails to separate the spontaneous experience of emotion from the artistic representation of it, the form or significance of the emotions cannot be communicated.

Many of the major practitioners and theorists of twentieth-century theater profoundly disagree about this issue. Stanislavski spent much of his career attempting to discover techniques for blurring distinctions between actor and character to allow the actor's real feelings to be identified with the character's fictional emotions.[17] Copeau and Saint-Denis followed Appia in the quest for authentic histrionic expression based on the natural connection between the performer's feelings and his corporeal means of expression. Craig imagined histrionic performance as a series of calculated effects, the actor manipulating his face, body, and voice as consciously as if he were pulling the strings of a marionette. The notion that the actor should be momentarily possessed by true emotion is portrayed as a vulgar fallacy of realistic theater.[18] In its place Craig substituted the idea of the actor as a signifier among many other signifiers: the marionette is an emblem of the idea that the actor is as much a part of the scenic spectacle as any of the visual elements. By *representing* rather than *impersonating* character, the actor might avoid the inartistic confusion caused by realist theater's insistence that acting should reproduce everyday behavior: "But I see a loophole by which in time the actors can escape from the bondage they are in. They must create for themselves a new form of acting, consisting in the main part of symbolical gesture. Today they *impersonate* and interpret; tomorrow they must *represent* and interpret; and the third day they must create. By this means style may return."[19]

In Craig's scheme, the actor would achieve power as a creative artist by initially abdicating from the conventional histrionic art of impersonation so that he might become an instrument for the symbolic representation of the director's vision; only then might he be free to create. In some respects Craig's vision of the theater of the future anticipated certain contemporary trends in devised theater, in which the performers themselves compose the performance without working from a preexisting text. Craig's Über-marionette evoked the image of the actor as a masked dancer-singer, performing actions in a manner that involves a degree of abstraction from ordinary life.

In championing the idea of the Über-marionette, Craig approvingly quoted Eleanora Duse's words, "To save the theatre, the theatre must be destroyed, the actors and actresses must all die of the plague. They poison the air, they make art impossible."[20] His immense admiration for Henry Irving nevertheless suggests that he did possess at least one specific historical example of the type of acting demanded by the new theater: "The perfect actor would be he whose brain could conceive and could show us the perfect symbols of all which his nature contains. He would not ramp and rage up and down in *Othello*. . . . he would tell his brain to enquire into the depths, to learn all that lies there, and then to remove itself to . . . the sphere of the imagination, and there fashion certain symbols which, without exhibiting the bare passions, would none the less tell us clearly about them. . . . Meantime do not forget that the very nearest approach that has ever been to the ideal actor, with his brain commanding his nature, has been Henry Irving."[21]

According to Craig, Irving's face was a mask, fully under the control of his mind; he was capable of manipulating the play of his features in order to express thoughts and emotions precisely: "The face of Irving was the connecting link between that spasmodic and ridiculous expression of the human face as used by theatres of the last few centuries, and the masks which will be used in place of the human face in the near future. . . . the mask is the only right medium of portraying the expressions of the soul as shown through the expressions of the face."[22]

Craig's view was so strongly antirealist that it paradoxically demonstrated the superior expressiveness of the mask over the face. In these early essays Craig went out of his way to emphasize the conscious control of the theater artist over the material of art, preferring the artificial material of the mask to the natural face of the nineteenth-century actor. For Craig, acting should be symbolic rather than mimetic; the actor should be a force of nature but should never try to appear natural. Later, in his book *Henry Irving* (1930), he described Irving as "the nearest thing ever known to what I have called the Über-marionette." Irving made his acting symbolic through the refined and deliberate cultivation of style: "From the first to the last moment that Irving stood on the stage each moment was significant. . . . every sound, each movement, was intentional—clear-cut, measured dance: nothing real—all massively artificial—yet flashing with the light and the pulse of nature. A fine style."[23]

In the essay "Stanislavski's System" (1937), Craig explained the nature of his objection to Stanislavski's attempt to teach actors how to be natural onstage: "It is unnecessary to devote years of a life to teaching would-be actors to be, above all things, 'natural,' since drama at its best is supernatural or 'spiritual' . . . It is therefore better that the actor should avoid *as far as possible* the attempt to interpret these plays in a 'natural' way."[24] Craig directly addressed a contradiction manifest in Stanislavski's inherently naturalistic approach to the performance of non-naturalistic drama, rejecting the comparatively new conventions of naturalistic acting in favor of a less literal attitude that attempted in a self-consciously modern way to revive the symbolic and ceremonial art of the past that persisted in non-Western cultures. While Craig did accept that there were realistic elements in the major works of world drama, he was opposed to the aim, which he understood as central to Stanislavski's system, of training and rehearsal to achieve naturalness in theatrical performance.

In fact Craig was skeptical of the very idea of teaching people to become actors. His notion of the actor is a Romantic one: "None but born actors should be trained to act. A very little training helps the born-actor: nothing can help the would-be actor who lacks the essence of acting in his composition. . . . I am opposed to the *'système Stanislavski'* and to every other system, for they threaten genius and stifle expression, and open but a small path to 'new talent' which they manage to mechanise—and that is all."[25]

These words reflect Craig's tendency to adopt the self-consciously dilettante attitude of the bohemian English artist with its exaltation of the amateur over the professional craft worker, yet he had been serious enough about the cultivation of the new artists of the theater to have spent years trying to establish a school (which actually did operate in Florence between 1913 and the outbreak of the First World War). In *The Art of the Theatre, The Second Dialogue* (1910), Craig's outline of his projected theater school reflected his desire to cultivate theater artists as innovators involved in experimentation toward the creation of new kinds of art, rather than to train specialists in preexisting techniques: "we shall have a college of experiment in which to study the three natural sources of art—Sound, Light and Motion—or, as I have spoken of them elsewhere, *voice, scene* and *action*."[26]

The thirty students in Craig's school were to be taught by a group of artists who were themselves engaged with Craig in making experiments in mise-en-scène. They would study a wide range of subjects, including movement, voice training, speech, music, drawing, scenic design and scene painting, dancing, mime, improvisation, lighting, the history of theater, and the skills of marionette theater. Craig's choice of subjects reflected his aims.

The students were to be trained as theater artists whose aesthetic sensibilities were to be developed in conjunction with their acquisition of craft skills. The description of the school evokes an ethos of research and experiment aimed at "infusing the life of imagination into every Art and Craft connected with the stage."[27]

There was no plan to teach the skills of characterization. In Craig's view, acting as mimetic activity could not or should not be taught. His criticism of the aims of Stanislavski's training remains worthy of serious consideration today, articulating a valid skepticism of any training that might encourage the acquisition of techniques at the expense of creative engagement with the form and content of artistic expression.

A Theater of Improvisation: Perishable Theater

There was one Moscow Art Theater actor whom Craig genuinely admired, a man named Artem. According to Craig, Artem possessed the capacity to be himself on stage as he shared the play with the audience, appearing perfectly natural without striving to submerge himself in the character. Craig described him in a manner that conjures up an impression of the kind of acting both Copeau and Brecht would have commended: "No one could say that he disguised himself so that he might be taken for another person—he was all persons in his own person, so that there was no need for any of those disguises so loved by second-class actors. All he tried for, then, was to express himself through the thoughts and words of Chekhov which he could understand so very well. His coming on—his talk—his facial play and his exits, were all like a single piece of drifting music or, as some might say, 'like a poem.'"[28] In describing the individual effects created by Artem, Craig implied the paradoxical relationship between the naturalness of acting without affectation, and the conscious framing and shaping of the performance necessary to render it as art. This is distinct from the slice-of-life illusion of naturalistic performance, as there was apparently no effort on Artem's part to conceal the fact that he was acting.

Throughout Craig's life, his comments on acting alternated between images of spontaneous play and ceremonial formality, reflecting a dualism in his thinking expressed in his distinction between the *durable* and the *perishable* theater. The durable theater required the actor to perform as Über-marionette in a formalized and ceremonial performance comparable to the Oriental and Asian theater forms about which Craig learned between 1908 and 1913. "I have been told . . . of a race of actors that existed (and a few today preserve that tradition) who were fitted to be part and parcel of the most durable theatre it is possible to conceive. . . . If the Western actor can become what I am told the Eastern actor was and is, I withdraw all that I have written in my essay 'On the Actor and the Über-marionette.' "[29]

Spontaneous improvised dramas were conceived by Craig as perishable theater. Examples of such performances were to be found in the commedia dell'arte of the fifteenth and sixteenth centuries, circus clowning, and contemporary vaudeville. Craig saw the main themes of such improvised comedy as the outwitting of the vain or pretentious fool and believed it provided the basis upon which sophisticated forms might be built: "It is seldom elegant, this comedy, and yet a perishable theatre would have to possess its improvised dramas that were elegant and even exquisite. Perhaps here we should drop speech and pass to the dance . . . dances based upon the movement of perishable things in nature . . . and, perhaps, the passing phases of childhood. . . . Not only the fact that a thing is perishable, but that it is mutable is of value."[30] Spontaneous dancing and singing (as in folk art) would represent aspects of this perishable theater, which would demand performers who possessed skills other than those of the performer of durable theater.

Notwithstanding his professed aversion to living actors in "The Actor and the Über-marionette," Craig maintained a conception of the paradoxical nature of acting throughout his career: while remaining critical of the realism typical of the late-nineteenth-century personality actor, his essays reflected his continuing interest in the possibility of a new kind of artist of the theater who might on the one hand execute the design of the author/director through a mastery of symbolic movement and, on the other, function as author of improvised performances. Both types of acting demanded that the actor be capable of refined forms of stylized performance. Craig's search was for forms of pure theater whose constituent elements would be derived directly from the theatrical medium rather than from literature.

Meyerhold's Innovations

Although the revolutionary Russian director Vsevolod Meyerhold was not aware of Craig's practical experiments or aesthetic theories until April 1907, he had been testing similar ideas about stylized performance since his first productions of symbolist drama in 1902–3.[31] In preparation for the production of *Tristan and Isolde* at the Marinsky Opera in 1909, Meyerhold had made a study of the theories of Wagner, Appia, and George Fuchs; in 1911 he witnessed a demonstration of eurythmics by Emile-Jacques Dalcroze and his students, who visited Moscow and Petersburg that year.

Early Experiments in Stylization

As an actor with the Moscow Art Theater from its inception in 1898, Meyerhold had exhibited a distinctive talent. After 1902, however, he found himself increasingly out of sympathy with the company's artistic policy, rejecting the widespread opinion that the MAT's productions of Chekhov were a vindication of the aesthetic of naturalism. According to Meyerhold, Stanislavski's acclaimed productions of Chekhov's plays had, at their best, revealed the dramatist as a master of the theater of mood.[32] Meyerhold's own aesthetic taste propelled him away from naturalism toward a theater of conscious stylization. His own early experience as a director led him from the abstract style of symbolism into a series of experiments with a wide range of aesthetic approaches including expressionism, theatricalism, futurism, and the grotesque. For Meyerhold, as for Craig, the essence of acting was movement. His early productions and essays reflected his insistence on the principle of rhythm as a factor that could unify the words, the scene, and the actor. In 1914 he wrote: "Movement is the most powerful means of theatrical expression. The role of movement is more important than that of any other theatrical element. Deprived of dialogue, costume, footlights, wings and an auditorium, and left with only the actor and his mastery of movement, the theatre remains the theatre. The spectator can understand the actor's thoughts and impulses from his moves, gestures and facial expressions."[33]

Unlike Craig, however, Meyerhold believed acting to be the primary element of theatrical performance: "The basis of the art of the theatre is acting."[34] In the final analysis, it was the interplay of actor and spectator that determined the theater event: "The actor, having assimilated the author's conception via the director, stands face to face with the spectator (with director and author behind him), and *freely* reveals his soul to him, thus intensifying the fundamental theatrical relationship of performer and spectator.[35]

While some of his early comparisons of the actor with a musical instrument are reminiscent of Appia, Meyerhold's conception of the relationship of the actor's speech and movement to the musical and visual rhythms of the whole performance was more subtle and varied. Where Appia stressed that the actor's performance was controlled by the principle of music, Meyerhold was sensitive to the way in which acting might signify independently of other theatrical elements, creating more complex effects in relation to music and scene when permitted to function as their counterpoint.

In a lecture on *Tristan and Isolde* (1909), Meyerhold drew clear distinctions between acting in realistic theater and in opera. Opera was seen as comparable to pantomime: in both forms "the rhythm of the movements, gestures and groupings . . . [should be] synchronized precisely with the rhythm of the music."[36] But Meyerhold observed that, by basing their performances on the libretto rather than the music, most opera singers "adopt the acting style of the realistic theatre," thus producing a discrepancy between the form of the work embodied in its musical structure and the style of its performance: "Stylization is the very basis of operatic art—*people sing.* Therefore no elements of real life should be introduced; as soon as stylization and reality are juxtaposed, the *apparent* inadequacy of stylization is revealed and the whole foundation of the art collapses."[37]

A new kind of actor was needed in order to achieve the synthesis of the arts that was the aim of Wagner's music drama. In response to Appia's ideas about word-tone drama, Meyerhold concluded that "the actor in the music drama must absorb the essence of the score and translate every subtlety of the musical picture into plastic terms."[38] The great singer Fyodor Chaliapin offered Meyerhold a model of the proper approach to acting in opera. "Chaliapin's acting is always *true:* not true to life, but theatrically true."[39] According to Meyerhold, Chaliapin created on stage a movement score that was in harmony with the musical score. The idea that "Man, performing in harmony with the *mise-en-scène* and the musical score, becomes *a work of art in his own right*" was a development of Appia's conception of the union of all the elements of theater. The image of the performer as a work of art in certain respects echoes Craig's idea that the actor should be transformed into an Über-marionette.

The Actor as Cabotin

Craig and Meyerhold had in common a sense of the problematic status of the performer as both the material of theatrical art and creator of the artwork—as both instrument and instrumentalist.[40] Both men believed that movement was the essential component of any performance. Meyerhold was, however, much more positive than Craig about the actor's capacity to accomplish the aim of the dramatist as translated into spatial and plastic terms by the director. Meyerhold's conception of stylized theater required the actor to utilize the skills of a dancer, and he cited the classical Noh theater of Japan as a historical example. Like Craig, he wished to revive the use of masks and improvisation in the creation of new theatrical forms, yet his notion of the actor as *cabotin,* or strolling player, sets his ideas apart from those of Appia, Copeau, and Craig.

While Meyerhold's earliest critique of naturalism coincided with his experiments in staging symbolist plays, he did not remain a champion of any single modernist approach, but explored an astonishing variety of theatrical styles in rapid succession. His first production of Blok's *The Fairground Booth* in 1906 demonstrated that the principle of stylization determined his approach as theater artist, rather than adherence to any particular style. His presentation of the Mystics in the play was received by the Russian followers of the symbolist movement as a deliberate affront.[41] Meyerhold himself described the grotesque effect created by his theatrical treatment of the Mystics: "In the first scene . . . there is a long table covered with a black cloth reaching to the floor and parallel to the footlights. Behind the table sit the "mystics," the top halves of their bodies visible to the audience. Frightened by some rejoinder, they duck their heads, and suddenly all that remains at the table is a row of torsos minus heads and hands. It transpires that the figures are cut out of *cardboard.*"[42]

The production of *The Fairground Booth* represented both a break with the symbolist aesthetic that characterized most of Meyerhold's early staging experiments, and a critique of it. Edward Braun analyses the features of the production that foreshadowed Meyerhold's mature approach to theatrical performance: "[The] style of acting was far removed from the *tableaux vivants* of his earlier productions. The disruption of illusion, the asides to the audience, all demanded a mental and physical dexterity, an ability to improvise, a capacity for acting not only the part but also one's attitude to it. These devices were all waiting to be rediscovered in the tradition of popular theatre stretching back to the *commedia dell' arte* and beyond. It was this theatre, the theatre of masks and improvisation which the experience of *The Fairground Booth* led Meyerhold to explore. It came to furnish the basis for his entire style, a style which in a word can be called 'grotesque.'"[43] Developing the theories of the Russian poet Bryusov in 1907, Meyerhold formulated a concept of conscious stylization that reflected discoveries he had made in working on his own productions: "[The] furtherance of stylization in the theatre . . . does not mean the conventional stylization of actors, who, desiring but lacking the ability to speak as in real life, resort to the unnatural emphasising of words, ridiculous gestures, strange sighs and the like. . . . Rejecting such thoughtless, stereotyped, anti-artistic stylization, he [Bryusov] wishes to see the growth of *conscious stylization* in the theatre as a production technique with its own distinct flavour."[44]

The Fairground Booth and subsequent productions in an overtly theatrical style demonstrated the power of the actor as *cabotin*. The concept of acting as *cabotinage* was antipsychologistic, emphasizing physical virtuosity in place of detailed characterization. New actors were to be taught the physical skills of traditional street entertainers—clowns, pantomime performers, minstrels, jugglers, and acrobats. Actors already experienced in the conventions of modern theater would need to be retrained in order to master this repertoire of physical skills and to learn how to interact spontaneously with an audience. According to Meyerhold, modern theater had substituted the reading of plays for their fully theatrical performance, naturalism requiring the actor to *live* on stage, rather than to *act:* "The cult of *cabotinage,* which I am sure will reappear with the restoration of the theatre of the past, will help the modern actor to rediscover the basic laws of theatricality . . . the actor of the future should . . . coordinate his emotional responses with his technique, subjecting both to the traditional precepts of the old theatre."[45]

Many of Meyerhold's ideas about acting appear to echo those of Craig. However, while Craig seemed increasingly skeptical of ever realizing the goals of a new theater, Meyerhold's writing, although critical about the theater of the time, reveals an infectious optimism toward the possibilities of creating a new actor and a new theater. There are also striking parallels with Copeau's attempts at a renovation of the theater of Molière, though Copeau himself was contemptuous of what he understood by *cabotinage,* and eschewed conscious stylization in favor of a realist approach to style as determined by the written text.

Toward a New Physical Technique: Commedia Dell'arte and the Truth of Masks

Between 1905 and 1922, Meyerhold and his actors explored a great variety of techniques in order to find new ways of reviving the theaters of the past in a modern context and with a modern consciousness. These explorations culminated in 1922 in Meyerhold's system of biomechanics, a method of psychophysical training that aimed to teach the performer to produce expressive movement with maximum efficiency. In the early stages of his career he experimented with an aesthetic of sculptural poses and groupings evocative of old masters, animated by repeated movements and gestures that were accompanied by hushed and rhythmically delivered speech ("coldly coined," according to Meyerhold). The principle of setting a precise rhythm to determine all aspects of the performance operated in a more complex fashion in *The Fairground Booth*. In this production each character was identified by typical vocal mannerisms and gestures, "prompted by the

inner rhythm of the role. The gestures always followed the words, complementing them as though bringing a song to its conclusion."[46]

On being appointed to the Imperial Theatres in Petersburg in 1908, he
established a theater studio with the musician Mikhail Gnesin in order to
conduct research into and teach actors the playacting or pantomimic skills
of theatrical theater. Meyerhold discovered (as did Copeau a few years
later) that the most important model for this kind of theater was the commedia dell'arte of the sixteenth and seventeenth centuries. While
Stanislavski was concerned with helping actors to acquire a psycho-technique that would allow them to create a character's mental landscape,
Meyerhold concentrated exclusively on developing the actor's technical
proficiency, stressing the skills of external mimicry at the expense of complex psychology. This is not to suggest that Meyerhold was naive in his
conception of theatrical signification. What distinguished his approach as a
director from that of Stanislavski was his view that the performance should
act as a stimulus to the spectator, who would complete, from his own
experience, the schematic outline of a drama that the actors were playing
in a nonrealistic style. Meyerhold was more sophisticated in his understanding of theater semiotics, for he realized (as did Craig) that it was the
spectator who constructed the meaning of the performance: "The stylized
theatre produces a play in such a way that the spectator is compelled to
employ his imagination *creatively* in order to *fill in* those details *suggested* by
the stage action."[47] Naturalistic productions often exhibited a tendency to
become too literal, with actors and directors fleshing out details of characterization and mise-en-scène that would be more powerfully felt if the
spectator were free to imagine them.[48]

In 1913 Meyerhold opened his own permanent studio, where he taught
stage movement alongside Gnesin's course in "musical recitation in drama"
and Vladimir Soloviev's historical and practical introduction to the techniques of commedia dell'arte (which later included the modern theatrical
application of traditional devices of seventeenth- and eighteenth-century
performance). Meyerhold's course aimed to teach the actor

1. spontaneous control of the body in space, with the whole body
   involved in every gesture;
2. to adapt his movements to the area available for the performance;
3. to distinguish between the various kinds of movement to music: in
   melodrama, circus and variety theatre; in the Chinese and Japanese
   theatres; the style of Isadora Duncan and Loie Fuller;

4. to imbue every action on stage with joy—the tragic as well as the
   comic;
5. the power of the grotesque ("the grotesque helps the actor to portray
   the real as symbolic and to replace caricature with exaggerated parody");
6. the self-sufficiency of the form of the actor's performance (his movements and gestures) in the absence of the conventional plot from an
   improvised mime, and the significance of this lesson for acting as a
   whole.[49]

The studio program reflected the physical basis of Meyerhold's approach
to actor training and included a list of thirteen subjects for discussion at the
studio, chosen "to demonstrate the value of the essentially *theatrical* elements
of the art of the theatre." The first subject was to be mimesis, "at its lowest
level—imitation devoid of creative idealization; at its highest—the mask; its
most profound variations—the comic, tragic and tragi-comic grotesque."[50]
This suggests Meyerhold's clear preference for the consciously stylized art of
mask acting over the naive practice of realistic imitation. It is significant that
he chose in 1915 to make a film of Oscar Wilde's novel *The Picture of Dorian
Gray,* for Meyerhold's ideas about the meaning and function of the mask in
theater seem in many respects to echo Wilde's philosophy of masks. In
rejecting the Stanislavskian idea that the actor should experience the emotions of the character in order that they may be successfully communicated
to the audience, Meyerhold quoted approvingly from Wilde's novel: "It is
time we reached some conclusion about the question of experienced emotions on the stage. Admirers of Oscar Wilde will have found the answer
already in the words of Sybil Vane in *The Picture of Dorian Gray:* 'I might
mimic a passion that I do not feel, but I cannot mimic one that burns me
like a fire.'"[51]

Here Meyerhold used Wilde to justify his own agreement with Craig on
the need for conscious artifice in theatrical performance. Meyerhold's
description of the qualities of the new kind of acting he wished to promote
invoked "the magical power of the mask." Describing some of the stock
commedia types, Meyerhold evoked an image of the mask as a fixed facial
and bodily attitude to character, even though the actors would not actually
wear the physical half-masks associated with Pantalone, Arlecchino,
Brighella, the Dottore, and others. The echoes of Wilde's paradoxical
"Truth of Masks" in the discussion of Molière's *Don Juan,* which forms part
of the essay "The Fairground Booth," revealed the subtlety and sophistication of Meyerhold's approach to acting. Where Craig envisaged the mask as

a means of depersonalizing the actor, Meyerhold saw it as a metaphor for the presentation of self in social life.

As an aesthetic attitude, the grotesque indicates the complex play of ambiguities that derive from the juxtaposition of an image and its opposite, of signifier and signified, form and content, mask and face. Mask acting can thus be seen as an essential component of Meyerhold's theater aesthetic. Since reality can never be as it appears, the only way of apprehending it in theatrical terms is through elaborate games of masking, in which the distance between truth and its semblances is enacted as irony.

In his celebration of theater as fairground show Meyerhold expressed a central tenet of modernism—the recognition of the artist's responsibility to do justice to the human experience of the world as irrational and disordered. In the words of Alexander Matskin: "Once he had met Blok, it became clear that for Meyerhold the grotesque was not merely *a means of expression,* a way of heightening colours, it was no less than the *content* of that reality, that dislocated world in which he found himself and which formed the subject of his art."[52] Mask acting was thus much more than a stylistic device for Meyerhold. It signified the manifold complexity of the human personality and of social interaction, and it expressed the equivocal nature of the phenomenal world. The mask was employed as an histrionic technique throughout Meyerhold's career. The commedia dell'arte provided Meyerhold, as it did Craig and Copeau, with the model of a theater of improvisation that foregrounded the virtuosity of the actor as street performer. All three were aware of the great discipline required of the actor in such a theater, and Meyerhold contrasted the self-indulgent approach of the contemporary "inspirational actor" who sacrificed technique in favor of "unconscious creativity" with the skill and invention of the professional entertainer.

In his essay "The Fairground Booth," Meyerhold distinguished between two kinds of puppet theater. The director of the first kind tries to make his puppets imitate human beings as closely as possible. The director of the second realizes that this is impossible and that the charm of the puppet lies in its very failure to resemble perfectly the human being that it is attempting to mimic: "[The] world of the puppet is a wonderland of make-believe, and the man which it impersonates is a make-believe man."[53] In one respect Meyerhold's view is similar to that of Craig: it is the artifice of the stage fiction that guarantees its expressive potential, not the degree to which it resembles reality. Craig's image of the actor as Über-marionette may well have prompted Meyerhold to formulate this comparison of realistic and consciously stylized acting in terms of puppet theaters. However, Meyerhold was concerned not so much with reducing the actor's function in performance to that of inanimate object as with emblematizing the complex signifying process of grotesque art in which meanings are self-consciously *constructed:* "the puppet . . . wishes not to copy but to create."[54] Paradoxically, for Meyerhold as for Craig, actors become creative once they have rejected the tendency to confuse realistic acting conventions with truth.

Biomechanics

Biomechanics was initially a project aimed at synthesizing the various elements of physical training that Meyerhold had derived from his study of European traditions of *cabotinage* and from Asian and Oriental theater techniques. Initially he sought to elaborate a system of bodily expression and training that not only employed the latest scientific ideas concerning the neurological functions of the human organism, but also advertised the Marxist ideology of work underpinning the new Soviet society: "In the past the actor has always conformed with the society for which his art was intended. In future the actor must go even further in relating his technique to the industrial situation. For he will be working in a society where labour is no longer regarded as a curse but as a joyful, vital necessity. In these conditions of ideal labour art clearly requires a new foundation."[55] As director of the State Higher Theater Workshop in Moscow and one of the theater workers most closely identified in the early 1920s with the creation of a new Soviet culture, the formulation of a Marxist approach to acting became important to Meyerhold. The new Bolshevik attitude to art and culture must inevitably have caused him to ignore or reject as bourgeois the introspective approach to human behavior being explored by Freudian psychoanalysis in favor of the strictly materialist principles of behaviorist psychology.

   The industrial organization of work pioneered in the United States in the form of Frederick Winslow Taylor's time-and-motion studies provided a model for early Soviet efforts toward the industrialization of the economy. Aleksei Gastev developed and promulgated Taylor's ideas in Russia, providing Meyerhold with an apparently scientific foundation for biomechanics: "In so far as the task of the actor is the realization of a specific objective, his means of expression must be economical in order to ensure that *precision* of movement which will facilitate *the quickest possible realization of the objective.* The methods of Taylorism may be applied to the work of the actor in the same way as they are to any form of work with the aim of maximum productivity."[56] In fact the whole approach to acting and actor training in Meyerhold's pre-Soviet period was based on the notion of the actor as dancer-acrobat, so the invention of biomechanics represented not so much a break with his earlier praxis as a development of it.

The word *biomechanics* itself provides the key to comprehending Meyerhold's project. In linking the principles of biology and mechanics, the system represented an attempt to exploit the nature of the human body as a machine.[57] In the drive toward the creation of a new industrialized Soviet economy the workers should not be alienated from the process and products of their labor (as Marx claimed they were in a capitalist economy), but should be reintegrated in the system of production in such a way that work might again become a natural expression of their human instinct to create. The actor as worker in the new Soviet theater would therefore achieve both maximum efficiency and joy when performing in accordance with the principles of the machine as determined by modern science. As Taylorism supplied a modern theory of industrial efficiency that explained how the actor's body could function economically, so Pavlov's theories of reflexology (derived from the behaviorist psychology of William James) offered Meyerhold a neurological model of the connection between physical behavior and psychological states.

According to Meyerhold, "the art of the actor is the art of plastic forms in space."[58] Rejecting introspective psychology in favor of a physical approach to performance composition, he insisted that "psychological states are determined by specific physiological processes."[59] Biomechanics would, he believed, exploit the function of the nervous system to produce the "*excitation* which communicates itself to the spectator and induces him to share in the actor's performance."[60] One of Meyerhold's most admired actors, Igor Ilinsky, explained how biomechanics helped the actor to create a physical basis for emotional expression: "The physical position of an actor's body determines his emotions and the expressions in his voice. He [Meyerhold] wanted actors to have easily excitable reflexes. . . . Acting consists of coordinating the manifestations of his excitability. Let us take this example: an actor representing fear must not experience fear first and then run, but must first run (reflex) and then take fright from that action. Translated into today's theatrical language this means: 'One must not experience fear but express it onstage by a physical action.' "[61]

From the time that Stanislavski began publicly to rationalize his own approach to acting at the First Studio (1909), Meyerhold seemed to have felt the need to define his own praxis as antithetical to that of his former mentor, and biomechanics was at first presented as an ideologically correct alternative to Stanislavski's system of teaching the actor to experience a role—to Meyerhold's way of thinking, an outmoded bourgeois approach.[62] In fact Stanislavski's elaboration of the method of physical actions in the 1930s, although very different in its precise aims, did have in common with biomechanics the fundamental assumption that acting exploited the psychophysical nature of the human organism.

As practiced, biomechanics was a series of exercises for individuals, pairs, or groups, each of which comprised a minimum of one acting cycle that involved the reflex function of the human nervous system:

> The coordinated manifestations of excitability together constitute the actor's performance. Each separate manifestation comprises an *acting cycle*. Each *acting cycle* comprises three invariable stages:
>
> 1. INTENTION 2. REALISATION 3. REACTION
>
> *The Intention* is the intellectual assimilation of a task prescribed externally by the dramatist, the director or the initiative of the performer.
>
> *The Realisation* is the cycle of volitional, mimetic and vocal reflexes.
>
> *The Reaction* is the attenuation of the volitional reflex after its realisation mimetically and vocally, preparatory to the reception of a new intention (the transition to a new acting cycle).[63]

Exercises were combined to create more complex études that were like short pantomimes involving one or more acting cycles. Repeated execution of the exercises was intended to cultivate in the actor qualities that Meyerhold observed in the movements of a skilled worker: (1) an absence of superfluous unproductive movements; (2) rhythm; (3) the correct positioning of the body's centre of gravity; and (4) stability. Movements based on these principles are distinguished by their dance-like quality.[64]

In 1922 Meyerhold introduced biomechanics at his studio as a psychophysical program of acting training. Biomechanical exercises supplemented training in sport and gymnastics. Meyerhold began with exercises involving first the positioning of the body (stretching, contracting, knee bends, work on the abdomen, diaphragm, and shoulders), then the positioning of head, arms, and leg (turns of the neck, balancing a ball, work on hands and fingers including juggling, work on the legs including extensions and knee bends, running, balancing a ball with the foot, and the Charleston). The simplest exercises, such as running and walking in different tempi, various kinds of falls, discus and spear throwing, led to the more complex études that were initiated by a fundamental exercise called the dactyl, used to start and conclude the session:

> 1. The actor stands in a state of full muscular relaxation, feet parallel and slightly apart. (The stance, reminiscent of a boxer's, is the opposite of

the turned-out position for exercises at the barre.) The knees are slightly flexed, the arms hang loose at the sides.

2. On a signal, the actor sweeps his hands swiftly upward, his body following until he is on the balls of his feet. The palms of the hands face each other near the forehead.

3. The hands are then brought swiftly and sharply downward to execute in rapid succession two short claps (parallel to the chest and the stomach), the momentum of the claps causes the knees to flex and the hands to be thrown back as they separate after the second clap.

4. This abrupt movement is transferred to the actor's entire body in a forward and downward motion as the energy is conveyed to his calves and feet. The actor is now prepared to perform the exercise.[65]

Meyerhold continually developed both individual and group exercises. In the first two years at the Meyerhold workshop, twenty-two exercises were taught: Throwing a Stone, Shooting the Bow, Falling and Catching, Leap onto the Partner's Back, Leap onto the Partner's Chest, Blow on the Nose, Slap in the Face, Exercises with Sticks, Bouncing a Ball in the Air, Pushing Down a Kneeling Figure with the Foot, Horse and Rider, Stab with the Dagger, Stumbling, Quadrille, Rope, The Jester, Bridge, Sawing, Scythe, Funeral, Leapfrog and Four Ice-skaters. Études were elaborated as sequences of action comprising elements of these exercises. The études were invariably accompanied by music, so that actors acquired sensitivity to rhythm, learning to shape the performance both in harmony with and in counterpoint to music. Meyerhold employed music as a significant structural element in all of his productions.

Biomechanics was a serious attempt to address a central problem of acting: the duality of the actor, whose mind was the creator of the performance and whose body was its material. Meyerhold referred to Coquelin's analysis of the significance of this duality, which had caused Craig to doubt whether theater art could be created using live actors. In answer to criticism that biomechanics was not a scientific application of modern physiology and that its gratuitous theatricality represented a betrayal of Taylorist principles of movement economy, Arkady Pozdnev, one of Meyerhold's students, pointed out that biomechanics was not actually a straightforward exploitation of Taylor's principles of work movement: "Taylor built his theory on the economy of the worker's energy, mainly by the natural reduction of the work gesture towards the *least and shortest trajectory*. In the theatre that is not only *not needed*, it is *harmful*."[66] Although actors shared with workers the general aim of eliminating superfluous effort in the execution of movement,

the actor's aim was not to *do* but to *represent* actions, so the economy of theatrical movement differed to a degree from that of ordinary labor. Biomechanics was the first modern system of corporeal training specifically
designed to transform the actor into a psychophysical instrument of expression. Biomechanics aimed not to teach a style of performance, but to train
the actor to be responsive and flexible enough to provoke in the spectator
the widest possible range of feelings. The objectives of each exercise were as
follows:

1. To enable the actor to feel the balance and center of gravity within
   himself, that is to develop complete control over one's own body.
2. To enable the actor to position and coordinate himself three-dimen-
   sionally in relation to the stage space, one's partner, and the stage
   properties. In other words to facilitate the development of a "good
   eye" so that the actor becomes a moving part of a harmonious whole.
3. To develop in the actor physical or reflexive arousal for instantaneous
   and non-conscious reaction.[67]

The point of the training was not to enable the actor to experience emotions (though that may have been a by-product of some of the études), but
to equip him to *evoke* feelings within the spectator through the efficient and
varied use of movement. Mikhail Korenev, one of Meyerhold's assistants at
the director's studio, characterized the loose yet precise kinetic quality promoted by the training as "moving on springs," and Meyerhold himself
referred to its "dancingness." Such descriptions gave the lie to the miscon-
ception that biomechanics encouraged militaristic displays of robotlike
gymnastic feats. While the movements were intended to be bolder and
stronger than the delicate gestures of pantomime, hands and fingers were
always to hang loose when not specifically engaged in gestic play. In performing biomechanical exercises, the whole body was required to participate in the movement of even its most peripheral member and there was to
be no superfluous movement.[68] Precision was the aim, and the movements
were to be practiced until they became reflexes. Actors accompanied biomechanical études with appropriate sounds, promoting the reciprocal relationship between sound and movement that has been a fundamental aspect
of modern actor training.[69] "Meyerhold based his biomechanics on the *rational* and *natural* use of movement. . . . He wanted biomechanics to be free
from any obtrusive style and manner. . . . Meyerhold valued highly the
expressivity of the body. He often demonstrated with a puppet. . . . This
masked figure, correctly used, could express everything that the mime can

express. . . . 'You must,' he said, 'know your body so that in any position you know exactly what effects it produces.' This faculty of the actor he called the 'self-mirror.'"[70]

Whether the études were indeed free of any stylistic signature is a moot point. Although Meyerhold was as dismissive of the balletic style as he was of the unintentional stylization that characterized the supposedly natural movement vocabulary of Delsarte and Isadora Duncan, photographs of études being demonstrated and descriptions and photographs of productions that utilized elements from selected études suggest that the kinesthetic vocabulary of biomechanics involved a theatricalization of Taylorist work movements. This contradiction is reinforced by Meyerhold's assertion, "Every movement is a hieroglyph with its own peculiar meaning."[71] On the one hand, he regarded the exercises as a purely kinetic method of provoking the states of excitability in the actor that would provide stimuli for the audience, while on the other, he appeared to view the movement sequences themselves as indexical or iconic, inherently imbued with affective content. Although the idea that "each exercise is a melodrama"[72] may have been useful as a means of fixing the shape of each étude for the performers, there is a confusion here between the use of movement to create mise-en-scène and the idea of a system of elements of motion, practiced in different combinations in order to develop the performer as a psychophysical instrument of expression.

Meyerhold's ideas were revolutionary. While in some respects anticipating Rudolf Laban's theory of eukinetics and choreutics (dynamic and spatial features of human movement) Meyerhold appears not always to have maintained a clear distinction between the elaboration of a system of psychophysical training for the actor and the cultivation of the performer's techniques of aesthetic composition. Unlike Laban, he undertook no research into the relationship between the spatial form of movement and its expressive content. Written statements by Meyerhold and his followers never clearly distinguish between physiological conditioning and performance composition. Meyerhold's own need to demonstrate biomechanics by quotations from selected études in *The Magnanimous Cuckold* (1922), *The Death of Tarelkin* (1922), and *The Forest* (1924) certainly increased the confusion over the significance and status of biomechanics.[73] The revolutionary film director Sergey Eisenstein was a student in Meyerhold's Director's Workshop in 1921 and 1922. He was profoundly affected by the genius of his mentor, developing his own approach to movement training and composition in theater and film by synthesizing biomechanics with Rudolf Bode's theories of expressive movement.[74] Although Eisenstein questioned some of the ways in which the practice of biomechanics had been rationalized, he believed that Meyerhold had discovered a fundamental truth about acting that made biomechanics the basis for systematic elaboration. From an entirely different perspective, biomechanics impressed the American director Harold Clurman, who witnessed a class in Moscow during his visit in 1935: "I had seen funny pictures and had heard abstruse explanations of the theory of Biomechanics, neither of which had interested me particularly. . . . To put it bluntly, this was the best body work for the actor I had ever seen. After seeing this I could understand why the Russian actors are so fluent and graceful on the stage. . . . The Biomechanics exercises are not only excellent in their purely physical elements for training the muscles through tension and relaxation, movement and the stopping of movement, but remarkable for their dramatic elements (without any artiness), for each of these exercises is a kind of play."[75]

In common with other major modernist theater practitioners, Meyerhold insisted that the actor should be educated as a creative artist. The various curricula of the Meyerhold workshop for actors and directors in the early 1920s presented biomechanics as one aspect of the movement course. The program included courses in voice and speech, dramatic literature, stage technology, music, and social sciences. Actors were required to study the theatrical function of stock character types. A table of type character roles was published by Meyerhold in 1922 as "The actor's emploi." Here the necessary qualifications of the actor were listed alongside examples of each type from the dramatic repertoire and the dramatic function of each type. In this way Meyerhold attempted to systematize his approach to the art of the *cabotin,* teaching the actors to become aware of their own particular physical and artistic predispositions and of how best to exploit them.

Acting for Meyerhold was a self-conscious art. All his productions exploited the technical virtuosity of his performers. The actor was required to indicate a quality of self-reflexivity in the moment of performance. What Meyerhold called *pre-acting* was a pause before the acting of a particular sequence, which would prepare the audience psychologically for what was about to happen: "[The spectator] comprehends the scenic situation fully resolved in advance and so has no need to make any effort to grasp the underlying message of the scene."[76] By revealing their attitudes to character and situation, the actors indicated their views of the action, attempting to influence the audience by means of such theatrical commentary. The idea of pre-acting anticipated a number of the devices that Brecht used in his plays and in production to break the flow of the action and promote the

spectator's self-conscious awareness with regard to the dramaturgical structuring of the narrative.

Meyerhold employed acting and mise-en-scène to create a performance
text that would form a counterpoint to the written text of a play. As with
Craig, the director was assumed to be the author of the performance. Elements of biomechanics contributed to the conscious stylization of productions such as *The Magnanimous Cuckold, The Forest,* and *The Government
Inspector,* which are usually ranked among Meyerhold's masterpieces. By
juxtaposing consciously theatrical acting against broadly realistic texts, Meyerhold demanded that the spectator play an active role in constructing the
meaning of the performance. Partly because of his view that the actor's performance should consciously convey an attitude toward what was being
shown, Meyerhold did not treat actors merely as puppets. Many actors who
worked with him testified to his sensitivity to their individual talents. In his
most successful productions, acting was never submerged by elaborate
scenic staging but animated the scenography through the interplay of movement, music, and vocal expression.

There have been few directors as ambitious or as eclectic as Meyerhold.
His deployment of the performer as an instrument provided a unique model
of how to counterpoint scenography and acting, exemplifying a self-
reflexive methodology of performance as artifice. Biomechanics was the
first attempt at a modern system of movement training for actors. The scope
of Meyerhold's influence is inestimable, but those inspired by his example
must surely include Peter Brook, Tadeusz Kantor, Jerzy Grotowski, Lev
Dodin, Peter Sellars, Yuri Lyubimov, Harold Prince, Richard Jones, and
Ariane Mnouchkine. Few avant-garde theater artists of the late twentieth
century did not in some way respond to the example of either Craig or
Meyerhold. The conception of actor as scenographic instrument has animated the work of Robert Wilson, the Wooster Group, the People Show,
Robert Lepage, DV8, Jan Fabre, and a large number of live and performance artists in the United States and Britain since the 1960s.

The Work of Anne Bogart

In the United States, Anne Bogart has during the last twenty years developed the *viewpoints* method of training and performance composition, in
order to enable actors to collaborate in the process of theater-making in
ways envisaged by Craig and Meyerhold. In her productions and in her
training and rehearsal methodology, Bogart explicitly aims to subvert and

disrupt what has become the clichéd naturalism of Stanislavskian performance, conceiving productions on analogy with visual arts such as dance and architecture. She consciously seeks to create mise-en-scènes from an eclectic range of sources, such as music, painting, photographs, and pop images. Her work is distinguished from that of many of her contemporaries by her determination to work in an open collaboration with actors, designers, dramaturgs, and musicians to create complex theatrical collages. In this respect, she is continuing a tradition of performance composition initiated by Craig and Meyerhold, and while her actual methods may not seem to derive from either of these innovators, her aim is to train performers in the same art of performance composition that Craig sought to develop at his short-lived school before the outbreak of World War I.

Bogart's technique of performance composition is postmodern in that her semiotically dense performance texts frame, counterpoint, supplement, comment on, and occasionally subvert the written texts she uses. As an example, her mise-en-scène for *South Pacific* in 1984 deconstructed Rodgers and Hammerstein's text, thus problematizing the naive optimism of its romantic narrative and musical themes. Instead of literally re-creating the intended atmosphere of the show's outdoor setting on the beach of a South Pacific island, she transformed the spectator's relationship to the action by playing the classic musical as a show-within-a-play set in the mental ward of an institution for wounded soldiers. A somewhat paternalistic affirmation of the superiority of liberal (and inevitably Western) values over racial prejudice became in Bogart's staging a much more disturbing interrogation of both the causes and effects of war—an exposure of the colonialist ideology partially obscured by Rodgers and Hammerstein's liberal rhetoric.

Bogart's collaborators view her work as a bold attempt to preserve the liveness of the theatrical medium—to assert its superiority as the vehicle for performance over the increasing banality consequent on the commercialization of the entertainment media by the film and television industries. Like those of Peter Brook, Jerzy Grotowski, and Eugenio Barba, her productions challenge the clichés of performance forms perpetuated without reference to content. Each new work she produces is simultaneously an experiment in exploiting the uniqueness of theatrical performance and a critique of existing formulae in American theater.[77] Although sensitive to the values of non-Western performance and the philosophies that sustain it, her conscious intention is to respond to American cultural forms *as an American*.

It is therefore understandable that Bogart is often asked why she chose to collaborate with the Japanese director Tadashi Suzuki in establishing the Saratoga International Theater Institute in 1992 as "a platform for multicultural expression in the theatre."[78] It seems likely that when she first encountered Suzuki's company in Togamura she was so impressed with the rigor of his training, and the power and precision of the company's performances, that she decided that the presence of the company at Saratoga every summer would be a stimulus and a challenge that might inform her own confrontation with conventional American attitudes to performance. As with the projects of Brook and Mnouchkine and the theater anthropology of Barba, a "dialogue with otherness" in performance terms has provided Bogart with the stimulus and the perspective to confront both the clichés and the creative possibilities of her own native tradition.

But remarkable though it is, Bogart's work as a director would not represent a major contribution to the art of the performer were it not for the influence that her viewpoints system has had as a way of preparing actors to collaborate in performance composition. In fact her way of working with actors in rehearsal involves three distinct phases: *(a)* source work, *(b)* the nine viewpoints, and *(c)* composition. Source work is Bogart's way of stimulating the various faculties of everyone in the company to do imaginative (rather than merely analytical) research on the subject and context of the play/performance. She believes that any significant piece of theater, be it the revival of an old work or the creation of a new, involves the discovery of a question. In striving to remove the clichés that have accreted around certain ideas—in order to penetrate beneath the answers that have in time begun to obscure the questions—source work aims to bring each individual member of the company into personal contact with the subject matter of the performance. The dramaturg and members of the group are asked to bring to early rehearsals material that expresses their own subjective associations with the core content of the production. These might include photographs, art objects, songs, historical documents, videos, or private memories that stimulate a *lived* relationship with the *play-world* being created on stage.

The source work is developed by exercises using both viewpoints and assignments in composition to create a system of playing with the initial research material in order to transform it into a theatrical vocabulary. The viewpoints provide a practical framework for exploration of the full range of movement possibilities in stage space. They are the core elements of a system of composition in space and time—"points of awareness that a performer or creator has while working."[79] In training, actors must use them to develop a stage presence sensitive to the kinetic possibilities of the body as an instrument of composition. Originally there were six viewpoints. The system was derived from two of Bogart's teachers—Mary Overlie, a dance teacher at New York University, and Aileen Passloff, who taught a composition class at Bard College. The viewpoints do not dictate a style of performance, but are the formal principles of staging that connect the work of actor, director, and scenographer. They allow actor and director to use a common language that has nothing to do with the actor's or character's feelings or psychology but, more properly, assists the actor to explore the effect of visual and aural composition (mise-en-scène) on the spectator.[80] By 1994, the number of viewpoints had increased from six to nine: spatial relationship, shape, gesture, architecture, topography, tempo, duration, kinesthetic response, and repetition.

The first five are viewpoints of *space;* the other four of *time.* Since 1994, Bogart has extended the viewpoints in order to apply her principles of composition to sound. The notions of shape, tempo, gesture, architecture, repetition, duration and kinesthetic response have been applied to sound and speech. Two new aural viewpoints have been added—*dynamic,* which relates to volume, and *pitch,* which relates to tone. Practice with all the viewpoints develops the actor's awareness of the varied aural and kinesthetic vocabulary possible when making a production. There is some overlap between categories, and their relative importance varies from one project to another; for example, repetition may be a major feature of one piece and hardly employed in another.

Spatial relationships, known in semiological terms as proxemics, refers to the distance between people and objects on stage and the compositional dynamics derived from their arrangement. *Shape* applies to the contour of the individual body as well as the pattern of a group of performers' bodies on stage. Bogart divides *gesture* into behavioral or expressive gesture. Behavioral gesture derives from social behavior and relates to its codes. It involves all the spontaneous actions we perform in everyday life. Expressive gesture is abstract or symbolic, expressing inner states or emotions. *Architecture* involves all aspects of the physical environment on stage in its relationship to the movement of the performer. *Topography* refers to the way in which the performers structure and use the floor space to create patterns that become visible to the spectator. It involves the creation of virtual space through movement as much as the actual physical arrangement of the space. The viewpoints of *time, tempo, duration,* and *repetition* are self-explanatory. *Kinesthetic response* is a spontaneous reaction to motion occurring outside the actor. It involves impulsive reactions to stimuli.

Parallel in some respects to the effort and spatial training of Laban, the psychophysical work of Michael Chekhov and the gestural/mimetic improvisations of Lecoq, viewpoints offer a method of physical training for imaginative work. There are no set exercises. By inviting actors to create group improvisations that incorporate selected viewpoints, Bogart's method simultaneously enhances the expressive potential of the individual and the ensemble, integrating exploration of the physical possibilities of the individual body with discovery of the principles of group composition in time and space. In her refusal to separate physical training from imaginative exploration, technique from expression, Bogart's approach echoes the praxis of Copeau, Saint-Denis, Laban, Brook, and Cicely Berry. According to Tina Landau, one of Bogart's frequent collaborators,

> [Composition] is the practice of selecting and arranging the separate components of theatrical language into a cohesive work of art for the stage. . . . [It] is a method for generating, defining and developing the theatre vocabulary that will be used for any given piece. . . . It is an alternative method of writing. . . . Composition is writing with a group of people on their feet. . . . [In] *No Plays No Poetry* we both employed the magic of Composition to have the company generate tons of material which we then sifted through as a film editor would. . . . In addition, in Composition work we study and use principles from other disciplines as translated to the stage. For example, stealing from music, we might ask what the rhythm of a moment is, or how to interact based on a fugue structure. . . . Or we'll think about film and ask, "How do we stage a close-up" . . . an establishing shot? A montage? In applying compositional forms from other disciplines to the theatre, we push the envelope of theatrical possibility and challenge ourselves to create new forms.[81]

Although her own work is in very few respects comparable with that of Suzuki, the absolute rigor of his physical training being far removed from the playful and improvisational quality she brings to her viewpoints training, the work of each constitutes a thoroughgoing critique of naturalistic performance.[82] In one particular respect, Suzuki training has proved helpful for Bogart's performers. The exacting physical discipline of the feet achieved through Suzuki's powerful stamping technique prevents performers from psychologizing the acting process. It enables actors to work with absolute precision on fixing and re-creating the movement score that is composed by the company in rehearsal. During the process of rehearsal Bogart's actors are theater-makers who collaborate fully with other members of the production team, rather than merely being used by the director.[83] In performance, they must be able to start from the secure basis of a fixed performance composition in order to be open and vulnerable in the encounter with the audience.

In an essay on her work, Eelka Lampe "conceive[s] of Bogart's encounter with East Asian performance traditions as the paradox of the circle. . . . Bogart has been opening herself up to Eastern traditions in order to come full circle, back to a deeper digging into and understanding of her own cultural background."[84] In this respect, her work is imbued with the spirit of cross- cultural exchange that distinguishes the present moment in theater practice. Bogart's questioning of the limitations of the tradition within which she herself works and her desire to extend the limits of that tradition is at the same time an interrogation of the meaning of theater. "I become more and more aware that there is one thing I have to say in theatre—I feel that every play has to ask the question, 'Why do we need theatre?' . . . I'm interested in the body, the human body that is the stuff of live theatre. For me it's the body, it's the meat."[85]

The increasing currency of Bogart's Viewpoints training system has challenged the pervasive influence of Stanislavskian approaches to rehearsal and training in the United States, and prepares actors to work as scenographic instruments in forms of total theater that continue the tradition of Appia, Craig, and Meyerhold into the twenty-first century.

4. The Legacy of Jacques Copeau

Opposed to theater-making as artificial process is an approach based on the premise that it is the most complex form of play. Although in Britain the approach is commonly associated with "playwright's theater," the actor being conceived as a physical and histrionic instrument whose function is to give kinetic and aural shape to the words of the text, it is based on a notion of theater deriving as much from improvisation and devising as from written text. The approach is inherent in both the praxis of Jacques Copeau and his many followers in France and the British tradition of Shakespeare productions initiated by William Poel through his "Elizabethan revival." Poel's approach was subsequently combined with modernist staging principles by his student Harley Granville Barker, forming a British tradition of Shakespeare production that still predominates.

In the 1930s, Copeau's nephew and disciple Michel Saint-Denis came to work in England, where he eventually settled. By working with many of the important young British actors of the 1930s and 1940s, Saint-Denis made an immediate impact on the English theater.[1] In the 1930s he set up a private school, the London Theatre Studio; after the Second World War he was responsible for establishing both the Old Vic Theatre School and the Young Vic Company.[2] Peter Hall's sponsorship of both Saint-Denis and the Cambridge don and director John Barton at the Royal Shakespeare Company paved the way for the employment of the brilliant teacher Cicely Berry as a permanent voice coach at the RSC. An aesthetic for playing the classics and modern plays was given concrete form; an official pedagogy determined a methodology of training and rehearsal that motivated the work of the RSC (and other subsidized companies in its train) until the 1980s.

One of the truly revolutionary theater practitioners in the twentieth century, Jacques Copeau (1879–1949) was also, paradoxically, a traditionalist. It was the religious zeal with which he pursued dramatic renovation that made his approach radical. Copeau's uncompromising idealism meant that he could not be satisfied by the series of theatrical triumphs achieved at the Vieux-Colombier before and after the First World War (1913–14 and 1919–24). When it seemed in 1924 that critical and commercial success might force him to compromise his artistic ideals, he retreated from Paris to establish a theater school in Burgundy in order to initiate the renaissance in performance he believed was necessary for the survival of theater as an art. Unlike Edward Gordon Craig, Copeau placed the human reality of the actor at the center of the new theater he envisaged. Like Craig, however, he saw the professional actor as the enemy of true drama. Completely convinced of the sanctity of the classic play-text (Molière, he believed, provided the exemplary model of a dramatist who *wrote* theater), Copeau was nevertheless the first director to conceive of improvisation as the means of developing the actor's imagination and histrionic sensibility. After his move to Burgundy, he even attempted to create a twentieth-century commedia dell' arte: with his actors, Copeau invented characters based on contemporary types and scenarios that would appeal to his country audiences.

What was Copeau's dramatic renovation? In essence it was an attempt to return to the sources of dramatic performance, in order to recover a theatrical economy in which dramaturgy was inseparable from theatrical form. "I see no true transformation possible in the theatre except through and by a social transformation. New dramatic forms will come from new ways of living, thinking and feeling. That is why I have never dared use the word renaissance. I always believed that our 'chapel,' our laboratory, our School, whatever one calls it—could not honestly be described as anything but a renewal or, even better, a preparation. Renewal of dramatic feeling through an understanding of the masterworks, and a renewed contact with the great technical traditions. Preparation of the means suitable to the play of a broader, freer and more audacious dramatic imagination."[3]

With his idea of the play of the dramatic imagination, Copeau initiated an approach to performance training and rehearsal that has in many ways been as pervasive as the system of Stanislavski. Copeau was reacting against both the factitious naturalism that was a product of twenty-five years of French imitations of André Antoine's once-revolutionary production style, and the deadly conservatism of the teaching at the Conservatoire.[4] Copeau had no interest in preserving the masterworks for antiquarian purposes, but hoped to stimulate the development of new dramatic forms that would come about through and by a social transformation. His project was of a radical nature. Just as much as Stanislavski, he believed that the creation of a new aesthetic for theater depended upon the establishment of an ethics of the stage. The return to a prelapsarian state of theatrical innocence was the precondition for the development of a drama that could express "new ways of living, thinking and feeling."[5]

Such a linkage of aesthetics with ethics—of art with life—is typical of theatrical reformers who conceive the attack on the outmoded conventions and clichés of contemporary theater as a return to the sources of performance. Stripped of the sophisticated accretions of theatrical and literary fashion, such performance is envisioned as authentically human. Copeau's own particular rhetoric finds echoes in many different contexts, from the radical credos and practices of Artaud, Grotowski, and Peter Brook, to British drama schools with their more mundane emphasis on sincerity of expression and fidelity to the writer's text and their disapproval of personal acting mannerisms and arbitrary interpretations.

Copeau was himself a versatile practitioner. At various times (and occasionally even simultaneously) playwright, critic, director, actor, teacher, and scenographer, his views on acting derive from concrete experiment in the workshop and before an audience. As a skillful playwright, however, he brought the perspective of an all-round theater-maker to his work with actors. His literary sensibility may have contributed to his extreme dislike of *cabotinage*. Such professional tricks of the actor's trade constituted precisely the approach to performance that Meyerhold admired. Although Copeau did not attempt to rationalize his practice by writing about it systematically after the manner of Stanislavski, he did leave a fairly large body of writing in the form of essays and lectures from different phases of his career. In these his views are explicitly stated. Certain recurrent themes constitute a cluster of associated concepts that entered the vocabulary of twentieth-century theater and animated its practice in many different contexts.

Scenographic Minimalism

A scenographic aesthetic of minimalism was embodied in Copeau's attempts to replace the proscenium-arch theater with a bare stage continuous with the space of the auditorium and therefore open to the audience. This was part of the attempt to abolish the illusionistic trickery he associated with *cabotinage*. Copeau desired to present the acting in full view of the audience with no attempt to disguise the fact of performance. Even when Copeau's actors performed in a realist play (which they often did) there was no need to engage in the naturalistic pretence that they were not acting. According to the American designers Kenneth MacGowan and Robert Edmond Jones,

Copeau "could build no ideal theatre, but he could make one in which his actors would escape the realisms and pretences of the modern theatre, and would play to and with the audience as their spirit demanded."[6]

Michel Saint-Denis described the renovated stage of the Vieux-Colombier thus: "The recollection of the Vieux-Colombier that first comes to my mind is of the stage itself: it was both wide and high and every part of it was open to the auditorium. A forestage—on the same level as the mainstage—projected into the auditorium to form an acting area, easily recognizable as such. It was designed for *physical* acting; its form, its many levels, its steps and aprons allowed for a great variety of staging. The whole stage was an acting area, in contrast to that 'box of illusions'—the proscenium stage. It gave equal authenticity to classical farce, poetic drama and realistic 'anti-theatrical' plays. It rejected any kind of naturalistic décor created by sets or complicated lighting."[7]

Copeau's *tréteau nu* was in effect Peter Brook's empty space—the stage that testifies to the theater audience that "there are no secrets." Brook, among many others, was profoundly influenced by Copeau's image of the presentational playing space and the distinctive possibilities it implied.[8] "The stage is the instrument of the dramatic creator. It is the place for the drama, not the equipment. It belongs to the actors, not to the technicians or the scene-painters. It should always be ready for the actors and for action. The reforms which we have accomplished . . . have this in view . . . to put an instrument into the hands of the dramatic creator, create for him a free stage which he can use freely, with a minimum of intermediaries. . . . Now what I need is to create a new stage in accord with the principles of a new drama."[9]

These words explain the intimate relationship of playwright, actor, and acting space that Copeau saw as a precondition for dramatic renovation. Prefiguring not only Brook's empty space but the poor theater of Grotowski and the environmental performance typical of much theatrical experiment from the 1960s onwards, Copeau articulated one of the fundamental tenets of radical stage practice in the late twentieth century: "what we need is not a masterpiece of stage machinery. We need a masterpiece of architectonic articulation."[10]

Acting as Instinctive Role-Play

For Copeau, the stage was a platform designed to allow the actors to share the theatrical presentation with an audience. Such acting made no attempt to pretend that it was anything other than a performance: "The question of decor does not exist for me. Forming a troupe of actors, having them act anywhere, renewing the actor's mind and soul: *that is inimitable.* No matter how we approach the problem of theatre, we come back to the problem of the actor as the instrument and perfect realiser of a dramatic idea."[11] Copeau's minimalist approach to decor found its histrionic equivalent in the simplicity and sincerity that he aimed to cultivate in the actor. "I care little for the great actor. If pressed I should say that in every age the great actor was the enemy of dramatic art. For great dramatic art what is needed is not a great actor but *a new conception of dramatic interpretation.*"[12]

Finding in children's games a model for the kind of *play* that might be useful in training the actor, Copeau was determined that actors' training should "preserve them from theatricality," and promised that his school would "fight against the encroachment of professional tricks, against all professional distortions, against the ossification of specialisation. In short, we shall do our best to re-normalise these men and women whose vocation is to simulate all human emotions and gestures. So far as it is possible for us, we will take them outside the theatre and into contact with nature and with life."[13]

The return to nature, the substitution of the normalizing influence of life in place of the artifice of artistic conventions, is a key motif in the Romantic artists' rejection of the formality of neoclassical values. Such a desire for complete authenticity in aesthetic representation had motivated Stanislavski's demand that the actor replace external mimicry by forms of characterization that attempted to embody essential spiritual or psychological truths. As a literary analyst Copeau was less naive than Stanislavski, but his implicitly religious quest for a *necessary* theater led him to conceive the function of the actor in equally universalist terms. For Copeau, there was an ethical foundation to good acting that he conceived in Christian humanist terms. Copeau differed from Stanislavski, however, in refusing to view the actor's process as a specialist technique divorced from other theater arts. Acting was viewed by Copeau as inseparable from the whole art of theater-making and as a function of the instinctive role-play that defines the social animal.

Although he shared Meyerhold's view of the actor as instrument, rather than creator of psychologically detailed characters, Copeau's dislike of overt theatricality was diametrically opposed to Meyerhold's taste for *cabotinage.* Copeau therefore formulated a concept of style that was distinct from the idea of conscious stylization.

Toward an Ideal Ensemble

For Copeau, actors were "servants of theatre" who needed to work in "an atmosphere of simplicity, honesty, comradeship and firm discipline."[14] The monastic ideal of a school and theater company living together in simple conditions away from the sophistication of an urban theatrical culture was partially realized by the company's various retreats to the country at different periods in Copeau's career. The first rehearsals of the Vieux-Colombier repertoire took place in the garden of Copeau's family home thirty miles outside Paris at Limon in 1913. The company lived in a country house in New Jersey in the summer of 1918 while rehearsing for their second season in the United States. In 1924 his retreat to Burgundy with a few members of the company and some students to pursue research led to the formation of the troupe, Les Copiaus, which was based in the countryside until its dissolution in 1929.

One of the recurrent themes of twentieth-century theater was the idea of the ensemble. Copeau's belief in the benefit to the theater ensemble of living and working like an extended family in a rural environment with close ties to the local community has been tested and reformulated in different ways by groups like the Living Theater, Joan Littlewood's Theatre Workshop, Grotowski's Theater Laboratory, Gardzienice, and Eugenio Barba's Odin Teatret. These practitioners of *third theater* have in common a desire to reinvent theatrical performance in a radical way that does not pander to what they regard as a pretentious fashion for avant-garde sophistication. The myth of a return to the origins of performance signifies a belief in theater as a primary cultural form, expressive of the most basic human instincts and needs.

To this end Copeau demanded of the actor not virtuosity or the arbitrary accumulation of performance skills, but honesty, simplicity, and sincerity. The student actor's work might often be unrewarding, and it demanded the kind of self-sacrifice that was a mark of personal integrity: "[It is] work which is done not only with the mouth, nor even with mouth and mind, but also with the body, with the whole person, all the faculties, and with the whole being."[15] Such an organicist notion of acting as an integration of all the faculties of the whole person is a myth animating most modern systems of actor training other than the explicitly critical and deconstructive approaches of Craig, Meyerhold, Brecht, and the postmodern practitioners.[16]

A potential danger attaches to the ubiquitous myth of the organic wholeness of good acting. Teachers and directors are tempted to assume the right to decide what kind of behavior best constitutes the truthful or unaffected expression of the whole person, and what kind of identity best manifests that wholeness. As it is easy for even the well-intentioned teacher and director to confuse their unconscious responses to the personality of an actor with particular ethical qualities, assuming authority as teacher to identify and mold the whole being is a bit like playing God. Acting teachers who are, like Copeau, serious in the aim of cultivating their students' wholeness of body, mind, and feelings are in danger of arbitrarily imposing an ideology at the most fundamental level of identity formation. Wholeness or balance are in practice words that conceal a speaker's complex of unconsciously determined feelings and prejudices that are never free of personal and social values.[17]

Notwithstanding the problems inherent in the belief that good acting is intimately connected with wholeness of being, its appeal to actors, directors, and teachers has been irresistible. Stanislavski's belief in the organic nature of the process whereby an actor becomes fused with the role to create a character (truth of characterization) parallels Copeau's valorization of honest representation as opposed to the professional tricks of *cabotinage*. While not concerned with detailed realism of characterization, Copeau is nonetheless as determined as Stanislavski to value *truthful* acting over stale conventions and theatrical clichés.[18]

The various notes on proposed and actual programs of actor training left by Copeau bear testimony to his ideal of teaching the whole person. He did not propose a coherent system along the lines of Stanislavski that would directly address all the problems of the actor in training and rehearsal, but more pragmatically developed an all-round program in theatrical and general culture that was to be combined with classes specifically directed to cultivating the imagination and skills of the performer. For one whose attitudes might appear strict and authoritarian, Copeau's pedagogical approach was in practice surprisingly liberal. In discussing his own use of rhythmic exercises, he quoted approvingly from Dalcroze: "It is the pupil who should teach the master, not the reverse. The role of the master is rather to reveal to the pupil what it is that he has learned."[19]

A New Kind of Theater School

As early as 1913, Copeau had expressed his belief in the need for a school as well as a theater to form actors capable of realizing his dream of dramatic renovation: "[Just] as a business cannot do without its laboratory . . . art becomes impoverished or confused if it does not have the principles of a school to depend upon. . . . School or laboratory [is] indispensable to the

theater which is both an art and a business. . . . [Stage] experience is worth
what it is worth. If it begins to roughen, it is theory's job to smoothe it
again. The stage alone makes the actor, just as it makes the author. But, it
unmakes them, too."[20]

Copeau's words were prophetic of the many significant initiatives
throughout the twentieth century to formulate revolutionary principles of
performance by exploration under the conditions offered by a laboratory or
school. His earliest plan for a Vieux-Colombier school in 1916 included
reading aloud, poetic recitations, literary and theater history, mime and
improvisation, games, study of the repertoire, athletics, and fencing. What
was remarkable about such a prospectus was not only the variety of types of
study (from purely physical to the intellectual) but also the prominence
given to different types of *play*. Improvisation and games were a central
aspect of Copeau's earliest thoughts about actor training. As he refined and
developed his ideas, he began to believe that such unscripted play could
mediate between the purely intellectual and wholly physical components of
the performer's curriculum, integrating intellectual and physical skills
through the development of the imagination.

Stanislavski devised improvisations in response to the immediate circumstances provided in the play text: these were clearly directed toward achieving concentration and imaginative belief in the fictional world of the character and situation. By contrast, Copeau's approach through games involved
the stimulation of the performer's creativity in a freer and less conscious
way. Playing games was a way of integrating body/mind functions in preparation for a type of acting that might exhibit qualities of spontaneity and sincerity. Copeau's notion of cultivating the imagination through play has
dominated twentieth-century British and French methods of actor training
and rehearsal in ways that explain why Stanislavski's teaching has not made
a significant impact in these countries.

Copeau's approach was motivated by the realization that older kinds of
actor training failed because they attempted to address concrete corporeal
problems by appealing to the actor's mind. He observed the phenomenon
that Stanislavski had addressed at different stages of his career—that actors
become self-conscious and indeed physically frozen when a director asks
them to express an interpretation that has been derived from a purely analytical study of the play ("work around the table"). The gap between the
actor's idea of the character's interior life (whether derived from reading and
analysis or via the psycho-technique) and its physical expression was a result
of having started with a reflective process. Whether the actor started from a
mental apprehension of character or a physical technique of characteriza-

tion, there remained a problematic gap between the conception of the character and its embodiment. What Copeau observed in the French theater was the actor's application of a stock of rhetorical speech modes as a substitute for a fully imagined interpretation.

The method of beginning rehearsals by reading the parts before attempting to illustrate them with gestures originated in the Renaissance theater at the point when playwrights became somewhat detached from the production process, giving each performer a script on which were written the speeches of his character, together with his cues. The conventions governing this process were those of rhetorical art, where the actor supplemented speech with persuasive gestures and movements. Movement and gesture continued to be conceived as an illustration and extension of rhetorical speech throughout the eighteenth and nineteenth centuries, even after the main emphasis of a theatrical production had become visually spectacular rather than controlled by the spoken text.[21] The advent of naturalism with its conception of action as behavior rendered anomalous the practice of adding stage business to *illustrate* the writer's speeches.

The courses proposed for the apprentice group of twelve student actors between the ages of fourteen and twenty describe a three-year program that, although it involved training in a wide range of skills, both technical and intellectual, was dedicated to the creation of a new dramatic form. In searching for a fundamental principle that might motivate the teaching, Copeau initially perceived that music could be taken as the foundation and guiding principle of dramatic training. Dalcroze's system of eurhythmics may well have been what Copeau had in mind at this point. What is clear is Copeau's determination to develop a philosophy that would integrate all the different activities of the school. He was critical of the methods of the existing Conservatoire, which provided for the accumulation of expertise undirected toward an artistic aim.

Every course in the new Vieux-Colombier school was planned to enable students to develop the dramatic imagination. In 1921 Copeau believed he might ensure the coherence of the teaching "in the linking of the preparatory teaching to a definite period in the history of theatre."[22] A study of the ancient Greek theater provided a focus for a series of courses and technical exercises in the first year. There was no pedantic aim of transforming the students into scholars of theater history but an attempt at "a close wedding of knowledge and practice, of renewing one's good faith in ancient traditions and rhythms, of reviving, not the actual forms of the past, but that spiritual bond which unfailingly puts us in contact with their principles."[23]

The first-year prospectus for the course commencing at the end of 1921 reveals Copeau's effort to focus the different aspects of the teaching toward a common end. In it, he did not address merely the technical and imaginative problems of the actor but suggests a series of complementary approaches aimed at providing an all-round theater education. Prosody, versification, and poetic technique were to complement the study of reading and diction. *Theory of theater* was coupled with *dramatic instinct,* both taught by Copeau. Acting was linked with mise-en-scène. There were courses in music and song as well as three different types of movement class—acrobatics, taught by the great circus clowns the Fratellini brothers; dance; and the Hébert method of physical education. Theatrical architecture was augmented by practical workshops in stagecraft, including costume, decor, and stage architecture. Clearly, the radical aim of Copeau's new school was to relate aesthetic principles and history to artistic practice.

Building on this range of courses, the prospectus for the second year (1922–23) was more specific with reference to the content of the courses: it clearly linked the development of aesthetic culture with training in artistic technique. Copeau's own course Theory of the Theater, while it may not appear scholarly from a present-day perspective, reflected his intention of educating the taste of the actor as an essential component of her training: "Religious origins and social significance. Birth and development of dramatic feeling, of the tragic form, of the instrument of theatre. The architecture and materials of the Theatre. Performance. The role of the actor and the arrangement of the stage. Written works."[24]

Taken together with the course entitled Schools, Communities and Civilisation, which began with the topic "The nation" and ended by examining how the daily life of societies expresses itself through poetry, music, and theater, this outline demonstrated the ambitious scope of Copeau's cultural program. Philosophical reflection on the function of the actor and the social significance of the arts formed a core of the theoretical courses. Significantly, acting was linked with scenic architecture and mise-en-scène, illustrating Copeau's aim of educating the dramatic imagination as a whole, rather than allowing the conventional (and, to his way of thinking) artificial specializations characteristic of professional theater. As Stanislavski's development of the psycho-technique was doing in Russia, and was later to do in the United States, Copeau's scheme for training the actor's imagination as a physical-emotional-intellectual whole was to transform the existing nineteenth-century modes of performer training and rehearsal, and to establish the terms of modern British and French theater training.

Under the heading "Dramatic Training" Copeau promised the "cultivation of spontaneity and invention . . . Story-telling, games to sharpen the mind, improvisation, impromptu dialogue, mimicry, mask-work etc."[25] Expanding on his earlier use of games and improvisation for actor training by the introduction of storytelling, mimicry, and mask work, Copeau's innovatory method of training the actor as a dramatic instrument became the foundation for major European traditions of text-based and devised theater.

Developing the Performer's Innate Capacity

Mask Work

Working in a mask has become for many practitioners an essential aspect of physical training as well as the basis of mime performance such as that practiced by Etiénne Decroux, a student of Copeau. Jacques Prenat's account of the work in Burgundy from 1924 to 1929 contains some reflections by Copeau on the function of the mask. The "corporeal impotence" that undermined the spontaneous individuality of his beginning students was, he believed, attributable to their modesty. Indeed, the actor, in tending to become unnatural while embodying a character, also tends to distort herself: thus arises her inner resistance as a human being.

A consideration of various periods in the history of theater (ancient Greece, Rome, Egypt) led Copeau to the conclusion that hiding behind the mask releases the actor from everyday social constraints: "In Rome, behind the mask, the audacity of the obscene mimes was multiplied and they ventured gestures and postures which they would never have dared with bare faces. . . . So, in order to loosen up my people at the School, I masked them. Immediately I was able to observe a transformation of the young actor. You understand that the face, for us, is tormenting: the mask saves our dignity, our freedom. The mask protects the soul from grimaces. Thence, by a series of very explainable consequences, the wearer of the mask acutely feels his possibilities of corporeal expression."[26]

The use of a full-face neutral mask for mime and improvisation was an essential stage in training the body as an expressive instrument. By denying the actor her natural means of communication with the audience through facial expression, the mask would oblige her to invent a vocabulary of physical and emotional characterization through the body, promoting the kind of precise yet abstract acting that Copeau desired as an alternative to spontaneous mimetic realism. Instead of actively impersonating a character, the masked actor would surrender to the character of the mask, which would gradually come to possess her as she experimented with simple poses, gestures, and movements.[27]

In the mid-1920s the Vieux-Colombier actress and teacher Suzanne Bing introduced Copeau to Japanese Noh drama. The rigorous discipline it required of the performer and the refined minimalism of its form—a kind of total theater of singing, music, mime, dance, and recitation performed in full-face masks on a bare wooden stage—appealed to his ascetic taste. In 1924 Bing chose a play called *Kantan* for the students to work on, which, according to Michel Saint-Denis, "was done, not in order to re-constitute a Noh, but to permit us to experience, to some degree, its ceremonial nature."[28] After the final rehearsal, the English director, actor, and playwright Granville Barker spoke to the cast on stage: "I have always doubted the legitimacy of a drama school, but now you have convinced me, and I no longer doubt that any progress can come from a school. If you have been able to do this in three years—in ten you can do anything."[29]

Noh theater offered Copeau a model of the synthesis of physical technique with art that he considered the essence of the actor's craft. Its stylized conventions of performance require the masked actor to perform with the gestic and musical precision of an instrument. The Noh actor expresses an interior drama of the psyche in images both abstract and dreamlike. The musical form of Noh drama seemed to reinforce Copeau's notion of music as a structural principle in theatrical performance—an idea derived from the theories of Appia and Dalcroze.

Eurythmics as a Model for Movement Training

In Burgundy, the actor's working day started with purely physical exercises "with the aim of achieving corporeal flexibility, control and balance of movements, and of breath control."[30] Exercises in which students invented mimes on given themes, were undertaken between 10:00 A.M. and noon, building imaginative work upon the basis of the physical training. As he became a more experienced teacher, Copeau discovered new ways of integrating intellectual and imaginative challenges with the physical training that started the day. Copeau continued to regard music as the key to the actor's expressive capacity. In the early phase of the school's existence, music and dance formed a significant part of the curriculum, but for some years he wrestled with the problem of how movement and music might constitute the core of the kind of training system he sought. His early thoughts were much influenced by his knowledge of the experiments of Adolphe Appia and Emile-Jacques Dalcroze. The employment of Dalcroze's system of eurythmics represented an attempt on Copeau's part to improve on the purely athletic training provided by Hébert's calisthenics. The aim was not merely to strengthen the body but to develop the actor's kinesthetic sense.

What impressed Copeau on reading about eurythmics was Dalcroze's aim of offering artistic challenges in order to develop the student's sensibil- • ity instead of merely training her to acquire technical skills: "One must not reshape the pupil but develop him. . . . [Technique] should be nothing but the means to art. . . . the aim of musical education should be, not the production of pianists, violinists, singers, but of musically developed *human beings*."[31] For Copeau, the aim was to "de-histrionicize" the actor; by a process of education that would promote self-knowledge through the harmonious training of his faculties, the actor was to become less specialized as a virtuoso in order to be more completely a dramatic artist. Eurhythmics aimed to sensitize the musical performer to music by encouraging its immediate experience in her body. Dalcroze compared the process by which the musician absorbs the structure of the music through rhythmic movement to the way in which, in reading, words are understood before they have been translated into mental images. Copeau's own employment of rhythmic exercises in the teaching of dramatic reading paralleled Dalcroze's idea. The similarities between the ideas of Dalcroze and the early thoughts of Copeau on actor training reflect their common purpose of cultivating artists rather than instructing performers.[32] Copeau's knowledge of the principles of eurythmics informed his continuing search for a proper basis for the actor's education, although he became increasingly aware of its limitations when utilized as part of his own teaching.

By contrast with Edward Gordon Craig, whom Copeau had met in September 1915, Adolphe Appia regarded the actor as the key to the artistic unity of performance. Where Craig's scenographic designs deliberately dwarfed actors, subordinating them as "Über-marionettes" to be manipulated by the director/designer, Appia's stage designs were scaled to achieve a subtle balance in the changing relationship between the actor's body and the three-dimensional volume of stage space. Lighting changed the shape and volume of space to show the actor in different relationships to it, so it was lighting that rhythmically dictated the overall structure of a performance in space and time. Copeau was introduced to Appia by Dalcroze in October 1915. While at first he felt there was nothing Appia could teach him about the use of music in the education of the actor, over thirteen years Copeau came to understand the deep affinities between them. As his own thinking developed, he realized the profound significance of Appia's theories of the relationship of stage architecture, scenography, music, and lighting as structural principles of performance.

Appia's ideas about music had clearly influenced Dalcroze, and both men stimulated Copeau's search to find a musical basis for dramatic performance and education. In a letter to Craig of December 6, 1915, Copeau quoted

Appia's view that music is the guiding principle in the search for a new drama and offered a commentary on Appia's ideas in defense of the actor: "You will say that human beings could never serve an artistic purpose as instruments do. They will, if they become instruments. I mean if they are in full possession of their bodies, voice and mind, of movement and expression, even to the finest shade, if they have *developed* their personality and *mastered* it enough to release it into more powerful hands. . . . music is to me the nearest, the keenest representation of an ideal dramatic action."[33]

The teaching that Copeau observed at Dalcroze's school in Geneva in 1915 provided an actual model against which he might test his own ideas and teaching practices. What struck him as original was Dalcroze's determination that the teacher should follow the student's lead in the learning process. Dalcroze's classes for children, Copeau commented approvingly in his notebook, began with the children's play and became progressively more structured without obviously imposing a technique upon the individual. It is a reflection of Copeau's rigorously functionalist attitude that he judged the pupils' failure to be a consequence of putting "too much feeling in the movements they are executing." He observed the difference between "achieving the union of body with music freely and spontaneously in time and space" and the mistake pupils made by consciously illustrating an emotional attitude.[34]

These words reflect Copeau's ideal of an actor's body as a musically expressive instrument. The agreement between Copeau and Dalcroze on this point represented a radical departure from the conventions of nineteenth-century performance in which the actor manipulated voice and body to express feeling. Copeau's goal was for the actor to learn to experience spontaneous and unaffected physical feelings that were to be produced in the body through a musical approach to movement and speech. When he observed a pupil of Dalcroze accompanying a verse recitation with interpretive movements, it struck him as affected and he regarded the exercise as unhelpful. When, on the other hand, pupils accompanied the climax of a series of movements with an exclamation, Copeau felt the exercise to be "natural and necessary."[35] In this instance, the sound produced seemed in keeping with the movement, a fulfillment of its expressive intention.

In some respects, the ideas of Dalcroze and Copeau prefigured later approaches to movement training—most obviously Laban's work on effort. They established the integration of vocal and bodily expression as an ideal that stimulated much experimental work in the 1960s and 1970s (such as Grotowski, Chaikin, Brook) and became a guiding principle for modern voice teachers (such as Cicely Berry, Kristin Linklater, and Patsy Rodenburg). Yet Copeau's actual experience of eurythmics as taught to his students and actors at various times between 1915 and 1921 proved disappointing. The teachers did not exemplify the artistic and moral values that Copeau believed Dalcroze was trying to inculcate. While Copeau continued to identify with the aims of Dalcroze, he came to see eurythmics as another specialized movement technique that, because it supplied a ready-made vocabulary of movement with its own idiosyncratic style, was in danger of dehumanizing the actor.

Although in 1921 Copeau still believed that the actor's being needed musicalizing "to the depths of its physical and moral constitution,"[36] he observed that eurythmics as it was currently taught merely added another set of skills to the actor's armory and was not *incorporated* or *internalized* in dramatic education. Typically, the terms of Copeau's criticism reflected the radical nature of his search for a primary principle of training that would ensure the actor's freedom from the *deformation* of existing movement vocabularies. The possibility of such an ideal system of corporeal training has frequently been called into question, many theorists insisting that there is inherent in every type of training a set of aesthetic values that imposes itself on and through the body of the performer.[37] Nevertheless a powerful myth prevails of a pedagogy and an aesthetic practice that is wholly organic and derives from the innate and natural expressiveness of the human being. This myth has motivated a great deal of twentieth-century theater practice.

Stylistic Unity in Performance

Dalcroze's response to some of Copeau's criticisms concisely summed up the aims of eurythmics and explained the appeal it held as a method of training. "I consider the displacements, gestures, attitudes, groupings as a kind of *orchestration* i.e. to the art of making use of each instrument's individual tonal quality with an eye to the ensemble effect, so I am sure that the knowledge of certain laws of muscular economy, sacrifice of personal effects, influence on space, elimination of useless effort, co-ordination of attitudes and immediate adaptation to various atmospheres, should allow the actor to blend his temperament with those of the ensemble and to regulate the relations between the soloist and the protagonists, as in a musical symphony."[38] Though it would never become a universally recognized basis of movement training, the values of eurythmics have certainly contributed to the formation of the ensemble ideal in French and British theater, and have informed systems of rehearsal and training predicated on the notion of the actor as instrument of the playwright.

Copeau adumbrated a concept of fidelity to the text that helped deter-

mine mainstream French and British actors' understanding of the purpose of
their art. In his *Testimony* written on the death of Appia in 1928, Copeau
pointed out that Appia's musical principle of dramatic staging was based on
spoken, as much as musical, action (i.e., opera) and treated the words of the
playwright as analogous to a musical score, with staging and acting implicit
in the written text itself. Here Copeau was not proposing a purely literary
notion of performance, but his words imply the primacy of the playwright's
conception and of the written text as a blueprint for performance. This conception of mise-en-scène motivates the work of mainstream British directors today (Trevor Nunn, Peter Hall, Richard Eyre, Adrian Noble, Greg
Doran, Dominic Cook, and their younger successors in subsidized theater)
and informs the approaches of British voice and acting teachers to speaking
the text.

> Tragedy, comedy, drama, if they are well conceived for the stage by a
> real dramatist (which is extremely rare), articulated in accordance with
> the movements, developed in accordance with the rhythms, organised in
> accordance with the architecture, are not only analogous to music but are
> the essence of music. Declamation in the classic theatre was written, as
> for example that of Noh theatre today. Notation is always postulated in
> the verse-form of great drama. . . . Even the divisions of free prose have
> a tendency to such formal shaping. A dramatic dialogue is not altogether
> expressive unless . . . it attains . . . harmony . . . by its spatial relationships,
> which control the elocution that is intimately linked to the action at hand
> and is a fact or function of space.[39]

Copeau's analogy with the performance of a musical piece demonstrated
the type of stylistic unity a theatrical performance would aim to achieve. A
well-written drama, he believed, implicitly contained its performance style
as an aspect of its linguistic form: the task of actors, director, and designer
was to realize it in material terms. Such an attitude to performance as
inscribed in a written text motivated Michel Saint-Denis's directing and
teaching in England, which focused on style in acting, an approach famously
summed up by John Gielgud: "Style means knowing what kind of play
you're in."

Above all, a truly great playwright conceived texts as blueprints for
actors. In this respect, it was Appia with whom Copeau had the strongest
affinity, as he demonstrated by quoting a letter to him from Appia that
included comments on a performance of Corneille's *Le Menteur:* "Finally,
finally, the actor and only the actor! . . . that is truth! You possess it in your

field. . . . I have it in mine . . . and the principle remains exactly the same!"[40] Because he viewed actors as instruments, Copeau did not wish them to re-experience the character's life in detail. The kind of acting he aimed for has been called presentational: "Presentational acting, like presentational production, stands in opposition to representational. The distinction is quite clear in painting. . . . An actor who admits that he is an actor, and that he has an audience before him, and that it is his business to charm and move that audience by the brilliance of his art, is a presentational actor."[41]

Writing of Copeau's performance of Ivan in an adaptation of *The Brothers Karamazov,* Harold Clurman evoked the sculptural and musical clarity of his style: "There is something inescapably incisive and defined in his performance, and the mystery of the character is not conveyed by any haziness or blurring in the means of presentation, but on the contrary, by their very austerity and directness. There is something almost awful in Copeau's clarity. . . . Copeau's emotionalism is largely a nervous emotionalism, dominated by mind. Copeau's acting is contained, tempered . . . his unmatched diction, pure and precise almost to a fault. Copeau's speech, however, derives its magic not merely from its clarity but from his very keen sense of rhythm which communicates itself to his movements as well, and which is one of his greatest gifts as a director."[42] In this kind of theater, actors are playing social and psychological types, not necessarily in a wholly abstract way, but with a recognition of the style in which the text has been conceived. There is a simplicity and directness in the indication of character, which is outlined rather than fully inhabited by the actor. The actor precisely delineates the character's personality, rather than attempting to evoke her inner world on stage.

Improvisation: The Search for a New Dramaturgy

Copeau's great love of Molière motivated his attempt to create an improvised comedy of social types. Molière's ability to make words *act* through the mastery of scenic writing—the principle of movement in his plays—was, according to Copeau, inherent in the performances of the Italian commedia dell' arte players who shared his playhouse. These performances profoundly influenced his dramaturgy. The physical virtuosity of the Italian comedians needed to be recovered in the modern playing of Molière. An exploration and rediscovery of the skills of commedia performance might create a new form of improvised comedy that would not only prepare actors for performing Molière but create a theatrical tradition that would provide a foundation for a new drama, just as in the seventeenth century the commedia dell' arte tradition had provided performance techniques and conventions perfectly appropriate for more sophisticated dramaturgical exploitation by Molière. In Burgundy, Copeau built on his earlier use of games and improvisations in attempting to develop a comedy of contemporary social types, a modern-day French equivalent of the commedia dell' arte.

The musicality with which the actor should invest her playing might be achieved in a comic register by applying the principles of dance to Molière and improvised comedy. Work with masks provided a foundation of body training that could contribute to the improvised comedy. Rejecting the rhetorical conventions embodied in traditional approaches to performing Molière, Copeau's return to the acrobatic style of popular farce represented another formulation of the idea of the actor as instrument. His correspondence with an early collaborator, Louis Jouvet, a member of the Vieux-Colombier before and immediately after the First World War, reveals his understanding of the potential value of *improvisation* as a method of helping the actor to absorb the gestic outline of the performance before dealing directly with the text. As an approach to working on a classical text, the practice actually originated with Jouvet, but Jouvet had already been influenced by Copeau, so the experiment was in fact a realization of Copeau's notion of dramatic play as a method of discovery.

In 1916, some years before Stanislavski had begun to formulate his method of physical actions as a rehearsal practice, Jouvet proposed to Copeau an innovation—improvisations around the characters and actions of a play. The intention was to help the actor incarnate the flow of character-in-action and avoid the prior imposition of a purely literary conception of character derived from textual study and rhetorical conventions of staging, which the actor later had to translate into scenic terms. "I have noticed that the actor becomes aware of the action and what he is playing—he is so accustomed by memory that he loses the scene; he has only the text left. . . . Declamation is typical of this. Don't you think that certain texts could be revitalised, regenerated by an exercise which would consist of reducing them to outlines, resumes or skeletal actions: which the actor should first improvise, animate and clothe by himself. . . . At least the director would no longer have to deal with mechanised actors. . . . What do you think of this Rousseauesque idea of giving the beginners only a copy, an altered and substantial text drawn from such and such a classic, then, later, as a final initiation, give them the real text in all its splendour and perfection?"[43] Jouvet's idea was strikingly similar to Stanislavski's practice of active analysis during the final years of his career. Copeau immediately adopted it as a training method, and it informed his work on classic texts as well as improvised comedy.

Games and improvisations, a synthesis of various practices of Copeau and Stanislavski, have since the 1960s been dominant in mainstream training and rehearsal. The approach has been central to such British directors as Joan Littlewood, Peter Brook, William Gaskill, Max Stafford-Clark, and Mike Leigh, and to Theatre Machine, Theatre de Complicité, and many other companies. Improvisation has been taught by Viola Spolin and her followers in the United States, and by Keith Johnstone and others in Britain. In furthering the Copeau tradition, Jacques Lecoq has employed play to develop the creativity of generations of theater-makers since the late 1950s. The common practice of starting rehearsals with a warm-up (either a purely physical workout or a game) is a product of Copeau's perception of the connection between physical and mental activity as aspects of the imagination. Copeau's scheme of alternating between purely physical and purely intellectual activity, mediated by games and improvised dramas that demand both physical and mental involvement, established a normative rehearsal convention for contemporary Western theater. Actors regularly use improvisation to make characters and actions their own.

In addition to Molière and improvised comedy, Copeau worked with his actors to revive another popular tradition: Greek drama and medieval religious plays—traditions of community theater that were *of* rather than merely *for* the people and quite possibly reflected the religious commitment reflected in his conversion to Roman Catholicism. These models provided the opportunity to explore the "symphonic" relationship between the soloist and the group that his acquaintance with the work of Appia and Dalcroze had enabled him to imagine. The ensemble here became expressive "of the great sentiments and attitudes of a people's collective identity."[44]

Corporeal Expression and Human Presence

According to Lee Strasberg, Copeau identified the primary problem of acting as "the battle with the blood of the actor": "The actor tells his arm, 'come on now, arm, go out and make the gesture,' but the arm remains wooden. The 'blood' doesn't flow; the muscles don't move; the body fights within itself; it's a terrifying thing."[45] In Copeau's words, "the problem of the actor is basically a corporeal one: the actor is standing on a stage."[46] Thus Copeau perceived the problem with which Stanislavski grappled between 1905 and the "discovery" of the method of physical actions in the 1930s—the relationship between intention and physical action. The gap between what the actor *feels* and what her body is doing results, in Copeau's view, from the false dichotomy between feeling and craft famously expressed in Diderot's *Paradoxe:* "The absurdity of the 'paradox' is that it sets the processes of the craft against the freedom of feeling and it denies, in the artist, the possibility of their coexistence and simultaneity."[47]

Copeau believed that the presence of the actor "certifies his authenticity." Eleanora Duse was for him the prime example of the actor whose "simple presence . . . [guarantees] that there is no possibility of deception. . . . It is a natural quality that can be enhanced by art but cannot be imitated by it."[48] Here the value of honesty and sincerity is quite clearly identified as the key to good acting. Copeau's craft was never systematized as a method of rehearsal in the manner of Stanislavski's, but it embodied an ethics of performance every bit as strict. The interweaving of art and craft would paradoxically ensure the freshness and clarity of the performance: "For the actor, the whole art is the gift of himself. In order to give himself, he must first possess himself. Our craft, with the discipline it presupposes, the reflexes it has mastered and holds at its command, is the very warp and weft of our art with the freedom it demands and the illumination it encounters. Emotive expression grows out of correct expression. Not only does technique not excuse sensitivity: it authenticates and liberates it. . . . Constancy in our accents, our positions, our movements, maintains freshness, clarity, diversity, invention, evenness, renewal; it allows us to improvise."[49]

Copeau's words were surprisingly prescient. Artaud, Grotowski, Julian Beck and Judith Malina, Brook, Barba, and Joseph Chaikin have all echoed such language. For the contemporary *third theater,* corporeal training is the key to creative expression, and the actor's giving of herself in the encounter with the spectator the raison d'être of the performance. Two types of praxis adumbrated by Copeau—respect for the text and the use of improvisation as a rehearsal and training method—are still predominant in mainstream French and British traditions of theater practice. In France, Copeau's legacy was promoted through the work of his students and those they trained and worked with—Louis Jouvet, Charles Dullin, Jean and Marie-Helene Daste, Jean-Louis Barrault, Jean Dorcy, Etiénne Decroux, and Jacques Lecoq. Copeau's "dramatic renovation" demanded actors as skilled in the use of the body as an expressive instrument as they were in the use of voice. Jean Dorcy and Étienne Decroux became influential teachers, establishing schools of mime and movement that had a profound influence on the development of French performance. Decroux's pupils included Jean-Louis Barrault and Marcel Marceau. Through the establishment of mime studies at a number of universities and in theater companies, Decroux's ideas were widely disseminated in France. In Britain, Copeau's ideas were developed and disseminated by his nephew, Michel Saint-Denis.[50]

5. Michel Saint-Denis and the English Tradition

English actors and acting teachers have characteristically maintained a pragmatic attitude to a craft established in an unbroken tradition that can be traced at least as far back as the late seventeenth century. The empirical method of post-Renaissance British philosophy is reflected in other fields as a habitual skepticism toward abstract theory and a preference for ideas that are the product of experience. New approaches have invariably been a reaction to the kind of acting that preceded them—either modifying the tradition or offering an alternative to what went before.

Edwardian Acting Styles

By all accounts, Edwardian actors perceived their playing as more realistic than that of their predecessors. They adapted the style of Victorian actors to suit the manners of the later era, but their notion of acting and training was no different in kind from that which obtained in the period of Tom Robertson's "cup-and-saucer" dramas. While early-twentieth-century English acting in many respects continued, rather than broke with, tradition, a new attitude to acting Shakespeare was evident in the three innovatory productions of Harley Granville Barker at the Savoy between 1912 and 1914, and was reflected in his *Prefaces to Shakespeare* (1927).

Granville Barker's approach derived from the experiments of William Poel, which had begun in 1881 with his Elizabethan revivalist production of the First Quarto *Hamlet*. However, Barker's principles of setting and staging the plays were as much indebted to the modernist scenography of Edward Gordon Craig as to Poel's insistence on a fixed architectural background, loosely based on the structure of the Elizabethan public playhouse, which replaced the changing scenes of the Victorian actor-manager with curtains and essential props.

Although Poel and Granville Barker were reacting against the operatic styles and pictorial realism of late Victorian actor-managers like Henry Irving and Herbert Beerbohm Tree, they did not so much invent a new kind of acting as employ existing styles in new ways. Poel was trained as a scholar rather than an actor. His performers were usually amateurs, and his attitude to acting Shakespeare was assumed to represent a critique of nineteenth-century performance styles. Granville Barker, on the other hand, was very much a man of the theater. A successful playwright and director and a talented actor, Barker was perhaps more pragmatic than Poel in adapting existing styles of realistic acting to suit his abstract and poetic conception of Shakespeare's drama. In fact, Poel's approach was more radical than his Victorian contemporaries were able to comprehend. What he lacked was an institutional context for teaching and promoting the type of acting that he deemed necessary for the effective performance of Shakespeare's plays.

In the 1860s a disciplined, ensemble approach to acting had been created by the Bancrofts in response to the realistic dramaturgy of Tom Robertson. Between the 1870s and the 1900s the production methods of the Bancrofts were successfully adopted by a number of managements, including John Hare, Charles Wyndham, and George Alexander, whose productions of well-made plays and comedies of manners promoted a natural vocal delivery very different from the idiosyncratic poetic diction that complemented the hypnotic illusionism of Irving and Tree. The carefully observed mimicry of social behavior had by the turn of the century become a recognizably English style of naturalistic acting *from the outside* that still today characterizes performances in realistic plays on the stage and on television. Oscar Wilde had remarked that the English were good at acting "between the lines," drawing attention to what has become a habit of emphasizing the subtextual implications of the drama. Playing the dialogue itself in a fairly uninflected way has the effect of foregrounding the behavioral nuances that the actor displays in continuous counterpoint to the spoken text.

While this became the dominant style of West End commercial theater and provided the basis of the acting that Granville Barker was obliged to integrate within his otherwise antirealist Shakespeare productions, Poel was enough of an outsider to the commercial theatre to have been able to ignore its conventions. As one might expect, this attitude did not immediately find favor with actors and reviewers, but it did allow him to be uncompromising in adopting a historicist approach to the performance of a Shakespeare play within the frame of its original conventions of production. Paradoxically, Poel's innovatory Elizabethan revivalist approach was a logical extension of the Victorian principle of archaeologically accurate settings. Poel, however, was no Victorian antiquarian. By performing Shakespeare's plays under theatrical conditions that pertained at the time of their original performances, he aimed to rediscover the principles that animated their dramaturgy. In the *Daily Chronicle* of September 3, 1913, he wrote: "It was just for acting's sake that the Elizabethan Stage Society was born. Some people have called me an archaeologist, but I am not. I am really a modernist. My original aim was just to find out some means of acting Shakespeare naturally and appealingly from the full text as in modern drama. I found for this that the platform stage was necessary."[1]

Poel challenged the visually oriented production methods of the Victorian actor-managers by giving performances in which the sound of the language predominated. By definition, his platform stage was largely devoid of scenic decoration; it was a chamber that sensitized the audience to hear rather than to view. Poel was not incapable of felicitous moments of visual staging through inventive groupings of actors costumed (usually) in Elizabethan dress. Robert Speaight has argued that "Poel's visual sense was as strong as Irving's or Tree's and far more selective."[2] Poel, however, employed the physical interaction of actors on stage to give shape and significance to their speech rather than rely on scenographic effects to illustrate moments of drama. There is a parallel here with Copeau, in that the bare stage is designed to foreground the nonillusionistic expressiveness of the acting. Just as Molière's theater provided Copeau with a model for a modern approach to staging, so did Shakespeare's theater offer Poel an example of an architectural environment that might challenge the pictorial illusions of late Victorian theater. Writing in the *Saturday Review* on February 18, 1928, Ivor Brown succinctly described Poel's achievement: "The Elizabethan platform was not only far larger than the average modern stage, but its triple division gave scope for swift alternations from one plane to another, both in structure and in temper. As soon as Mr Poel recreates his platform-stage he recreates the flow, the rhythm, and the energy of Elizabethan drama."

Poel cast plays as though he were choosing singers for operatic roles, assigning parts according to his sense of the balance of musical registers in the play (roles were conceived as sopranos, contraltos, baritones, etc). Actors were given strict instructions as to the delivery of their lines, considerably more rehearsal time being devoted to practicing the delivery of the verse according to "tuned tones" than to the blocking of movement, which would be determined by the structure of the platform stage, or to work on physical characterization. He also insisted upon a delivery swifter than was conventional in the Victorian theater. Poel's emphasis on the meaning of the words at the expense of their beauty or histrionic effectiveness constituted a decisive rejection of the application of melodramatic acting styles that had predominated in the English theater since the Romantic period: "As with the other arts, so it is with good acting, its excellence lies in restraint and in knowing what to surrender. If elocution is to imitate nature, a dozen or more words must be sacrificed so that one word may predominate and thus give the keynote to the tune of the whole sentence. In this way only can the sound be made to echo the sense. But the last thing, apparently, the actor cares to do is to give up making every word tell."[3]

Significantly, Poel paid little attention to the details of psychological motivation so central to Stanislavski's acting system, and which, in accordance with their own pre-Freudian intuitions, had illuminated the characterizations of Irving and Beerbohm Tree. In this respect, he provided a model for Granville Barker of a nonnaturalistic approach to Shakespeare in which attention to the music and sense inscribed in the prosodic structure of the language might determine stage interpretation. In some respects this approach is consonant with Copeau's view of the written text as a musical score for performance. This is an attitude that informs mainstream British assumptions about acting Shakespeare today. Because he was a scholar rather than a professional actor or manager, Poel directed actors by teaching them how to speak the text. His ideas had a profound influence on the English theater, not only as promulgated by Granville Barker (who acted Richard II for him in 1899), but through the generation of actors who went on to direct and act in Shakespeare after working with Poel—Lewis Casson, Robert Atkins, Nugent Monck, Ben Greet, and Edith Evans being among the most illustrious. In 1927, Ivor Brown claimed that "the better type of Shakespearean presentation to-day is simply Poel popularised without acknowledgements."[4]

If the majority of the theater establishment remained skeptical of Poel's achievements for the duration of his career, it took Granville Barker less than two months to convince audiences of the theatrical effectiveness of the new approach to staging Shakespeare. While his production of *The Winter's Tale* that opened at the Savoy on September 21, 1912 caused a stir, it was not universally admired. Some critics disapproved of Barker's attempt to break the illusion of proscenium arch theater by building an apron stage over the orchestra pit in order to bring the actors into closer proximity with the audience. Many criticized the fast pace of the speaking. However, his production of *Twelfth Night* (first night, November 15, 1912) met with almost universal approval. John Palmer was one critic who immediately recognized the "Elizabethan" qualities inherent in Barker's staging concept:

The value of Mr Barker's revival . . . rests almost wholly upon his projection of the stage into the auditorium. . . . Mr Barker's innovation . . .
is not a merely a topographical trick of stage management. There were
precious moments in the Savoy Theatre on Saturday when it was possible to be thrillingly conscious of precisely the appeal Burbage made as he
issued from the tiring-house to the vacant platform before Elsinore. . . .
Gone was the centuries-old, needless and silly illusion of a picture-stage,
with scene and atmosphere ready-made, and mutoscopically viewed. I
had no illusion, and could wait receptively for Shakespeare to build it.
Never before had his splendid rhetoric, his glamour of resistless verse, the
true and vivid illusion upon which he alone had so successfully relied,
reached me in a London theatre.[5]

Barker's productions re-created the spirit of Elizabethan staging as conceived by Poel's productions, but presented in the terms of an entirely modernist scenographic style by Norman Wilkinson (settings) and Albert
Rutherston (costumes). In effect, they demonstrated the revolutionary
nature of Poel's theories by dispelling any sense of antiquarian revivalism
that may have undermined Poel's own productions. Although Barker was
both resourceful and adventurous in finding modern methods of approxi-
mating the rhetorical conventions of Elizabethan acting, his approach was
not elaborate or monumentalist in the manner of Reinhardt or Craig, nor
did he deploy his modernist vocabulary to effect the grotesque theatricalism
typical of Meyerhold. Barker's aesthetic was as refined and spare as that of
Copeau. Given how closely his own search for a form of theatrical production appropriate to the performance of Shakespeare resembled Copeau's
experiments in creating a modern equivalent of the theater of Molière,
Barker's admiration for the work of the Vieux-Colombier school on *Kantan* in 1924 is unsurprising.[6] Despite the very high reputation Barker
achieved as an actor, playwright, and director, he retired prematurely from
professional work in the theater, choosing to pursue his interest in Shakespeare production not by working with a company of actors but by writing
Prefaces to Shakespeare, in which he interpreted the plays as he imagined they
were intended to be performed. But the legend of his Savoy productions
together with the *Prefaces* did exert a profound influence on the acting and
production of Shakespeare in Britain, establishing a tradition in which simple, uncluttered staging gave priority to the actors' speaking of the text.
    It was this tradition (most famously exemplified in the early perfor-
mances of John Gielgud as Hamlet and Richard II) that anticipated the visit

of Michel Saint-Denis's Compagnie des Quinze to London in 1931, ensuring the instant receptivity of British theater professionals and audiences to their work. While Barker did not develop any specific system for training actors to speak Shakespeare, his actors were clearly successful in achieving the approach that he desired. The reviewer of *The Winter's Tale* in the *Saturday Review* on September 28, 1912, noticed that the dramatic structure of the play was embodied in the tempo of speech and action: "It varied dramatically with the play's rhythm—the rhythm not alone of the verse but of the play's procedure and emotion." Barker himself stated his aim of substituting a more subtle and flexible style of speaking for the slow declamation of the Victorian actor: "The whole merit of Elizabethan verse . . . [is] its consonantal swiftness, its gradations sudden or slow, into vowelled liquidity, its comic rushes and stops, with above all, the peculiar beauty of its rhymes."[7]

Although his close reading of the plays did result in new interpretations of roles that had for decades been played according to unquestioned conventions, there is no evidence to suggest that Barker's reforms with regard to the speaking of the text provoked an overall reassessment of techniques of acting. Respect for the text is the cornerstone of Barker's approach to playing Shakespeare. "When it comes to staging the plays, the speaking of the verse must be the foundation of all study."[8] Barker's idea that the text *instructs* the actor in its own performance is akin to that of Copeau: "The actor, in fine, must think of the dialogue in terms of music; of the tune and rhythm of it as at one with the sense—sometimes outbidding the sense—in telling him what to do and how to do it, in telling him, indeed, what to *be*."[9]

Barker consolidated a modern tradition of acting Shakespeare that combined the understatement of Edwardian drawing-room realism with Poel's musical approach to speaking the text. The style of the performance was a compromise between an abstract theatricality of visual design and a simplicity of acting style. Unlike Copeau in France, Barker did not feel the need to establish a school or theater laboratory to train actors for a new kind of theater, but in a pragmatic fashion was content to modify existing techniques.

In the English theater, acting in Shakespeare's plays had by the late eighteenth century become the ultimate test of the great actor. An unbroken theatrical tradition was dominated by definitive performances in the major Shakespearean roles, successive generations of actors seeking to challenge the preeminence of their predecessors by establishing new approaches to well-known roles. Even in an intensely commercial theater system, the cultural kudos represented by success in a great role has been enough to attract

English actors to appear in Shakespeare. In the twentieth century this ensured that drama schools would privilege training in the performance of Shakespeare despite the fact that this training might not be directly relevant to an actor's usual work in theater, film, or television.

The cultural prestige of Shakespeare meant that the revolution in production represented by Poel's experiments and Granville Barker's revelatory productions would have a major impact on English acting. While the realistic tradition of acting in the purely commercial theater continued to be modified by succeeding generations in order to reflect new styles of social behavior, the new approach to playing Shakespeare came to be regarded as a tradition of classical acting. The terms of great acting in twentieth-century English theater were thus founded on a notion of Shakespearean performance. This was the tradition of acting that in the mid-1930s Michel Saint-Denis was to inherit and transform. His promulgation of Copeau's approach established a tradition of modern British acting dedicated to realizing the playwright's vision.

Saint-Denis in London

The founding of the London Theatre Studio by Saint-Denis in 1935 marked a new approach to actor training in Britain. While the studio may not have made an immediate impact on the professional theater as a whole, Saint-Denis more than anyone was responsible for establishing the principles that would in time shape the curriculum of the modern British drama school. Although more willing than Copeau to negotiate a compromise with the actual conditions of professional theater, Saint-Denis had nevertheless inherited his uncle's idealism. Unlike most progressive British practitioners of the time, Saint-Denis's pragmatism did not extend to compromising his own idea of theatrical performance, which meant that he spent more of his energies in setting up and running theater schools in London, Strasbourg, Montreal, and New York than directing professional productions. This may, paradoxically, have been the reason why his impact on the British theater has been so pervasive. His work at the Old Vic Theatre School between 1947 and 1952 influenced a generation of actors and teachers during a period of great change in British theater. In a foreword to Saint-Denis's *Training for the Theatre,* published posthumously in 1982, Peter Hall assessed his impact: "[His] influence on British theatre has directly touched and changed all of us over the age of thirty-five and indirectly the generations to come. Four major theatres—the Royal Court, the National Theatre, the English National Opera and the Royal Shakespeare Company—all owe part of their way of working to him."[10]

The first appearance in 1931 of Saint-Denis's Compagnie des Quinze at the Arts Theatre in Noé and Le Viol de Lucrèce by André Obey was received with enormous enthusiasm by London audiences, who were amazed at the freshness of the performance and the simplicity of the staging. The integration of mime, movement, song, dance, and speech proved a revelation to audiences accustomed to the limited vocabulary of well-made British realism: "The eruption on to the London stage of this anti-naturalistic form of drama demonstrated that a new realism based on action and *physical* expression was possible."[11] Saint-Denis, it appears, was able to translate and adapt Copeau's approach to acting into terms that progressive English actors, directors, and designers found sympathetic and even inspiring: "I had come to realise that by tradition as well as temperament the English have a more down-to-earth understanding of theatre than the French—they react directly and sensitively to poetry. . . . Shakespeare to them is *alive*—not intellectually—but concretely. Consequently they were much better prepared to accept an art in which psychological, intellectual and literary preoccupations were not the primary considerations."[12]

Saint-Denis did not believe in training actors in isolation from other practitioners: the curriculum of each of his schools was devised with the aim of giving every practitioner an experience of the collaborative working of a proper ensemble. Saint-Denis followed Copeau in the belief "that whether or not a student could become a genuine actor depended intimately on the nature of the student's character and the richness of his temperament."[13] For Saint-Denis as for Copeau, training involved more than the acquisition of technical skills. Training theater practitioners to be part of an ensemble represented a radical break with current British practice: "The general idea is to unify the various elements of the theatre in the school: that is to say, the intention is not to turn out young actors and actresses, after the average model, to enable them to act in average plays in the West End; but to produce a homogeneous group of people working in the theatre—a troupe that can work by itself and for itself; with writers, musicians, mechanics trained to support it. As well as being a school, it will be a dramatic centre and will attract to itself many people who are already in the theatre."[14]

The Actor as Flexible Instrument

Two connected ideas underlie Saint-Denis's practice: the actor should be a flexible instrument, malleable in rehearsal into whatever form the play

John Gielgud in André Obey's *Noah* directed by Michel Saint-Denis, 1935. Courtesy of the Theatre Museum Picture Library, London.

demands, and style as a key to performing the text. These ideas derive from Copeau, although Saint-Denis employed them in very different ways and in many different contexts. Both ideas remain fundamental assumptions among the majority of working professionals and teachers in Britain.

Saint-Denis's approach to theater was more eclectic than that of Copeau. Possibly as a result of having to locate himself in a new cultural context, he moved away from the Copeau-inspired aim of the Compagnie des Quinze of having actors collaborate with a playwright in devising performances. In London, Saint-Denis concentrated on developing new systems of training and rehearsal that would equip actors to play any kind of drama according to performance conventions inscribed within the written text. This ideal of flexibility (often valorized as freedom) is the aim of mainstream British approaches to acting and actor training today: "Of course our first, and most essential, desire was to serve the contemporary theatre; but in order to do this we needed to prepare actors capable of interpreting *all* styles without letting style deflect from truth. . . . We were searching for the proper way to give . . . [the actor] a sense of creative freedom."[15]

To achieve creative freedom the actor had to escape from the prison of self. One of the enduring myths inherent in this approach is the idea of "stripping down" the actor—of ridding him of the mask of personality that is assumed to constitute a social defense mechanism, so that he can engage the play text as if he were a blank page to be inscribed with a characterization determined by the playwright. Many of the methods pioneered by Copeau were employed by Michel Saint-Denis. The *noble mask* (which has come to be known as the neutral mask) was employed to effect the stripping down of the actor. According to Saint-Denis, improvisation played the most important part in integrating all aspects of training, being "a means to discover in oneself the sources of acting."[16]

Saint-Denis made a distinction between two types of actor—an *actor/interpreter* who works with an existing text, and an *actor/improviser* (e.g., clown, music hall entertainer) who creates his own text. In the conventional theater the actor was normally an interpreter, required to comprehend the play text through objective analysis at the same time he expresses his character by means of his own subjectivity. Like Stanislavski, Saint-Denis saw the confrontation between the subjectivity of the actor and the objective existence of the role as an essential problem in acting: "The connection between the subjective and the objective, the absolute necessity of constant exchanges between these two attitudes, conditions the entire progression of the work."[17]

Whereas Stanislavski had devised his method of analysis through actions and objectives in order to enable the actor to project himself into the character's pattern of intentions, Saint-Denis maintained the tension between subjective and objective responses to characterization as necessary, thus ensuring that while his humanity animates the role, the actor does not superimpose his own personal identity on it: "From the conflict and reconciliation of these two attitudes, one can gradually obtain an interpretation which will be both faithful to the text and vitally alive."[18] In order to cultivate the imagination of the actor/interpreter, it was necessary for him to be trained as an actor/improviser. It was improvisation that was to develop the actor's inventiveness and enhance his ability to create character through physical means.

Saint-Denis's reflections on improvisation as a means to school the actor in the interpretation of all styles of performance manifest a paradoxical traditionalism akin to Copeau's: "The challenge is two-fold: how to bring the actor's need for truth gradually up to the level of the finest classical texts, and how to prevent this need for truth from clashing with the remoteness and the unfamiliarity of the *form* of these texts."[19] The assumption here is that the classics are inherently superior to modern realistic texts, and that the truth expressed according to naturalistic conventions of verisimilitude is limited, in comparison with the universal truths of the classical texts. What Saint-Denis was attempting to confront was the conflict between post-Stanislavskian conventions of theatrical naturalism (which purport to represent truth) and the overtly rhetorical conventions of prenaturalistic drama. His language betrays a value judgment that is not relevant to his argument, but it is characteristic of the humanist cultural tradition to place special value on the performance of the classics. This attitude reflects a culture that assumes the necessity of state subsidy for the arts as national treasures—and it is an attitude that Saint-Denis's work in Britain did a great deal to promote. His assumptions were, in their refusal to acknowledge that the meaning of a text changes over time, naively unhistorical. The quest for authenticity in productions of the classics runs the risk of nostalgically idealizing the past as a golden time. In reality such a desire for fidelity often results in revivals that have the values of museum exhibits rather than challenging theater, although it was certainly not Saint-Denis's intention to produce such revivals. The tendency to romanticize the classics in this way finds an echo in the attitude of many British critics and practitioners who claim the authority of the written text as primary in the process of theater-making.

In one respect, Saint-Denis's approach did, however, reflect and anticipate an important trend in the contemporary understanding of drama—one that is more modern than Stanislavski's essentially bourgeois nineteenth-century conception of character. The structuralist view of human agency rejects the bourgeois construction of the individual personality as an integrated character, and instead posits the speaking subject as the locus of human identity. In order to characterize a speaking subject the actor creates an appropriate context and manner of enunciating his speech utterances. Beckett's drama represents a powerful demonstration that the fictional presentation of human agents need not necessarily involve the construction of historically consistent or psychologically integrated characters.

Training the Actor as Expressive Instrument

Although Saint-Denis insisted that the actor study the arts, history, religion and social life of different periods as a prerequisite for understanding the cultures from which plays derive, his outline of the content and aims of such courses was vague. The ethos of the drama school as he described it was admirable and certainly inspired many idealistic attempts at creating institutions with similar values, although pressure of time and conflicting agendas within many British acting schools means that such principles are often honored more in the breach than the observance. "The development, at the very heart of the school and of the company, of a human and artistic milieu, which, because of its invisible pull on everyone, quite naturally breeds a climate where the quality of the professional training, the adherence to the guiding principles, the multiplicity of critical and theoretical exchanges, will spread a sense of individual responsibility, which will ultimately merge with the school's sense of ensemble. I believe that this milieu . . . could impress students more profoundly than the study of even the most advanced techniques."[20] Saint-Denis was echoing Copeau in his aim of training "simultaneously, from the beginning, the mind, the technique and the spirit of the actor to serve the imagination."[21] Again following Copeau, it was improvisation that would develop the actor's invention and spontaneity; these qualities should be cultivated before work on interpreting texts was begun. Movement, voice, and speech were the three fundamental disciplines involved in training the actor as an expressive instrument. For Saint-Denis, as for Copeau, these disciplines should not be taught as specialized techniques, but should be interrelated. Technique should be taught in such a way that students would experience it as a tool of creativity that, once acquired, became second nature.

In *Training for the Theatre,* Saint-Denis outlined his four-year curriculum. This was to proceed from a *discovery year* in which the student learns to recognize what talents he possesses and what techniques may need to be acquired in developing them, to a *transformation year* in which he employs the various skills of physical, vocal, and imaginative expression to transform himself into other characters. In the third year, the student applies the expressive techniques developed in the second year to the interpretation of a wide range of plays. In the fourth, *performing year,* students have an opportunity to perform a wide range of plays on various stages and for different kinds of audiences. This would culminate in a two-week repertory season for audiences and theater agents.

Where Saint-Denis's approach to training differed from that of the average English stage school of the 1930s and 1940s was in his insistence that in every one of the twelve terms of the course classes in technique should run side by side with classes aimed at developing the imagination. In his outline curriculum, classes in technique are listed as body, voice/diction, and speech/language: under the heading *imagination* are improvisation, interpretation, and imaginative background/miscellaneous.

Developing Control of the Body: An Organic Approach

Saint-Denis followed Copeau in comparing the actor's control of his body with the musician's control of his instrument. Work on the body was intended to enhance the student's awareness of the body, both physically and as an expressive instrument. Relaxation exercises should enable students to release tension, and classes should also enable students to enhance muscular strength and flexibility. Building upon the foundation of the purely physical training were classes in which different parts of the body were isolated so that students explored how each could be made expressive. According to Saint-Denis, different parts of the body can make gestures that signify a range of different emotional attitudes.[22] At the early stage of training, it did not matter whether the expression was crude or obvious; the point was for the student to practice using the body to express a wide range of feelings and attitudes. This kind of work was parallel to exercises entailed in Stanislavski's method of physical actions. The difference was that whereas Stanislavski focused on the body's expression of intention (feeling would be displayed as an involuntary concomitant of the actor/character's success or failure in achieving his objective), Saint-Denis was concerned with making the whole body expressive through movement.[23]

Saint-Denis stressed a principle that has become axiomatic in movement training: "The student should . . . learn that in whatever he does, however small the gesture he uses, a kind of current, *life,* must go through the *whole* body. He will gradually discover that his entire body takes part in the gesture even if it does not move with it. The originating motor of movement should be in the centre of the body, from which all movement passes to the extremities, creating a continuous flow."[24]

This notion of the organic relationship of the center to the extremities of the body in movement is one of the constituent myths of the tradition that stems from Copeau.[25] The participation of the whole body in any movement of one of its parts is a corporeal sign of the human presence of the actor in the performance, a guarantee that movement is not being made mechanically, without the full expressive engagement of the artist. Directors and teachers sometimes tell actors or students they are faking their responses when the whole body is not supporting the expressive gesture of the isolated part, projecting a system of ethical judgments on to the kinetic field. It is assumed that the authenticity of the actor's engagement is assured when the impulse to move comes from the center. The metaphor of the center expresses the imperative of organicity that underlies this particular conception of acting.

During the 1960s, Saint-Denis added the Alexander technique to the curriculum. This was intended to help the student overcome habitual bad posture and to afford a method of addressing the body-mind split that undermined most students' attempts to be immediately and spontaneously alive in their expressive acts.

> The Alexander technique, briefly, is a method of showing people how they are mis-using their bodies and how they can prevent such misuses, whether it be at rest or during activity. This information about USE is conveyed by manual adjustment on the part of the teacher, and it involves the learning of a new Body-Grammar—a new mental pattern in the form of a sequence of words which is taught to the pupil, and which he learns to associate with the new muscular use which he is being taught by the manual adjustment. He learns to project this new pattern to himself not only whilst he is being actually taught but when he is on his own. This procedure is *not* a method of manipulation in which the subject is a passive recipient and goes out none the wiser about how to stop himself getting into a tension-state again. It is a method by which he is taught to work on himself to prevent his recurrent habits of misuse, and by which he can learn to build up a new use-structure.[26]

The principles behind the Alexander technique are not only consonant with Copeau's ideal of the organic interrelationship between mind and body, thought and movement, but provide an explanation of the healthy functioning of body-mind in the terms of anatomical and physiological science. Saint-Denis was thereby provided with a pseudomedical principle in support of his notions of integrated corporeal expression.

In the second term, movement classes were intended to demonstrate that sloppy or tense movement was inexpressive by contrast with "controlled *free* movement." Here again, Saint-Denis's terminology implied that freedom might be realized through a technical control of the body, which should ideally achieve a kinesthetic golden mean between tension and inertia. Typically, such a myth of organicist practice was employed to naturalize a particular physical technique. Exercises were also designed to allow students to explore different attitudes to space, time, and rhythm as manifest in life. In the third term, acrobatics was to be added to the general movement work. At the start of the second year, a new movement teacher was to be introduced. The earlier classes were to continue, but more demands made of students in generating energy and developing stamina. Unarmed stage combat was to be introduced. There would be three ninety-minute movement classes every week during the remainder of the course, with various additional elements emphasized in different terms. In the seventh term, for example, the focus would fall on the relationship between words and movement, and a tap-dancing class was to be added. A dance-drama project was to be undertaken, in which students might have an opportunity to concentrate on expressing moods and feelings through movement. There were to be further projects in stage combat (now armed), and different qualities of movement were to be explored in different terms.

Integration of Voice and Body

The work on voice and diction was to proceed in tandem with work on the body from the first term onwards. Saint-Denis believed that voice training should be based on singing "in order to obtain a vocal quality . . . that is strong, clear, rhythmic and musical."[27] Saint-Denis was opposed to the teaching of elocution, emphasizing that his approach was designed, not to stress beauty or musicality for its own sake, but to promote a vocal flexibility and control that would enable an actor to respond instantly to the demands of a text. According to Saint-Denis, vocal tone rather than pronunciation was what has an immediate emotional impact on the audience.

In order to be capable of performing any kind of play, the actor should possess a powerful voice with a mastery of a wide range of tones, supported by good breath control. The teacher of voice at the Old Vic Theatre School was Jani Strasser, who was originally a singing teacher. Acting students began by singing a phrase or verse to piano accompaniment, then repeated the words without the melody. In this way students developed resonance and tonal variety, as well as breath control. Strasser's exercises were accompanied by body movements like swinging the arms or skipping around the room while speaking or singing, an early version of the kind of method now commonly employed by voice and acting teachers, who try to avoid treating the voice as an instrument artificially separated from the rest of the body, as had been the practice of elocutionists and traditional singing teachers.

Saint-Denis believed that voice classes should continue throughout the four years of the course, in order to provide a student with a method of working that he could practice during the whole of his professional career. In the first term, classes would introduce students to the functioning of their vocal equipment—the organs of speech, breathing mechanism, and resonators. Each student was gradually to be helped to discover the natural pitch of his voice, and there would be elementary work on articulating vowels and consonants to produce clear diction. The approach to voice training adopted by Saint-Denis was progressive in its insistence on treating each actor as an individual whose own vocal personality should be gradually enhanced rather than transformed into the standard voice that the elocutionist had previously demanded. In subsequent terms, students were to become aware of inflection and would exercise to develop pace, vocal power, modulation, and rhythm. Work on projecting the voice would begin near the end of the second term. Classes in voice, diction, and singing were to be interwoven through each term's work.

Exercises on rhythm were designed to sensitize students to the danger of elocuting a text—the result of giving equal stress and length-in-time to every syllable. As always, Saint-Denis advocated the interrelationship of movement and sound as a means of creating an experience of rhythmic variety in the whole body, and suggested that during a particular phase of the term, work on rhythm might be scheduled to take place in the movement, voice, and speech classes. In a way that parallels the exercises in bodily expressivity, exercises in modulation aimed to teach students to express feeling through sound: "Great attention should be given to establishing a relationship between thought, feeling and speed. In learning how to modulate the voice, the student, following a given feeling indicated in a text, plays with the voice in order to translate this feeling melodiously, but in a direct way, into the right kind of sound."[28] For Saint-Denis the stimulation of the actor's *vocal-aural imagination* was as important as the development of vocal skills. As improvisation was to be used to help an actor develop kinesthetic imagination, so vocal play would enhance the actor's vocal-aural imagination. In the early part of the training, physical work, voice, and speech were to be taught in parallel, but would gradually merge as the student began to employ all aspects in integrated acting exercises. An important component of such vocal training was the use of nonverbal sound: "If we dispense at first with words, it is only to make clear that words are the *result* of an inner state, an inner, physical state, related to the senses, which conditions the spoken word. So the first exercises should aim at making the student's voice expressive without using words."[29]

Sound exercises were recommended, using humming, clicking, or nonsense words to express different feelings. Other vocal sounds could be employed that might make use of natural sounds such as wind, rain, waves, or animal noises. After exploring the emotive potential of these sorts of sounds, students were to begin to employ short words like "yes" and "no," used as answers to a great range of questions in many situations. The words should then get longer, until students could begin to use phrases from pop songs, poems, plays, and prose in different contexts and to express different moods. Students were asked to think the words silently, to whisper them, to sing them, and to speak them, and then, within a phrase, to change from singing to whispering or speaking. The idea was to develop a sensitivity to the relationship between mood or feeling and vocal tone, so that students were intuitively able to use the voice to color and modulate a complex dramatic text when they encountered one. Students would also be made aware of how different relationships between speaker and listener were reflected in the voice in different situations, for example, intimate or public—conversations in a pub, a street, an open field.

Work in speech and language classes was to be directed toward developing within the student an intuitive apprehension of style. The course was designed not only to facilitate the student's progress from nondramatic prose readings through more difficult poetic texts whose structure would provide more complex challenges, but at the same time to ensure that he actually experienced the vocal and linguistic demands of the range of dramatic forms and styles that he would eventually encounter as an actor. Few technical demands were to be made on the student in speaking and reading texts in the first term, the idea having been to make the experience of reading as enjoyable as possible in order to cultivate sensitivity to the literary use of language. No plays were to be read until the third week of the second term, in order to prevent students from taking shortcuts before they were adequately prepared.

L'Expression Parlée

According to St Denis's plan, the third term was to begin with the introduction of a sustained speech project called *l'expression parlée,* which consisted of a series of poetic texts (poems and speeches from plays) that students were to enact solely through the voice. No emphasis was to be placed on characterization and no direction was given; instead students were required to explore the ways in which they could dramatize the shape and sense of the language by using the resources of speech: "In rehearsals of a play our principal interest is in 'doing,' but in these specialized exercises on poetic texts we are more concerned at first with obtaining a complete expression of meaning through the use of the voice alone; with finding a way of acting which is based, almost entirely on the use of the *voice*—on tone, phrasing, pace and rhythm."[30]

The texts were to become gradually more demanding in the fourth term as the students applied the vocal skills they had been developing to "the significant question of style: the relationship between form and meaning."[31] *L'expression parlée* was Saint-Denis's most obvious application of Copeau's approach to harnessing the actor's expressive ability in the interpretation of the text. An elaboration of Copeau's notion of the text as a blueprint for performance, the method was intended to teach the actor how to *submit* himself to the form of the text, thereby intuitively achieving a performance style consonant with the playwright's intentions. This was a training method that aimed to realize the ideals of Poel and Granville Barker with respect to the way the text should control the actor's performance. Students were also required to practice speech gymnastics (which involved speaking against noise or while performing an unrelated activity) in order to improve their coordination and develop the ability to function simultaneously on the conscious and unconscious levels. In this way, the student would learn to integrate speech with the performance of his bodily activities.

Over a number of terms, *l'expression parlée* was to employ a wide range of types of writing so that students might develop sensitivity to different moods and tones of speech and an ability to signify the various relationships between the speaker and the content of his speech, for example, sympathetic, detached, ironic, passionately engaged, and so forth. In essence, this approach to speaking the text was opposed to the psychological attitude to characterization elaborated by Stanislavski. Following the psychological approach, an actor reads the text to discover a character's mental states and motivations for action, and speaks it as an aspect of that network of action. Apparently Saint-Denis did not wish to ignore the psychological aspects of character inscribed within a play text; however he was seeking an approach to performance that would privilege the rhetorical form of a written text, while allowing actors to find non-naturalistic ways of indicating psychology.

His insistence that the student actor should not impose gestures and movements upon the speech in attempting to *enact* it but should be free to move spontaneously whenever he felt it necessary, reflected Saint-Denis's aim of providing the actor with an experience of how a text *demanded* to be played in certain ways and thus of how the playwright might *direct* the actor. At advanced stages of the acting course, this method was to be applied to the enactment of speeches and scenes from comedies, farces, and different kinds of tragedy, in order to afford practice in finding vocal attitudes and tones of voice appropriate to the performance of different dramatic styles. Saint-Denis was among the first practitioners consciously to adhere to a principle of rehearsal that subsequently became firmly established in British theater— that the actor should not learn the words before rehearsals begin. An important function of rehearsals according to this method of working is the exploration of the relationship between speech and gesture/movement (blocking). This might be varied from one rehearsal to the next in a process of trial and error until the actor and director were convinced that the correct relationships had been established.

Clearly the aim of body, voice, and speech training was not merely to provide a technical preparation for the work on the imagination: Saint-Denis arranged the sequence of courses in such a way that creative and expressive challenges were tackled *as part of* the physically based body and voice exercises. In Saint-Denis's scheme, work in these technical subjects led inevitably to the classes in improvisation, interpretation, and *imaginative background* by means of which the imagination was to be developed. Copeau's approach to training the actor was thus systematized by Saint-Denis, whose own scheme of training determined a carefully planned process of experiential learning through which the student progressively discovered how technique and imagination should be interwoven in creative work. The classes were designed to manifest the ways in which technique might become expressive and in which the imagination might express itself in physical terms.

Improvisation as Training and Rehearsal Method

As in the work of Copeau, improvisation underpinned all aspects of the teaching. What the English theater learned from Saint-Denis was a method, pioneered by Copeau, of harnessing the instinct to *play* as a way of stimulating the imagination and facilitating the actor's unself-conscious exploration of creative problems in games.[32] In a student's first term, two-hour improvisation classes were timetabled immediately after the early morning movement classes. The work was to start with nonverbal improvisation aimed at providing a basic experience of the nature of acting by learning to express action and ideas without words.

Improvisations using simple activities drawn from daily life were intended to enhance the student's skills of observation and their inventiveness. The improvisation exercises became more complex and varied in the second term, when students were asked to portray people with different occupations, for example, tailors, mechanics, waiters, painters, and so on. When the student had discovered the characteristic movements of the person's craft, he then presented the character in an appropriate place. The next step was to create a particular mood for the character, concentrating on how this would dictate a rhythm of physical performance. Eventually an incident was added that would have the effect of changing the mood and rhythm of the performance. The improvisations were to remain simple and last no longer than ten minutes. Saint-Denis believed the exercise should be stopped if it led to "a kind of self-imposed theatricality lacking in truth."[33] These silent improvisations resembled some of Stanislavski's early exercises in truth and belief. The emphasis on rhythm, which probably derived from Copeau's explorations of music as a key to performance training, was akin to Stanislavski's work on tempo-rhythm. The requirement that the execution of the improvisations be simple and untheatrical reflected Copeau's underlying idea that honest acting was grounded in a bodily integrity that did not depend on sophisticated forms of pretence.[34]

The next phase of work on silent improvisations involved the composition of more complex scenarios: the student was to plan and rehearse each scenario in segments before attempting to play the whole of it. Once devised, the scenario was edited and shaped by means of a few short rehearsals. During this exercise, the student should begin to develop an understanding of dramaturgy by learning how to structure action and to communicate significant details of setting and mood. At this stage, Saint-Denis himself regarded as relevant Stanislavski's approach to the development of the imagination by means of exercises involving sense memory and concentration.

The actor was then to work on a sequence of improvisations designed to teach him to transform himself physically into different types of people. Exercises in performing simple activities "in character" drew on the student's observation of people as well as physical skills of mimicry. One of the standard silent improvisation exercises employed by Saint-Denis—transformation into animals—entered theatrical legend as a result of Peter Ustinov's hilarious description of his becoming a salamander during a class at the London Theatre Studio. Despite humorous accounts of what happened during some of the animal transformations, the rationale behind the exercise is pertinent: "To start this work of transforming his body, the student begins by precise observation of the chosen animal. . . . He must not reduce these observations to the obvious, but rather *select* those elements that can register on the stage and which capture the temperament, the essence of the animal. He must not try *to be* the animal in the abstract; he must get the feeling of the animal in his body and *lend himself* to it."[35]

Apart from the purely physical experience of a different quality of movement from his own, the student had to create an impression of character in a somewhat exaggerated way, expressing through the body the typical attitude of the animal without resorting to straightforward mimicry.[36] As with so many of the exercises, animal transformations were intended to assist the actor through a process of physical exploration to achieve a spontaneous recognition of style in performance.

Work on animal transformations gave way to improvisations around the personae of different entertainers, introducing the student to more overtly stylized forms of performance. Playing a particular type of entertainer provided an experience of conscious role-play, challenging the student to create an illusion of virtuosity in evoking the entertainer's performance while at the same time maintaining a sense of the humanity of the person beneath the act.

Improvisations on dreams encouraged the student to experiment with the dramatization of different levels of consciousness, the relationship between conscious and unconscious states being figured in contrasting styles of performance that might be generated by the imagination in conjunction with memory, rather than being a product of deliberate artistic decisions: "[These exercises] prepare the actor/student for those styles which are not naturalistic. . . . our goal . . . is to train the student to become as creative as possible in the interpretation of all styles."[37]

Group improvisation work was to commence in the third term, beginning with only two people, and gradually progressing to larger groups. Exercises were to be undertaken to enhance sensitivity to space and positioning with respect to others in the space. Saint-Denis believed that the actor needed to cultivate his memory of space and proxemic relationships and to experience the spontaneous transmission of feeling through a group by physical work in which a number of individuals learned to function as a coordinated ensemble. In group improvisations, there were no individual protagonists: the drama centered on a community and action was largely mimed, although key words from texts might be used at particular points.

Group improvisation provided a foundation for the devising of new theater pieces. During the process, new verbal texts might be devised or the performance might utilize sound, music, gesture, dance, clowning, and other nonverbal forms to generate new forms. Saint-Denis advocated the use of the improvised language called *grummelot* that mimics the sound of foreign languages ("the music of meaning") to enhance expression and free the performers from the constraints of actual speech where necessary. These improvisations represented a purely theatrical drama that sprang from the histrionic potential of actors spontaneously collaborating in the theatrical use of their imaginations. Saint-Denis believed that dramatists could learn much by watching how a physical and musical language of theater emerged in the shaping of such spontaneous dramas. In the 1960s, the work of Peter

Brook on *US,* the Open Theater's *The Serpent* (directed by Joseph Chaikin), and Keith Johnstone's improvised plays afforded Saint-Denis examples of the kind of theater generated by this method of devising. More recently work that has been created in Britain according to this group approach has been presented by Joint Stock (at times in collaboration with Caryl Churchill and other writers), Theatre de Complicité, Forced Entertainment, Frantic Assembly, and Improbable Theatre.

Neutral Mask Work

Work with the neutral mask was to run in tandem with group improvisation. This course represented a summation of everything learned in different phases of the improvisatory work. For Saint-Denis, Copeau's discovery of the noble mask as an instrument of actor training provided the key to his approach to acting. The neutral mask, as it became known, demanded of the actor at one and the same time a passionate commitment of feeling and a rigorous control of form: "At the very moment when the actor's feelings beneath the mask are at their height, the urgent necessity to control his physical actions compels him to detachment and lucidity."[38]

The alien identity of the neutral mask would energize the performer, demanding that he discover how to focus the emotions by way of the body with the utmost force and clarity. There were four distinct types of neutral mask, with features suggesting adolescence, adulthood, mature age, and old age. A student was to spend time studying the four masks before choosing one with which to work. Significantly, Saint-Denis regarded mask work as "anti-psychological." Playing in a mask required the student actor to draw on unconscious impulses; however, there was no attempt to portray the psychology of character in a literal way. The process whereby the actor reacted to the features of the mask before deciding to put it on and then experimenting with how his body should *perform* it was intuitive: the aim was to break the socially conditioned connection of inner impulse and bodily expression (which in social behavior is normally registered involuntarily through facial expression) in order to compel the actor to discover a wholly aesthetic vocabulary of posture, gesture, and movement through which the mask/character could signify.

During the improvisatory process in which the student was composing mask scenarios, he was obliged to make spontaneous aesthetic choices about the appropriate forms through which his feelings might be expressed. He would experience the difference between the socially conditioned acting that was learned as part of the repertoire of everyday behavior of his culture, and the terms of an aesthetic vocabulary in which such spontaneous behavior might be reconstituted for expressive purposes.[39] The aim of improvised mask work was to produce the discoveries through a *trial and error* process during which the learning might take place in the student's *body,* rather than being understood intellectually first and then translated into corporeal form. As in any process of creative art, feeling or intention might arise *after* the form had been sketched out: the student's playing might create movements that produced feelings appropriate to the mask under the circumstances precipitated by the improvisation.

The question of whether actors should work on a role from the inside (through empathic identification with the character's psychology) or from the outside (by manifesting character through physical imitation of observable social behavior) was rendered irrelevant in Saint-Denis's work with neutral masks. Such an inner/outer dichotomy often troubles actors who train in Strasberg's Method but spend most of their working life having to act to order as a consequence of the technical requirements of stage, television, or film. Mask work was to teach the student actor an improvisational process that integrated the consciousness of aesthetic form with the experience of subjective impulse in performance. By developing a corporeal economy appropriate to expressing the personality of the mask, the student would acquire a physical discipline that prepared him for the performance of a wide range of dramatic styles.

Since it was posited on the assumption that the body in space is more expressive than the face and eyes, Saint-Denis's approach was clearly designed to suit the circumstances of theater rather than film and television. The mask training most obviously distinguished his approach from other training systems. Saint-Denis may well have been able to make the powerful impact on the British theater that he did because neither of its dominant performance traditions—the art theater (Shakespeare and revivals of the classics) and the mainstream commercial theater—had ever fully embraced the aesthetic practice of Zolaesque naturalism as exemplified in the productions of the Théâtre Libre and the Moscow Art Theater. The "jerky, staccato delivery"[40] that Saint-Denis noted as typical of the realist acting in British commercial theater was itself a style of physical acting that effectively reproduced the external features of English social behavior, leaving the audience to construe the details of psychological motive and subtextual emotion.

Within this theatrical context, Saint-Denis's approach offered ambitious and idealistic young actors an opportunity of developing and transforming a British tradition of acting that was based more on social observation than on psychoanalytic insight. Until the 1960s, on the other hand, Stanislavski's ideas—to the extent that they were actually known or understood in Britain—seemed needlessly psychologistic, promising a type of naturalism that struck English practitioners as heavy-handed and irrelevant. The kind of training introduced by Saint-Denis has produced actors like Judi Dench, Diana Rigg, Ben Kingsley, Ralph Fiennes, Maggie Smith, Emma Thompson, Daniel Day-Lewis, and Kenneth Branagh, whose style, intelligence and vocal/bodily technique has enabled them to give detailed and technically brilliant performances in Shakespeare, the well-made West End play, or naturalistic film and television drama. In contrasting a production performed according to the principles of Strasberg's Method with the acting that his own system of training aimed to produce, Saint-Denis threw into relief the characteristic features of modern English acting, and at the same time indicated ways in which the influence of American film and television threatened to transform it: "[The actors'] faces, their gestures and words were far less important to them than their nervous systems, their secret 'stirrings,' the meaning behind the words. Though a photograph of life was intended, only the negative was being shown, not the finished print. Our feeling is that the student, in his acting, should *present* rather than *impersonate* and should give first place to objective gesture rather than to the study of subjective psychology."[41]

According to Saint-Denis, mask work would continue alongside improvisation classes during the whole of the second year, but in the fourth term students were to be introduced to character and comic improvisations in *character masks,* which covered only the upper part of the face. This work was an introduction to the techniques of performing comedy and farce; the approach was very different from the work with neutral masks, involving traditional techniques derived from commedia dell' arte, music hall, and circus clowning. Students were to create the features of a mask character through a bricolage process in which elements from scenic and wardrobe stock were assembled. They were encouraged to use random combinations of props, costumes, and even musical instruments until an embryonic idea of character emerged out of the relationship between the mask and the various props. The point of this exercise is to encourage inventiveness. In the early stages of improvisation, the student would try out a range of possible vocabularies and speech styles for characterization. In contrast to the work with a neutral mask, he would use a mirror to check the effect on the mask of different attitudes to performance.

The experimentation with character masks was a playful but conscious rehearsal of roles intended to foster the objectivity necessary for effective comic acting. Once a coherent identity had been fixed, the student was to practice a repertoire of physical and vocal tricks in the personality determined by the mask. While work with the neutral mask constituted useful preparation for the performance of classical tragedies, improvisation in character masks taught the skills essential for playing comedy and farce. One has only to look at the films of Charlie Chaplin, Buster Keaton, the Marx Brothers, Jacques Tati, or Peter Sellers to observe the kind of comic acting that employs such mask techniques. The modern actor may not actually wear the half-mask of the Italian commedia dell' arte, but the indication of role in comedy and farce through stylization of facial expression and vocal/bodily attitude still reveals its kinship with masked performance.

Interpretation

Structurally, the core of Saint-Denis's drama school curriculum was the course he named Interpretation. In essence, this was a program of play productions over the four years of the course, to which every other strand of the curriculum was in every term more or less directly related. Beginning with a *discovery play project* in the first term, students were to encounter the fundamental problems of acting by rehearsing a wide range of different types of play throughout the four years of the course. The discovery play project aimed to demonstrate to the students why they needed training, and it provided an opportunity for teachers to identify individual students' abilities and needs. This project familiarized students with the most basic rehearsal methods. The teacher was not to direct the students with the aim of leading to a finished performance. The project was to be viewed by the faculty as a way of monitoring student progress. In the second term, classes focused on the reading of three plays written in contrasting styles; the third of these was to be rehearsed in a relaxed way, shown to the faculty, and discussed.

From the third term onward, rehearsals and performances were to become more formal, although, apart from the faculty, no audience was to be permitted to see the performances until the end of the fifth term, when a farce was performed for the rest of the school and some invited guests. In the seventh term, a play would be toured to schools and colleges; the general public was to be admitted to performances for the first time in the penultimate term of the program, and the final term would conclude with a two- to three-week repertory season of four or five plays to be performed for an audience that included the general public, the press, and professional agents. During the twelve terms of the program a student should have performed a play involving mime and mask work (e.g., Obey's *Noah*), two realist plays, a Shakespeare, a farce, a Chekhov, a Jacobean tragedy, a

Restoration play, a Greek or Shakespearean tragedy, another classic, and an experimental piece. During the performance of these plays, a student would have encountered a wide range of performance styles. By allowing students to learn the most basic aspects of the rehearsal process in the first few informal production projects, and then progressively making the discipline of rehearsals stricter as the challenges offered by the plays increased, the program ensured that a student learned through his actual experience of rehearsal and performance, rather than merely through class exercises. As in other aspects of the course, sensitivity to style was to be acquired by the student through exposure to the stylistic demands of a wide range of texts in performance.

Fundamentally, Saint-Denis's approach to rehearsal and training was motivated by a belief in the efficacy of the actor's intuition in the process of becoming acquainted with the text. Most of his methods of training and rehearsal imply the rejection of the possibility of finding an appropriate mode of performance through rational analysis of the text in favor of a less conscious process in which the actor's imagination is stimulated by the playful exploration of its potential for enactment. Its form in performance is discovered through a series of concrete attempts to enact it that gradually acquire focus during a process of osmosis between actor and written text. By that means the play is simultaneously apprehended and expressed through the whole imagination of the actor, rather than merely his intellect.

There is clearly a parallel here with Stanislavski's method of physical action, although, by cautioning against improvising the action of the play until after the first reading of it, Saint-Denis differs from the practice adopted by Stanislavski in his last years: "I have sometimes seen rehearsal improvisations done by actors who were not really familiar enough with the play and this has, of course, its hazards as it can lead the actor away from the role."[42] This awareness of the potential dangers of improvisation as a rehearsal method has been and is echoed regularly by British practitioners, and reflects the principle that a performance must remain faithful to the written text—a principle that determined Saint-Denis's approach to rehearsal and training. Saint-Denis did not assume that the character created by the actor in this rehearsal process would be realistic: in fact the whole process was designed to allow the style of the performance to manifest itself through working with the text. At the same time, Saint-Denis's approach implied a rejection of conscious stylization, insisting that a performance style should arise organically from the written text.

The final component in Saint-Denis's program of training was a course that introduced students to the social and cultural contexts of the plays performed as well as important phases of theater history. Although it consisted of lectures and research projects intended to complement the interpretation course, Saint-Denis was convinced that this should not involve a purely abstract intellectual approach. Rather, information about the culture of different periods and societies should be communicated in such a way that it would stimulate the imagination of the student actor, whose task was to apprehend intuitively the world that determined a character's particular set of social assumptions, as opposed to achieving a purely theoretical understanding of a play's context.

The Impact of Saint-Denis's Teaching

The outline of a model drama syllabus developed by Saint-Denis in the 1960s was a modification of ideas he had developed during his apprenticeship with Copeau. Adapted to take account of mainstream English attitudes to acting, it incorporated and transformed elements of practice that had characterized the work of Poel and Granville Barker. Whereas in the 1930s the work of the London Theatre Studio was viewed with a degree of skepticism in some quarters, by the 1960s the fundamental principles embodied in Saint-Denis's training had become the accepted basis of the teaching at most British drama schools and dominated approaches to rehearsal in subsidized British theater. Privileging experience over analysis—*doing* over *thinking*—this approach reflects the typical British attitude to training for the arts in general, the hostility to theory and analysis being an aspect of an empiricist tendency deeply rooted in the culture. Saint-Denis's approach has been consolidated by the work of drama schools and mainstream theaters since the 1960s. In Britain during the 1960s and 1970s the theory and practice of Brecht appeared to offer a major alternative, but by the mid-1980s Brecht's influence on actor training and production methods had become marginal.[43]

Whereas the Stanislavskian approach to acting has stressed the identification of actor with character and thus approached the process of acting as a psychophysical re-creation of real experience—whether drawn from the actor's memory or from imagination—the English and French tradition deriving from Copeau has emphasized the actor's role as an expressive instrument, employing all the physical, emotional, and intellectual faculties of the imagination to create a unified style of playing for each production through which the form of a drama manifests itself as performance. It is not that Stanislavski entirely ignored the factor of style in performance, or that Copeau and Saint-Denis reject psychological characterization. The difference in their starting points, however, has determined the very different qualities of acting within these two major traditions.

Many contemporary actors and performance artists have studied with Lecoq, whose synthesis of Copeau, commedia dell' arte, and clown training has been instrumental in the formation of two generations of practitioners who employ the "principle of play" to create theater from improvisation or by working with written texts. The teaching of Jacques Lecoq has over the past fifteen years made a significant impact on acting, directing, and writing in France and Britain. By an irony of history, the enormous success of Lecoq-inspired companies like the Theatre de Complicité in London in the 1980s and 1990s has helped to reintroduce the radical aspects of Copeau's practice into British training in a way that Michel Saint-Denis had not fully managed to achieve in the 1950s and 1960s. Lecoq himself learned Copeau's methods from various teachers who had been trained by members of the Vieux-Colombier or Compagnie des Quinze.[44] Paradoxically, by the mid-1980s groups like Theatre de Complicité, Steven Berkoff's London Theatre Group, Footsbarn, and the Moving Picture Mime Show constituted a performance-based alternative in British theater to the orthodoxy of the text-based tradition that Michel Saint-Denis had done so much to establish at the Royal Shakespeare Company, the National Theatre, and the Royal Court.

6. British Approaches to the Teaching of Speech and Movement

A number of sociocultural factors contributed to a transformation of the British theater from the mid-1950s to the 1970s. The most obvious manifestation of this change was the nature of the plays being written and staged, but by the early 1960s a new generation of actors (most notably Albert Finney, Rita Tushingham, Tom Courtenay, and Richard Harris) had introduced working-class styles and attitudes to acting that challenged the upper-middle-class manner of the great actors of the day—Gielgud, Olivier, Redgrave, Edith Evans, and Peggy Ashcroft.[1] George Devine's English Stage Company at the Royal Court theater and Peter Hall's Royal Shakespeare Company were not merely responsive to Continental European influences (most immediately Brecht's theater and the French avant-garde drama that came to be labeled *absurdist*) but also sponsored and promoted many of the innovations in writing and performance. However, the attitude to acting in even the most progressive British theatrical institutions remained rooted in the tradition of "respect for the text," and the vast majority of British actors had no experience of the approaches of Stanislavski, Strasberg, Meyerhold, or Brecht and no knowledge of Artaud.

When arguing in 1959 for a London base for the RSC at the Aldwych Theatre, Peter Hall insisted on the need for the company to perform new plays alongside those of Shakespeare. To prevent the company from becoming merely a museum for the preservation of Shakespeare, actors and directors would confront Shakespeare's plays with an informed awareness of the contemporary world; conversely they would employ the rhetorical techniques of speaking Shakespeare in exploring the linguistic variety of contemporary drama. This idea clearly reflected the philosophy of Michel Saint-Denis (together with Hall and Peter Brook, one of the RSC's triumvirate of directors): "From your modern standpoint you must assimilate the reality of past styles. . . . There is a two-way action. The proper realistic approach we have today can be of great benefit to the interpretation of classical works. At the same time, training and practice in the classics is essential to enrich and inspire realism which is otherwise in danger of becoming sensational, sentimental or merely empty."[2]

By the early 1970s the Royal Shakespeare Company had come to represent a new orthodoxy with respect to acting in the noncommercial theater. The English theater's tradition of privileging Shakespearean performance as the ultimate challenge for the serious actor was reinforced by the prestige that the company enjoyed internationally.

John Barton and the Royal Shakespeare Company

The person who did most to shape the RSC's approach to acting Shakespeare was John Barton, appointed by Peter Hall as a director in 1960 and becoming an associate director of the company in 1964. A don who had built up a reputation for directing Shakespeare at Cambridge, he was largely responsible for establishing an approach to speaking the text that combined a scholarly respect for the detail of its structure with a modern attitude toward the communication of meaning. Hall and Barton were opposed to an excessively musical style of delivery that they believed was a superimposition of vocal mannerism upon the texts: instead they taught their actors to concentrate on the syntactical shape of the argument in each speech. This produced an unsentimental and muscular approach to speaking the text that stressed *sense* rather than *sound* in a way that seemed to reflect the values of Brecht's epic theater. In the early years of the RSC, actors were contracted for three years. This enabled the directors to create a genuine ensemble and to provide the training in speaking Shakespeare's language believed by Hall and Barton to be essential if the company was to revitalize the approach to performing Shakespeare.

John Barton's ideas about acting Shakespeare reflect the traditionally empiricist attitude of British practitioners who prefer to arrive at a viable practice through intuition and experiment and are skeptical of a completely theorized methodology. Directors at the RSC and voice and acting teachers at drama schools have embraced this approach with characteristically British pragmatism. In *Playing Shakespeare,* the book based on his television series of that name, Barton presents his own working practice as a compromise between the assumptions one might suppose an Elizabethan actor to have made about acting and the attitude with which a modern actor, conditioned by the habits of naturalistic performance, might approach Shakespeare. In this respect, his work is located within the historicist tradition of Poel and Granville-Barker, attempting to formulate modern principles of acting and staging Shakespeare as a response to historical knowledge of the conditions and conventions of the Elizabethan theater: "One thing we would all like to know, of course, is how Shakespeare's actors rehearsed a part and what way their minds worked. I have suggested in this book some of the things they must have instinctively gleaned from the text, and how an actor today can easily do the same."[3]

Given the great gap between the signifying context of Shakespeare's theater and that of today, Barton's concern to qualify his assertion is understandable, yet he does not seem troubled by the contradictory nature of his theoretical stance: "But I must confess I have never worried over-much about the precise accuracy of what I may say in the rehearsal room. The test there is not whether a given statement is objectively true but whether it helps, stimulates and releases an actor at a particular rehearsal."[4]

The problem here is that Barton is *not* merely exploring Shakespeare's texts in a pragmatic way. No one would question the right of a director to experiment freely with different ways of speaking a passage of text, but Barton's method and his authority is grounded in his scholarship, so ignoring the system of Elizabethan prosody when it does not suit his immediate purpose in rehearsal calls into question its validity as a guiding principle. Behind Barton's belief "that in the Elizabethan theatre the actors knew how to use and interpret the *hidden direction* Shakespeare himself provided in his verse and his prose"[5] is an assumption deriving from both Poel and Copeau that it is possible for an actor to be directed by the play text itself: "If the textual points are ignored, then it's pretty certain that Shakespeare's intentions will be ignored also or at least twisted. Something else will be put in their place, valid in itself but none the less a distortion. I'm not trying to knock that kind of work. It can be rich and exciting in its own right. But if it ignores the verse it leads to an alternative to and not a realization of Shakespeare. Shakespeare *is* his text. So if you want to do him justice, you have to look for and follow the clues he offers. If an actor does that then he'll find that Shakespeare himself starts to direct him."[6]

The contradictions inherent in Barton's approach are apparent in his introductory explanations about the method of textual exploration: "There are few absolute rules about playing Shakespeare. . . . We want to test and to question. Particularly we want to show how Shakespeare's own text can help to solve the seeming problems in that text. Of course much of it is instinct and guesswork. . . . I shall hardly talk at all about directing, and at first I shall try to keep clear of interpretation. We won't talk much about individual characters, and we shall say even less about plays as a whole. We shall simply concentrate on finding out how Shakespeare's text *works*."[7]

Given Barton's education at Cambridge in the 1950s it is hard to avoid noticing echoes of the Leavisite tradition of literary criticism, which employed an empirical method of close reading rather than historical analysis in identifying the values of a literary text.[8] The desire to avoid "interpretation" does not make much sense, since finding out how a text *works* is indistinguishable from finding out how and what it *means*. Barton himself is at times forced to admit that directorial decisions about interpretation and actors' decisions about characterization must be made in order to give any sense whatever to the speeches of the different characters that constitute the text. The language of a play cannot be treated as language in a poem; its rhetorical structure is located within a dramaturgical and theatrical framework, and an individual speech makes complete sense only as an utterance within a larger context of enunciation.

In order to demonstrate his thesis, however, Barton feels compelled to contrast this Elizabethan tradition of acting as rhetoric with the modern approach, which emphasizes relationships, character, and intentions: "Our tradition is based more than we are usually conscious of on various modern influences like Freud and television and the cinema and, above all, the teachings of the director and actor, Stanislavski. . . . I think the most basic thing in all that is the importance of asking the question 'What is my intention?' "[9]

According to Barton the twentieth-century attitude to realistic characterization in drama was foreshadowed in some respects by Shakespeare, which makes his plays accessible to modern actors: "That's why I believe we'll find that the problem of how to marry the two traditions in fact doesn't exist once you get to know how Shakespeare's text *works*."[10] Having stated at the outset that "an actor in Shakespeare has simply to marry the two traditions of heightened language and naturalistic acting,"[11] Barton spent most of the television series working on methods of speaking verse and prose that presume that the meaning of the dramatic performance is inscribed within the written text from which it is derived. Although a character's motives are at different times during the series acknowledged as relevant to an actor's way of delivering lines, the conclusion of the only sustained attempt to work on character is that the different characterizations of Shylock by David Suchet and Patrick Stewart are a result of their "individual imaginations and personalities."[12] Barton reinforces the idea that the director is a kind of midwife, not actively interpreting, but bringing the inherent meanings of the text to life through the medium of the actors.

The underlying assumption that directors and actors oversimplify by *consciously interpreting* Shakespeare's plays derives from the abiding myth of

Shakespeare as universal genius, whose inexhaustible richness transcends the limited perspective of any individual interpretation. A controversial argument in support of this attitude was published by John Russell Brown in 1971 in an essay entitled "Free Shakespeare":[13] "The choice of a unifying idea for a production, and its expression in settings, costumes, interpolations, by-play, verbal emphasis, manner of performance, limits the presentation of what Shakespeare has written. It concentrates on one single meaning for every ambiguous line. It enlarges one incident and diminishes, or cuts completely, some other incident that is capable of contrary emphasis. The productions are not myriad-minded; Shakespeare is not free."[14]

Russell Brown proposed an experiment in staging Shakespeare that might allow audiences to find meaning in the plays without having their responses manipulated by the director's deployment of acting and scenography. Audience and actors would be in the same light, and plays would be presented in a "smallish" theater on a thrust stage. Rehearsal periods would be shorter than they conventionally are so that performances might assume an improvisatory attitude, with movement and interpretation not being absolutely fixed, but partially discovered in the moment of performance.

Ironically, John Barton and Peter Brook—who professes an almost mystical notion of Shakespeare's inclusive vision—are among the directors castigated by Russell Brown for manipulating Shakespeare's texts to support their particular interpretations. The theoretical stance underlying Russell Brown's proposal, however, is shared by Barton, Brook, Peter Hall, Trevor Nunn, in fact by most of the major British directors who have worked at the RSC since the 1960s. Even what seemed to be the most Meyerholdian production of a Shakespeare play in Britain during the last fifty years, Brook's *A Midsummer Night's Dream,* was claimed by the director to be the product of a process of textual exploration rather than the result of a directorial concept. There is no doubt that some of the most exciting and well-acted productions of Shakespeare (and other dramatists) were produced by the Royal Shakespeare Company between 1964 and the early 1980s when it had a world reputation for unparalleled excellence.

The Teaching of Cicely Berry

By the early 1970s the prestige of both the RSC and the National Theatre, under the directorship of Laurence Olivier, reinforced the belief in the effectiveness of the British approach to actor training and rehearsal, with its pragmatic insistence on textual exploration as the key to good acting. As company voice director at the RSC, Cicely Berry conducted daily voice and text classes that made a significant contribution to the quality of acting in productions in the 1970s and early 1980s. Her work at the Central School of Speech and Drama and at her own private studio had already influenced a generation of young actors and teachers. Her approach to speaking the text supported the views of Hall and Barton, and demonstrates the impact of Saint-Denis on British notions of actor training. In *The Actor and His Text,* she expressed succinctly the rationale for using Shakespeare as a foundation for actor training: "It seems to me there is so often a gap between the life that is going on imaginatively within the actor in order to create the reality of the character he is playing, and the life he gives the text which he finally has to speak. It is as if the energy and excitement that an actor feels when working on a part is not released fully when he commits to words, when he is bound by the language set down. . . . Whatever the style of writing the actor has to find the right energy for that particular text. . . . I do believe that work on Shakespeare is the surest way of learning about text."[15]

Berry has identified a problem that Stanislavski believed the actor would need to address when she progressed according to the method of physical action from improvisation toward speaking the writer's text. Copeau's idea of improvised play around the text was the first thoroughgoing attempt to resolve the problem, while Saint-Denis's system of rehearsal was a refinement of Copeau's idea. Berry is characteristically undogmatic in explaining that it is this problem that renders voice and speech work central in contemporary British training.

Many of the principles that motivate the work of Cicely Berry and other contemporary voice and speech teachers in Britain are those that underpin the approach to training adumbrated by Michel Saint-Denis. These include the rejection of elocution and the linking of voice work with movement training. The centrality of "text work" derives from the importance Saint-Denis accorded *l'expression parlée* as a way of teaching the actor how the relationship between form and meaning in dramatic texts manifests itself in performance as style. In *Voice and the Actor* and *The Actor and His Text,* Berry reflects on her experience of working with acting students and professionals, and outlines a wide range of exercises designed to help the actor communicate effectively. Rejecting the idea of an ideal standard of voice production toward which the actor should aspire, Berry insists that the actor's voice should express her own personality. The actor should not think of her voice as an instrument, but as an extension of herself. The guiding principle for the development of vocal technique is not virtuosity but freedom from tension and clarity of delivery. Control of the vocal apparatus is achieved through exercises in text work that create a link between technical and imaginative challenges. The attitude to performance that informs such ideas can be traced back to Copeau's organicist notion of the dramatic imagination. Technique is related to the need to express thoughts and feelings: it involves a harnessing of the energy of the voice to produce the sounds inherent in the words: "The exercises have nothing to do with making you technically more accomplished. They are for the purpose of freeing the voice so that it is able to respond to the instinct of the moment. . . . if the voice has not the breadth and experience of resonance and ways of making sound its response will be limited. It can only respond to the extent that it is capable of making sound."[16]

Berry identifies three stages in the development of the voice. The first involves exercises for relaxation, breathing, and increased muscularity of the vocal organs. During the second the vocal play gives way to the speaking of texts for the benefit of an audience. This is the most complex part of the work because it involves the relationship of the voice to all other aspects of the acting process. The actor must confront the personal reasons for all the tensions that prevent her from communicating freely in learning to achieve the "unity of physical and emotional energy" that produces expressive sound. The third stage is one of simplification, in which the student moves beyond the difficulties of the second stage to reexperience the earlier exercises more straightforwardly. Berry regards *listening* as an important aspect of vocal development. By this she does not mean listening to the "external sound of your voice," but suggests that a kind of aural sensitivity is required to monitor the relationship between sound and sense while speaking.

Berry invokes the organicist myth of human creativity in explaining the importance of text work: "Just as breathing is a vital function, so the need to make sound to convey our needs is vital. Words came about because of the physical need to express our situation. . . . The words are rooted with the breath. . . . It always seems to me a waste of time to work on any text that is second-rate; the better the text the more possibilities will open up."[17]

In making a connection between the production of words and the life-giving energy of breath, she is asserting the primacy of speech as a basic human function, as well as making certain assumptions about "good" texts, which she implies are more effective with respect to "the physical need to express our situation" than second-rate texts. An aesthetic of "naturalness" is implicit in her method of cultivating the voice and in her notion of the usefulness of good texts. Like Copeau, Berry implies that learning how to vocalize a text is a process of eliminating the blocks caused by years of bodily and mental tension in order to free the actor to release the energy of sound determined by the meaning of each word.[18] Speaking a text may therefore require movement work as much as vocal exercise, because the voice cannot be separated from the body in the act of speaking. Text work thus becomes a kind of key to work on the whole being of the actor, engaging her mental, emotional, and physical energies. Berry, in common with other voice and acting teachers, recommends the Alexander technique to assist the actor to develop a tension-free approach to bodily activity, but there are clear parallels between her work on text and the approach of Laban to the enhancement of the individual's capacity for expressive movement.[19]

By insisting that the student work on interesting texts from an early stage of her training, Berry ensures that the exercises are never purely mechanical, but that what is being expressed, shapes the means of its expression: "We have to make the breath and the muscular formation of the words the means by which the thought is released. . . . However, unless this work connects organically with an ever-fresh and developing response to language, it remains a technical accomplishment, which makes the voice stronger and more resonant, but does not necessarily make the speaking more interesting."[20]

Much of Berry's work on the relationship of sound to meaning and on exploring the energies of a text aims to help the actor go beyond conscious responses to meaning by sensitizing her to the sensuous experience of producing and hearing speech. This ensures that the literal meaning of language is not allowed to repress the unconscious dynamic of each word. Many of her exercises encourage the discovery of levels of meaning that cannot be grasped rationally, but which are manifested through a spontaneous play of movement and voice. Berry acknowledges the influence of Peter Brook (with whom she worked on *A Midsummer Night's Dream* in 1970) on this aspect of her work.

Through practice the student actor discovers many of the techniques of prosody that create heightened speech: Berry's method requires the actor to experience the effects of different kinds of linguistic structure in order to acquire competence in using language rather than to study the rules of prosody. In the acting of Shakespeare, Berry favors a balance between *presenting* and *experiencing* feeling and thought. She refers to Brecht when discussing the idea that the actor might share with the audience an awareness that goes beyond that of the character, yet still cautions against playing simply for effect. Even though the balance between *being* and *presenting* varies from one play to another, it is always important that the actor shares the text with the audience in an appropriate way. Berry identifies two common approaches to speaking Shakespeare: exaggeratedly emotional and poetic delivery, or its opposite—rational, unemotional speaking. The first is a response to the heightened quality of the language, the second to the difficulties of understanding it. According to Cicely Berry, a balance between the two approaches is necessary: "it is the thinking that gives the feeling its strength; the thought itself is passionate."[21]

It is Berry's belief that if the actor learns to trust the sound of the language, she will not have to work much at creating the thoughts and emotions, for these are embodied in the speech, an idea that is very much in keeping with the belief of Copeau and Saint-Denis that the text *directs* the actor. What Berry offers the actor is a structured approach to developing the vocal and corporeal flexibility and sensitivity that will initiate the two-way process in which the actor energizes the words in response to the stimulus that the text itself provides. According to Berry the structure of speech within a dramatic text depends on the following:

1. How the metre is disposed within a line, and how the sense stress works with the metre stress.
2. The through energies of line, thought phrase, and whole thought structure. We have to be aware of how each of those three contributes to the movement forward.
3. How the thoughts are broken up, be it in prose or verse, directly related to the emotional state of the character.
4. The substance of the word—i.e. the number of syllables, the length of vowel and the quantity and type of consonants; all this within one line gives it its particular character, and this tells us of the quality of the thought.
5. The use of antithesis, and how this sets up the parameters of the thought.
6. The logic of the imagery, and how the finding of the image is directly related to where the character is placed in terms of the laws and structure of his particular world, and of nature. And also how very often there is a ladder of imagery set up which leads us through a scene or a part of a scene.
7. We have to be aware of word games and patterns. There is often for instance a double meaning to a word, and sometimes this is used overtly for its humour; at other times it is used more suggestively for subversive reasons.
8. How, nearly always, the statement of the premise is made at the beginning of the speech. The opening out of the theme then follows in a kind of debate, and some conclusion is reached.

9. The tempo of the whole, which is governed by the matter in hand, the debate.[22]

Berry is enormously creative in inventing physical exercises and games that allow the student actor to experience the structures of speech in the form of dramas played out through the whole body and in interaction with others. By performing a variety of activities, using mime, singing, whispering, percussive movement, and a wide range of sounds, she initiates a process of play that in subliminal ways opens actors to the complexities of a written text they might fail to grasp through pure analysis. Berry observes that actors will usually have worked out their interpretations of the characters and the play analytically or in kinetic terms before they do any serious work on speaking the text, so that her task is often to draw attention to the linguistic forms in which a character's thoughts and feelings manifest themselves.

Berry has made a unique impact on British acting. Her books and her practice offer concrete demonstrations of a method of rehearsal and training that has become synonymous with the British approach to the classics and has certainly provided a method of working for a number of major British actors, directors, and teachers. Questions of psychology are not directly addressed in her work, which assumes that well-written plays provide the key to a character's attitudes and motives in the pattern of speech created for them by the dramatist. In this respect her work is rooted in the tradition of Copeau and Saint-Denis rather than Stanislavski. Berry's avowed political commitment demands that actors see "theatre as a serious political force in the context of the society we live in," and her working method is an expression of the ideology of romanticism deeply ingrained in the English artistic tradition.[23] Although she may not have theorized her approach completely, her practice has been thoroughly consistent with her aims and has undoubtedly helped generations of actors since the 1950s to express thoughts and feelings through vigorous, passionate, and unaffected speaking.

Expressive Movement for the Stage: Laban's Praxis as Model

Michel Saint-Denis's insistence on an integrated approach to voice and movement training had a profound impact on the development of voice teaching in British drama schools. Whereas earlier elocutionists had taught the actor to cultivate the voice in order to produce beautiful vowels and clear consonants, demanding that students master the so-called Received Pronunciation as the standard form of spoken English, virtually all voice work at drama schools for the last thirty-five years has aimed to make the student actor's natural speaking voice flexible and expressive. There has not been such a clear consensus about the correct approach to movement teaching, which is still often split between the Alexander and Feldenkrais methods (designed to cultivate the body wisdom that helps an individual to move without stress) on the one hand, and specific kinds of skill training (e.g., fencing, tap dancing, T'ai Chi, mime, and mask techniques) on the other. Although only the Drama Centre and East 15 specifically acknowledge the use of Laban's system as an aspect of their teaching, Laban's praxis is widely known to teachers of contemporary dance and physical education, and many acting teachers integrate some aspects of his system in their work.[24] In my view, Laban offers a coherent approach to *expressive* movement that embraces many of the values of the "organic" approach to voice and text. As a complement to Berry's holistic approach aimed at freeing the actor to meet the expressive demands of the text, the teaching of Laban enables the performer to enhance her natural movement capacities in such a way that she develops the sensitivity to qualities of movement hitherto beyond her control. The dynamic quality of movement constitutes a direct expression of feeling and thought.

In Germany, Laban established a tradition of *Tanztheater* whose exponents include Kurt Jooss and Pina Bausch. In Britain, Laban's investigations into human movement were chiefly applied in the fields of industry, dance training, and choreographic analysis; during the 1950s and 1960s, they influenced the pedagogy of physical fitness at elementary schools. His concept of "effort actions," however, offers a potentially useful method of cultivating the bodily expressivity of the actor and provides an approach more sophisticated and flexible than that of either Dalcroze or Meyerhold to the actor's cultivation of physical expressiveness. Laban developed a system of movement education that aimed to enhance the individual's own capacity to move without imposing on her body a stylistic imprint as do such training systems as ballet, Martha Graham, or Noh drama.

One professional theater company whose work was profoundly influenced by Laban's ideas was Joan Littlewood's Theatre Workshop, based initially in Manchester and later at Stratford East in London. Although in the 1940s and 1950s she was very much an outsider to the theater establishment, Littlewood is today regarded as one of the two most important British directors of the last half-century. She used improvisation as both a method of script development and as a rehearsal method for actors, her left-wing political beliefs prompting her to create an idiom that brought working-class life onto the stage in a direct and physical style—a startling contrast to the refined and at times attenuated performance styles of the British theater of the early 1950s. Theatre Workshop did more to challenge the predominant mode of acting in the British theater than any other company of its time.

Littlewood's intuitive feeling for the use of movement onstage made her immediately receptive to Laban's ideas:

> After a session with Laban you began to look at the world with different eyes, as if it had changed its colours or its shapes. . . . you watched for the slightest gesture which could give away a secret. After a while, with some degree of accuracy, you could tell what people did for a living, or analyse their state of mind as they passed you on the street. . . . To our good fortune Laban remained in Manchester throughout the war and whenever possible we attended his studio. . . . When he came to Blackburn to see us, I was on tenterhooks all night—his good opinion meant more to me than all the rave reviews in the world. . . . Mostly he was surprised at how much I knew without having trained with him. . . . He had seen the way I played with time and space, converting every day actions. "What about voice?" he asked me. "Can my efforts theory be applied to the voice?" "Yes, of course." He had discussed this problem with Kurt Jooss at Stuttgart and thought the dancers' range would be extended by the use of vocal efforts, though not in pure dance.[25]

Born in Bratislava in 1879, Laban had become the leading choreographer and dance master in the Weimar Republic, and through his students Kurt Jooss and Mary Wigman he influenced the development of *Ausdruckstanz,* which revolutionized dance in Europe. Laban was forced to escape to Paris from Germany in 1938 and was soon invited to join Kurt Jooss, whose company was based at Dartington Hall in Devon. In Britain the first application of his theory of effort was in industry, and his book *Effort* was jointly written with the factory consultant F. C. Lawrence. According to Littlewood, it was his colleague from the Ballet Jooss, Lisa Ullman, who encouraged him to promulgate his system as part of the physical education program in primary schools, so that in Britain his ideas had more immediate impact on industrialists and educationalists than on theater practitioners.[26]

Laban's system was based on the idea that movement is a result of the body's capacity to channel latent energy in order to effect motion in specific directions and with different qualities. This capacity he called *effort.* Movement is a function of living organisms; inanimate objects might be in motion, but are not capable of initiating or directing movement. Laban's establishment of an approach to kinesthetic expression on the basis of general principles of human movement, distinguishes his system from that of earlier theorists.[27] His observation of the energy utilized or manifested in the neuromuscular functions of the body was not translated into aesthetic categories, but was analyzed as the basic principle of organic existence, from which all human functions could be seen to derive.[28]

Although Laban spoke of the *inner* qualities and *outer* forms of human movement, effort is a psychophysical phenomenon. Only in the process of reflection can it be analyzed into its inner and outer components. Effort is focused energy, its spatial forms being a manifestation of its dynamic as bodily experience. Effort, "with all its manifold shadings of which the human being is capable, is mirrored in the actions of the body. But bodily actions performed with imaginative awareness stimulate and enrich inner life."[29] By conceiving the human organism as alive through movement, Laban was able to identify the interrelatedness of mental, physical, and emotional activity. The harmonious functioning of the human being depends on the integration of these aspects. Fully expressive movement is a sign of a healthy organism. This does not mean that the healthy body functions in a manner that is observable as peaceful or gentle or relaxed, but that it participates fully in the complete range of efforts of which the organism is capable.

"The components making up the different effort qualities result from an inner attitude (conscious or unconscious) towards the factors of movement, Weight, Space, Time and Flow."[30] A person can either *indulge in* or *resist* each of the motion factors. The two contrasting attitudes to weight are lightness (resisting) and strength (indulging in); to space, directness (resisting) and flexibility (indulging); to time, suddenness (resisting) and sustainment (indulging); to flow, bound (resisting) and free (indulging). The eight basic effort actions are a result of the different possible combinations of attitudes to weight, space, and time. These are *press* (strong, direct, and sustained), *wring* (strong, flexible, and sustained), *glide* (light, direct, and sustained), *float* (light, flexible, and sustained), *thrust* or *punch* (strong, direct, and sudden), *slash* (strong, flexible, and sudden), *dab* (light, direct, and sudden), and *flick* (light, flexible and sudden). An attitude to flow is typically, though not invariably, associated with each effort action. The words signifying each effort action were chosen by Laban for their onomatopoeic qualities; their sounds help the student recognize the effort quality of each type of action. A movement personality can be identified in an individual's "body shape" and "movement habits" that result from inherited predispositions toward certain effort qualities and the fixing of habitual bodily responses to environmental factors in early life. Through effort training it is

possible to enhance the individual's capacity to perform the kinds of movements that are not a part of her habitual movement vocabulary.

Any form of purposive movement—work or expressive—evinces effort
characteristics. Because it is possible to choose an attitude to each motion
factor, the worker or performing artist can find the most appropriate effort
for the performance of any particular task (instrumental or expressive). The
performing artist can, through observation and analysis of the habitual attitudes of others to the motion factors, learn to recognize these as "the basic
indications of what we call character and temperament." Laban's approach
ensures that the actor does not merely imitate the superficial features of a
person's movement as the physical basis for characterization, but that she
characterizes movement on the basis of its "inner attitude" to the motion
factors. Instead of merely imitating behavioral mannerisms or reproducing
conventional forms of posture and gesture, the actor is provided with a
method of grasping and expressing in the body what motivates an individual to move. Laban's new way of identifying the elements of movement distinguished his system from all previous approaches to movement training
and provided a new perspective for the observation and reproduction of
movement for expressive purposes. The actor can only become capable of
subtlety and restraint in movement if she has learned how to be expressive
as a moving being within the full range of effort actions. Movement training then becomes the key to expressiveness for the actor.[31]

Laban conceived movement as the fundamental principle of theatrical
expression, and mime as the origin of theatrical art: "Human movement,
with all its physical, emotional, and mental implications, is the common
denominator of the dynamic art of the theatre. Ideas and sentiments are
expressed by the flow of movement, and become visible in gestures, or
audible in music and words."[32]

Laban was not primarily concerned with signification. He did consider
the semiology of stage movement, but he was wary of attempts to translate
the meaning of culturally determined signs into words. What he wished to
comprehend and notate was the *sheer experience* of movement as shared by
performer and spectator. Movement may be more or less stylized according
to the signifying codes of the different arts, but the engagement of the spectator with the performance occurs on both a phenomenological and a semiotic level, so that, whatever the aesthetic code, the expressiveness of the
movement is fundamentally a function of its effort characteristics: "It is the
arrangement of effort expression of everyday life into logical yet revealing
sequences and rhythms which gives a theatrical performance its special character."[33] Laban believed that, as a consequence of the logocentrism of West-

ern culture, artists and spectators had become less sensitive to the phenomenological than the semiotic aspect of movement. Yet intuitively the spectator is always responding to the effort content of the movement.

Speech is, according to Laban, "audible movement," which implies that effort determines the quality of vocal sound as it does the form and quality of movement: "The art of the stage developed from mime, which is the representation of inner movements by visible outer motions. Mime is the stem of the tree that has branched into dance and drama. Dance is accompanied by music, and drama by speech. Both music and speech are produced by movements which have become audible. Musical sound arouses emotion; spoken words express thought. But the musical quality of speech also colours words with emotion. . . . in reality there exists no speech without bodily tension. Such tension is potential movement, revealing sometimes more of a person's inner urges than do his words."[34]

The investment of a simple action or word with a particular type of effort in performance will convey a specific emotional or mental attitude.[35] Laban believed that the clichés that had become apparent in both melodramatic and naturalistic acting resulted from performers' failure to express the range and gradation of effort inherent in the movement vocabulary of each style. In order to enhance the performer's sensitivity to the effort quality of movement and the inner attitudes that effort expresses, Laban recommended that she learn movement as a musician learns music, acquiring a sense of its structures through analysis, and its kinesthetic qualities through practice. The psychosomatic experience of an effort action is called a movement sensation. While the movement sensation is merely an accompanying factor in functional actions, it becomes of primary importance in expressive situations. For the factor of weight, the movement sensations are heavy or light; for time they are momentariness or endlessness; for space, narrowness or everywhereness; for flow, fluidity or pausing.

Movement is not always characterized by complete effort actions. If two of the motion factors are latent, the effort action will be "incomplete." Laban names the six combinations of two motion factors as *awake* (space and time), *dreamlike* (flow and weight), *remote* (space and flow), *near* (weight and time), *stable* (space and weight), and *mobile* (time and flow). What Laban calls *drives* occur when one of the motion factors is dormant. When flow is dormant, Laban speaks of the *action drive* (the eight effort actions are variants of the action drive). When the weight factor is replaced by flow, the *vision drive* results. The *spell drive* is a result of time being replaced by flow. The *passion drive* results from the replacement of space by flow. Laban also relates each motion factor to a type of *inner participation*. The inner participation in relation to space is attention (concerned with "where" and affecting the power of thinking). The inner participation of weight is intention (concerned with "what," affecting the power of sensing). The inner participation of time is decision (concerned with "when," affecting the power of intuiting). The inner participation of flow is progression (concerned with "how" and affecting the power of feeling).

Laban accounts for the infinite variations in the quality of movement in terms of these combinations of effort attitudes revealed in deliberate action and in the unconscious "shadow movements" that accompany it: "The shapes and rhythms which are formed by basic effort actions, movement sensations, incomplete effort, movement drives, give information about a person's relation to his inner and outer world. His mental attitude and inner participations are reflected in his deliberate bodily actions as well as in the accompanying shadow movements."[36]

The system at first appears complicated; however, students do not encounter it in purely theoretical terms: by practicing the different components as movement sequences, they gradually acquire competence in executing and recognizing the dynamic qualities of the effort attitudes and the differences between them. Its originality as an approach to the communication of emotions via the body is that it avoids the arbitrary association of particular gestures or movements with specific emotions. By separating the semiology of expressive movements (invariably the product of ideology) from a phenomenology of movement forms, Laban was able to avoid the confusion of the kinesthetic qualities of stage action with its semiotic coding. The spectator may interpret an actor performing the effort actions of slashing and punching in one narrative frame as hatred and in another as despair. The construction of meaning will be a function of the codes that operate in that particular performance, which are in turn determined by the cultural context within which the performance is situated. But the bodily experience of slashing and punching is the primary phenomenon experienced kinesthetically by the spectator. The movement sequence may acquire more complex layers of meaning in the process of being "read" according to semiotic codes, but the force of the performance cannot merely be reduced to the level of signification.

The vocabulary Laban chose as a means of indicating qualities of effort deliberately avoids reference to the overdetermined language of emotions beloved of popular nineteenth-century acting manuals (e.g., fear, rage, delight, surprise). His aim was to suggest the dynamic quality of bodily action, not to hypostatize states of feeling through gestural or postural attitude. Certainly, the mastery of the effort "scale" enables a performer to convey the range of feelings a character may experience. But more importantly, an actor or a dancer who is capable of encompassing the full range of effort qualities in her movement will provide a stimulus for the spectator's emotional engagement. Laban's approach thus reinforces Meyerhold's view that it is the spectator who experiences emotions in performance; whether the performer experiences them in the same way is irrelevant, so long as her body is fully engaged in the execution of the appropriate action.

Laban distinguished the personal space surrounding every individual (the kinesphere) from the general space of the surrounding environment. The kinesphere "travels" with the body, so that in their personal space the performer is always facing forward ("forward" being the direction ahead of wherever the body is facing, no matter where in the room the performer has traveled). Sensitivity to space involves the ability to relate the dimensions of the kinesphere (up, down, forward, backward, right, left) to that of the public space, which does not "travel" in the same way. The student must not only learn how to use the immediate dimensional scale of the kinesphere but also acquire a sensitivity to the articulation of the body as it makes pathways in public space. Invented by Laban in the 1920s, *kinetography* or *Labanotation* is a system of notation now widely used for recording modern dance. It enables an observer to notate precisely the movement of individual body parts as well as the pathways traced by the body in space. Laban identified two scales of movement in space—the dimensional scale for directions (high-deep, left–right, backward-forward) and the diagonal scale for movement along diagonal pathways: right-high-forward, left-deep-backward, left-high-forward, right-deep-backward, left-high-backward, right-deep-forward, right-high-backward, left-deep-forward. Each of these scales can be performed with either the right or the left side of the body leading. The diagonal scale for the left side becomes left-high-forward, right-deep-backward, right-high-forward, left-deep-backward, right-high-backward, left-deep-forward, left-high-backward, right-deep-forward. In performing the dimensional scale the body is in an upright vertical position (as in normal walking) so this is regarded as a *stable* scale, whereas each movement in the diagonal scale is experienced as a pull in three directions and is therefore always slightly off-balance, making this scale *labile*.

According to Laban, each of the six fundamental directions of the dimensional scale has as a "secondary tendency" an association with an effort dynamic, as follows:

1. The direction upwards is associated with a feeling of lightness.
2. The downward direction is associated with strength.

3. Movement directly across the body from one side to the other is associated with restriction (directness).
4. Movement of opening the body from one side to another is associated with freedom (flexibility).
5. The direction backwards is associated with a feeling of suddenness.
6. The direction forwards is associated with a feeling of sustainment.

While it is possible to perform a movement in any of the six directions with a dynamic quality opposite to its secondary tendency, the movement in each direction is normally characterized by the associated feeling that is its "natural" dynamic. An actor may choose for dramatic purposes to perform a movement upwards with the quality of strength: this would create an impression of extreme intensity as it would be very much in defiance of the downward gravitational pull. (This could of course be utilized by an actor who wishes to move with intensity in a very dramatic situation.)

Laban mapped the two scales as a cube that represents the space of the kinesphere. Correspondingly the dynamic scale of effort actions can be located on this cube, using the secondary tendencies to plot direction thus creating what Laban called the dynamosphere. By practicing movement in the diagonal scale with an awareness of the effort dynamic of the secondary tendencies, the performer learns the most economical or natural way to articulate those effort actions in spatial form, making each effort action into a dance step. Once this is learned by the body, the performer is capable of indicating all the nuances of effort shading that lie somewhere between one complete effort action and another and are usually indicated by the shadow movements that are unconscious or involuntary expressions of the individual's state of being. For an actor, Laban training promises an enhancement of her own neuromuscular functions, as well as increased kinesthetic awareness, both in the body and through observation.

The performer learns to vary the quality of energy applied in the performance of any movement or gesture through the choice of specific effort attitudes. Because the shape of a movement is related to a sense of its dynamic qualities, the actor acquires an ability to characterize any activity with effort in order to evoke the "inner" emotions or attitudes that she may be required to signify by means of the behavior specified in the text. This approach allows a performer to characterize any kind of stage action or movement with its appropriate effort qualities, no matter what style of playing is demanded. Classical ballet makes use of a particular repertoire of spatial and dynamic forms, but it is necessary for the dancer to perform with proper engagement in the dynamic qualities of the movement if the steps are to have any emotional impact on the audience. The conventional steps of the ballerina may especially emphasize the attitudes of lightness and flexibility, involving a combination of gliding, floating, and flicking actions, and the stylization of the form will require the dancer to articulate the shape of the movement in space as clearly as possible. But without the proper expression of the effort components of the movements, the dancer will merely give an empty display of technical virtuosity.

At the other extreme, a particular naturalistic drama might require an actor to use a far wider range of effort actions and incomplete efforts than the ballerina, but these may be expressed mainly in the shadow movements whereby the character accompanies the deliberate actions that she employs to execute her intentions. The shadow movements will be small movements that are not very precisely articulated as spatial forms. Although a character may not be conscious of exhibiting these shadow movements, they nevertheless manifest dynamic qualities, revealing the concealed or unconscious attitudes connected to her main actions. The performance of a Greek tragedy will be somewhere between a ballet and a naturalistic play, requiring the actor to delineate the effort qualities in terms of clearly articulated movement forms, but allowing for the use of a certain amount of accompanying shadow movement. Proper effort training will equip the actor for any style of performance. The degree of stylization of movement would be a matter of judgment by the actor or director with respect to every production, but the acting will be inexpressive if the effort qualities of movement and speech are not delineated.

The performer learns to vary the mood of scenes through practice of sequences of movement and speech in different rhythms: "The elements of movement when arranged in sequences constitute rhythms. One can discern *space-rhythms, time-rhythms,* and *weight-rhythms.* In reality these three forms of rhythm are always united, though one can occupy the foreground of an action."[37] The performer is required to repeat exercises in the different measures that are the metrical forms of rhythm in order to acquire sensitivity to them before beginning to experience the variations of rhythm in a range of dramatic situations. Laban recommended simple improvisations to teach the student an awareness of how different emotions or temperaments manifest themselves in the rhythms of movement. The initial performance of an improvisation is always repeated and analyzed so that the student is able to fix the pattern of movement that represents its dynamic structure in the body and the imagination.

Although Laban did attempt in *Choreutics* to indicate the mathematical foundation for the laws of human movement that he believed he had discovered, his approach was based on rigorous empirical observation. While certain theoretical aspects of his system may be purely speculative, there is no doubt that he invented a viable language for observing and analyzing movement. Before Laban, one could talk of movement either in purely technical terms (as in the language of classical ballet) or in the vague and subjective terms of emotional affect.[38] His system provides a basis for comprehending the functional and expressive aspects of movement. At present its use in acting training may be restricted to the work of experts teaching at a few drama schools, but there is no doubt that his approach is susceptible of a wide range of uses by actors and teachers.

Class work in movement usually begins with bending, stretching, and twisting different parts of the body (e.g., head, arms, legs, chest) in different directions. By developing an awareness of the movement possibilities of different parts of the body, the student comes to understand that movement involves far more than merely locomotion and conventional hand gestures. Each individual works with a partner, observing and mirroring their movements, learning to correlate the experience of her own movement with observation and analysis of another's. Students are encouraged to improvise simple movement sequences, chosen to provide an experience of the particular elements being studied at the time.

In recommending the use of basic themes of movement rather than the repetition of set exercises, Laban revolutionized the approach to dance education.[39] His is the opposite of the approach to classical ballet training, in which the dancer must practice a traditionally established set of exercises until she is capable of performing each movement in the preestablished form that is conventionally acceptable: "While the movements of everyday life are directed towards the accomplishment of tasks connected with the practical needs of existence, in dance and play this practical aim recedes into the background. In the first case the mind directs the movement, in the other the movement stimulates activity of the mind."[40] The actor must master both approaches to movement, being required to perform the occupational actions specified for a character in a dramatic situation, while at the same time evoking the emotional and mental attitudes with which each movement sequence is invested. As in those types of actor training derived from Copeau, the principles of play and exploratory improvisation are important in Laban's pedagogical approach.

An actor would benefit from working in sequence on Laban's sixteen movement themes for movement education. These involve a progression from the simplest theme of awareness of the body to the most advanced, which are "concerned with the expressive qualities or moods of movements." The sequence of themes is as follows:

1. Awareness of the body
2. Awareness of resistance to weight and time
3. Awareness of space
4. Awareness of the flow of the weight of the body in space and time
5. Adaptation to partners
6. Instrumental use of the limbs of the body
7. Awareness of isolated actions
8. Occupational rhythms
9. Shapes of movement
10. Combinations of the eight basic effort actions
11. Space orientation
12. Shapes and efforts using different parts of the body
13. Elevation from the ground
14. Awakening of group feeling
15. Group formations
16. Expressive qualities or moods of movements.[41]

Movement improvisations based on the first eight themes assist in the acquisition of fundamental bodily awareness and control; the last eight are more advanced and involve more concentration on the expressiveness of the body in space. Although themes 13 to 15 are specifically concerned with the aesthetic aspects of dance, 14 and 15 can help the actor acquire sensitivity to proxemic relationships, spatial composition on stage, and interaction within an ensemble. The final theme is most directly pertinent to acting. Laban regarded the last eight themes as advanced. Such an approach to movement education is completely different from the kind of formal technical training in dance techniques like ballet or tap. Its emphasis on the development of an awareness of the body in space and of the economy and expressive possibilities of well-focused effort derives from the assumption that there is no ideal body-shape or perfect model of kinetic performance: movement education is a process of disciplined and playful experimentation in which each individual discovers her own movement capacities before engaging in coordinated or choreographed group work.

Laban's approach to movement has in common with mainstream British approaches to acting a belief that theatrical performance should be based on organic principles. As a pioneer of modern dance (or free dance, as he sometimes referred to it), he was convinced that expressive movement should be based on "natural" laws of physics and physiology. Not only can Laban training improve the student actor's general neuromuscular coordination and control, it also provides a structured approach to acquiring the kinesthetic awareness of spatial and dynamic forms necessary for effective movement on stage. However tendentious some of his more abstract theories may appear, there is no doubt that his systematic empirical observation and analysis of movement provides a complementary approach to the text work advocated by Cicely Berry. The fact that one may not entirely agree with the Romantic ideology of either does not invalidate the usefulness of their practice.

The slogan of "respect for the text" combines a principle of abstract minimalism in staging with a rhetorical approach to the performance of plays, aiming to integrate "fidelity" to the play text with an imaginative economy of means that emphasizes the flexible use of the actor's voice and body. The notion of a free exploration of the text through bodily and vocal play had by the 1960s become so firmly established that when Peter Hall became director of the National Theatre in 1973 he appointed John Russell Brown as literary manager. Although there have been very few systematic attempts to allow the text to speak through the actors, unmediated by directorial "interference," this idea does underpin much voice and movement training and has inspired the production approach at Shakespeare's Globe Theatre on London's South Bank.[42]

7. Improvisation and Games for Devising and for Performer Training

New approaches to performance began to manifest themselves, in different ways, both in the British and in the American theater of the late 1950s. In the United States, playwrights such as Tennessee Williams and Arthur Miller followed a tradition of serious drama established in the 1930s by the Group Theater. Their work addressed the individual's personal experience of moral and political issues in ways that government censorship of performed drama in Britain rendered unimaginable. The most talented British playwrights of the interwar years, Noel Coward and Terence Rattigan, tailored their drama to suit the middlebrow requirements of a commercial theater Establishment. Nevertheless, by the end of the 1950s, the success of the English Stage Company at the Royal Court and the Theatre Workshop in Stratford East had inaugurated a renaissance of new writing for the stage. The impact on the British theater of a new generation of European modernist dramatists, in particular Bertolt Brecht, Samuel Beckett, Jean Genet, and Eugene Ionesco, was a significant catalyst in the promotion of new attitudes to dramaturgy and performance. As a result, British drama regained the status of a serious art form that it had achieved in the Edwardian heyday of George Bernard Shaw. An indirect yet important consequence of this new movement in theater was the abolition of stage censorship in Britain in 1968.

Two traditions of acting were dominant in the American theater of the 1950s. The older tradition was based on a more rough-and-ready nineteenth-century attitude, combining techniques of melodramatic and comic acting in a broadly theatrical style still successfully employed in the Broadway musical—the native American form that had by the 1930s eclipsed its British and European antecedents. This approach was based on the nineteenth-century idea that acting was a craft that could be cultivated by purely technical means. In the early part of the twentieth century, American performers were renowned for the athletic quality of the singing, dancing, and acrobatic skills that they exhibited in popular shows. The "serious" acting tradition had since the 1940s been almost entirely derived from the Stanislavskian approach to psychological realism, Strasberg's Method having become the canonical approach by the 1950s. In the late 1950s, critics identified as a problem the fact that American actors were either exclusively introspective creators of psychologically detailed characters, or barnstorming virtuosos with a purely external technique inappropriate to the performance of sophisticated drama. Method actors were said to lack basic techniques of voice and speech production, while musical theater performers could *perform* but not *act*.

New Approaches to Performance in Britain and the United States

Although Brecht had lived in California during the war and had actually succeeded in mounting a production of *Galileo* with the actor Charles Laughton in 1947, his theories of dramaturgy and production made no serious impact on the American theater until the advent of avant-garde companies such as the Living Theater and the Bread and Puppet Theater toward the end of the 1950s. The success of *The Threepenny Opera* off-Broadway in 1954 (it ran for six years) was attributable more to the growing popularity of Weill's music and the legendary performance of his widow Lotte Lenya than to Brecht's contribution. The grossly oversimplified and reactionary attitude to Brecht prevalent in Britain and the United States insisted that his theater was flawed by a type of didacticism consequent upon a wrongheaded allegiance to Communism.

By the early 1960s, however, a new generation of American theater practitioners had begun to absorb the influence of European avant-garde performance of the 1920s and 1930s. These approaches were soon transformed into alternative American performance styles. The publication of Artaud's *The Theater and its Double* in English in 1958 had a major impact on this generation of theater artists. Although the British theater establishment had been somewhat skeptical of both Brecht and Stanislavski until the mid-1950s, the visit of the Berliner Ensemble to London a few days after Brecht's death made an immediate impact on young British playwrights and directors. By 1964 the theories of Brecht, Artaud, and Stanislavski were being hotly debated among the new generation of theater practitioners in both the United Kingdom and the United States. New approaches to rehearsal and training, involving improvisation and game-playing, were being explored in progressive theater companies and drama schools.

In the United States, interest in the new European drama together with an awareness of the modern theories of performance caused a reassessment of Stanislavski's ideas and a critical reevaluation of the Method. Practitioners began to distinguish more clearly between the Method, as promulgated by the Actors Studio, and Stanislavski's actual praxis. The publication of Erving Goffman's *The Presentation of Self in Everyday Life* (1959) heralded the introduction of a new sociological perspective on the performative nature of social interaction, chiming with the tendency in avant-garde theater and art toward a blurring of the boundaries between performance and everyday behavior.

The use of improvisation as a means of cultivating spontaneity and enabling actors to achieve full identification with characters was popularized by the Actors Studio in the 1950s and 1960s. The improvisation of scenes by actors employing *given circumstances* to explore how characters would interact under specific conditions was an important aspect of Method training. Plays such as Jack Gelber's *The Connection* and Edward Albee's *Zoo Story* were very much a product of such improvisational approaches to acting, attempting to evoke the surface of everyday experience with its randomness and apparent lack of psychological coherence. Indeed many alternative American theater groups and experimental filmmakers of the early 1960s used improvisation as a way of "writing" the performance.

Another aesthetic tradition that exploited the idea of improvisation as central to performance derived from the experiments of the futurists, dadaists, and surrealists and was initiated by dancers such as Merce Cunningham (in collaboration with the composer John Cage) and Ann Halprin, and visual artists such as Allan Kaprow, Claes Oldenburg, Jim Dine, and Robert Whitman. Kaprow's *18 Happenings in 6 Parts* introduced the word *happening* into the lexicon of modern performance. People invited to the Reuben Gallery in New York in the autumn of 1959 encountered a loft divided into three rooms by plastic walls. Chairs were arranged in circles and rectangles, thus forcing visitors to face in different directions. Program notes were in the form of instructions to the visitors, which explained that the performance was in six parts, each part containing three happenings that would occur simultaneously and would start and end with two strokes of a bell. The participants were asked to follow their instructions, which suggested that they might move from one room to the next after the first two parts and again after the second two.

The performance utilized music, live painting, slides, readings from placards and recitations of monosyllabic words. It lasted ninety minutes. Over the next few years, a large number of varied performance events were labeled Happenings by the press. These events were not consciously part of a coherent artistic movement, but they usually involved an idea of performance as a spontaneous and unrepeatable event that explored the relationship between chance and design and the shifting boundaries of art and everyday experience. By breaking down the overt distinction between performer and spectator, and between one art form and another, Happenings called into question conventional notions of the theater event. Improvisation itself had become performance.

The Work of Viola Spolin

First published in 1963, Viola Spolin's *Improvisation for the Theatre* has probably done more than any other book to popularize improvisation as a theatrical activity and as a basis of actor training in the United States. Notions of spontaneity, chance, and the overlap between everyday reality and performance animated Spolin's use of improvisation, but her work arises directly out of a tradition of sociological thinking rather than from experimental performance. Although many of her ideas originated with Stanislavski, her emphasis on the game-playing aspect of improvisation was very different from the self-absorption of Method exercises. Her own practice demanded openness to the audience and a dedication to the problem-solving function of games that had more in common with educational methods than with naturalistic theater.

Spolin's work was inspired by the experiments of the Chicago-based sociologist Neva Boyd: "I received from her an extraordinary training in the use of games, story-telling, folk dance, and dramatics as tools for stimulating creative expression in both children and adults, through self-discovery and personal experiencing."[1] Spolin's approach was based on the idea of learning through experience.[2] Theater games were designed to enable the participants to make discoveries in the act of playing. Spolin insisted that a game should not be manipulated by the teacher to ensure a predetermined outcome but that participants should be encouraged within the limits established by basic rules to solve problems through meeting the immediate challenges encountered in playing the game. Spolin's use of the word *player* rather than *actor* signified an attitude to theater games as a tool for learning rather than as a purely aesthetic technique: "Playing a game is psychologically different in degree but not in kind from dramatic acting. The ability to create a situation imaginatively and to play a role in it is a tremendous experience, a sort of vacation from one's everyday self and the routine of everyday living. We observe that this psychological freedom creates a condition in which *strain* and *conflict* are dissolved and potentialities are released in the spontaneous effort to meet the demands of the situation."[3]

Spolin believed that the intuitive (as opposed to intellectual or physical) faculty was neglected in conventional education systems and that playing improvisational games was a way of freeing the intuitive faculties of players to function creatively in unfamiliar situations. At times her philosophy was reminiscent of Copeau's: "Through spontaneity we are re-formed into ourselves. It creates an explosion that for the moment frees us from handed-down frames of reference, memory choked with old facts and information and undigested theories and techniques of other people's findings. Spontaneity is the moment of personal freedom when we are faced with a reality and see it, explore it and act accordingly."[4]

The process of learning engaged all aspects of the whole person (physical, intellectual, and intuitive). The acquisition of skills occurred without conscious effort but was part of the fun of the game. The players' agreement to abide by the rules of the game obviated the need for discipline to be imposed in an authoritarian manner; individuals would learn to collaborate by playing in a group. The games thus constituted models of social and psychological interaction that provided a kind of rehearsal for real life. Spolin was determined that the games be used to break down the authority structures that pressure students into seeking approval from teachers, insisting on the equality of teacher-director and student, and exhorting facilitators to allow them to learn through the experience of the game rather than through the mediation of an authority figure. As a facilitator, the open and flexible attitude of the teacher director permitted him to learn from the game alongside the student.

The audience was to become an essential part of the learning experience. Spolin rejected the convention of the fourth wall, separating actors from spectators: theater games were always played with the goal of communicating with an audience. Players were to acquire the necessary techniques through playing the games, rather than being taught specific vocal or bodily techniques—a radical application of the principle of learning through experience that lay behind Copeau's use of improvisation to develop the imagination. Early stages in the game-playing process taught students to appreciate the power of sensory perception and to express relationships in concrete, physical terms. Spolin appears to have integrated elements of Stanislavski's early ideas on truth and belief with the method of physical actions to develop an approach to theatrical communication as a physical process: "Reality as far as we know can only be physical, in that it is received and communicated through the sensory equipment. . . . Nor need we be concerned with the feelings of the actor, for use in the theater. We should be interested only in his direct physical communication; his feelings are personal to him. . . . A player can dissect, analyze, intellectualize, or develop a valuable case history for his part, but if he is unable to assimilate it and communicate it physically, it is useless within the theater form. . . . When a player learns he can communicate directly to the audience only through the physical language of the stage, it alerts his whole organism."[5]

Spolin's approach privileged the *process* of improvising rather than its end result as a group-devised performance. Indeed she advised the workshop leader to prevent improvisations from becoming devised dramas (she referred to this as playwriting) or unscripted but preplanned performances. Her method exploited the player's ability to invent material in response to the immediate stimuli of ever-changing situations. By insisting on the importance of spontaneity, she aimed to create a process of playing that integrates unconscious impulses with conscious decision-making about character and action. Ideally, characters would always be in action during improvisation games, thus guaranteeing that the outcome would be a surprise rather than a prearranged denouement. The method was a theatrical equivalent of the automatic writing sponsored by the surrealists, except that theater games were collaborative by nature and involved immediate responses to a range of human and environmental stimuli. The rules of playing were to be acquired in an orientation process that consisted of playing simple games, didactic instruction being kept to a minimum. The teacher-director was to perform as a kind of team coach, monitoring the improvisations on behalf of the group through "side-coaching." This involved giving simple, practical advice aimed at preventing the improvisation from losing focus or becoming theatrically contrived. The teacher would participate from the sidelines rather than as a pure spectator, becoming an adjunct to the team as on the sports field.

Each game was set up by establishing a point of concentration that acted as a kind of focus for the players—an aim that gave shape to the playing. Once the game had been explained, the players were to decide the answers to the questions—Where? (establishing the place of action)—Who? (establishing character)—What? (establishing the nature of the problem/action itself). The way in which the games operated can be illustrated through the example of the Hero exercise for two or more players. The group would choose a physical object and make a decision about where the action took place, who they were, and what they were doing in the imagined situation. The point of concentration was to play the action in such a way that the chosen object (which would be an actual stage prop) became the hero of the scene. The situation was to be suggested by the nature of the object and action should revolve around it. According to Spolin, many fairy tales are structured on such a principle.

The teacher-director was to initiate an evaluation of each game when it was complete but was to take care to avoid value judgments regarding the artistic merits of the performance, the intention being to develop critical awareness within the group about the effectiveness of both the problem solving and the players' communication with the audience: "Was concentration complete or incomplete? Did they solve the problem? Did they communicate or interpret? Did they show or tell? Did they act or react? Did they let something happen?"[6]

In her book Spolin provided numerous examples of different games, from the simplest orientation games such as tug-of-war with a mimed rope, to those in which one player mirrored the other's movements, to games involving communication through gibberish, games played blind, and games designed to develop awareness of space, the use of the voice, body, and different kinds of emotional expression. Spolin introduced the performance of improvisations created at the suggestion of the audience, an idea developed by her son Paul Sills in his professional work as co-director of The Compass, which he founded with David Shepherd in 1955 as the first company dedicated to improvisatory theater. This approach gave rise to a popular form of theatrical entertainment. Members of the company like Elaine May and Mike Nichols achieved great popular success in the early 1960s and directly influenced a major tradition of American stand-up comics. The audience request format has more recently become the basis of the long-running British television series, *Whose Line is it Anyway?*

Sills and Shepherd were influenced by Brecht's praxis: their intention was for The Compass to function as a working-class theater for culturally deprived communities. They began by creating shows on the principle of the commedia dell' arte, with performances based on preplanned scenarios that determined plot but relying on improvisation for the elaboration of individual scenes. In addition to their main show, the actors also performed shorter "Living Magazine" pieces and improvised sketches at the suggestion of the audience. In 1959, Sills set up the Second City Company in collaboration with Bernie Sahlins and Howard Alk. Second City became famous for its presentation of devised shows and on-the-spot improvisations, but Sills left the group in 1967 to establish Game Theater with his mother, and in the 1970s created the highly successful Story Theater that employs improvisatory methods in combination with preexisting narrative material.

Notwithstanding the success Sills has achieved within the professional theater, he has remained true to Spolin's original aim of facilitating the self-
actualization of the participants. In this respect, their work is comparable to
that of Augusto Boal, Keith Johnstone, and the exponents of Theatre-in-
Education in Britain.

The Influence of Keith Johnstone

In Britain, Michel Saint-Denis's call for performances devised from actors'
improvisations found an answer in the work of Keith Johnstone. His *Impro*
has had an impact on the teaching of drama in Britain comparable to that
which Viola Spolin's book had in the United States. While Johnstone is
very much aware of the praxis of both Brecht and Stanislavski, his formative
artistic influence was George Devine, a student and later assistant of Saint-
Denis. It was Devine who invited Johnstone to teach improvisation and
mask work for the Royal Court Writers' Group and Actors' Studio alongside the director William Gaskill. Johnstone became director of the studio
in 1963, and founded an improvisation group called Theatre Machine,
which he directed between 1967 and 1971, with Roddy Maude-Roxby,
Ben Benison, Ric Morgan, and John Muirhead as performers. In some
respects Johnstone's ideas are similar to Viola Spolin's, although he did not
know of her work until 1966. There are, however, significant differences
between them.

Both are dedicated to fostering the individual's creative imagination,
encouraging originality and freedom from social conformity by any means.
Spolin's method is characterized by a recognizably American liberalism that
assumes the importance of every individual's freedom. Her games are modeled on a self-regulatory principle of social interaction based on the belief
that conflicts between individuals within the group are resolvable by playing the game honestly, thus assuming that one individual's freedom may be
maintained without suppressing the rights of others. Johnstone is more critical of the social pressures that shape individual behavior and repress the free
flow of the imagination. For Johnstone, improvisation and game playing
represent ways of liberating the spontaneous processes of the imagination to
allow fantasy to transform reality in an unrestricted play of fears and pleasures. His intense awareness of the manner in which social conformity is
reinforced by the educational system leads him to devise games that both
mimic and transgress the hierarchical structures of society in order to enable
the performer to rediscover the spontaneity of the child.

The most influential aspect of Johnstone's practice is his idea of the status transaction, which presents social interaction as a function of the different ways in which individuals enact their perception of the position they occupy in the social hierarchy. Like Spolin, Johnstone is wary of analytical discussion of creative problems and, whether working with writers or actors, adopts Brecht's habit of asking actors to express ideas in rehearsal by demonstrating them rather than talking about them.[7] In this respect Johnstone shares with Copeau, Saint-Denis, Spolin, Brecht, Boal, and practitioners of Theatre-in-Education a view of drama as in itself a form of dialectical thinking. The word *play* becomes a key term, improvisation being the game in which the whole intelligence of the performer engages with the complex and changing nature of reality. He is extremely critical of the way conventional education suppresses spontaneity by encouraging students to imitate preexisting methods of solving problems. Johnstone cultivates the individual's powers of observation as a stimulus to the imagination, harnessing the unconscious by employing free-association games and recalling hypnagogic images (those that arise in the mind at the threshold of sleep). Johnstone acknowledges the influence of his teacher Anthony Stirling, who introduced him to the wisdom of the *Tao te Ching:* "The sage keeps to the deed that consists in taking no action and practises the teaching that uses no words. . . . When his task is accomplished and his work done the people all say, 'It happened to us naturally.' . . . I take no action and the people are transformed of themselves."[8]

There are clear parallels between this philosophy and the ideas of Michel Saint-Denis, who emphasized the importance of the imaginative process through which the actor discovers for himself how to embody the various aspects of the role by physically engaging with the drama in rehearsal. Johnstone believes that the director should never interfere with the actor's imaginative process by demonstrating how any aspect of the role should be performed, but that the actor should feel that he has made all the creative discoveries himself. Johnstone's innovative approach to improvisation through status transactions originated as a strategy designed to help actors create convincing relationships on stage. When asked to improvise a scene, actors tended to indulge in lengthy discursive exchanges that did not resemble real conversation at all. Johnstone's response to the Moscow Art Theater production of *The Cherry Orchard* was that it was too theatrical because the objectives that the actors chose to motivate their characters were too strong. Instead of asking students to play objectives in each scene as a way of indicating the motives that determined the action, they were to create relationships by enacting minimal status differences. This immediately had the effect of making the interactions among characters on stage more alive, the focus of every scene becoming the battle among the characters to negotiate the gaps in status. Because these gaps were not clearly or immediately apparent, the actors would surprise themselves and one another in the improvisations as they reproduced the mechanisms by which status is transacted in social situations.

Status in improvisation is not what the character *is* but what he *plays*. It is a function of relationships, a habitual defense mechanism, rather than a completely fixed aspect of character. An aristocrat may be a low-status player; a servant may prefer to play high-status. A low-status player can be as effective in manipulating the outcome of a situation as a high-status player: "My belief . . . is that people have a preferred status; that they like to be low, or high, and that they try to manoeuvre themselves into the pre-ferred positions. A person who plays high status is saying 'Don't come near me, I bite.' Someone who plays low status is saying 'Don't bite me, I'm not worth the trouble.'"[9]

Johnstone's observations regarding the significance of status in human relationships reveals a somewhat cynical view of human nature: "When we tell people nice things about ourselves this is usually a little like kicking them. People really want to be told things to our discredit in such a way that they don't have to feel sympathy. Low-status players save up little tit-bits involving their own discomfiture with which to amuse and placate other people."[10] Playing status focuses the attention of the audience on power and the way it is negotiated within the social hierarchy, and, by contrast with American approaches to improvisation that concentrate on the psychologi-cal aspects of behavior, it foregrounds social relationships.

To stimulate spontaneity and liberate the imagination in developing action and narrative out of simple human interactions, Johnstone advocates a method parallel to the playing of status games by which he aims to help performers express intentions in social situations. His observation of the way in which social inhibitions tend to prevent adults from accepting invitations to allow free reign to their fantasies in improvised actions leads Johnstone to devise games of improvisation in which one performer makes an "offer" to another who can accept or block it. Accepting an offer does not mean say-ing yes to the suggestion; it means agreeing to collaborate in inhabiting the imaginary situation that the offer conjures up: "I call anything that an actor does an 'offer.' Each offer can either be accepted, or blocked. If you yawn, your partner can yawn too, and therefore accept your offer. A block is any-thing that prevents the action from developing or that wipes out your part-ner's premise. If it develops the action it isn't a block. . . . Once you have established the categories of 'offer,' 'block' and 'accept' you can give some very interesting instructions. For example, you can ask an actor to make *dull* offers, or *interesting* offers, or to *overaccept,* or to *accept and block* and so on."[11]

The variations on the possibilities of blocking and accepting offers are virtually limitless. Elaborating scenarios on the principle of blocking and accepting offers enables actors to free themselves of the inhibitions that make it difficult to collaborate imaginatively with others, but also develops awareness of the strategies of cooperation and avoidance that shape all social exchanges. The possible permutations of behavior involved in responding to offers add to the repertoire of social strategies that Johnstone introduces to the actor in the form of status games, stimulating spontaneity in imaginative activity and providing insights into the terms of social transactions.

Johnstone believes that "the imagination is our true self,"[12] so he devises improvisational games to remove the stress involved in consciously trying to be imaginative, and to circumvent the censorship mechanisms by means of which the education system represses the free working of the imagination. In teaching narrative skills as part of improvisation, Johnstone asks the student to ignore content. "Once you decide to ignore content it becomes possible to understand exactly what a narrative is, because you can concentrate on *structure.*"[13] In approaching narrative structure, Johnstone asks the improviser to allow the story to take him anywhere, encouraging him to free-associate in order to produce fragments of unconnected material as a starting point. Only later does the improviser "connect" and "reincorporate" in order to shape the initial material into a satisfying structure. This is often achieved by splitting a group of students into pairs: one person begins a story for thirty seconds, leaving gaps in the narrative, which is then completed in thirty seconds by the other, who has the task of filling in and reincorporating earlier narrative strands to make a satisfying ending. Having worked in pairs, performers can then do the same thing on their own: "[T]his game . . . encourages you to write whatever you feel like; it also means that you look back when you get stuck, instead of searching forwards. You look for things you've shelved and then reinclude them."[14]

Johnstone encourages spontaneous imaginative activity by playing a range of free-association games. These include making lists of objects that come into your head spontaneously; associating an image with one offered by a partner; working in groups of three to name a character and attempt to invent his history and personality in a process of instantaneous consensus; a type of automatic writing prompted by a rapid series of questions; the invention of dreams while lying on the floor with eyes closed (again being prompted by a questioner); a surreal game of interviewing "experts" who have to give direct answers to absurd questions; games of verbal chase, requiring precise answers to a series of questions about being in particular situations; word-at-a-time game in which a story is made up by the members of a group each adding one word to the previous one.

According to Johnstone, blocks occur in improvisational storytelling because people's conscious aesthetic and conceptual judgments inhibit the free flow of the imagination. The editing function—an aspect of the conscious mind—is overdeveloped, shaping material before it has been concretely imagined. In solving this problem, Johnstone advises the storyteller to think of the story as a routine that is interrupted. (*Red Riding Hood,* for example is an interruption of the routine "taking a basket of goodies to Grandma.") In order to introduce the element of surprise or to change the direction of a routine, it must be interrupted. The interruption may in turn become another routine that will need to be interrupted. To enhance the narrative structure of an improvisation, each actor in a scene can be asked to surprise his partner with a prearranged interruption. Johnstone cautions actor-writers creating narrative structures on stage against allowing conversation to move the focus of attention to thoughts of another time and place, thus diverting the development of action from the here and now, and against "canceling" the story by setting up a narrative line that is resolved before it can lead anywhere. As soon as it becomes recognizable as a new routine, Johnstone advises the actor-writer to interrupt it.

Johnstone's method of generating narrative in improvisations is based on the idea of out-maneuvering the conscious mind in its habit of controlling the imagination. He advocates immediate responses to questions in order to exploit the faculty of free association and to stimulate subconscious reactions in as many ways as possible. The final part of *Impro* is devoted to the evocation of trance states in mask work derived from Copeau and Michel Saint-Denis via George Devine. Mask work as a way of enabling total possession of actors by characters has made a less immediate impact on British practitioners than Johnstone's games of status and his method of developing improvisations through making offers. While the theory animating his practices reflects a view of creativity as a kind of imaginative anarchy, his romantically anti-authoritarian attitude to the process of improvisation has profoundly influenced generations of theater-makers from the early 1970s to the present day.[15]

The Work of Clive Barker

In many ways the most coherent introduction to the principles and practices of training and rehearsal that had begun by the early 1980s to influence teaching methods in British drama schools and in the more progressive areas of theater is Clive Barker's *Theatre Games*.[16] Barker's work reflects the ethos of the British Drama-in-Education and Theatre-in-Education movements of the 1960s and 1970s that represented a growing recognition of the value of drama as an educational tool.[17] Although *Theatre Games* may not have had as immediate an impact on theater practitioners as Johnstone's *Impro,* it demonstrates a method of integrating improvisation and game playing with contemporary British practices in voice and movement training so as to offer the first British account of a holistic approach to actor training. Theoretically, the approach is grounded in the idea that the psychophysical process of acting largely depends upon the subconscious activity of the back brain. The foundation for the technical training of the actor's instrument is a combination of the kind of speech work done by Cicely Berry with the movement teaching of Laban.[18] Barker translates the type of exercises that Laban and Berry introduced as ways of developing the expressive potential of body and voice into the form of children's games. Students and actors replace their self-conscious struggles to learn with the unself-conscious pleasures of playing a game.[19]

Stanislavski is acknowledged by Barker as the first to recognize that the central problem of the actor is to access the process of the subconscious through the conscious activity of the will. Barker's synthesis of various training and rehearsal practices was a response to the various difficulties he himself experienced while acting with Joan Littlewood's Theatre Workshop Company.[20] Although he acknowledges the pioneering work of Stanislavski in identifying and attempting to help the actor resolve the fundamental problems of performance, Barker eschews a systematic approach in favor of a pragmatic response to the specific problems of the individual actor. This necessitates the invention of training programs to suit each actor's particular needs. While in general terms the fundamental problem of integrating the mental and physical functions of the actor within the psychophysical act remains a constant factor, each actor experiences this problem as a symptom of his particular set of vocal, bodily, and intellectual limitations. Just as Laban thought that the performer should not be pressured to surrender his individual movement personality in the process of acquiring a greater expressive capacity, and Cicely Berry believes that the actor should aim to enhance his own vocal personality rather than attempt to transform it into a standard voice, so Barker rejects any ideal standard of performance in favor of a cultivation of each actor's own skills of coordination and expression: "The ideal of the completely flexible actor is Utopian and detracts from the main purpose which is to enable the individual actor to find the best use of his mind/body resources. In this respect, there is no such state as 'normal-ity.'"[21]

Stanislavski had recognized two separate but linked aims in training: to develop the actor's ability to translate conscious intentions into physical actions and to stimulate and enhance the actor's imagination. The achieve-ment of both these aims demands the activation of the complex neurologi-cal link between mind and body, which it is the function of the back brain subconsciously to effect. "The kinaesthetic sense, or *body/think* is the process by which we subconsciously direct and adjust the movements of our bodies in space, either in response to external stimuli, or to intentions aris-ing in the mind."[22]

The chief difficulty, according to both Stanislavski and Barker, is that any willful intervention by the conscious mind in the psychophysical processes of acting is bound to result in self-conscious performance that is either uncoordinated or appears as a mechanical contrivance of theatrical effect: "[The] kinaesthetic sense, or *body/think* acts automatically unless it is dis-turbed, and . . . it is regularly disturbed by impulses from the front brain. Conscious thought regularly disturbs the working of the *body/think,* which automatically rights itself when, and only when, conscious thought and direction cease."[23]

The various games invented by Barker to help the actor in every kind of training, rehearsal, and performance situation aim to remove blocks to the spontaneous functioning of the psychophysical apparatus. In his description of the appropriate way to learn physical skills, Barker echoes the movement theorist Moshe Feldenkrais: "The keynote of all the work is that it is a process of exploration and discovery, not the direct acquisition of practical skills which the actor does not possess. The acquisition of skills is the by-product of the work. By starting from this premise we concentrate on the processes of action and not on the results we want to achieve."[24]

The most basic games are designed to improve neuromuscular coordina-tion by means of natural processes, the actor experiencing the appropriate kinetic sensations in the body before analyzing what she is doing or how coordination is achieved. The essential aim is to enable the actor first to experience the satisfaction of executing the psychophysical task sponta-neously before attempting to discover how to reproduce the movement in a more self-conscious fashion.

In recognizing the nature of the problem of how to behave naturally or spontaneously in performance, Barker once again echoes Stanislavski, but his solution is not to suggest exercises in truth and belief (which he believes might make the actor conscious of trying to produce effects). The game provides Barker with the model of the kind of process that the actor–character will have to experience in performance. By learning to perform the game through the subconscious activities involved in play, the actor internalizes in his body the kinesthetic sensations appropriate to the dramatic action.[25] "The central part of the acting process embodies the paradox of recreating spontaneous patterns of action and activities, when the outcome is already known, and doing this wilfully. Nothing in the performance takes place unless the actor is instrumental in setting the processes in motion. But this should not be confused with 'making it happen,' which is what sometimes occurs, and from which many problems spring. . . . The result is never achieved and can never be achieved. The harder you try consciously to achieve, the further you get from allowing the natural processes to happen."[26]

Although Barker believes Stanislavski and Laban contributed greatly to the understanding of the fundamental psychophysical processes of acting, he also fears that an analytical explication of the rational basis of the system would interrupt the instinctive flow of the performer's kinesthetic and imaginative processes: "Laban-based or not, the best teachers teach movement, not the system."[27] The system exists to direct and rationalize the teacher's methodology. Conscious awareness of its logical basis will usually not be of benefit to the student or actor during performance.

In effect, Barker takes issue with the skills-based approach to training prevalent in some more traditional schools in the late 1970s, and *Theatre Games* offers learning strategies for working actors who are experiencing blocks at any stage of their career, as well as an approach to training the young actor. One of Barker's basic principles is the use of observation to enhance the performer's ability to recognize and tackle his own inhibitions and limitations in bodily and vocal performance. This constitutes a development of Laban's method of promoting kinesthetic sensitivity by asking the student to alternate the invention of his own patterns of movement with the imitation of others. The student's level of kinesthetic awareness is progressively enhanced as he learns to recognize his own characteristic attitudes and movement habits by comparison with those of fellow students and to extend his movement range by assimilating the movement habits of others. By harnessing the intuitive ability to adjust his own performance through practicing the imitation of another's, the student is protected from the danger that criticism may introduce an excessive self-consciousness that would interfere with the flow of the psychophysical process. Movement observation and imitation becomes a way of allowing the actor to objectify and adapt his own movement habits without having consciously to correct bad posture, gesture, and movement. Work is carried out, then, as a process of alternately doing and watching other actors do. The whole process is a complex interweaving of exploration and observation, repetitions, imitations, and experimentation with alternative ways of acting in a given situation. Through this, rather than mechanical exercises, the actor learns and develops.[28]

The first game that Barker describes in *Theatre Games* constitutes a paradigm of the way in which games can function to develop both the performer's skills of neuromuscular coordination and control, and the imaginative ability that enables him convincingly to re-create patterns of action as performance. Adapted by Barker from a classic Peking opera, this game, The Fight in the Dark, has been widely used in drama classes over the last twenty-five years. Chairs are laid out to demarcate a square with one entrance point. One of the two players guards a precious object placed in the center of the square. The other participant plays a thief whose aim is to steal it. The players must imagine the room to be completely dark. Neither guard nor thief can see the object. Guided by sounds, the guard must try to catch and kill the thief. The game is first played (as in Peking opera) in the light with the participants' eyes open, after which they play it blindfolded. Other pairs of players play the game in turn so that everyone has an opportunity to both observe and participate.

The Fight in the Dark provides a key example of how Barker's games create learning situations for the player/observer, the blindfold version promoting the use of the faculty of body/think in a spontaneous way as the guard and the thief blindly struggle to achieve their objectives closely watched by the observers, the acted version challenging the performers imaginatively to re-create the experience of being in the dark. In the acted version, performers initially "play the result," trying to illustrate their generalized impression of movement in the dark without actually experiencing the heightened sensitivity that is an immediate consequence of being in the dark. According to Barker, playing the game with blindfolds forces the actor to express intentions rather than to pursue effects. As successive pairs enter the square to play the game, the participants are progressively sensitized to the various challenges involved in re-creating the actual situation through the processes of observation and experience. By performing first the acted version and then the blindfold version of the game, players and spectators learn with both their bodies and their eyesight the difference between the "real" experience and its fictional enactment. Kinesthetic awareness and skill is further enhanced if the players are challenged to correct their first acted version after having experienced the game blindfolded.

Barker encourages the teacher to study children's games in order to build up a repertoire of theater games. The principle is simply to replace any technical training exercise with a game that obliges the players to employ the same faculties without being conscious of its being merely an exercise. The effectiveness of The Fight in the Dark derives from the excitement of its inherent drama. Participants and observers are caught up in the thrill of the conflict situation, so that the learning becomes a function of their heightened involvement rather than a result of the repetition of difficult movements for their own sake. The overall aim of an extended program of games is for each performer to progress from personal experience of his abilities and limitations to awareness of and sensitivity to the dynamics of the group, starting from purely physical aspects of performance and gradually learning to encompass the more complex social and psychological processes of human interaction that will arise as a natural consequence of playing in a group. The games introduce the problems and the possibilities of their resolution by providing fictional models of human action and interaction, the experience of which subconsciously stimulates the learning process. The developmental shape of this program echoes the pattern Laban had advocated for the teaching of movement themes, starting with the individual's personal experience of his own body in space and ending with complex improvisations of different types of interaction that create the ability to work as an ensemble in a shared space.

As the first stage in a program of theater games, Barker recommends playing five different types of movement games that help to "break down self-consciousness and free the actor's *body/think* mechanisms."[29]

1. Playing games with *simple aims and objectives* allows the actor to forget about the technical demands of moving while concentrating on achieving the objective of the game. Various forms of *tag* are used to provide pleasure in the violent release of energy while running around the playing space.

2. Competition is a principle of game playing that is used to generate a large variety of games that remove the actor's focus of attention from himself and project it onto winning. Barker advocates the performance of all sorts of movement motifs (e.g., hopping, skipping, jumping, crawling) within the framework of relay races to develop the actor's physical skills of balance and locomotion while he focuses on the goal of winning rather than on the quality of his execution.

3. The use of external objects (e.g., a ball) forces the actor to project attention onto the object instead of himself and can help in improving neuromuscular coordination and the development of ensemble

playing. Many variants of playing with objects can be introduced, and each game can be enhanced by introducing more complex rules as the actor's skill and concentration increases.

4. The use of *other people* as *partners* is a further way of removing from the actor the pressure of performing skillfully. This category includes varieties of tug-of-war with one or more partners, and a game called Fox and Grapes, in which one person tantalizes a partner by holding an object high above his head and moving it out of the partner's grasp every time he reaches for it. Other games can be built out of various kinds of coordinated activity with a partner, such as a two-person somersault, or standing back-to-back and lifting the partner on to one's back. Barker adds voice work to this last game, observing that the voice is released freely in that situation, as there are no tension stops along the spine because the head, neck, spine, and pelvis of both players need to be flattened to achieve the lift.

5. Possibly the most important category of games to free the actor's physical apparatus involves the use of *imagination*. Imaginary scenarios are designed that will necessitate the kind of movements that need to be practiced. These scenarios ensure that the performer concentrates on the imagined situation rather than on the technically correct execution of the action. Games such as Crossing the Ice, Being a Balloon or Crossing the Kalahari Desert are useful for exploring different kinds of effort qualities as well as for practicing balance and reducing excess tension in the antigravitational muscles.

By applying imaginative transformations to any of the other kinds of movement games, the teacher can vary them in order to maintain the interest of student actors, and can begin to integrate the imaginative process with the complex of neuromuscular activities involved in purely physical action. Once performers begin to tire of a game, it can be made more challenging by introducing more discipline into it, making the performers more aware of the technical considerations involved in perfecting its playing. Awareness of technique should not be permitted to inhibit the spontaneous satisfaction derived from each game until the unself-conscious pleasure of playing it has been exhausted.

In explaining the social and psychological significance of games as learning activities, Barker refers to the ideas of Roger Callois:[30] "The elements of play, as defined by Callois, are also the seeds of drama because they are expressive forms of human personal and social behavior, and because drama is itself a game or a play activity. The use of games is therefore not only a means of technical training and of exploring human behaviour and acting, but a springboard for exploring the nature of drama and theatre. This creates the bridge over which one may cross in rehearsal from improvised games to the performance of the structured play."[31]

In many respects Barker synthesizes ideas inherent in the practice of Stanislavski and Copeau concerning the use of improvisation as a means of preparatory exploration of a written text. Although Barker does not deny the efficacy of improvisation as a way of imaginatively and physically exploring in rehearsal the dramatic situation encoded in a written text, he cautions against the "magic faith" that some practitioners have in improvisation to solve performance problems without engaging in serious work with the text. The chief problem in doing improvisations on situations analogous to those in the play, or in improvising the play in the actors' own words, is the possibility that a play will be created different from that determined by the written text. After the excitement and freedom of the improvisation sessions, actors often encounter the same blocks they initially experienced when confronted by the text. Their substitution of a mere facsimile of the *results* of the improvisation may threaten to generalize or replace the dynamic performance of particular actions as structured by the text: "The fallacy lies in believing that improvisation is a process of pure inspiration and intuition. The body/think will only react as it has been programmed to react. If it has not been programmed with a mass of material about the play, the situations, the characters and their interrelationships it will only produce the material it has, which will naturally relate directly to the here and now, the situation in which the actor is actually present, along with a mass of cliché responses he has learned from other situations. This is not improvisation. It is 'mugging.'"[32]

Similar skepticism about the value of improvisation in the performance of written texts was expressed by Michel Saint-Denis. From the perspective of a voice and speech specialist, Cicely Berry's explanation of the actor's difficulties in articulating, through the language of the text, points of characterization initially discovered by means of analysis and improvisation reflects the problem that Barker is identifying.[33] Barker's games and improvisations are undertaken not so much to discover in the written text what may easily be gleaned by reading and analysis, but to free the actor's psychophysical apparatus (including the faculty of imagination) so that it is unhindered by the stress that is a normal part of daily life and by the nervous tension that Stanislavski first recognized as a central problem occasioned by the performance situation.

According to Barker, "Theatre centres upon the ritual transformation of one human being into another, conditioned by considerations of time, space and character which are not those of the person undergoing the transformation."[34] Games based on incarnating the process of evolution, or pretending to be a child, a monster, or one of the seven deadly sins, are used to free the imagination through taking on the physical and mental characteristics of another creature without the inhibiting self-consciousness produced by a detailed or subtle character study. Barker's games of imagination and fantasy stimulate the performer to express internal states of thought and feeling in terms of overt physical sensation, thus preventing the mind/body split that can occur when an actor has analyzed a character and has to translate his mental image directly into stage action. Starting from relatively simple imaginative transformations, the actor can progressively be led to construct more difficult transformations into complex characters.

Once actors have begun to develop strategies for imagining and externalizing character, they will need help in shaping the action and interaction contained within the scenes of a play. *Theatre Games* includes games that create different models of meetings and encounters as well as communication improvisations to enable actors to learn how to deal with interaction in performance. The Chairs is a game designed to teach an actor the effect of making eye-to-eye contact (i.e., establishing a relationship) with another actor while attempting to execute an action when his mind is preoccupied with something outside the immediate situation. The aim is for one player to move another (who does not resist) from a seated position in one chair to others set at intervals of three or four yards apart. When the game is repeated, the player who leads must think about something unconnected with the actual situation. During a second repeat the leader must move his partner as quickly as possible—orienting himself toward a future intention.

After reversing roles, another group repeat the exercise with one variation during the first and second repetitions. The player being moved is required to catch the eye of his partner at some point, invariably causing some kind of break in concentration. Barker regards this as an extremely important exercise. Since it involves all the major elements of dramatic performance, including intention, subtextual thought, and character interaction focused on specific physical activity, it models the state of divided attention experienced on stage, testing the performer's ability to interact spontaneously with other actors while executing a learned pattern of physical activity.

He describes other games directly designed to make performers experiment with eye-to-eye contact, before outlining the game of Touch your Partner, which involves attempts to touch one's partner in the small of his back without letting him touch one's own back. No other physical contact is permitted. Touch your Partner is an elementary conflict game that requires each opponent to assess the behavior patterns of the other in order to plan a successful attack and maintain a satisfactory defense. The most primitive instincts are also brought into play, but faculties of calculation and observation are employed in a highly sophisticated way. Barker believes that the audience experiences a performance kinesthetically: The "strongest audience response comes when the actors are meeting and interacting on the stage, and imaginatively invoking in their bodies the kinaesthetic sensations of the dramatic encounter they are portraying. If the actors are merely repeating the patterns of some past situation (as will happen if the production is "fixed" definitively in rehearsal), or if they are consciously preoccupied with reflective thoughts or intentions, then the audience cannot respond to the flow of interaction. All they can do is follow the stage pictures and the literal meaning of the spoken text."[35] In order to engage the empathy of each spectator to the fullest possible extent, Barker believes the performers must be fully interactive, allowing character to reveal itself in action rather than being illustrated in a series of posed tableaux.[36]

Conflicts in meetings and encounters can be made more complex by varying the basic game structures so that a group plays them as street scenes. Explorations of triangular relationships are possible through the enactment of situations in which three performers attempt to communicate without the use of words. The dynamics and strategies of social interaction are experienced in the actors' bodies, with emphasis varying from direct physical activity to more internalized mental and emotional conflicts, adjustments, and interrelationships. Communication improvisations are employed to assist in the process whereby the actor *inhabits* the words designated for the character to speak. Barker recognizes a widespread tendency among actors to repeat the text mechanically after learning the lines, even after a lengthy period of improvisation. "The principal use of improvisation, as far as I am concerned, is to overcome the actors' failure to penetrate the text to the actions which underlie it."[37] He is, however, fairly skeptical about the usefulness of free improvisation to rectify the problem, because he observes that on returning to the text after doing the improvisations, actors still tend to become inhibited by the sheer technical difficulty of using the writer's words to express intentions and feelings that they have discovered for themselves in the games and improvisations. Although Barker refers to various types of improvisations currently used to promote convincing communication by means of the prescribed words of the written text, he identifies potential problems inherent in each approach.

A common solution adopted by directors to the difficulty of speaking the words in such a way that they appear to spring spontaneously from the characters' interactions within a scene, is to ask the actors to paraphrase the dramatic situation in their own words. According to Barker, this often ends up in a very vague approximation of the interactions within the scene if (as is usually the case) it is too early in the rehearsal process for the actors to have a full grasp of the detailed intentions and circumstances of the characters in the play.[38] If used later in the rehearsal process, the improvised dialogue can end up being mere verbalization, since the actors become anxious to account for everything that is expressed in the scene in their own words. Barker finds the work of the sociologist Erving Goffman particularly helpful as a basis for exploring interactions in which characters are disguising their intentions from one another.[39]

Improvisations on analogous situations to those in the play are not favored by Barker, because they threaten to substitute for the terms and tensions of the specific scenic interactions, imagined details of other situations that can never satisfactorily match the precise actions that give rise to the actual words of the text. Barker considers the use of exercises in which nonsense words replace the actual words of the text, but points out the danger that such exercises may encourage excessive emotional coloring of language (although he accepts that such coloring may be appropriate when working with banal texts). Barker does, however, favor "non-existent languages" as a way of sensitizing actors to the multidimensional role of language within situations of human interaction.[40] By improvising a situation from a play in a pastiche of an existing language that they cannot speak but will have heard (such as Russian), performers can be made to simulate the real thought processes that express themselves in speech rather than merely parodying speech acts in a nonsense language. Games are devised with such nonexistent languages to approximate real communication situations in which people have to communicate without speaking one another's language, thus placing emphasis on the psychological and social impulses to communicate that determine actual speech.

Barker's adaptation of children's games for actor training gives precise and detailed content to the ideas of Copeau and Saint-Denis concerning the play of movement and speech. It is Barker's view that actors perform a function akin to that of social scientists. Since play is a fundamental learning activity, the actor is an expert in the strategies of observation and imitation of human behavior through which social and psychological insight is acquired in everyday life, and is therefore in a unique position to provide raw material for analysis and theorization by sociologists and psychologists.

Theater games offer concrete action structures through which psychological and sociological theories can be experimentally tested and demonstrated. The practice of Joint Stock Theatre Company (directed by William Gaskill and Max Stafford-Clark) in many respects exemplified Barker's notion of the actor as social scientist. When Caryl Churchill asked the actors of Joint Stock to improvise material that they had derived both from their own life experience and from their reading about and observation of other cultures (the behavior of people working in the stock market in the mid-1980s for *Serious Money;* the people's liberation from the Ceauşescu regime in Romania and its impact on social life in the early 1990s for *Mad Forest*), she was in effect employing actors as anthropologists, utilizing their various performance skills to enable genuine research into human behavior under particular historical circumstances. The fact that these same actors later performed the plays for which this research was the starting point gave a heightened sense of precision and authenticity to the theatrical performance.

From the 1970s onwards, a number of British practitioners (most famously Mike Leigh) have worked with actors to create plays and films from improvisation and game-playing exercises. The methods of these practitioners involve an extension of work initiated independently by Stanislavski and Copeau, and utilize the approaches to the performer's process of work of contemporaries such as Spolin and Johnstone in order to develop new ways of making theater. Leigh's adherence to naturalism as a theatrical form has perhaps allied his work closely with the improvisations aimed at fleshing out a character invented by Stanislavski, but British groups such as Theatre Machine, Theatre de Complicité, Trestle, and Improbable Theatre have explored the use of improvisation and games in the tradition of practice stemming from Copeau and exemplified in the teaching of Spolin, Johnstone, and Lecoq. In this tradition, practitioners invent dramatic scenarios that possess a surrealistic logic as a means of creating non-naturalistic languages of physical theater.[41]

The Impact of Jacques Lecoq

The training school that exerted the most profound and widespread influence on Continental European and British theater-making during the 1990s is the École Jacques Lecoq in Paris. A majority of contemporary British and French theater groups who devise performances on the basis of improvisation derive their working methods from the practice of Lecoq. His teaching has stimulated the growth of companies devoted to devised or physical theater around the world. As a result of the international prestige of companies such as Ariane Mnouchkine's Théâtre du Soleil, Steven Berkoff's London Theatre Group, and the London-based Theatre de Complicité, his methods are being disseminated in many areas of mainstream theater.[42]

Play as Methodology

Lecoq died in 1999, but his influence continues to spread. His work was neither entirely original nor thoroughly systematic. His genius was to provoke and inspire students with a non-naturalistic alternative to devising and improvising performance. At its core was Copeau's notion of play as first principle of the dramatic imagination. Like Copeau, Lecoq made no hard-and-fast distinctions between writing, acting, scenography, and directing. Performance was for him indistinguishable from all other facets of theater-making. Acting was performance, and performance incorporated a full range of skills of improvisation, devising, writing, and scenography. Lecoq's school inculcates in its students the aesthetic values of simplicity, authenticity, and creative play acquired by Lecoq during the course of his own training at the hands of disciples of Copeau. His own particular improvisational and clowning skills were elaborated while working in Padua and (with Giorgio Strehler) in Milan between 1948 and 1956.[43] His initial training as a teacher of physical education predisposed him to regard movement as the basis of actor training; in its own way Lecoq's approach can be comprehended as a bridge between movement training and the improvisational games of practitioners such as Keith Johnstone. Lecoq seems not to have direct knowledge of Laban's praxis; nevertheless many of his ideas are parallel to those of Laban, overlapping at times, but never achieving the systematic coherence of Laban's conceptual framework. The advantage of Lecoq's approach is that the play principle guarantees fun and appeals to the actor's imagination in ways that Laban's systematic but rather dry exposition seldom does.[44]

Although not scientific in the same sense that Laban or Stanislavski attempted to be, Lecoq nevertheless clearly established an underlying rationale for the deployment of the strategies represented by each of his exercises:

- The developmental method, going from the simplest to the most complex;
- The transfer method, moving from physical technique to dramatic expression (dramatic justification for physical actions, transfer of natural dynamics to characters and situations);

- Expansion and reduction of gestures, from equilibrium to respiration;
- Scales and levels of acting;
- Linking of gesture and voice;
- Economy of movements, accidents and detours;
- Passage from the real to the imaginary;
- The discovery of play and its rules (the rules arising out of play itself);
- The method of constraints (spatial, temporal, and numerical).[45]

In utilizing an approach via the principle of play, Lecoq encouraged the student actor to treat performance as a psychophysical process, interrelating the psychological, physical, and social aspects of the performing body, through an experience of the integration of all the faculties of the histrionic instrument in relation to the surrounding space. Lecoq's approach was underpinned by Copeau's fundamental belief that acting was not a technology that could be acquired through a purely mechanical training, but an art that deployed the complete resources of the imagination. It therefore involved the actor's cultivation of the means of corporeal expression as an aspect of his whole being.

Discovering the Performing Identity

Lecoq's experience as director and movement trainer led him to explore a wide range of theatrical styles and modes, which were formative in his development of a non-naturalistic approach to performance. Two specific approaches can be seen as keys to the comprehension of all of Lecoq's training strategies. The discovery of the individual performer's unique stage identity (or clown) was the aim of the "psychological play" undertaken at the earliest stage of training, just as the deployment of the neutral mask (developed from Copeau's noble mask) aimed to *form* the actor's instrument of corporeal expression into a "poetic body." Insofar as Lecoq could have been said to have a *system* of training, self-discovery occurred by means of the interweaving of these two approaches. Each utilized the trial-and-error playing that motivated the process of Copeau's training for the dramatic imagination. Mask work effected an apparently organic process in which the aesthetic (as opposed to the social body) is recognized and cultivated, while psychological play abstracted from social experience to identify and perfect the persona that most succinctly expressed each performer's creative attitude. Both creative strategies aimed to distance the actor from the factitious mimesis characteristic of film and television naturalism. In place of the literal mimicry of everyday behavior they privileged the type of histrionic play that is a fundamental human instinct. Whether grotesque, comic, surrealist, or realistic, Lecoq's approach was never naturalistic, since it was based on the notion of *performing* rather than *imitating*.

Like Copeau and Michel Saint-Denis, Lecoq did not aim for the methodical inculcation of a coherently structured system, but promoted learning through a psychodynamic process of directed play that stimulated each performer to discover his own individual potential by actual experimentation with the performing body in space and time. The acquisition of technique was not divorced from the processes of rehearsal or creation. A holistic process of theater-making was the basis of the learning experience, so that learning might occur both consciously and unconsciously through practice of the art form in protected situations. The performer learned to be fully present in each moment. Spontaneity in performance was a result of risk-taking in the moment-to-moment decisions that determine improvisational acting. The performer learned to maintain the sense of immediacy in performance by preserving the danger that made him vulnerable in the situation of live performance. Having to respond immediately in the act of performance to other performers and to the audience, the individual perfected the skills of ensemble performance. Performers were to experience the truism that the whole is greater than the sum of its parts through the arduous experience of developing their abilities in front of others. In order to facilitate the process of learning through actual creation, the syllabus of the École Jacques Lecoq included the *auto-cours,* a year in which students devoted themselves wholly to the production of their own creative work.

Lecoq conceived the particular strategies for actualizing the methodologies of improvisation and corporeal training as a journey. Beginning in the first year with silent "psychological play," the student progressed a little later to neutral mask work. This facilitated a sequence of work that involved corporeal expression of responses to stimuli encountered in the natural environment, or derived from artworks and social interaction.

Work on style continued by way of exercises on gestural languages, and was formalized through the exploration of Lecoq's five chief generic categories ("dramatic territories") of melodrama, commedia dell'arte, *bouffons,* tragedy, and clowning, in the second year. The third year was entirely dedicated to the *auto-cours.*

Psychological Play

Lecoq's idiosyncratic use of the terms *play* and *replay* explains his notion of psychological play. At the most basic level, improvisations were created on the basis of the performer's observation of other people's social behavior:

Students at the Lecoq School improvising with larval masks. Photo by Patrick Lecoq.

"Replay involves reviving lived experience in the simplest possible way. Avoiding both transposition and exaggeration, remaining strictly faithful to reality and to the student's own psychology, with no thought for spectators, the students bring a simple situation to life, a classroom, a market place, a hospital, the metro. *Play* [acting] comes later, at a point when, aware of the theatrical dimension, the actor can shape an improvisation for spectators, using rhythm, tempo, space, form. . . . *Play* may be very close to *replay* . . . but it must never lose sight of the root anchoring it to reality."[46] The relationship between play and replay signaled the equipoise between the close observation of reality and the performer's free embracing of theatrical style. As soon as the performer had quoted reality in the form of "restored behaviour," he was encouraged to shape it through the application of a wide range of artistic techniques and theatrical styles.[47]

As always, Lecoq's emphasis was on the material and social world rather than on the introspective exploration of subjective experience. Many of his games involved the reintegration of the performer within a harmony of the physical environment at an elemental level. The neutral mask allowed the actor to step back from the habits acquired in the spontaneous experience of social life and to deploy an expressive movement vocabulary. The actor was thus taught to play characters from the outside rather than to attempt a psychological identification with a role. Although not a self-conscious distancing as in the Brechtian *verfremdungseffekt* this strategy provided the performer with an artistic perspective. This transcendence of the everyday process of mimicry that characterizes social role-play promoted the actor's ability to *interpret* and *portray* characters rather than spontaneously to *incarnate* them.[48]

The Neutral Mask as Catalyst

Lecoq's development of Copeau's noble mask as the neutral mask has made a great impact on the physical training of performers in Europe during the last twenty years. Once the performer had begun to experience the "poetic" body through the distancing created by the wearing of the mask, he was liberated to start creating, from a position of complete artistic freedom, a neutrality that did not efface his personality but allowed him consciously (aesthetically) to exploit and channel the body/mind as an instrument. A series of phases of corporeal training followed as a logical extension of work with the neutral mask. Like Craig, Meyerhold, Copeau, Saint-Denis, and Eugenio Barba, Lecoq assumed the primacy of the performer's body as an aestheticized instrument divorced from the artist's social persona. This approach was opposed to the underlying assumption common to Stanislavski, Vakhtangov, Strasberg, Laban, Boal, and Grotowski that the performer's histrionic personality is an extension of his socialized body. While demanding that the performer learn to identify a principle of neutrality that motivates the corporeal level of performance, Lecoq wisely avoided the temptation to valorize neutrality as an ethical principle in performance—a temptation to which Copeau's asceticism rendered him peculiarly susceptible:[49] "Of course students also need to have their own point of view. In their work they must have ideas and opinions. . . . Starting from an accepted reference point, which is neutral, the students discover their own point of view. Of course there is no such thing as absolute and universal neutrality, it is merely a temptation."[50]

The wearing of the mask would permit the student performer to distance himself from his everyday (socialized) sense of self. The social personality could be placed in parenthesis through an effacing of physiognomy that at the same time foregrounded the whole body as expressive instrument—"so the face becomes the whole body."[51] Central to the ethos of experiential learning, the neutral mask taught the student principles of "balance and economy" in movement. For Lecoq, work with the neutral mask offered a significant model of "indirect" learning. It allowed the teacher to hold back—to eschew didactic explanation that restricted the flow of a student's imagination, preventing individual creative discoveries by inculcating the notion of a right way of performing an exercise or mastering a technique. There was in the corporeal training outlined by Lecoq a strong relationship between the phenomenological factors of space and time and the actor's own sensibility. Neutral mask work was not concerned with human relationships but with the individual's participation in the world. Actions and themes were essentialized in the neutral mask, freeing the performer to become a psychophysical instrument engaged in a spontaneous process of artistic composition/selection.

Lecoq adumbrated a series of simple themes to be performed by the masked performer. Starting with farewells, the student progressed to the core motif in neutral mask work—"the fundamental journey" in which the individual performer progressed through a day in the natural world, miming the physical challenges of all the different geographical and ecological conditions. The student learned to participate through the body in different natural conditions, so that the next stages of work in the mask could develop different "identifications." Work on the *elements*—air, water, earth and fire—enabled the performer's body to participate in their dynamic qualities, while exercises on *materials* created a physical engagement with the sensuous textures of reality. The performer learned to participate in natural "life" processes by experiencing them in and through the body. Direct mimicry of objects and forces of nature helped the performer to identify with and embody the *qualities* of energy and the phenomenological textures experienced in nature. Students observed everyday materials such as liquids (e.g., water, mercury, acids, honey) and solids (wood, glass, paper, rubber) in preparation for a representation of their *qualities*. Physical representation of the form of these materials, and the possibilities of transforming them, developed a sensibility that located itself in the actor's body. As students progressed through the first year from a bodily exploration of the world of nature to a psychophysical engagement with the arts, they acquired a vocabulary of felt experiences that enabled the cultivation of the "universal poetic sense."[52] In so doing, student performers learned to become "architects of the inner life." At that point the phase of neutral mask training was complete.

Lecoq used the *transference method* to transpose the dynamic qualities of natural phenomena or animals onto human behavior or to ground it in the energy of natural elements, animals, or materials. By exercises in transposition, performers learned to access the kinds of energy "engraved" in their bodies, activating the many "traces" of experience stored in body-memory. Although Lecoq focused on the body as site of the imagination, he was skeptical of mime's development into a virtuoso art form. He was therefore careful to distinguish his use of *open mime* and its *mimages* (physical expressions of inner states) from mime as a generic form. Lecoq's manifold use of miming had more affinities with Laban's practice of effort dynamics and with Brecht's composition through *gests* than it did with the stylistic vocabulary of Noh drama or the French art of mime as exemplified by Marcel Marceau. "To mime is literally to embody and therefore to understand better. . . . The action of miming becomes a form of knowledge. . . . Every true artist is a mime. . . . There is a submerged form of mime which gives rise to different creative acts in all the arts. . . . For me mime is an integral part of theatre, not a separate art form. The mime which I love involves an identification with things in order to make them live, even when words are used."[53]

In working with the neutral mask, the performer acquired a body memory of all the identifications made through the miming of elements, materials, and animals. In this way, the body became a psychophysical locus inscribed as a living network of experiential traces, incorporating the various identifications felt in the body in its empathic relationship to the world around.

Dramatic Territories

Lecoq's own early theater experience encompassed a wide spectrum of dramatic modes and theatrical styles. The stylistic eclecticism that underpinned his approach to training implied a rejection of dominant traditions of naturalistic acting and a desire to recuperate the full range of dramaturgical conventions manifest throughout history. Thus the two-year training specifically addressed the five principal "dramatic territories" Lecoq had explored in his early professional work: melodrama, commedia dell'arte, *bouffons* (Lecoq's term for the type of grotesque humor that combines parody and mystery with a Rabelaisian attitude to the social body), tragedy, and clowning. In addition, he aimed to teach the varieties of comedy, although he never made a clear distinction between clowning and other styles of comic acting. These "dramatic territories" he had himself explored in various ways, using mime and contemporary music for political agit-prop, and investigating silent film acting, Greek tragedy in outdoor theaters, varieties of clowning and acrobatic skills, and later researching the impact of architecture on the spatial dimension of performance.

In many respects, Lecoq's artistic and pedagogical principles involved a systematic application of Copeau's approach to training the dramatic imagination through improvisation and play, although it is evident that Lecoq was less puritanical and more eclectic in developing the histrionic sensibility. Since Copeau, practitioners and educationalists have exploited the inherently human propensity for play in many different ways, utilizing the creative potential of games to promote learning as well as artistic creation.

8. Brechtian Theater as Political Praxis

Bertolt Brecht is arguably the single most influential figure of twentieth-century European theater. Virtually all left-wing theories of political theater since the Second World War have owed something to Brecht's praxis. As playwright and director, his innovations in the fields of dramaturgy, acting, theater theory, production, and design were both subtle and radical, involving a new attitude to the form and function of theatrical art. Given the widespread knowledge of a number of Brecht's plays, it is ironic that his production praxis has been a subject of persistent misunderstanding.

One of the many misconceptions of Brecht's theater is that it is didactic and, therefore, inevitably dull. Apart from the Puritan opposition of learning (serious) versus entertainment (frivolous) that underlies this prejudice, it misses both the tone and the fundamental attitude of Brechtian performance, which he himself never tired of emphasizing. *Fun* (in German, *Spass*) was the word he had used since the early 1920s to describe the means through which the performer should engage the spectator, and he used it in his last note to the Berliner Ensemble as they prepared for their first visit to London in August 1956, ten days before he died.

Even before Brecht first used the term *epic theater* and began reading Marx, he had written a number of essays and reviews outlining his desire for a "smoker's theater" where the stupefied inertia induced in the audience by the escapist fantasies of the bourgeois art theater would be replaced by the alert, detached and critical attitude of spectators at a boxing match: "*A theatre which makes no contact with the public is a nonsense. Our theatre is accordingly a nonsense.* . . . There is no theatre today that could invite one or two of those persons who are alleged to find fun in writing plays to one of its performances and expect them to feel an urge to write a play for it. They can see at a glance that there is no possible way of getting any *fun* out of this. No wind will go into anyone's sails here. There is no 'sport.'"[1]

As a writer, Brecht was reacting to the "hypnotic" effects induced by the sophisticated performance conventions of the modern German drama, whether naturalistic or expressionistic in form. Whereas naturalism stressed the total coherence of the theatrical illusion, expressionism emphasized the subjective power of the spectator's complete identification with the emotions of the leading actors. Both theaters functioned by exploiting the empathy between actor and spectator. The necessity of replacing the bourgeois theater with a form that actually expressed the realities of twentieth-century life was felt by no practitioner more urgently than Brecht: "The theatre of our parasitic bourgeoisie . . . 'conjures up' the illusion that it is reflecting real-life incidents with a view to achieving more or less primitive shock effects or hazily defined sentimental moods which in fact are to be consumed as substitutes for the missing spiritual experiences of a crippled and cataleptic audience."[2]

Clearly, Brecht's aim was to create an alternative to this theater of emotional manipulation and escapist illusions. Laughter was a necessary weapon in the armory of the new type of theater. Years later, in the *Messingkauf Dialogues,* Brecht expressed this view succinctly: "A theatre that can't be laughed in is a theatre to laugh at. Humourless people are ridiculous."[3] As a spectator, Brecht found a sense of *Spass,* not in any of the sophisticated art theaters, but in popular entertainment forms such as cabaret, silent films, sports matches, music-hall clowning, and street performance.

From Popular Entertainment to Epic Performance

One of Brecht's early idols was the playwright and cabaret singer Frank Wedekind. While his own early plays *Baal* (1918), *Drums in the Night* (1922), and *In the Jungle of the Cities* (1923) reveal the influence of Wedekind's grotesque and ironic dramaturgical style, Brecht's tribute to Wedekind, published in the local Augsburg newspaper three days after his death in March 1918, clearly indicated the qualities Brecht valued—and even imitated—in a performer:[4] "[Wedekind] sang his songs to guitar accompaniment in a brittle voice, slightly monotonous and quite untrained. No singer ever gave me such a shock, such a thrill. It was the man's intense aliveness, the energy which allowed him to defy sniggering ridicule and proclaim his brazen hymn to humanity, that also gave him this personal magic. . . . His greatest work was his own personality."[5] One can recognize, as early as 1918, the characteristics that were to become definitive features of the Brechtian mode of performance. Employed by Brecht as a component of his Marxist aesthetic from 1927, this approach originally constituted a spontaneous reaction against the "feigned intensity" of the "panic-driven, artificially whipped-up band of actors" he described eight years later in an article in the *Berliner Boursen-Courier*.[6]

Above all, Wedekind's performance was marked by his personality. The idea that the actor should present a strong personality to the audience was the first tenet of Brechtian acting. Whereas Stanislavski went to great lengths to invent techniques to submerge the actor's personality so that only the character remains apprehensible, Brecht demanded that the actor maintain the attitude of a popular entertainer who consciously *shows* us the character and *tells* us the story. There is no hint of the depersonalized attitude or flat delivery often assumed to typify the earnest didacticism of Brechtian performance—quite the contrary. Brecht admired the vitality and energy of Wedekind's delivery. But equally, he emphasized the performer's extraordinarily direct contact with the audience: "when I heard him give a reading of *Herakles,* his last work, I was amazed at his brazen energy. . . . he read those verses . . . looking deep into the eyes of each of us in turn as we listened to him."[7]

The direct relationship with the audience—again, a complete contradiction of Stanislavski's idea that the actor had to develop techniques that would permit her to seem wholly unaware of its presence—was to become another definitive feature of the Brechtian actor's art. Brecht's admiration of the songs, sketches, and comic mimes performed by the Munich comedian Karl Valentin in a beer hall suggests that cabaret and music hall performance, rather than traditional theater, was an important source of Brecht's developing notion of theatrical performance. Brecht commented that as "one of the most penetrating spiritual forces of the period, [Valentin] brings vividly before our eyes the complexity of the interconnections between imperturbability, stupidity and *joie-de-vivre,*"[8] and praised the comedian for his "virtually complete rejection of mimicry and cheap psychology"—a characteristic jibe against the fake authenticity of naturalistic theater.[9] In 1949, he proudly claimed that as producer he had copied "the music hall comedian Karl Valentin's groupings," which suggests not only how sophisticated the comedian's art may have been, but also how alert Brecht was to the possibility of exploiting popular art forms in creating his own intellectually complex mise-en-scènes.[10]

The fusion of high art and popular entertainment is an index of Brecht's modernity, a further example of the way he rejected the strict division between upper-class and working-class culture that had developed in the mid–nineteenth century. The same attitude informed his enthusiasm for the films of Charlie Chaplin. In his diary, he noted his response to Chaplin's

The Face on the Bar-Room Floor, which he saw in Berlin in 1921: "the most profoundly moving thing I've ever seen in the cinema: utterly simple. . . . it's unadulterated art . . . of a quite alarming objectivity and sadness."[11] Already one can sense in the paradoxical juxtaposition of objectivity and sadness the dialectical tension between reason and emotion that characterized Brecht's approach to the actor's presentation of feelings.

Chaplin's technique of silent comedy offered an example of the kind of physical acting that would be useful in creating an epic theater performance. Brecht's notes to his play *Man Equals Man* explained how the epic actor physically demonstrates the logic of contradictions that informs the changing behavior of a character as conceived in an epic drama.[12] In them he asserted, "The actor Chaplin . . . would in many ways come closer to the epic than to the dramatic theatre's requirements."[13] Three years later, in an interview given for a Danish newspaper, Chaplin is used as the model for epic acting: "[The] only form of acting that I find natural [is] the epic, storytelling kind. It's the kind the Chinese have been using for thousands of years: among modern actors Chaplin is one of its masters. . . . The actor doesn't have to *be* the man he portrays. He has to describe his character just as it would be described in a book. If Chaplin were to play Napoleon he wouldn't even look like him; he would show, objectively and critically how Napoleon would behave in the various situations the author might put him in. In my view the great comedians have always been the best character actors."[14] Clearly, Brecht's notion of epic performance exploited the comedian's attitude and technique as a method of presenting character. His unreserved enthusiasm for a range of popular performance forms argues for a notion of performance based on wit, irony, and clowning, in short, the objectivity of the comic performer. However, his unqualified admiration for Chaplin includes an acknowledgment of his pathos, giving the lie to criticism that suggests that the seriousness of Brecht's political project and its stress on reason must inevitably render his theater cold, unemotional, and boring.

Brecht's Reasons for Theorizing His Practice

Attempts by practitioners to perform Brecht's plays routinely founder on the failure to understand the relationship between his dramaturgy and his theories of performance. In desperation, many actors and directors deliberately ignore anything Brecht said or wrote about the theater in order to find their own solutions to the problems of staging the plays. Lacking understanding of Brecht's peculiar attitude to dramatic form, the majority of such approaches undermine the political meanings in the plays and, as a result of their failure to grasp the specifically Marxist ideas inscribed within Brecht's numerous idiosyncratic dramaturgical effects, end up eliciting empathy from the spectator instead of promoting the required critical attitude.

An alternative approach is to follow Brecht's instructions precisely, using notes and photographs that he left in the form of *Modellbücher* (model books) for a number of plays in order to re-create as closely as possible how the Berliner Ensemble might have performed them under Brecht's direction. This method commonly results in productions that are boring and lifeless, with actors mouthing the words as political slogans, in a determined effort to act as the author's mouthpiece, rather than entering into the dialectical game that provides the pleasure of the play as a performance. Since it is well known that Brecht regularly rewrote both his own and other people's plays as well as revising productions in relation to changing historical circumstances, it is hardly likely that he would have recommended slavish adherence for all time to his own model of production. On the other hand, it would make no sense to create a detailed record of a production if one did not intend it to have any function in establishing guidelines for interpreting the work in performance.

The theoretical essays that Brecht produced throughout his working life were intended to explain to actors and directors the rationale behind his new approach to dramaturgy and theatrical staging—a new aesthetic he correctly assumed would be neither recognized nor appreciated by the majority of practitioners and theatergoers in Germany and elsewhere. In reply to the repeated criticism that his theory was "over-intellectual, clever-clever . . . abstract . . . [and had] nothing to do with real life," identified in Brecht's "Short List of the Most Frequent, Common and Boring Misconceptions about the Epic Theatre," he explained his understanding of the relationship between his practice and its theory: "In fact it arose from and is associated with many years of practical activity. . . . The plays . . . were acted by working-class groups and by stars; there was a special theatre, the Theater am Schiffbauerdamm, with a company of actors . . . who developed these principles. Piscator's two theatres developed some of them too."[15] Some years later, he commented, "Most of the remarks, if not all, were written as notes to my plays, to allow them to be correctly performed."[16]

While a bourgeois audience in a capitalist society was bound to be not merely baffled by Brecht's aesthetic, but actually hostile to it, his ideas eventually came to define the terms of the major modern tradition of oppositional theater. Early in his career Brecht understood clearly that his new form of dramaturgy could not succeed without a total renovation of the existing forms and conventions of the theater, and from 1927 he consciously set about trying to transform both the theater institution and the attitudes of its audience: "The modern theatre mustn't be judged by its success in satisfying the audience's habits but by its success in transforming them. It needs to be questioned not about its degree of conformity with the 'eternal laws of the theatre' but about its ability to master the rules governing the great social processes of our age; not about whether it manages to interest the spectator in buying a ticket—i.e. in the theatre itself—but about whether it manages to interest him in the world."[17]

Brecht summed up the modernity of his approach to theater in the slogan "theatre for a scientific age." By this he meant the Einsteinian science of relativity rather than the positivistic certainties of nineteenth-century science. He argued for a theater that was not only capable of grasping and interrogating economic and political processes as conceived by twentieth-century social science, but one whose very form might induce in its spectators an attitude of active engagement with the world and the possibilities for changing it.

During the Cold War the overtly Marxist nature of Brecht's aesthetic praxis caused as much of a problem for Western scholars and practitioners as the unfamiliar form of his dramaturgy had done for German audiences before the Second World War. Since many of the plays that Brecht had written in exile between 1933 and 1947 (after which he resumed his work as a director in Europe) were acknowledged as masterpieces of dramatic writing, various strategies were employed by Western critics to interpret his plays in the terms of bourgeois theater. The most common was the idea that Brecht's best plays did not actually adhere to his own theories, that his instincts as a dramatic poet somehow allowed him to triumph over the dogma and didacticism of his Marxist ideology.

Ironically, Communist critics were simultaneously taking Brecht to task for what they perceived as his formalism—a refusal to represent the victory of Communism in the prescribed form of socialist realism that became the aesthetic norm of the Stalinist period. Brecht had first expressed his divergence from Communist aesthetic orthodoxy in 1938 in a rejoinder to an essay on the realist novel by Georg Lukács, who in 1934 had initiated what became a long-standing debate between expressionism and realism in the German émigré journal *Das Wort:* "Literary forms have to be checked against reality, not against aesthetics—even realist aesthetics. There are many ways of suppressing reality, and many ways of stating it."[18]

It must be borne in mind that Brecht's praxis was a response to particular historical circumstances. As those circumstances changed, so too did his political and aesthetic attitudes. While a Marxist orientation determined the fundamental principles of his practice, this orientation was one that itself emphasized the effects of changing historical circumstances on people's beliefs and behavior. Logically, it is only to be expected that Brecht's ideas were constantly developing in a dialectical relationship to changing circumstances. Communist orthodoxy was certainly not a possible option for an artist as sophisticated as Brecht.

Principles of Epic Performance

The term *epic* was first applied to the theater by the innovative director Erwin Piscator, who was largely responsible for making the Berlin theater of the 1920s the most technologically advanced in the world. Brecht worked as a dramaturg and co-director on a number of Piscator's productions, so he acquired knowledge of this new approach to theater production at first hand. The major innovation of Piscator's epic theater was the idea of framing the drama with relevant social and political information conveyed by means of modern communication technology such as still photographs and documentary films. By supplementing the fictional situation through which the playwright had represented social reality with facts about that society, the production provided a commentary on the representation that was intended to provoke the spectator to interrogate the playwright's argument. The sophisticated scenic technology included advanced electric lighting, a semicircular screen (cyclorama) at the rear of the stage for film projection and captions, revolving stages, and a conveyor belt. This technology was openly displayed to the spectator's view, signifying the theater's determination to represent the economic, social, and political factors motivating the action of the play in modern scientific terms.

Brecht shared Piscator's belief in the new methodological possibilities offered by epic theater as an instrument for analyzing social reality and a forum for promoting social change. Brecht, however, was to transform this concept into the image of theater as a laboratory for experimenting with the possibilities of changing society. By refunctioning not merely the technical methods of production, but the form of the fictional representation itself—both dramaturgy and acting—Brecht revolutionized every aspect of theatrical production. In the works that he wrote with Kurt Weill, notably *The Threepenny Opera* (1929) and *The Rise and Fall of the City of Mahagonny* (1930), Brecht experimented with a radical redefinition of the Wagnerian *Gesamtkunstwerk,* a model of musical drama that dictated the "high art" conventions of the German musical stage.

By exploiting the spectacular devices of Piscator's total theater, including elements such as music, song, and dance, Brecht deconstructed a form that he regarded as "culinary theatre" whose aim was to gratify the hedonistic needs of the bourgeoisie for escapist pleasure. Instead of trying to replace this musical theater with a purely didactic form of epic theater, Brecht and Weill attempted, as it were, to subvert the bourgeois form of opera from within, by parodying its decadent romanticism and satirizing the gross materialism of its audience: "As for the content of this opera [*Mahagonny*], *its content is pleasure.* Fun, in other words, not only as form but as subject-matter. At least enjoyment was meant to be the object of the enquiry even if the enquiry was intended to be an object of enjoyment. Enjoyment here appears in its historical role: as merchandise."[19]

Burlesque of the decadent form of opera produced a grotesque metatheatricality intended to destroy the old form. By revealing its emotional intensity as a tawdry lie, opera was exposed as an escapist palliative that masked reality in order to keep the bourgeois consumer satisfied with the political and cultural status quo. *The Threepenny Opera* mocked the debased consumerist version of the *Gesamtkunstwerk,* substituting the rude vitality of street performance and cabaret for the portentous and intrinsically vulgar sentimentalism of early-twentieth-century opera. Whereas the Wagnerian form aimed at the synthesis of all other art forms (acting, music, poetry, painting, dance) Brecht and Weill separated each of the forms, juxtaposing one element against another in distinct opposition, allowing the lyrics, for example, to comment upon the music rather than being absorbed into its effect: "When the epic theatre's methods begin to penetrate the opera the first result is a radical *separation of the elements.* . . . so long as the arts are supposed to be "fused" together, the various elements will all be equally degraded. . . . The process of fusion extends to the spectator, who . . . becomes a passive (suffering) part of the total work of art. Witchcraft of this sort must of course be fought against. . . . *Words, music and setting must become more independent of one another.*"[20]

Brecht's Literarization of the Theater

Piscator's exploitation of documentary techniques was refunctioned to create an effect that Brecht named *literarization.* Brecht utilized the spectatorial effect of Piscator's epic form, without adopting its genuinely documentary aims of supplying information extrinsic to the dramatic scenes. Piscator's method of framing more-or-less naturalistic scenes with documentary film and still photographs was replaced by consciously literary devices in the form of cryptic or ironic titles announcing scenes and songs. These broke the flow of the narrative and forced the spectator mentally to change gear in order to reflect on the implications of the narrative at regular intervals during the show. By such means the spectator was made now to watch the acting, then to listen to the songs that commented upon it, and at other moments to read the captions that explained key themes in each scene as well as anticipating its outcome. In this way the spectator was provoked to question the motives and significance of action in each scene, rather than having her emotions manipulated with respect to its outcome. These devices all aimed to disrupt the habitual empathy induced in the spectator by the performance and to subvert its "culinary" values, promoting instead a critically alert attitude that awakened the rational faculties and made the individual spectator actively responsible for constructing an interpretation of the performance.

In contradistinction to the Stanislavskian notion of theater, in which the drama is primarily conveyed through the interaction of characters created by the actors, with scenographic and other effects providing a convincing environment for the acting, Brecht, like Meyerhold, saw theatrical performance as a complex form of communication, in which acting constituted one among many sign systems. It was important for the actor to accept that the main aim of the performance was to communicate the point of view of the play, rather than to seduce spectators into an illusory belief in the reality of the characters' world. Acting was one of a range of different devices for telling a story that provoked reflection on its social and political meaning. Although it appears that Brecht had not yet found much opportunity to work with his actors to create the new style of acting required, his casting of such entertainers as Lotte Lenya and Ernst Busch, rather than conventional opera singers, was a startling divergence from traditional practice. The originality of Weill's counterpointing of popular and serious music and the gestic quality that allowed the music to comment upon the singing and the acting, coupled with the self-referential quality of the acting (with actors interrupting the action within a scene, as they visibly changed function to become singers), were ambitious attempts to realize Brecht's developing notion of epic performance in the fullest possible way.

Ironically, the enormous commercial success of *The Threepenny Opera* meant that, contrary to being shocked and offended by its critique of capitalism, the bourgeois audience it attacked was amused enough to accept it tongue-in-cheek. As a result, Brecht abandoned attempts to subvert the "culinary" theater, in favor of a more ascetic approach that addressed itself, not to the bourgeoisie, but to a proletarian audience. Once again, Brecht was clever enough to retain the methodology he had invented during his Piscatorian experiments, but without their quality of large-scale spectacle.

He was at this moment to employ his new theatrical devices to construct a much sparer form of didactic drama or *Lehrstück,* intended as a pedagogical method of politicizing the working class. These plays were to have no spectators. Instead students or workers were to perform the plays for themselves, as exercises in learning how to analyze reality in Marxist terms. Viewed as written texts, these little plays may appear abstract and rather dry. But performed with a full understanding of Brecht's innovative praxis, they constitute a richly suggestive model of Brechtian performance, and were indeed the matrix in which the complex, dialectical mode of his mature masterpieces was formed.

Acting became even more crucial to the success of the *Lehrstück* than it had to the large-scale epic plays, and Brecht's experiments in the writing and staging of these plays in the early 1930s are clearly reflected in the three major essays on acting written in the middle to late 1930s.

Epicizing: Acting as Storytelling

Piscator's productions had employed the device first used by constructivist art and theater of making the spectator aware of the materials from which the production was constructed in order to initiate a self-reflexive discourse on the material and technological economy of the modern. In *Man Equals Man* (1926), Brecht began to exploit this principle in even more sophisticated and self-reflexive ways to heighten the spectator's consciousness of the act of spectating in order to promote a critical awareness of the issues at stake in the drama being presented. For the actor, this meant *demonstrating* rather than *being* the character, illustrating and telling the story rather than merely being part of it. Here was Brecht's first deliberate dramaturgical exploitation of the self-conscious style of narrative presentation he had admired in the performances of Wedekind, Valentin, and Chaplin, now being employed to demonstrate the Marxist notion that the individual human ego is produced by economic and social forces, and that human beings change and can be changed according to the imperatives of specific forms of social organization.

In his notes to *Man Equals Man,* Brecht responds to criticisms of Peter Lorre's seemingly incoherent method of playing the central role of Galy Gay by pointing out that Lorre was not attempting to present the character according to the traditional methods of the "dramatic" or "Aristotelian" theater. Instead of shaping the behavioral details of the role supplied by the writer into one coherent pattern of motivation and action, Brecht explained that Lorre had used an epic style that involved grasping the dialectical relationship of the various contradictions within the character's behavior, and playing each episode as a separate *gest,* a piece of physical demonstration that showed the precise nature of the character's social attitude under the given material circumstances at that moment. The short film that Brecht had made of the "nodal points of the action"

> shows surprisingly well how exactly Lorre manages in these long speeches to mime the meaning underlying every (silent) sentence. . . . The epic theatre, with its wholly different attitude to the individual, will simply do away with the notion of the actor who "carries the play"; for the play is no longer "carried" by him in the old sense. A certain capacity for coherent and unhurried development of a leading part such as distinguished the old kind of actor, now no longer matters so much. Against that, the epic actor may possibly need an even greater range than the old stars did, for he has to be able to show his character's coherence despite, or rather by means of, interruptions and jumps . . . the various phases must be able to be clearly seen, and therefore separated; and yet this must not be achieved mechanically.[21]

The technique of the epic actor aimed to reveal not "a single unchangeable character," as was the case with naturalism, but "one which changes all the time and becomes more and more defined in course of 'this way of changing.'"[22] The problem was that since modern Aristotelian theater was founded on the double identification of spectator with actor and actor with role, the average spectator would perceive epic acting as merely incoherent. Like seventeenth- and eighteenth-century European theater, but in direct opposition to nineteenth- and twentieth-century naturalist and expressionist theater, epic theater had to use every device of dramaturgy, acting and production to prevent the flow of empathy between spectator and performer. To achieve this, the actor had to avoid becoming identified with the character she was representing, but had to use her own personality as the basis for a dramatic role that involved her as both storyteller and character. Obviously such acting demanded a conscious awareness of the audience, and a technique of playing directly to it—the technique of the popular entertainer rather than the conventional twentieth-century actor.

In "A Dialogue About Acting" published in the *Berliner Borsen-Courier* in 1929, Brecht wittily summed up the demands that his new form of epic theater made on actors.

> The actors always seem to score great successes in your plays. Are you yourself satisfied with them?
> No.

Because they act badly?

No. Because they act wrong.

How ought they to act then?

For an audience of the scientific age.

What does that mean?

Demonstrating their knowledge

Knowledge of what?

Of human relations, of human behaviour, of human capacities.

All right; that's what they need to know. But how are they to demonstrate it?

Consciously, suggestively, descriptively.

How do they do it at present?

By means of hypnosis. They go into a trance and take the audience with
them.

Give an example.

Suppose they have to act a leave-taking. They put themselves in a leave-
taking mood. They want to induce a leave-taking mood in the audience. If the séance is successful, it ends up with nobody seeing anything further, nobody learning any lessons, at best everyone
recollecting. In short, everybody feels.

That sounds almost like some erotic process. What ought it to be like,
then?

Witty. Ceremonious. Ritual. Spectator and actor ought not to approach
one another but to move apart. Each ought to move away from himself. Otherwise the element of terror necessary to all recognition is
lacking.[23]

The quality and style of epic performance is succinctly captured in
Brecht's injunction to actors to perform "consciously, suggestively, descriptively." The epic actor consciously *describes* character and *suggests* salient
details to evoke the situation in a style appropriate to a street-singer or
stand-up comic rather than a naturalistic actor. More than twenty years later
in rehearsals at the Berliner Ensemble, Brecht was in the habit of using a
verb he had coined—*epicize*—in order to indicate the precise quality of epic
performance. *Episieren* indicated the actor's art of *telling* the scene rather than
inhabiting it. Although Brecht was not in the habit of encouraging discussion of his theories when rehearsing, the actor Ekkehard Schall remembered
that he often directed actors to "epicize": "He'd say, 'Just tell me the
scene.'"[24]

The first phase in the development of Brecht's mature theory was complete once he had formulated his concept of *Verfremdung*, an idea that was already latent in his thinking as early as 1926. The significance of *Verfremdung* and the strategies for producing the *Verfremdungseffekt* were outlined in the three major essays that Brecht wrote in exile between 1935 and 1940, "Alienation Effects in Chinese Acting," "The Street Scene," and "Short Description of a New Technique of Acting which Produces an Alienation Effect."

Verfremdungseffekt as Production Praxis

"To Show the Showing"

The basic strategy of Brechtian performance is *Verfremdung*—most accurately rendered in English by the clumsy formulations *strange-making* or *distancing*, but more commonly translated as *alienation*. Initially, Brecht employed the term *Entfremdung*, which had become especially significant in Marxian analysis, but in the essay "Alienation Effects in Chinese Acting," written after seeing the actor Mei Lan-fang in Moscow in 1935, he first used the term V*erfremdung* as more appropriate for his own purposes.[25] The strange-making device is a technique that makes the everyday appear strange by defamiliarizing both the whole act of performance and individual moments within it.[26] The defamiliarization of the act of performance was the initial and most basic V-effect, by means of which the actor indicated that she was *presenting* the character in the scene, and not *being* the character. Early in Brecht's career he had shown an intuitive predilection for the spontaneous V-effect that is a function of the artist's "astonishment" at the way things are. This preference for an art capable of "dislocating our stock associations"[27] led Brecht over the next ten years to formulate a strategy to produce performances whose strangeness might startle the spectator out of the assumption that a certain way of behaving is natural or that the sociopolitical status quo is inevitable:

> Show that you are showing! Among all the varied attitudes
> Which you show when showing how men play their parts
> The attitude of showing must never be forgotten.[28]

Not only did the new form of epic performance need to *show* rather than transparently *reflect* reality, it had to "show the showing"—it had to be doubly self-conscious in reminding the spectator that what she was watching was not in itself reality but the playwright's and actors' view of it. Astonishment was the effect that Brecht's actors were initially to provoke in the spectator—a sense of surprise that the everyday behavior of ordinary people in the everyday world is the way it is. The everyday had to be defamiliarized as the first stage in the process by which the spectator would come to recognize that present-day social conditions were neither natural nor inevitable, and that human behavior was amenable to being changed, as were the structures of society.

In the essay "Alienation Effects in Chinese Acting," Brecht's account of the acting of the great Mei Lan-Fang is somewhat selective, but his analysis of the demonstration given by the Chinese actor in Moscow served as a striking illustration of the kind of acting style that he characterized as epic: "Above all, the Chinese artist never acts as if there were a fourth wall besides the three surrounding him. He expresses his awareness of being watched. . . . The audience can no longer have the illusion of being the unseen spectator at an event which is really taking place. . . . A further means is that the artist observes himself."[29]

What Brecht admired most about the performance was its complete self-consciousness. Unlike the acting in what he had begun to refer to as the Aristotelian theater, the Chinese actor made no covert appeal to the spectator's unconscious. Like other types of popular art (e.g., fairground shows and paintings), the actor makes the speeches and the actions of the characters appear strange rather than natural, seeking to amaze the spectator with the unfolding of the narrative: "Everyday things are therefore raised above the level of the obvious and the automatic. . . . The performer's self-observation, an artful and artistic act of self-alienation, stopped the spectator from losing himself in the character completely, i.e. to the point of giving up his own identity. . . . Yet the spectator's empathy was not entirely rejected. The audience identifies itself with the actor as being an observer, and accordingly develops his attitude of looking on."[30]

This is one of the most fundamental tenets of epic acting, promoting a type of spectatorship capable of infinite degrees of self-reflexiveness. The split function of the actor as both presenter and character, together with her own self-observation, is noticed by the spectator who not only observes all three separate aspects of the actor-in-performance, but is marginally aware that the actor's critical persona as presenter may be a performance constructed by a real person with somewhat different views from those that the playwright requires her to adopt in performing the role. At the same time, the performer will have made the spectator aware of the contradictions within the character's behavior, and will obviously elicit varied reactions from different spectators. The actor's act of self-observation, which is the V-effect through which the actor shows the act of acting, prevents the spectator from simply empathizing with the character being portrayed. It ensures a critical attitude on the part of the spectator, reminding her that social reality is not given but constructed.

Actors and critics often presume that the V-effect entails a stylized form of acting, and thus adopt an exaggerated style of caricature when performing Brecht's plays. Aware of the danger that his notion of the V-effect might be misconstrued in this way, Brecht himself wrote: "The alienation effect does not in any way demand an unnatural way of acting. It has nothing whatever to do with ordinary stylisation. On the contrary, the achievement of the A-effect absolutely depends on lightness and naturalness of performance. . . . [The actor] can always be corrected by a comparison with reality (is that how an angry man really speaks? is that how an offended man sits down?) and so from outside, by other people. He acts in such a way that nearly every sentence could be followed by a verdict of the audience."[31]

It is the collaborative nature of the relationship between actor and spectator that is crucial to the creation of the V-effect. This is not a form of stylization but the method by which the actor initiates a tacit dialogue with the audience in order to promote judgment on the character's actions and attitudes. Stylization may be employed as one of a number of devices through which the actor encourages the spectator to notice the performance *as a performance,* but it is by no means an essential part of the process. Some of the acting in Brecht's productions such as *The Threepenny Opera, Man Equals Man,* and *The Good Person of Szechwan* might have been thought of as stylized. Film and photographic records of masterpieces such as *The Mother, Galileo, Mother Courage,* and *The Caucasian Chalk Circle* suggest that the acting, though spare and subtle rather than naturalistically detailed, was by no means grotesquely stylized, even when scenography and music utilized subtle modes of stylization to create gestic effects. In Brecht's view, the Chinese theater's use of emblematic rather than pictorially realistic conventions, its employment of devices such as flags, masks, and symbolic gestures to delineate action and situation, was not arbitrary aesthetic stylization but a straightforward method of ensuring the spectator's active participation in the construction of every element of the fiction.[32]

Historicization as V-Effect

Brecht compared the astonishment of the performer to the questioning attitude of the scientist, which is "an attempt . . . to interfere with the course of nature" in order ultimately to render it "intelligible, controllable."[33] According to Brecht, art should exploit its own techniques to find answers to the apparently inexplicable aspects of social behavior. Brecht claimed that

the modern German epic theater had introduced the V-effect by "histori-
cizing" the incidents of contemporary life. Epic theater replaced the uni-
versalizing tendency of the bourgeois theater to portray instances of social
behavior as essentially human with a curiosity that permitted the spectator
to see individual instances of human behavior as historically determined—
dialectically related to the social and economic conditions of which they are
an aspect. A Marxist concept of history underpinned the epic theater: "The
idea of man as a function of the environment and the environment as a
function of man, i.e. the breaking up of the environment into relationships
between men, corresponds to a new way of thinking, the historical way."[34]

By portraying every incident in a play as a unique response to a given historical situation, Brechtian performance avoids the simplistic and sentimental tendency to generalize the action into becoming representative of human
behavior at all times and places. Many of Brecht's plays create this kind of
V-effect by analyzing a present-day reality (e.g., twentieth-century European war in *Mother Courage*) through a presentation of a different but comparable historical situation (the Thirty Years' War in seventeenth-century
Europe). This requires the actor to think historically about a character's
relationship to the environment. By portraying the archaic and unfamiliar
aspects of a character's behavior as plausible, and the familiar as odd, the
actor creates an effect of historicization, allowing the audience to grasp the
process of historical change, and to notice both the parallels and the differences between one epoch and another.

The V-Effect and Characterization

Brecht realized that, in order to "epicize" rather than dramatize the narrative, the performer needed to acquire the habit of separating her viewpoint
from that of the character and to make the audience notice the difference
between these two positions. Stanislavski had taught his actors a technique
to align the actor's intentions and those of the character. Apparent correspondence between the feelings of character and of actor was created
through the actor's empathy with the character, which ensured that the
spectator empathized with the actor/character, actor and character being
indistinguishable to the audience.

Realizing that Western actors had become habituated to empathizing
with the characters of serious drama, Brecht wrote "The Street Scene" to
provide a model by which an actor could judge the character's behavior and
present it in a way that would in turn provoke the spectator to judge.[35]
"The Street Scene" is, in effect, a practical analysis of the process of artistic
selection as it pertains to theater-making. It constitutes an exposition of the

experiments in acting and dramaturgy that Brecht had conducted during the making of the *Lehrstücke* during the early 1930s. Brecht attempted to combat the pervasive influence of naturalism on modern actors, challenging its assumption that all forms of acting depend on the complete transformation of performer into character.

According to Brecht, the concept of acting as detailed realism of characterization entailed a major problem. The pervasive naturalistic approach substituted the characters created by the actors for the play written by the dramatist. From the playwright's perspective, the roles specified in the script do not exist as complete characters. They are fragments of behavior by specific agents placed in particular relationships within a selected series of incidents, designed to communicate a certain view or argument about social reality as conceived by the writer. In Brechtian theater, the job of the actor is to *describe* the action as vividly as possible so as to animate as lively as possible a debate with the spectator concerning the validity of the play's representation of social reality. Such a form of representation requires performers who, rather than being Romantic artistic geniuses, possess powers of observation and analysis that would be effective in a law court.

In this essay, Brecht describes the epic theater in terms of the kind of demonstration eyewitnesses might give in recounting an accident that had occurred at a street corner. Brecht doubts the usefulness to the epic theater of the traditional skills of the actor: "[It] is important that he should not be too perfect. His demonstration would be spoilt if the bystanders' attention were drawn to his powers of transformation. He has to avoid presenting himself in such a way that someone calls out 'What a lifelike portrayal of a chauffeur!' . . . He need not dispose of any special powers of suggestion."[36]

The most important skill of the actor is that of observation. A theatrical performance is compared to a courtroom reenactment of a street accident, in which the actors' task is not to evoke the emotional excitement of a conventional drama. That excitement is inherent in the real incident that is being reenacted. The actor must focus the spectator's attention on the rights and wrongs of the decisions made by people involved in the incident—on the causes and effects of each person's actions. Characterization is a matter of delineating how the typical attitudes of each participant affected the outcome of the event, not how they were feeling that day, or how they behave in other moments of their lives—unless these other personal characteristics are directly relevant as causes of the accident. The aim of epic acting is not to present character (what a person *is*) but to show the relationship between people's behavior and the events that issue from it (what people *do*). Thus a certain amount of imitation is required of the actor, but this is more appropriately achieved through a method of social observation and analysis than through any process of psychological identification with the character. Indeed, too much identification of the actor with the role being portrayed will render the actor incapable of judging her behavior properly.

This essay is more radical than anything else Brecht wrote in its apparent rejection of all the talents traditionally considered necessary for stage acting. During the last nine years of his career, when he was working regularly as director of his own plays, he repeatedly modified some of his more extreme views, suggesting that his most radical statements were written as correctives to the overstated naturalism and crude emotionalism of 1920s and 1930s German theater. However he might have exaggerated his objections to traditional forms of acting, "The Street Scene" did clarify the different function of acting in the epic theater, and it proposed techniques to aid the epic actor in replacing stage illusion with the kind of demonstration that Brecht intended.

One important aspect of Brechtian performance articulated in the essay is the notion of acting in the past tense. Since Brechtian theater concentrates exclusively on the analysis of social reality rather than on the creation of a fantasy world of artistic illusion, a performance takes on the quality of a reenactment of something that is presumed to have happened in the real world: "The street demonstrator's performance is essentially repetitive. The event has taken place. What you are seeing now is a repeat. If the . . . theatre follows the street scene in this respect then the theatre will stop pretending not to be theatre . . . the whole machinery and the whole process of preparation . . . all becomes plainly apparent."[37]

So even when a Brechtian play does not actually represent historical events, it is performed as though it does. Paradoxically, this connects the spectator more immediately with the concrete reality of the everyday world because the form of fictional representation is seen as merely a method of demonstrating something that has actually happened in the world. Brechtian theater deliberately denies the spectator the pleasure of narrative closure. The actor demonstrates what happened in the real world in order that the spectator may decide what to do about it in the immediate future. The narrative is never brought to a satisfying conclusion, but the realities of social inequality and human selfishness are starkly exposed as problems for the spectators to resolve outside the theater.

By exposing the process whereby the demonstration has been conducted, the actors remind the spectator that the performance itself is the product of a series of political and artistic choices, which represent the points of view of the actors, director, and playwright, thus enhancing the spectator's sense of responsibility for engaging in the argument about society that the playwright has initiated by writing the play. The happy endings in Brecht's plays are patently theatrical jokes—as in the absurd arrival on horseback of the royal messenger in *The Threepenny Opera*. Other endings are deliberately incomplete, provisional, and often ironic, as in *Mother Courage, Galileo,* or *The Good Person of Szechwan*. The impact of the ending is very much dependent on the attitude of the actor, as various productions of *Mother Courage* have shown. If the actor playing Courage chooses to elicit sympathy for the character's desolate state at the end of the play, this can have the effect of undermining one of the major points that the action has demonstrated—that she consistently refuses to learn from the terrible consequences of her own misplaced selfishness. Brecht's concern to describe the kind of acting demanded by his new form of theater did not reflect a purely theoretical interest in performance, but was a concrete response to the way actors can rewrite written texts through the devices of performance.

Techniques for Distancing Actor and Role

Written in 1940, "A Short Description of a New Technique of Acting which Produces an Alienation Effect" is a summation of Brecht's thoughts on how the V-effect operates as a function of epic acting. Apart from restating the main ideas of the two earlier essays on acting, "A Short Description" elaborates specific methods to assist the actor in producing the appropriate V-effects in performance. In the essay Brecht states that the performer need not entirely avoid empathy as a means of representing human behavior on stage, but that empathy will be employed only as part of the actor's process of imagining the character's motives and attitudes during rehearsals. However, in performance the *aim* of the acting should not be to produce empathy, but to promote critical reflection.

Four rehearsal strategies are suggested by Brecht to prevent actors from spontaneously empathizing with the role and to enable them to achieve the requisite critical distance from the character:

1. There should be a longer period of "reading rehearsals" before the actor learns the text and begins to impersonate the role. This permits the actor, before attempting to incarnate the role, to understand the network of relationships enmeshing the character in the narrative as well as the factors affecting the character's actions.
2. The actor should memorize her first impressions of the role, in order to notice what first surprised her about the attitudes that motivated the character's actions.

3. The actor should read the part at rehearsal with the attitude of a person who is astonished and who disagrees with the character. The actor must memorize not merely the words spoken by the character but also her reactions of astonishment at the particular shape of the story and her impulses to contradict the peculiar decisions the character makes. In other words, the actor must in rehearsal employ a technique that allows her to incorporate and expose her own personal responses to the way the action unfolds as a consequence of the character's choices.

4. The technique that Brecht referred to as fixing the "not . . . but" should be employed in order to enable the spectator to notice the alternative possibilities for action latent within the narrative but overlooked in favor of the actual choices of action made by the characters. This method operates both at the level of the performer's artistic choices ("she chose *not* to move downstage left *but* to move upstage right instead") and at the level of the narrative fiction (the heroine did *not* immediately fall in love with the handsome airman *but* first asked his friends how much money he earned before responding to his amorous advances).

Whereas in "The Street Scene" the form of characterization appropriate to epic theater is to be achieved simply by acting in the past tense, in the later essay "acting in quotation marks" permits a further development of this mode of performance: the "actor speaks his part not as if he were improvising it himself but like a quotation. At the same time he obviously has to render all the quotation's overtones, the remark's full human and concrete shape; similarly the gesture he makes must have the full substance of a human gesture even though it now represents a copy."[38]

Three particular methods of rehearsal were useful in achieving the effect of performance as quotation:

1. Transposition into the third person.
2. Transposition into the past.
3. Speaking the stage directions out loud.[39]

At rehearsal the actor is asked to deliver her lines as though they were passages of direct speech in a story, for example, "Hamlet shouted in anger against his own self-preserving cowardice, 'O what a rogue and peasant slave am I.'" This would not only detach the performer from the role that she was demonstrating, but would ensure that the attitude of the commentator modified the tone of speaking. At rehearsal the actor should examine the stage directions to see what light they shed upon the attitude of the speaker, and also read the play carefully to find remarks that commented upon the character. The clash between the two modes of voice—narrative and direct speech—would also alienate the text of the play: "This style of acting is further alienated by taking place on the stage after having already been outlined and announced in words. Transposing it into the past gives the speaker a standpoint from which he can look back at his sentence. The sentence too is thereby alienated without the speaker adopting an unreal point of view; unlike the spectator, he has read the play right through and is better placed to judge the sentence in accordance with the ending, with its consequences, than the former, who knows less and is more of a stranger to the sentence."[40]

The multiplicity of V-effects created by the ostensibly simple act of reading a speech in a play has the consequence of promoting a complex play of ironies in performance, and it is true to say that the Brechtian performer is an ironist, displaying her superior knowledge of the playwright's judgment throughout the performance in a way that provokes the spectator into a battle of wits with the actor. The spectator, without the actor's privileged knowledge of the play, actively applies her own critical faculties to seeking forms of action that might be effective in promoting a satisfactory outcome to the problems posed within the drama. Thus Brechtian theater begins by identifying problems that exist in the real world and ends by returning the spectator to that world, after having conducted a kind of experiment in how to solve those problems under laboratory conditions. In this way, theater becomes an exercise in thinking politically—a rehearsal for acting politically in everyday life.

As part of the appendix to the "Short Description," Brecht had included some "practice scenes for actors." These overlap to a certain extent with the much more extensive "Exercises for Acting Schools," which appear to reflect the content of lessons given by Brecht's wife, Helene Weigel, at a Finnish theater school, and which John Willett appended to his translation of "The Street Scene."[41] As listed, most of the exercises are cryptic headings for improvisations or activities, without much explanation of their content. Brief though they are, however, they are typically suggestive of the values Brecht wished to inculcate in training actors for the epic theater. Characteristically, he required that actors being taught conjuring tricks also be expected to study the attitudes of spectators, a kind of rehearsal in the strategy of *showing* that is the foundation of epic performance. Such an exercise demands that the actor learn the effect the trick has on each spectator at the same time as she learns how to perform it.

The aim of most of the exercises was to promote the actors' powers of observation and mimicry.[42] Interestingly, Brecht introduced a kind of V-effect into apparently simple exercises like "folding and putting away linen" and "various attitudes of smokers." The first one required women to observe a household activity that is traditionally performed by women— something so common and undramatic that actors probably never bother to think what might be expressed by different ways of executing it. The V-effect is doubled by then having men, who normally have no experience of folding linen, perform it. A similar effect would be achieved in the smoking exercise that women are asked to perform once male actors have done it. These seemingly straightforward exercises become sophisticated lessons in social observation precisely because they subject to close scrutiny everyday activities that are not normally thought of as dramatic and enable the actor to develop a critically self-conscious attitude to the simplest details of social behavior.

By obliging actors to take notes of such details of gestures and tones of voice, Brecht would teach them to become critically aware of the way in which social attitudes are expressed through physical behavior. The process of taking notes about gesture and vocal tone is the opposite of the conventional method whereby the actor learns to copy by empathizing with the character in the fictional situation. The example that was given of "exercises in imagination" also highlights the conscious observation of behavior: "Three men throwing dice for their life. One loses. Then: they all lose." With the simplicity of a biblical parable, the portrayal of an extreme situation encourages actors to notice how people really act in life-and-death situations, what their most basic instincts are, and the difference in one's attitude when one's own life, rather than someone else's, is under threat.

The "exercises in temperament" also present a significant variation on the conventional naturalistic improvisation. Again, the ordinary action of women quarreling is alienated by the fact that they are calmly folding linen, after it gradually becomes apparent that they are merely feigning "wild and jealous" behavior in order to fool their husbands, who are in the next room. Later the quarrel becomes genuine. The exercise therefore aims to investigate in practice the subtle differences between a real quarrel and an acted one. It also provides a model of the layers of self-consciousness that Brecht intended all epic performances to exhibit.

All the exercises were clearly designed to inculcate an attitude of self-consciousness and precise analysis in the process of imitation. Most of the exercises in mimicry aimed to train the performer to express inner attitudes through precisely executed physical actions—vocal or gestural. The quick-change competition would allow the actor to perfect her technical skills of mimicry by stressing the speed of the change from one imitation to another. Rhythmical verse-speaking while tap-dancing would sensitize the student performer to the structure of a verse speech and a stylized movement sequence. The rhythmic pattern of the one form alienates that of the other, forcing the performer to create an appropriate relationship between the two. The exercise in characterizing another actor offered further opportunities to practice the self-consciousness of the epic performer's act of mimicry, transforming actors themselves into objects of imitation, and allowing them to see how they appear to their peers. The operation of the V-effect was yet again built into the exercise in eating with an outsize knife and fork and then a very small knife and fork, which would create V-effects that could distance the act of eating and focus attention on the attitude of the character.

Brecht also recommended that students learn to search for the "nodal points" in a scene, an anticipation of his detailed work during rehearsals at the Berliner Ensemble to find and fix every *Gestus* in a play. He proposed that students devise a theatrical presentation of a street accident in order to learn the limits of justifiable imitation, or alternatively perform the traditional song "A Dog Went into the Kitchen," a long-winded and maudlin burlesque of an epic ballad. Presumably this would teach the actor how to select which elements of the narrative to act out, and how to describe them with well-chosen gestures.

Gestus as Acting Method and Dramaturgical Principle

Inherent in the foregoing discussion of epic acting is Brecht's notion of *Gestus,* translated into English as "gest." The term had been introduced by Kurt Weill in an essay written in 1929. A year later Brecht employed it in "The Modern Theatre is the Epic Theatre," in relation to the use of gestic music as a technique of epic theater. In German, *Gestus* means both "gist" and "gesture." The term was used by Brecht and Weill to indicate the effect this new kind of music had in reproducing the physical character of an action on stage in expressing an unequivocal attitude toward the action being represented. Brecht elaborated his own notion of the *Gestus* as a performance strategy aimed at giving physical form to the "nodal points" in the drama. His work in California with Charles Laughton on *Galileo* (1947) and the famous productions at the Berliner Ensemble (1949–56) gave him scope to develop the technique in concrete terms.

The gest is a piece of physical action on stage that conveys social meaning. The story of a play (Brecht called this the *fable*) is communicated on stage through the sequence of gests performed by the actors. Each gest is an embodiment of a social attitude or a complex of attitudes in the form of a physical action or gesture. What distinguishes the gest from a purely physical action is its deliberate indication of a social attitude. Thus the action of a man sweeping away a bothersome fly is not a gest, while the action of chasing away a dog may become one, in a situation where the dog is a watchdog and the man is badly dressed, and it is clear that he is in the habit of fending off such dogs. In the second instance, the gesture of chasing away an animal possesses implications (the man's poverty, the keeping of dogs to protect the property of the rich, the habitual nature of the man's experience of being chased by such dogs) that express a social meaning.

Many types of art represent human situations, for example, someone crying in pain, but the common way of representing such an action as art is to generalize the gesture to such a point of abstraction that the social and historical context disappears and one is left with a gesture that communicates nothing more than the universal human emotion of pain. This type of representation offers no explanation for the pain and no possible analysis of how it may be prevented, but merely communicates how it feels in the most vivid and general manner. Brecht wished to restore the social and historical significance to the action, by structuring it so that its essential social meanings were revealed as part of its physical form, and its other facets became incidental: "The realm of attitudes adopted by the characters towards one another is what we call the realm of gest. Physical attitude, tone of voice and facial expression are all determined by a social gest. . . . The attitudes which people adopt towards one another include even those attitudes which would appear to be quite private, such as the utterances of physical pain in an illness or of religious faith."[43]

The fable is communicated in physical terms through breaking it down into a series of specific episodes. Each one of these episodes is identified as a *Grundgestus* (the interpretation of its fundamental action) by the dramaturg, director, and actors. In order that the actions that shape the presentation of the fable function properly as gests, Brecht required actors to disrupt the normally seamless flow of action typical of traditional "Aristotelian" drama. Each *Grundgestus* should have the character of a tableau whose significance might be clearly read by the spectator even if she could not hear the actors speaking. The physical action should be shaped so as to emphasize both the artistic nature of its composition and the social attitudes that inform its social meaning. In other words, the performance of a play should be artful rather than spontaneous. No matter how subtle, the construction of the fable and the manner of its unfolding should be clearly apparent to the spectator. Each gest should therefore be alienated from its surrounding context in order to promote the effect of astonishment at the particular set of social relationships that determined the characters' behavior in the episode and at the contradictions between successive gests. Brecht's habit was to note or record these nodal points or *Grundgesten* so they might be analyzed. As early as 1926, he had made a film of the nodal points of Peter Lorre's performance as Galy Gay in *Man Equals Man,* and the *Modellbücher* (model books) produced by the Berliner Ensemble in the 1950s contained a series of photographs intended as a visual record of major gests in each production.

In discussing how he and Laughton built up the role of Galileo in the play's premier production in California, Brecht provided an insight into the detailed choices of gest that were eventually recorded in the written text. Brecht appreciated Laughton's wonderful craftsmanship as an actor, and, notwithstanding their quite appreciable ideological differences, used a number of his suggestions as to ways of building up the gestic outline of the performance. Brecht's approach as a theater artist was pragmatic. "The proof of the pudding," he was fond of saying, "is in the eating." Because of the language barrier between Laughton and Brecht, their method of translating the text and creating individual gests was in itself gestic: "[He] spoke no German whatever, and we had to decide the gest of each piece of dialogue by my acting it all in bad English or even in German and his then acting it back in proper English in a variety of ways until I could say: that's it. . . . This system of performance-and-repetition had one immense advantage in that psychological discussions were almost entirely avoided. Even the most fundamental gests, such as Galileo's way of observing, or his showmanship, or his craze for pleasure, were established in three dimensions by actual performance."[44]

The designer of most of Brecht's productions was Caspar Neher, who collaborated fully on the construction of the gestic pattern of the production, watching the actors in rehearsal and creating settings that would reinforce or counterpoint every gest to create the most refined and significant tableaux throughout the course of the play: "His sets are significant statements about reality. . . . In his designs our friend always starts with 'the people themselves' and 'what is happening to or through them.' He provides no 'decor,' frames and backgrounds, but constructs the space for 'people' to experience something in. . . . But above all he is an ingenious story-teller.

. . . he is always content to give indications wherever something 'plays no part.' At the same time these indications are stimulating. They arouse the spectator's imagination, which perfect reproduction would numb."[45]

Brecht's description of the level of abstraction achieved by Neher's stage designs could apply equally well to the kind of indications that epic acting achieved in eschewing the naturalistic reproduction of character, and presenting only the physical details that convey the social gests significant to the narrative. Brecht desired the spectator to appreciate the beauty of the sculptural compositions achieved through blocking, to notice the economy of the exposition of the various gests, rather than to respond unconsciously to their verisimilitude as physical action: "The grouping of the characters on the stage and the movements of the groups must be such that the necessary beauty is attained above all by the elegance with which the material conveying that gest is set out and laid bare to the understanding of the audience."[46]

The chief task of the actor and director in rehearsal was to discover the appropriate physical form for the communication of each gest, while the designer and the director would frame and orchestrate the sequence of gests so as to draw attention to their significance and their aesthetic qualities.

Epic versus Dialectic

During his period of exile from Germany after 1933, Brecht only occasionally had the opportunity to test his ideas in practice. He spent his time in non-German-speaking countries (Denmark, Finland, and finally the United States) elaborating and testing his praxis by writing plays—a number of which are considered to be his mature masterpieces (*Galileo, Mother Courage, The Caucasian Chalk Circle, The Good Person of Szechwan*). The dramaturgy of these plays both exemplified and advanced his own notion of theater, so that by the time of writing *A Short Organum for the Theatre* in 1948, his presentation of the opposition between epic and Aristotelian theater as an absolute dichotomy had given way to the model of a theater that represented a witty refunctioning of many of Aristotle's concepts, rather than a wholesale rejection of them. This new approach may have been occasioned as much by the confusion in some quarters over his earlier elaboration of the principles of epic theater as by his own desire to revise his previous ideas. According to the director Manfred Wekwerth, in his later years Brecht was in the habit of referring to the revised model of his practice as "dialectical theater," and he entitled a collection of theoretical writings (published posthumously) "Dialectics in the Theatre." Wekwerth remembered Brecht saying, shortly before his death, "Narrating a story on the stage was really at the same time a 'dialecticising' of the events."[47]

Dialectics captures better than the term *epic* the playfulness of Brecht's deconstructions of traditional forms of naturalism and expressionism, the sense of fun that was essential to the pleasure of theater. Learning, as Brecht himself pointed out, was for Aristotle the definitive human pleasure. By the late 1940s, Brecht had therefore entirely integrated his intuitive sense of the fun to be had in observing and representing the contradictions in human behavior with a Marxist conception of the pleasure to be derived from learning how the world might be changed. Dialectics in the theater was a kind of game through which the future could be rehearsed. Its fun was not the degraded escapism of the bourgeois entertainment industry, but the active pleasure of laughing at contradictions in society's status quo, and exploring ways of resolving them through social change. One of the appendices to the *Short Organum* makes the point: "The theatre of the scientific age is in a position to make dialectics into a source of enjoyment . . . they heighten both our capacity for life and our pleasure in it."[48]

All of Brecht's writings on epic acting in the 1930s took the Stanislavskian approach as a paradigm of Aristotelian performance, and proposed a method of epic acting in direct antithesis to it. As this opposition appeared to him in time to be simplistic and overstated, Brecht reformulated his notion of acting, stressing the fact that the prevalence of naturalistic assumptions about performance had at the time made it necessary for him to frame his notion of acting as a direct alternative to the Stanislavskian approach in order to clarify his own somewhat paradoxical and unfamiliar ideas. In the late 1940s, Brecht began to reconsider the aspects of Stanislavski's technique that would be useful in the elaboration of his dialectical approach. Brecht admired Vakhtangov for having developed Stanislavski's methods in such a way that he avoided Stanislavski's emphasis on the mimetic re-creation of real experience as well as Meyerhold's over-schematized abstraction. However, Brecht believed that, while the theatricality that Vakhtangov's actors achieved in "demonstrating" characters was potentially useful, a spectator learned nothing from his productions.[49]

Although Brecht always remained convinced of the futility of training actors to achieve total immersion in the character with the concomitant truth and belief in the reality of the fictional world being represented, he admired the conscientious exploration of social reality that Stanislavski demanded of his actors, and approved of his insistence on shaping the production to embody the play's governing idea or superobjective. He believed that the later elaboration of "Stanislavski's 'method of physical actions' is most likely his greatest contribution to a new theatre."[50] Stanislavski's method of analysis through physical actions has a number of features in common with Brecht's practice of creating the performance through the elaboration of a sequence of gests. However, Stanislavski's approach was entirely based on a psychological conception of character motivation, while Brecht stressed the social attitudes embodied in every action performed by the characters. Again, Stanislavski's actors were asked to resolve the contradictions between one objective and another in the light of the character's superobjective, while Brecht's V-effect was designed to highlight the social factors that create contradictions within a character's behavior. Stanislavski's detailed work on finding precise physical actions to express intentions might well have influenced Brecht's later approach to working with each actor to build up the sequence of gests that constitutes her role in the drama.

Having admired a Stanislavski production still in the repertoire of the Moscow Art Theater when he visited Moscow in 1955, Brecht was said to have commented ironically that Stanislavski's practice contradicted his theory. In practice, Brecht believed, Stanislavski's productions "represented reality as full of contradictions." "He grasped the diversity and complexity of social life and knew how to represent it without getting entangled. All his productions make sense."[51] Brecht recognized (as had Meyerhold as early as 1905) that Stanislavski's practice was not consistently naturalistic, that his own sensibility allowed him to grasp the poetic significance of a play's form and eschew the factitious reproduction of real life: "In S's theatre a splendid naturalness went arm-in-arm with deep significance. As a realist he never hesitated to portray ugliness, but he did so gracefully."[52] Typically, Brecht stressed the contradiction between the content and method of presentation that was central to his own conception of maintaining the appropriate distance between the actor and the role. Although the aims of Brechtian performance were very different from conventional forms of realistic theater, many of Stanislavski's actual techniques might be refunctioned to produce precisely the kinds of effects Brecht intended.

Function of the Emotions

One of the aspects of Brecht's praxis that has caused critics and practitioners most difficulty is its approach to the emotions. The third of the "misconceptions about the epic theatre" that Brecht listed was that it is "against all emotions." Brecht's own response was blunt: "The epic theatre isn't against the emotions; it tries to examine them, and is not satisfied just to stimulate them. It is the orthodox theatre which sins by dividing reason and emotion, in that it virtually rules out the former. As soon as one makes the slightest move to introduce a modicum of reason into theatrical practice its protagonists scream that one is trying to abolish the emotions."[53]

The emotions play an important part in Brechtian theater, but they are not its raison d'être. In this regard, the epic theater aims to *clarify* emotions. This is achieved by subjecting the characters' feelings to the critical analysis of the actor, who conveys her attitude toward the character's emotions so that the spectator may reflect on their appropriateness to the dramatic situation.

From as early as 1926, Brecht made it plain that the portrayal of feelings was a significant part of the epic theater's function. However, it was the manner of their (re)presentation that was critical. What was to be avoided at all costs was the exploitation of empathy by which actors of the time commonly manipulated the audience into identifying themselves with the actor/character's feelings.[54] Brecht's plays often deal with extremely powerful feelings (e.g., a mother's desire to save her child from physical injury in *The Caucasian Chalk Circle,* the unrequited passion of Shen Te for Yang Sun in *The Good Person of Szechwan,* the terrible moments in *Mother Courage* when Courage is successively confronted by the deaths of her three children and, on one occasion, forced for the sake of her survival to pretend not to recognize the corpse of her son). These are moments that would usually evince primal feelings. However, in each situation, Brecht emphasizes the tension between the character's feelings and the spectator's reason. By maintaining the concrete particularity of social and historical context, by refusing to separate a person's suffering from the factors that led to it, the plays create what at times is a terrible conflict within the spectator between reason and emotion. Contrary to the conventions of Aristotelian drama, Brecht refuses to permit the suspension of the spectator's rational faculty at moments of powerful emotion. Indeed he specifically requires that the actor direct the audience to adopt contradictory emotions to those of the character.

In a paragraph headed "Emotions," written during or shortly after 1953 and forming a section of the notes to his production of a contemporary play, Brecht expressed a modified version of his earlier attitude to the representation of emotions. Although he reemphasized the difference between the actor's feelings and those of the character, it appears that he had reconsidered his early preference for the "cold" and "classical" qualities of epic acting: "[Our] mistakes are different from those of other theatres. Their actors are liable to display too much spurious temperament; ours show too little of the real thing. Aiming to avoid artificial heat, we fall short in natural warmth. We make no attempt to share the emotions of the characters we portray, but these emotions must none the less be fully and movingly represented, nor must they be treated with coldness but likewise with an emotion of some force: thus, the character's despair with genuine anger on our part, or his anger with genuine despair as the case may be."[55]

The Brechtian Actor in Performance

In his own practice, Brecht had never made the mistakes of those followers who read his own attacks on the actor's exploitation of empathy as implying a rejection of feeling or an emotionally neutral attitude on the part of performers. During the first phase of his work in the 1920s and early 1930s, he worked with actors whose innate talents included the ability to project strong personalities on stage. He wanted actors to appear as real people (not refined, artistic types) with the vitality and individuality of Wedekind, Valentin, and Charlie Chaplin. There was no question of the actor effacing her personality to adopt a neutral persona in order to ventriloquize the playwright's point of view. The early Brecht performers were all striking personalities, who brought seemingly idiosyncratic attitudes to the world on to the stage with them before they attempted to demonstrate the characters' actions and attitudes indicated in the written text. Perhaps Brecht's preference for casting strong personalities in productions of his own and other playwrights' plays was so fundamental to his practice that he never thought it necessary to rationalize this assumption in his theoretical essays.

The idea that an actor should bring a strong personality to bear on her role is implicit in Brecht's theoretical essays, challenging the commonplace bourgeois disjunction between serious art and fun. However, this approach did not mean that Brecht favored the standard typecasting of traditional theater: "Parts are allotted wrongly and thoughtlessly. As if all cooks were fat, all peasants phlegmatic, all statesmen stately. As if all who love and are loved were beautiful. . . . It is pure folly to allot parts according to physical characteristics. "He has a kingly figure." What does that mean? Do all kings have to look like *Edward VII*? . . . Can one go by temperament? One can't. . . . True there are gentle people and noisy, violent ones. But it is also true that every man has every variety of temperament. And the more of an actor he happens to be, the truer that is. And those varieties which he is repressing may be particularly effective when brought out."[56] What Brecht seemed to value in a performer was the kind of intelligence with which she exhibited her attitude to the character—a combination of relish of the character's human vitality with a critical perspective on her social attitude.

In exile, Brecht often referred to a group of chosen performers as though they were collaborators in the creation of a new mode of acting. In an issue of the *Left Review* (1936) he claimed that "the training of a whole generation of young actors for the new style of acting, the epic style, took place."[57] In that essay, the actors mentioned were Oscar Homolka, Fritz Kortner, Carola Neher, Alexander Granach, Ernst Busch, Helene Weigel, Peter Lorre, and Lotte Lenya, all of whom were forced to leave Germany when Hitler came to power. None of them possessed the histrionic intensity or romantic glamour that typified the star actors of the day. Oscar Homolka, the Viennese actor who created the role of Baal, was "burly," and it was with him in mind that Brecht conceived the roles of Azdak and Galileo. Ernst Busch, who was in fact to play both Azdak and Galileo at the Berliner Ensemble, was also a large man. Busch's performing persona was shaped by his working-class background, his leftist activism, and his experience as a cabaret singer: "This Azdak," said Brecht, "is the product of Busch's whole life . . . his struggles in the Weimar Republic and in the Spanish Civil War, and his bitter experiences after 1945."[58]

According to the theater manager Aufricht, the physically small actor Peter Lorre (who later became famous in Fritz Lang's film *M* and as the Chinese Mr. Moto in numerous Hollywood "B" thrillers) "looked like a tadpole" but combined a distinctive style of playing with a sharp intelligence that Brecht admired, particularly in the role of Galy Gay in *Man Equals Man*. Lotte Lenya, who as Kurt Weill's wife was later to become the most famous interpreter of his songs, startled audiences by using her distinctive but untrained singing voice to originate a number of roles in Brecht-Weill operas and musicals. She used an acerbic manner and striking but unconventional looks to project the tough and realistic persona of a working-class woman, an attitude that usefully contradicted the naive or greedy escapism of the characters she portrayed. All these actors possessed a down-to-earth ordinariness, appearing on stage as ordinary working people rather than as bourgeois artists. Even the famous film star Charles Laughton, with whom Brecht worked in the United States after the war, possessed no conventional "Hollywood" glamour. Brecht stresses Laughton's cultivation of an appetite for food as a sensual manifestation of his artistic temperament; his large girth was used in the performance to highlight the contradiction between Galileo's hunger for knowledge and his willingness to compromise his principles in order to survive.

The exemplary Brechtian actor was Helene Weigel. An Austrian Jew and a Communist, Weigel made her professional debut in Frankfurt in 1919, met Brecht in the early 1920s, and married him in 1928. She gave definitive

performances in a number of his plays (Widow Begbick in *Man Equals Man,*
Wlassowa in *The Mother,* Antigone in Brecht's version of Sophocles' play,
and Mother Courage) and was the manager of the Berliner Ensemble from
its inception in 1949. It is probable that Brecht learned as much about the
pragmatics of epic acting by observing her performances as she learned by
appearing in his plays. She was not tall, but had a strong, narrow face with
a high forehead and prominent lips. Brecht described her voice as "rich and
dark, and pleasant, even in sharpness or in a scream. Her movements are
definite and soft."[59] Implicit in his words is the contrast between the intensity of a character's feelings and the artistry of the performer's execution. In
"A Dialogue about Acting," Brecht used his recollections of her performance in Jessner's 1929 production of Sophocles' *Oedipus Rex* to exemplify
his concept of the epic style of acting he was aiming for: As the servant,
Weigel "announced the death of her mistress by calling out her 'dead, dead'
in a wholly unemotional and penetrating voice, her 'Jocasta has died' without any sorrow but so firmly and definitely that the bare fact of her mistress's
death carried more weight at that precise moment than could have been
generated by any grief of her own."[60]

Weigel epicized the role, telling the story of the events the character had
witnessed, rather than interpolating the character's supposed emotions
between the suicide and the spectator's response. In order to convey the
impact of the event on the character, she used makeup to whiten her face,
thus employing a visual device to illustrate the feelings of the character
rather than employing an empathic process: "With astonishment she
described in a single clear sentence the dying woman's ranting and apparent
irrationality. . . . And as she held up her arms in conventional lamentation
she was begging at the same time for pity for herself who had seen the dis-
aster, and with her 'now you may weep' she seemed to deny the justice of
any previous and less well-founded regrets."[61]

While completely unsentimental in its depiction of a terrible event,
Weigel's performance was not cold but economical, the actor's attitude
encouraging the spectator to notice the various surprising features of people's behavior in such an extreme situation. The subtlety of Weigel's conception consisted in its separate presentation of every gest. Each of the character's reactions was focused in a distinct visual sign or gesture, allowing the
spectator to react to each moment individually, rather than being immersed
in an overall wave of empathy for the character.

Weigel's performances were distinguished by the "ease and lightness" of
playing that Brecht had always advocated. Not naturalistic, but natural, her
approach to characterization was highly selective in its use of gesture, vocal

effect, and well-chosen props as a focus for the chief gests of the play. The economy of her playing directed the spectator to the attitudes appropriate to the point of view being communicated through the narrative, rather than to a generalized realism of characterization. Brecht had criticized the tendency of actors schooled in naturalistic techniques to find an irrelevant subtext to play "between the lines."[62] Many twentieth-century actors, especially those habituated to television and film, believe it is their task to elaborate a non-verbal subtext in order to flesh out the unexpressed aspects of their characters' lives. This Stanislavskian approach to characterization is often (but not always) appropriate for naturalistic plays, but has repeatedly undermined productions of Brecht's plays in Britain and the United States, and appears to have been the major cause of Stanislavski's own lack of success with Shakespeare. Weigel's real artistry lay, according to Brecht, in the intelligence with which she directed her great skill and talent toward a social purpose: "Many artists make their audience blind and deaf to the world with their superb skill. Weigel's achievement was that she now made the audience see more and hear more than just herself."[63]

In the final analysis, Brecht's admiration for particular performers was based on the use to which they put their skills. Like Stanislavski and Copeau, Brecht's notion of theater entailed an ethics of performance, although in Brecht's case this ethics implied a political struggle for social justice: "[The] persecuted who heard her [Weigel] forgot their own troubles, but they never forgot the causes. And always, they left the hall stronger for their fight. This was because Weigel showed them her own wisdom and her own goodness."[64]

Rehearsal as Collaborative Experiment

The establishment of the Berliner Ensemble allowed Brecht to stage his own dramatic masterpieces and, at the same time, to put his aesthetic principles into practice. For Brecht, rehearsal was a method of making mise-en-scène. Since the theater he was creating required the performer to maintain an open and playful acknowledgment of the spectator and a critical attitude to herself and the character, rehearsals were not conceived as a process of nurturing the imagination of the actor. Instead actors invented and tested different gests to discover the best way of elaborating arguments about society in action. "The directorial method was based on investigation and varied experimentation that could extend to the smallest gestures—eyes, fingers. . . . Brecht worked like a sculptor on and with the actor."[65]

Like Copeau, Saint-Denis, and Brook, Brecht's approach to rehearsals

Helene Weigel as Mother Courage performing the famous *Gestus* of the silent scream. Photo by Hainer Hill, used by permission of the VG Bild-Kunst, Bonn/Design and Artists Copyright Society (DACS), London, on behalf of Akademie der Künste Archiv, Brecht-Weigel Gedenkstätte, Berlin.

was entirely pragmatic, the only consistent method being trial and error. On joining the company the director Carl Weber was surprised at the loose way in which Brecht worked in rehearsal, but soon realized that such an open approach was essential to the experimental nature of rehearsals, during which Brecht encouraged actors to demonstrate their ideas in practice rather than discussing them. Whereas Stanislavski's rehearsals enabled the actor to achieve progressive identification of actor and role through a structured psychological process, Brecht's method was self-conscious and public. Rehearsals at the Berliner Ensemble were devoted to the painstaking exploration of alternative performance possibilities implied by the written text, in order to choose one that was most effective in demonstrating the complex and contradictory nature of social reality. After having invented the various gests that constituted her role, the actor's task was to practice their execution until she was capable of playing them with ease.

Since the ideal Brechtian performance was itself a kind of three-dimensional political debate, dramatizing various possible ways of behaving in society rather than merely discussing them, Brecht conducted rehearsals so as to mimic the structure of such a performance, encouraging intervention and argument, provoking actors to "rewrite" the performance by showing alternative stagings of scenes or gests. Indeed, his ideal performance resembled a rehearsal, concentrated but not too intense, in principle permitting the kind of interventions and arguments provoked during the actual rehearsals of the Berliner Ensemble. The presence of the designer at rehearsals and his contribution to the production process was another instance of the open and collaborative nature of Brecht's practice. The making of the performance should be as much fun for the actors as the performance itself should be for the audience, the playfulness of dramatic art being a definitive element of its performance and creation.

Brecht's notes on the "Phases of a Production" printed in the Berliner Ensemble's illustrated volume *Theaterarbeit* in 1952 reveal an attitude to the rehearsal process that eschewed mystification and emphasized collaborative experiment and productive analysis as the key elements of a fundamentally social activity. Brecht listed fifteen phases, beginning with the analysis of the play and ending with the first night. Many of the principles laid down are now standard production practice in Western theaters, but it is significant that the production process was analyzed purely pragmatically, to ensure that the gestic expression of the narrative would be effectively shaped. There was to be no special treatment for the actor, who was regarded simply as one of the team of skilled workers who assembled the performance through the elaboration and linking of significant details. A few notes are of particular interest. Brecht suggested that casting should not be irrevocably determined at the outset, implying that the process of working as a group would determine the proper balance of casting. Since Brecht saw drama as exploring sets of social relationships and as a method of discovering how society determines individual character, casting should be determined by the early phase of rehearsal rather than reflecting a mistaken sense of the absolute equivalence of actor and character.

During the reading rehearsal, actors should attempt to convey the meaning of the lines and avoid "expression" or characterization. This implied that the actors should avoid fixing interpretations by means of stock line readings or character conventions. Characterization was a function of the construction of gests that should begin to emerge during the rough indication of attitudes at the positioning rehearsal, but even then "continuity of characterisation" should be avoided. The bulk of rehearsal time was to be devoted to balancing detailed work on specific moments against run-throughs and tempo rehearsals dedicated to establishing an effective rhythm for the whole performance. The notes reveal Brecht's remarkable concern for the precise physical form of each detail and with the tempi that create overall rhythm.

Five notes on acting at the end of *Theaterarbeit* reveal both the extent of Brecht's concern with all the practical minutiae of performance, and his conception of acting as a physical process. The first two notes suggest some parallels with Stanislavski's method of physical actions, and also with Craig and Meyerhold's views of the actor as a physical instrument. The first note, which carries the heading "If you want to master something difficult take it easy," is concerned with the achievement of bodily relaxation through rehearsing the physical shape of the performance. The dividing up of the part and arrangement of movements are "tasks for the senses, and his [the actor's] training is of a physical kind."[66] The second note, which carries the heading "Control of stage temperament and improvement of stage diction," warns the actor in precise terms against certain habitual mannerisms, namely the mechanical exploitation of generalized displays of temperament, and the blanket adoption of the "rhetorical voice." Both of these mannerisms superimpose a fake histrionic personality that masks the precise expression of particular attitudes. These two notes illustrate Brecht's sharp awareness of typical actors' clichés and his sense that the decorum of stage acting must constantly change in tandem with social change. ("Great forms only get a new lease of life when they are continually nourished from a continually changing reality.")[67]

The third note, on "taking the tone," expresses Brecht's sense of the collaborative nature of acting, succinctly describing the need for each actor to match and contrast the vocal tone of her partner on stage, in order that she genuinely appear to be taking part in a conversation, rather than performing speeches in isolation from the other actor or actors—a very common fault among inexperienced and vocally insensitive actors, and as Brecht pointed out, a technique commonly misused by experienced actors: "Deliberately sometimes, an actor will perform entirely for himself, beginning each remark afresh and simply annulling the preceding remark by his partner. This sort of actor is also liable to insert those small and deadly gaps into the dialogue, quite tiny hesitations which follow one's partner's remark and cut off the new remark from the rest, emphasising it, underlining it and giving its speaker a monopoly of the stage."[68]

Under the fourth heading, "Common tendencies for actors to guard against," are points concerning the actors' spatial relationships on stage, such as "detaching oneself from groups in order to stand alone," or standing too close to other actors. These points chiefly address conventional actors' insensitivity to the ensemble playing that properly indicates the relationship between one person and another in social interactions, and their tendency to generalize action and character and to suppress their own critical attitude to the character. Clearly Brecht believed the best form of actor training was on the job. He had no sympathy for training that removed actors from real life behind a "monastic wall," and he introduced preview performances so that productions could be tested before an audience as the final stage of rehearsal.

Under the leadership of Brecht and Weigel, the Berliner Ensemble came to be regarded as the most important European theater company to have been established since the Moscow Art Theater. The "complex simplicity" of its performances and its ensemble approach to production provided a model that a number of major Western theater practitioners have attempted to emulate.

The Influence of Brecht's Praxis

Although Brecht's success in transforming the political attitudes of bour-geois audiences is questionable, his work has undoubtedly been a major influence on many theater practitioners until the present day. Immediately after the Second World War, the plays of German-language playwrights such as Max Frisch, Friedrich Dürrenmatt, and Peter Weiss revealed Brecht's dramaturgy as the predominant influence on German, Austrian, and Swiss theater; in the 1960s and 1970s a new generation of German-speaking playwrights such as Peter Handke and Heiner Müller explored the inherent postmodern possibilities of the Brechtian aesthetic in conducting their own dramaturgical experiments, as has the avant-garde German chore-ographer Pina Bausch. The most important postwar Italian stage director, Giorgio Strehler, was a great admirer of Brecht, and from the 1950s to the early 1990s staged a large number of Brecht's plays at his Piccolo Teatro in Milan. A Brechtian aesthetic has informed the work of major French the-ater directors, such as Roger Planchon, Ariane Mnouchkine, and Simone Benmussa, and European film directors such as Jean-Luc Godard, Lindsay Anderson, Wim Wenders, and Rainer Werner Fassbinder. Since the 1960s, Brecht's ideas have informed theoretical debates about theater and film and inspired performances by avant-garde groups in the United States such as the Living Theater in New York, the Bread and Puppet Theater in San Francisco, the Wooster Group, and others.

The visit of the Berliner Ensemble to London a fortnight after Brecht's death in 1956 made a profound impact on the new generation of theater writers and directors that emerged in the mid-1950s, exerting an immediate influence on the production aesthetic at the Royal Court and the Royal Shakespeare Company, and reinforcing the incipiently Brechtian approach of Joan Littlewood at the Theatre Royal, Stratford East. During the 1970s, productions by left-wing theater groups all over Britain were informed by Brecht's theory, while his practice provided a model for writers such as John Arden, Edward Bond, David Hare, Howard Brenton, Trevor Griffiths, Howard Barker, Caryl Churchill, Timberlake Wertenbaker, and directors such as William Gaskill, John Dexter, Lindsay Anderson, Howard Davies, Max Stafford-Clark, and many others. Feminist and gay theater groups have found his ideas particularly useful, and aspects of Brechtian praxis have contributed to the development of feminist and queer theory in the United States and Europe since the 1970s.[69]

9. Augusto Boal and the Theater of the Oppressed

The work of Augusto Boal has become enormously influential among alternative theater groups with a socially and politically progressive agenda. In South America, the United States, Canada, and Europe the arsenal of strategies that Boal names *theater of the oppressed* (TO) has provided a new approach to the development of a wide range of techniques in the fields of theater education, social work, dramatherapy, political activism, and theater for development.[1]

From the *Lehrstück* to Forum Theater

As director of the Arena Stage in São Paulo between 1956 and 1971, Boal developed an indigenous Brazilian form of antirealist theater, much influenced by Brechtian praxis, which he called "the joker system." The system aimed to undermine the power of dominant systems of theatrical representation such as naturalism whose photographic images reify a bourgeois view of the world as a given material reality. The commonsense attitude of the spectator to society is subverted through a confrontation not only with the multiplicity of possible constructions of "reality" but also with the infinitely various artistic forms through which these constructions might be represented. The drama offered fantasy in place of the realism that dominated Brazilian theater.

The system was characterized by the function of the joker and by four theatrical techniques:

1. Following Brecht, actors were separated from the characters they played, developing "masks" in the form of generic repertoires of mechanized gestures, vocal habits, costumes, and props to indicate rather than inhabit types of social attitude and behavior.

2. Actors functioned as narrators of the action. All the actors interpreted—and, on occasions, played—all the roles, thereby emphasizing collectively created social meanings rather than nuanced psychological interpretations achieved through the empathic relationship of a single actor with his character.

3. A kind of artistic chaos was created by the extreme stylistic eclecticism. The surprising juxtaposition of a variety of dramatic genres and theatrical styles (e.g., surrealism, soap opera, circus, expressionism, tragicomedy) offered stylistic relief to the spectator, stimulating fresh responses to what was being expressed.

4. Music was used as an independent theatrical language to counterpoint or contradict the other sign systems.

Boal's aim in developing this new approach was to connect individual experience and universal significance in order "to find the typical particular."[2] The opposition between the "ethical" function of the protagonists who represented the particular details of concrete reality and the "dianoethic" function of the wild card or joker who generalized the significance of the action formed the dramaturgical core of the new form. The system of the joker exploited all the discoveries in the areas of dramaturgy and staging made by Boal's company at the Arena Stage.

The new form provided a carnival of unmasking. The polyvalent function of the joker allowed him to shift roles, assume the function of a *raisonneur,* step outside the play to comment on the action, or become directly involved in it. The joker thus promoted an active and critical attitude within the spectator, encouraging him to question all social rituals and public forms and motivating him to challenge the status quo and resist the banal clichés of official discourse. Through the clash of opposing styles, contradictions between different social attitudes and interest groups were revealed, and the falsifying mythologies of bourgeois expressive forms were exposed as fictions.

After the military coup of 1968, political repression in Brazil became so extreme that Boal was led to question the value and efficacy of his middle-class agit-prop theater. He believed that such theater was limited as political activism by its failure to challenge the traditional assumptions built into the bourgeois model of theatrical performance whose privileging of the actor over the spectator unwittingly reproduced the hierarchical power structure of class-based society. By 1971 his innovation of *forum theater* enabled Boal to explore techniques for creating performance that later came to be known as the theater of the oppressed.

Brecht's influence on Boal's mature conception of theater appears to have been profound. During the earlier phase of Boal's work, when he was exploring the possibilities of the joker system, his exploitation of Brechtian dramaturgical techniques appears to have been overt, even though it lacked the subtleties of Brecht's own theatrical dialectics. However, Brecht's idea of the *Lehrstück* as learning experience *for the performer* later provided a practical and theoretical paradigm from which Boal's own praxis developed. Following Brecht's suggestion, Boal transformed the spectator into an actor—a spect-*actor*—for the purpose of motivating and educating each individual to take direct responsibility for effecting change in both the personal and social spheres of his life.

Two Brechtian principles underpin Boal's praxis. The first is that theater should promote concrete political action. A performance should represent actual life, not for the purpose of allowing contemplation of powerful artistic fictions, but to provoke and rehearse interventions that might change those aspects of society that oppress individuals and groups. The second is the notion that dramatic performance in itself constitutes a dialectical process of learning. Although Boal has asserted that he had begun to formulate the techniques of forum theater before he met Paulo Freire, he acknowledged his debt to the ideas of the radical educationalist by naming his own method of theater after Freire's "pedagogy of the oppressed." In any event, Boal's praxis represents a fusion of the Brechtian conception of theater as an instrument for political education with Freire's idea of learning as a process of self-actualization. Freire's goal as an educationalist was to promote a process of *transitive learning,* through which the student is actively engaged in the act of learning rather than merely a vessel for receiving knowledge from the teacher. Boal's aim as a political activist paralleled this purpose, creating performance strategies that would enable the individual to identify the conditions contributing to his oppression and to use theater as a means of improvising alternative ways of changing them.

In a number of respects, Boal took up the idea of political activism inherent in the *Lehrstück* at the point where Brecht left it in the 1930s. On the surface Brecht's artistic employment of more traditional theatrical forms after his return from exile in 1948—albeit to a Berliner Ensemble located in a Communist state—might appear to have been a retreat from his radical praxis in the early 1930s. Brecht restricted the dialectical process of political education to the *symbolic* level of the dramaturgical fiction, which in turn he rendered progressively more sophisticated in its capacity to represent the complex of contradictions through which social reality is articulated. Boal, on the other hand, developed the *Lehrstück*'s inherent theatrical possibilities in precisely the opposite direction. Forum theater is innovatory in its methods of concretely *staging* the self-education process that had been merely implicit in Brechtian theater.

By requiring the spectator to intervene in the acting out of social and personal problems, Boal adds another layer to the Brechtian process of analyzing human action in social terms in order to educate the spectator about effective ways of promoting social change. The spectator is obliged not merely to *think* through the problems and possibilities of effecting change, but also to identify himself with the protagonist's desire for change to the point of physically reenacting his oppressions and testing possible solutions. The techniques of the theater of the oppressed are potentially therapeutic, operating not solely intellectually, but emotionally and physically, to remove the barriers of fear and insecurity through which many people collude in their own oppression.

Forum theater was the first format of the theater of the oppressed to be devised by Boal. It is, however, more complex than some of the other strategies that Boal subsequently introduced, and therefore not normally employed until participants in TO workshops have worked through the first two stages of "knowing the body" and "making the body expressive." From 1974 Boal regarded forum theater as a third degree of the third stage of work dedicated to the participants' discovery of "theater as a language." Forum theater represents the highest degree of direct participation of the spectator in the performance:

> The procedure is as follows: First, the participants are asked to tell a story containing a political or social problem of difficult solution. Then a ten- or fifteen-minute skit portraying that problem and the solution intended for discussion is improvised or rehearsed, and subsequently presented. When the skit is over, the participants are asked if they agree with the solution presented. At least some will say no. At this point it is explained that the scene will be performed once more, exactly as it was the first time. But now any participant in the audience has the right to replace any actor and lead the action in the direction that seems to him most appropriate. The displaced actor steps aside, but remains ready to resume action the moment the participant considers his own intervention to be terminated. The other actors have to face the newly created situation responding instantly to all the possibilities that it may present. . . . Anyone may propose any solution, but it must be done on the stage, working, acting, doing things, and not from the comfort of his seat.[3]

The central scene of forum theater is called the *anti-model,* so as to imply its unsatisfactory nature as a solution to the protagonist's problematic situation. Its real purpose is not to suggest a solution, but to provoke a contest between various alternatives. The actual participation of the spectator who wishes to propose a different solution to the problem is crucial, as he is confronted with the real difficulties posed by his idea of change in the concrete terms in which they would be experienced by an oppressed individual. Theorizations of revolutionary action are tested in the living situation in which the individual must act, promoting realistic attitudes toward the difficulties of effecting change, and stimulating impassioned arguments about strategies for intervention. Typically, intervening spectators learn that their initial solutions to the protagonists' problems do not take full account of the complicated nature of actual social and political injustice. They are obliged to revise their first proposals in the light of new problems posed by the other actors' responses to the new situation created by the intervention. As the scenario progresses—usually to a further impasse—another spectator will be aroused to stop the action and intervene as spect-actor to create yet another possible version of resistance to the oppression suffered by the protagonist, and so the forum game continues.

Even though it is unlikely that any individual will come up with an entirely satisfactory solution in terms of purely individual action, the forum graphically illustrates the workings of an oppressive system in the terms in which it is actually experienced by individuals, and rehearses putative responses that may be individual or collective. The forum is controlled by a *joker* who acts as a kind of master of ceremonies, introducing a degree of commentary upon decisions made by those who intervene in the enactment, where necessary generalizing the social and political significance of the action, provoking response from spect-actors and making sure that the participants are correctly interpreting the rules of the forum game. As a theatrical strategy, forum theater develops even further Brecht's notion of rehearsals as a process of collective creation by involving the audience as decision makers in the rehearsal and construction of a drama that is oriented toward direct intervention in the situations of everyday life.

Logically, a materialist theater aesthetic might be assumed to promote interaction between the living bodies of actors and spectators in the process of social change, so Boal's method of direct rehearsal of the process of change might be seen as an extension of Brecht's materialist theater praxis. In developing the forum theater format through which the spectator as spect-actor employs his own body to remake the actor's performance, Boal created a form of performance that not only bridges the gap between the fictional world of the play and the real world of the audience, but gives the right to author the play to actors and spectators alike. In this way the conventional hierarchy of bourgeois performance, with its formal separation of writer, actors, and audience, is subverted. Forum theater entertains alternative solutions to social and personal problems at the level of action rather than merely as ideas. Whereas Brecht's actors aimed to present a performance to an audience *as though it were a rehearsal,* forum theater promotes a series of reenactments of situations from real life in a way that arms proletarian actors and spectators to *rehearse* the resistance or revolution that is their desired future.

> Aristotle proposes a poetics in which the spectator delegates power to the dramatic character so that the latter may act and think for him. Brecht proposes a poetics in which the spectator delegates power to the character who thus acts in his place but the spectator reserves the right to think for himself, often in opposition to the character. In the first case, a "catharsis" occurs; in the second, an awakening of critical consciousness. But the *poetics of the oppressed* focuses on the action itself: the spectator delegates no power to the character (or actor) either to act or think in his place; on the contrary, he himself assumes the protagonic role, changes the dramatic action, tries out solutions, discusses plans for change—in short, trains himself for real action.[4] In this case, perhaps the theatre is not revolutionary in itself, but it is surely a rehearsal for the revolution. The liberated spectator, as a whole person, launches into action. No matter that the action is fictional; what matters is that it is action! . . . I believe that all the truly revolutionary theater groups should transfer to the people the means of production in the theater so that the people themselves may utilize them. The theater is a weapon, and it is the people who should wield it.[5]

Boal's personal charisma and his generosity have been an inspiration to many thousands of participants in the many workshops he has led around the world. First published in 1974, *The Theater of the Oppressed* has made an enormous impact on political theater practitioners and educationalists. Nevertheless it must be said that the theoretical chapters that precede Boal's outline of his TO techniques in *The Theater of the Oppressed* are contradictory and at times inaccurate. Given its Marxist approach, the book is surprisingly thin on detailed historical analysis, providing simplistic, idiosyncratic, and biased accounts of Aristotle's *Poetics,* Machiavelli, Shakespeare, Hegel, and Brecht by way of introduction to the discussion of Boal's own practice.[6]

A Materialist Aesthetic

Transformations of the Body

In Boal's theater, the materialist aesthetic that motivated Brecht's sculpting of actors' bodies to form a pattern of *gests* expressing in dramatic form the social and economic relationships being analyzed is manifest in the spect-actors' own actual (as opposed to fictionalized) bodies. Utilizing the notion of the *Lehrstück* as a learning experience *for the actors,* Boal's forum theater transforms spectators into performers of their own life dramas. In the various forms of theater of the oppressed, the concrete liberation of the body from its deformations is both a precondition for and a rehearsal of the liberation of the person from the conditions of oppression that created those deformations. In this respect Boal's attitude to revolution is very different from that of Brecht. Brecht scrupulously restricts the function of his epic and dialectical theater to provoking a critical deconstruction of the contradictions of capitalist society, exhorting the spectator to action by the negative force of his picture of the alienation experienced by the individual under capitalism. Boal's praxis, on the other hand, implies that the political act of liberating oneself from social or economic oppression at the same time constitutes a process of therapy or healing. In spite of various denials, Boal does appear to harbor a Rousseauistic ideal of effecting a return to a paradisial (precapitalist) state of being in which an individual's bodily health is the emblem of society's.

By contrast, Brecht appears to have maintained a healthy skepticism about the possibility that psychological change within individuals could provoke changes in the social structure. From *Man Equals Man* (1926) onward many of Brecht's plays explicitly addressed the problematics of the relationship between personal identity and social structures, but they did not suggest an automatic correlation between the social order and the psychic structure of the individual human being.[7] This is why he never proposed an acting training designed to enhance the actor's bodily or vocal expressiveness. Brecht maintained a rigorous historicism, treating performers as individuals already formed by their personal and social histories. While he might certainly have tried to influence their artistic or ideological choices in the composition of a performance, he saw no point in trying to mold the performers' artistic temperaments. On an ideological level, he wished his performers to adopt a Marxist point of view, but nevertheless appeared to relish the larger-than-life personalities of many of his actors: Brechtian theater emphasized the contradictions between the performer's attitude and that attributed to the dramatic character. So long as the actor did not conflate his own persona with the social attitude of the character he was portraying, the critique of the character's actions and decisions would be effective.

Like that of Copeau, however, Boal's praxis does in certain respects imply that acting is a way of remaking the body to recover the essential humanity deformed through centuries of social conditioning. Although Boal's political orientation is directly opposed to the conservatism of Copeau, their parallel pursuit of a utopian ideal of *communitas* renders their theatrical praxis similar in this one important respect. In *The Theater of the Oppressed* the process of transformation of spectator into actor proceeds in four stages, from exercises to enhance his awareness of his own body, through a series of games and exercises aimed at making the body expressive, to a third stage in which the techniques of theater as a language are acquired, culminating in a fourth stage involving the staging of theatrical spectacles directed toward the deconstruction and demystification of traditional modes of social and political discourse.

Unlike Copeau, however, Boal is careful not to impose an image of the neutral or ideally liberated body. The aim of the first stage of exercises is not to construct a new body image, but to make each individual participant *conscious* of the peculiar pattern of nervous and muscular habits that constitute his physical identity. The process of physically "disjointing" his own movements allows the TO participant to achieve greater flexibility and range in adopting and controlling patterns of movement characteristic of other social classes and occupations. Philip Auslander explains the rationale for this aspect of Boal's work: "What Boal seems to be after . . . is not so much a Brechtian gestic body educated and shaped by its experience of class struggle, as a body that can step aside momentarily from its particular ideological regimen to try on others for size. This is not necessarily with the intention of adopting them, but as a means of exploring other configurations. . . . The Boalian body never comes to rest in a neutral state; rather the point is for the spect-actor to be able to move from one mask to another while retaining a critical distance from all masks. The spect-actor cannot exist outside ideology and doesn't even attempt to, but can only try on different ideological positionings as they are inscribed on the body."[8]

Knowing the Body

In order to avoid alienating or imposing theatrical techniques upon TO participants, Boal advises the facilitator to begin by asking them to use the individual's primary expressive instrument—the body. Boal offers a series of games—the slow-motion race, cross-legged race, the wheel race, and a boxing match in which participants engage in a mock fight with the proviso

that they never touch. In another exercise he calls *hypnosis,* pairs of participants face each other, one putting his hand a few inches from his partner's
face, and moving it in all directions while the partner attempts to maintain
the exact distance between his face and his partner's hand. A Wild West
scenario invites the participants to perform a silent mime version of a bad
Hollywood western, in which every participant in a typical barroom brawl
must react in character to every action or movement performed.[9] All these
exercises attempt to disturb the habitual movement pattern of each participant, challenging him to reassemble kinetic components in new formations.
He thus achieves a temporary experience of other possible body images,
while identifying the peculiar features of his own. Thus each person is
enabled to discover for himself the extent to which physical behavior patterns are determined by the demands of work, in its turn a function of class.

Making the Body Expressive

The second stage implies a critique of the logocentrism of modern culture
and in my view represents a further example of Boal's elaboration of the
Marxist notion of the relationship of base to superstructure. Boal views the
body as the primary instrument of human expression (in the way that material conditions form the base structure), while speech is expressive at a secondary level (just as ideology is manifest as superstructure). Implicit in Boal's
view is a politics of presence. The assumption is that human being is centered in the body, so that speech is more "truthful" or more fully expressive
when rooted in the somatic presence of the person, rather than in the "free-
floating" form of written text. In order to educate or reeducate the body to
be expressive, Boal devised games that force the participants to use sensuous
and physical apprehension to engage with others, rather than conventional
verbal language. Many of these exercises involve imitating animals. Typically, participants are required to work in pairs, one person watching while
the other person treats him like a specific animal. The partner must respond
as the animal he assumes is being imagined. At a certain point, the players
reverse roles, so that all have a chance of being animals. The game can cre
ate much hilarity if partners do not guess what kind of animal is being portrayed, but it invariably stimulates the direct physical engagement of participants in performance. Participants are encouraged to invent their own
games to add to the repertoire already suggested by Boal.

Theater as a Language

According to Boal, any TO technique must initially derive from the experience of the individual before it progresses to a more general level of discourse. A full exploration of an individual case of oppression or repression leads spectators to understand the social laws governing all cases. Theater is a language that should function in the present to bring about change in the future rather than creating an image of a life already past. To this end he identifies three "degrees" of theater language: (1) simultaneous dramaturgy, (2) image theater, and (3) forum theater. The sequence of techniques requires progressively greater degrees of active engagement in the movement toward changing the conditions of oppression experienced by the participants.

Simultaneous dramaturgy invites the spectator to intervene in "rewriting" a short scene improvised by actors at the request of a spectator who desires to confront a problematic situation. At the moment of crisis, the actors stop performing and ask the spectators to propose solutions, each of which the actors immediately improvise with the aid of the audience, who have the right to correct aspects of the performance as it proceeds. The audience discusses the pros and cons of each improvised solution with the benefit of concrete illustrations provided by the performers' enactments. Elements of the discussion can be played out as performance, revealing all the inherent possibilities of action *in the form of action.* The action ceases to be presented in a deterministic manner as something inevitable—as fate: "Everything is subject to criticism, to rectification. All can be changed, and at a moment's notice. . . . The actor . . . goes on being the interpreter. If formerly he interpreted the solitary author locked in his study . . . here on the contrary he must interpret the mass audience . . . he must give expression to the collective thought of men and women."[10]

Image theater was developed in 1973 when Boal participated in a national literacy campaign in Peru. The body, rather than spoken language, is the expressive instrument, allowing the participant to engage in the dramatization of his oppression at the most fundamental level. Physical expression functions as a language for communicating the most basic types of oppression felt as bodily experience and manifest in kinesthetic images created by the oppressed body. Although image theater was only identified as a specific strategy after the form of forum theater had been devised, Boal subsequently utilized image theater as a preparatory technique in forum theater workshops. It is now viewed as the key to TO games and exercises, providing a basis for Boal's development of "the rainbow of desire" techniques in the late 1980s. Participants start with physical warm-ups and are then invited to express their feelings and picture their experiences by sculpting images on their own and others' bodies. These images enable the participants to recognize clearly the nature of oppression as a *real* experience rather than as an abstract concept. An image theater workshop normally starts with games and warm-up exercises aimed at building participants' confidence in the use of their bodies, before sensitizing the body to the difference between repression and liberation. Image theater itself then proceeds from the sculpting of individual images of oppression to a group tableau, collaboratively created. This is followed by a process of "dynamization" in which the image is transformed into one in which the oppression is contested and liberation achieved. The pressures of daily life might have habituated individuals to their own oppression, encouraging a passive acceptance of that which seems impossible to change. Image theater encourages participants to identify the most fundamental types of oppression in their own lives. It also gives them the opportunity to create images of ideal situations where the oppression does not exist.

Forum theater (which has been previously discussed) is the most complex and actively interventionist of the three types of theater language and builds upon the motivation for change provoked by the TO participants' experience of the first two. Image theater exercises constitute a useful preparation for forum theater work, enabling participants to recognize both their own oppression and the desired solution before attempting to rehearse strategies for transforming actual situations.

Theater as Discourse

Boal quotes approvingly George Ikishawa's view of formal theater as a bourgeois conception: "The bourgeoisie already knows what the world is like, *their* world, and is able to present images of this complete, finished world. The bourgeoisie presents the spectacle. On the other hand, the proletariat and the oppressed classes do not know yet what their world will be like; consequently their theatre will be the rehearsal, not the finished spectacle. . . . it is equally true that the theatre can present images of transition."[11]

Boal deconstructs a number of traditional theater forms, refunctioning them so that they question and subvert the bourgeois status quo, rather than reinforce it. Boal's list of formal theater techniques includes newspaper theater, invisible theater, breaking of repression, masks and rituals, photo-romance, and myth theater. His utilization of these techniques involves different methods of deconstructing the "inevitable" logic of traditional narrative and discursive forms. For example, the speaking of newspaper reports in the rhythmic forms of popular song disrupts the seemingly natural connection between sound and sense. Playing out the news in apparently inappropriate theatrical styles defamiliarizes the conventional rhetorical relationship between its form and content, thereby exposing the ways in which bourgeois forms of expression naturalize the arbitrary basis of the social status quo. In every case, theatrical techniques are utilized to reveal the class interests that determine social interactions. In order to expose the contradictions within each individual's experience of social existence, different social roles are externalized through the overt deployment of props or costumes. In Boal's enactment of each form, the original narrative or discursive structure is taken apart to expose the oppression it reinforces, before being reassembled by the spectators-actors so that it can be made to represent a preferred social order.

The most widespread technique of the fourth stage is *invisible theater*. Actors rehearse scenarios they will perform in appropriate public places, where they make interventions in everyday life situations in order to provoke actual conflicts and generate real debate. So, for example, a group of actors might rehearse a performance about price-fixing by supermarkets that they perform at a supermarket in the guise of shoppers. It is essential that none of the onlookers know they are acting. They must appear like irate customers, complaining about the price of groceries. The drama should evolve in such a way that other customers are spontaneously drawn into the situation so that they too become involved in the arguments. If the store manager attempts to suppress the fracas that breaks out, the actors have to be prepared to engage more shoppers in the moral questions entailed in the restriction of freedom of speech. Such "spontaneous" theater (which must never be revealed as theater by the performers) effectively teaches actors the possibilities and difficulties of engaging in real political activity, encouraging a positive and critical attitude toward social change as it provokes passers-by into actual political discussion and debate.

From the "Cop in the Head" to the "Rainbow of Desire"

Throughout all the phases of Boal's work, a relationship has persisted between material oppression on one hand, and mental/psychological oppression on the other. Boal started by teaching his techniques to those groups obviously deprived of freedom or power, such as working-class women, gay people, peasants, and laborers. Gradually he moved toward more complex confrontations with the many subtle forms of oppression attendant upon the sophisticated hegemonic mechanisms of late-twentieth-century capitalism. While in exile from Brazil and Argentina between 1976 and 1986, Boal had the opportunity to develop the TO strategies to fit new social contexts. The "cop in the head" strategies described in *The Rainbow of Desire,* were codified between 1988 and 1993 and derived from Boal's experiences of conducting TO workshops in Western Europe.

Initially hostile to the overtly therapeutic use of theater (like Brecht he believed the dominant Aristotelian mode of Western theater exploited the process of catharsis to make the spectator passive in the face of social injustice), he came to realize that the protagonist's (and, in turn, spect-actor's) experience of catharsis was in fact a liberation, an unblocking of the repression that prevented him from taking action to address his own oppression. Just as the illiterate Peruvian farm laborer is materially enslaved by his economic exploitation at the hands of his boss, so are many individuals in Western societies crippled by the psychologically internalized power of late capitalist ideology to manipulate and control consciousness

While working in Europe in the late 1970s, Boal came to understand the peculiar forms of alienation that created suffering among relatively affluent Western people. Oppression is internalized, manifesting itself in feelings of loneliness, helplessness, or emptiness rather than in violence; such suffering might be painful enough to provoke suicide. Boal characterizes such internalized oppression as "the cop in the head." Its actual causes, he believes, exist outside of the individual consciousness, but the ideology of late capitalism is so sophisticated that it has developed psychological mechanisms that repress the individual's desires and encourage him to censor himself. To tackle the oppression one has first to challenge the self-censoring device. Thus social change is linked to psychic change. In 1991, Boal described the relationship between social and psychic change in terms of therapy: "politics is the therapy of society, therapy is the politics of the person."[12]

Theater of the oppressed is a tool for transforming individuals and groups into active participants in their own social and personal destinies. While it does not pretend to offer global solutions to macrocosmic problems, it provides effective strategies for transforming the passive victim of oppression or repression into an active protagonist with a faith in the possibility of changing the concrete circumstances of his oppression. According to Boal, the cop in the head is an introjection of the external agent of oppression that seeks to objectify the individual victim. But the oppressor cannot completely reduce the individual to an object, for oppression produces in the victim not only submission but also subversion. The goal of TO is to remove the propensity to submit, and consequently dynamize the impulse to subvert.

Utilizing the transitive relationship between stage and auditorium, TO empowers the participant, encouraging her to take control of the dramatic action with the help of the spectators. *Metaxis* is the process that allows the participant to play within the potential space of art while at the same time inhabiting the real world. This provides him with the opportunity to experiment with alternative possibilities, in the process of discovering better ways of being. The experience of an individual's oppression must be translatable into terms that can be shared by others; if it is entirely singular, it may not be amenable to group analysis and reenactment. Boal employs the principle of *analogical induction* to allow others to identify with the essential human content of the drama. By offering alternative suggestions and perspectives, the others promote a distanced analysis of the participant's problem: "Theatre . . . is this capacity . . . which allows man to observe himself in action. . . . The self-knowledge thus acquired allows him to be the subject (the one who observes) of another subject (the one who acts). It allows him to imagine variations of his action, to study alternatives. . . . Man can . . . feel himself feeling, think himself thinking."[13]

The distinguishing feature of the rainbow-of-desire strategies employed to counteract the cop in the head is that the oppressed individual performs the act of liberation himself, thus being enabled to undertake it in everyday life. Improvisations are performed with the oppressed person as both protagonist and director of the drama in order to help him to identify his own will and the forces that are preventing its realization. "Points of crisis" at which the protagonist makes choices must be analyzed to understand why he normally chooses inappropriate alternatives. The other actors and spect-actors provide a perspective on the protagonist's choices, offering suggestions for alternative ways of responding to circumstances and creating a sense of the shared experience of sympathetic supporters to counter feelings of isolation and oppression. The polysemic property of an image means that different participants offer different interpretations of it. Boal's work may be distinguished from other forms of drama-therapy because it directly involves the group in offering alternative perspectives on the individual's problem. The rainbow of desire aims to enable individuals to overcome their sense of isolation by participating in a shared experience of the fear and self-censorship manifest as the cop in the head. The collaborative nature of such theatrical activity produces feelings of personal liberation and self-esteem. The overriding effect produced by a Boal workshop, whether undertaken to address conditions of material oppression or psychological repression, is an experience of carnival. Being able to express negative feelings in a protected space with the support of a sympathetic group liberates the sense of emotional well-being consequent on a proper understanding of human rights and promotes the confidence to assert them. The intention is to enable the participants to change the negative patterns of their daily lives.

Since being elected member of the Rio de Janeiro Chamber of Vereadores (equivalent to a city council) as a Workers' Party representative in 1994, Boal has employed forum theater techniques to create a form he calls "legislative theater." Legislative theater gives communities the tools to identify social problems that urgently need addressing. Through the use of TO techniques, participants discover the specific conditions of injustice or hardship that new legislation would address, in order to assist in the effective framing of the law. Lawyers then draft legislation that the *vereadore* (Boal himself, during the mid-1990s) can put forward in the chamber to address specific injustices or hardships. Legislative theater thus becomes a way of motivating and persuading politicians to recognize the need for new and more effective laws.

Boal's own circumstances presented him with the opportunity to utilize the TO techniques in new ways. It is nevertheless a measure of his resourcefulness and commitment to progressive social change that he has discovered new contexts in which the basic principles of TO might be of value. Boal has redefined the profession of the actor, linking overtly artistic functions of theatrical performance with traditions of Drama- and Theatre-in-Education, dramatherapy, and forms of political activism that had previously been viewed as unconnected activities.

10. Antonin Artaud, the Actor's Body, and the Space of Performance

Within the sphere of avant-garde performance, the intensity of Artaud's life and the force of his writing still radiate incandescently. Yet Artaud's career constitutes a paradox. Notwithstanding the enormous impact his notion of a theater of cruelty has made on performance practitioners during the last fifty years, his own specific attempts to achieve such a radical theater were failures. The extraordinary suggestiveness of his writing on theater was a response to what he believed to be the decadence of a Western culture that he felt powerless to destroy.

The Existential Drama

The potent myth he created of himself as victim of a blindly oppressive society was his unique way of expressing—often through the medium of his own tortured body—his overwhelming sense of rage and humiliation at the rejection of his radical ideas by the French intellectual establishment. Reading Artaud can be a bewildering experience. His language is dense, vague, repetitious, poetic, and, on the surface, self-contradictory. Multiple images of a theater of cruelty accumulate so rapidly in his essays that the forms and devices they are intended to indicate dissolve at the moment one feels one has grasped them, leaving one only with a sense of the writer's violent energy and compulsive desire to annihilate the power of established culture. It may indeed have been the explosive negativity of his views on theater that cleared the space in which avant-garde dramatists, performers, and directors in the 1960s and 1970s were able to conduct their own Artaudian experiments against the grain of Western traditions of performance.[1] Artaud voiced impossible demands of the contemporary French theater system. This may have done more to provoke new initiatives by succeeding generations of practitioners than the carefully modulated ideas and subtle nuances of practice offered by many of his contemporaries. A survey of much post-modern performance would suggest that a number of the most notable contemporary practices are new methods of realizing notions of the body in performance originally formulated by Artaud.[2]

Artaud's ideas are, however, opposed to one tendency in postmodern performance—that of theater as the unrestricted play of signification, with unlimited potential for mediatization. In this respect Artaud's praxis can be seen to initiate a tradition identified by Eugenio Barba as third theater, which is opposed to the related but different tradition of postmodern performance deriving from Craig and Meyerhold. By espousing an aesthetic of performance as presence, the third theater follows Artaud, ignoring or rejecting the deconstructive turn of postmodern performance manifest in games of self-reflexivity, quotation, mediatization, and pastiche, as Artaud had rejected the hermeneutic games of representation that characterize literary theater. While he was very aware of the playful nature of theatrical representation, Artaud became disillusioned not only by the theater's literary qualities but also with the idea of performance as spontaneous play through which dada and surrealist art had aimed to capture the flow of the unconscious. His break in 1926 with the surrealist movement marked the point at which his unique conception of theatrical performance as *event* was formulated in earnest.

In an essay written that year to introduce his proposed Théâtre Alfred Jarry, Artaud explained the power of the theater event by picturing a hypothetical police raid on an "ordinary-looking house":

[From] inside the house there emerges a group of women walking single file like beasts to the slaughter. The plot thickens: the police net was intended not for a gang of criminals but only for a group of women. Our emotion and our amazement are at their peak. . . . For surely we are just as guilty as these women and just as cruel as these policemen. . . . Well this spectacle is ideal theater. This anguish, this feeling of guilt, this satiety gives the tone and feeling of the mental state in which the spectator must leave our theatre. He will be shaken and antagonised by the internal dynamic of the spectacle, and this dynamic will be in direct proportion to the anxieties and preoccupations of his whole life. . . . it is not to the minds or the senses of the spectators that we address ourselves but to their whole existence. Their existence and ours. We stake our own lives on the spectacle that unfolds on the stage. . . . The spectator who comes to our theater knows that he is to undergo a real operation in which not only his mind but his senses and his flesh are at stake. Henceforth he will go to the theater the way he goes to the surgeon or the dentist. . . . He must be totally convinced that we are capable of making him scream.[3]

From this moment in the development of his thinking, performance, as opposed to writing, became Artaud's model for the form and function of art. Performance was not simply a game of make-believe but demanded a peculiar interpenetration of reality and theater. The essays of the 1930s published as *The Theater and its Double* proposed the notion of a theater of cruelty whose essence as art consisted in an unrepeatable action or gesture that destroyed itself in the moment of its creation. It was typical of Artaud's thinking that his theater of cruelty is in concrete terms unrealizable—a demand for an art of pure gesture that is self-consuming. He believed it was only by destroying theater that a true theater could be born. Derrida's explication of Artaud's ideas concluded that Artaud attempted to replace theater (as a mode of representation) with performance (as a mode of presence).[4]

Theatrical performance was for Artaud a limiting point of human experience: in theater the fullness of pure being is experienced at the moment of its own extinction. Artaud's shifting and difficult notion of the double offered a possible explanation of this paradox. "If the theatre is the double of life, life is the double of the true theatre."[5] The theater of cruelty is born to create life from the human residue of a dead civilization but at the same time as the act of theater animates its double (life) in the event of performance it becomes the double of life, the dead form that shadows the living.

During the last two years of his life, after a nine-year incarceration in the mental asylum at Rodez, Artaud came to believe that his few appearances as a public speaker were a more authentic demonstration of the power of a theater of cruelty than the actual productions by means of which he had earlier attempted to exemplify this idea. Life came to "double" theater as theater had been intended to "double" life: the unrepeatable event that he desired theater to be was created by the intensity of Artaud's heightened public display of his own suffering. The physical and mental pain that persisted throughout Artaud's life as a consequence of his various addictions to drugs originally prescribed to control his psychotic states was to be figured abstractly in a theater that would reveal the complacency of bourgeois society for the terrible lie he knew it to be.

The Theater of Cruelty

The originality of Artaud's notions of performance did not reside in any innovations with respect to concrete theatrical devices or techniques that he proposed. Most of those described in "The Theater of Cruelty: First Manifesto" were not in fact new. The idea of theater as a total artwork, which is repeated in so many different ways in his essays, is common to the ideas and practices of a number of major modernist directors whose productions he had seen (e.g., Meyerhold, Piscator, and Copeau) or whose writing on theater he was familiar with (e.g., Appia and Craig). He was influenced by the performances and written texts of a number of expressionist plays (he assisted Ivan Goll with a production of his play *Methusalem,* and he had directed Strindberg's *A Dream Play* and *The Ghost Sonata*). Even the first project intended to realize his own theatrical ideas was named after a radical practitioner of the fin de siècle, Alfred Jarry.

What defined Artaud's notion of performance as *cruelty* was its authenticity as event, the visceral nature of the encounter between spectator and spectacle—its power to release the demons that it was the normal function of social conventions to repress. Uniquely, Artaud's writings on theater possess the power to convey the idea of a theater that may never have existed and that may be unrealizable. The essays in *The Theatre and its Double* read like texts for incantation in an Artaudian theatrical event. Artaud evoked the qualities of this total art form in a language so rich in sonority and so concrete in its evocation of sensuous images that one could imagine it being conjured into existence by a mere reading of the essays.[6] "I say that the stage is a physical and concrete place which demands to be filled and which must be made to speak its own concrete language. . . . To make a metaphysics out of spoken language is to make language express what it does not usually express. It is to use it in a new, exceptional, and unaccustomed way, restore its possibilities for physical shock, to divide it and distribute it actively in space, to use intonations in an absolutely concrete manner and to restore their power to hurt as well as to manifest something."[7]

The essay "On the Balinese Theater" evokes Artaud's impressions of the Balinese dance-drama that he witnessed at the Colonial Exhibition in Paris in 1931. Artaud rendered its sensuous and physical form in a manner that transformed the event into a concrete demonstration of his own theatrical project:

> [The] Balinese are carrying out with the utmost rigor the idea of pure theater, in which everything, conception and realization alike, has value or existence only in terms of its degree of objectification *on the stage.* . . . The situations are vague, abstract, extremely general. What brings them to life is the complex profusion of all the artifices of the stage, which impose on our minds, as it were, the idea of a metaphysics derived from a new utilization of gesture and voice. What is really curious about all

these gestures, these angular and abruptly broken attitudes, these syncopated modulations formed at the back of the throat, these musical phrases that break off short, these flappings of insect wings, these rustlings of branches, these sounds of hollow drums, these creakings of robots, these dances of animated puppets, is this: that out of their labyrinth of gestures, attitudes, and sudden cries, out of gyrations and turns that leave no portion of the stage unused, there emerges the sense of a new physical language based on signs rather than on words. These actors with their geometric robes seem like animated hieroglyphs.[8]

Among the many vivid images through which *The Theatre and its Double* envisioned the theater of cruelty, one provides a significant insight into the phenomenology of performance. Artaud wrote of the unity of body-mind in the experience of performance as a proof of the "metaphysical identity of the concrete and the abstract." This was not merely a statement of his estimation of the value of performance as a therapy for the disintegrated self, but reflected the view adumbrated at various points in the book, that matter cannot be separated from thought and feeling. According to Artaud, it was a primary function of performance to recuperate the ontological wholeness that Western civilization had caused the individual to lose: "Nothing is left to chance or to personal initiative. It is a kind of superior dance in which the dancers are, above all, actors. . . . *this revelatory aspect of matter* . . . seems suddenly to scatter into signs in order to teach us the metaphysical identity of the concrete and the abstract. . . . the realistic aspect of matter is known in Western Theater, but here it is carried to the nth power and definitively stylized."[9]

In certain respects this was a development of the notion of performance envisaged in Craig's vision of the actor as Über-marionette. Artaud went much further than Craig, however, in theorizing the epistemological purpose of such art and in giving a precise value and significance to the humanity of the performer: "The domain of the theater is not psychological but plastic and physical. And the point is not whether the physical language of the theater is capable of arriving at the same psychological resolutions as the language of words, whether it can express feelings and passions as well as words; the point is whether there are not in the domain of thought and intelligence attitudes which words are incapable of capturing and which gestures, and everything that partakes of the language of space, express with greater precision than words. . . . The point is not to do away with speech in the theater but to change its function, and above all to reduce its role?[10] Here Artaud was rethinking not merely the aim of Western theater but inventing a new model of dramaturgy to express that aim. The total theater proposed by Artaud was a corporeal and spatial event, in which all the actor's faculties of bodily expression animated the empty space of performance. The synesthesic effect of the performance provoked an experience that reintegrates the spectator's mind and body in a primordial unity of being.

Artaud's own scenarios and texts for a theater of cruelty, together with the classic texts he listed for possible future productions, provided a suggestive image of what such a theater could be. His scenario for *The Conquest of Mexico* and his adaptation of *The Cenci* from works by Stendhal and Shelley demonstrated the violence of the attack he aimed to conduct on the existing French literary culture. The only production he actually staged was his own version of *The Cenci,* which eliminated much of the lyrical beauty of Shelley's verse in favor of horrifying visual spectacle. Although its performance does not seem to have been entirely successful, the visceral nature of the text's concrete language of sound and gesture insisted on the performance as an event rather than a dramatic reading. Typically Artaud proposed to stage a gory Elizabethan tragedy (he cited *Arden of Faversham* as an example) but indicated that he would cut most of the language to expose the barbarity of its core action and atmosphere of violence and terror. Other proposed texts include the gruesome story of Rabbi Simeon from the *Zohar,* the erotic horrors of Bluebeard, the sacking of Jerusalem and a story by the Marquis de Sade. His early scenario, *The Spurt of Blood,* although extremely fanciful, proposed to fill the stage with concrete physical images, while the later scenario, *The Philosopher's Stone,* is more stylized and condensed in presenting the struggle of Harlequin and Isabelle to maintain their instinctual vitality in the face of Dr. Pale's relentlessly abstract logic. The repressive rationalism of patriarchy was presented as a sustained series of ritualistically eroticized acts of violence.

Although the violent atmosphere of these putative events appears extremely intense, Artaud himself believed that action in the theater should be symbolic, not literal, and specifically asserted that cruelty was a metaphysical rather than a physical phenomenon. Many of Artaud's contemporaries and critics regarded his radio piece *To Have Done with the Judgement of God* as the most successful demonstration of his theatrical ideal.[11] Although recorded in November 1947, its broadcast was banned on the grounds of obscenity and political offensiveness. Even today the range of vocal textures and sounds—screams, animal noises, staccato speech, roars, yelps, tom-toms, and "xylophonics"—produces a shock. The density of sound and the incantatory quality of the declamation of obscenities, poetic prose, and non-

sense language by Artaud and three other actors remains a startling demonstration of the concrete aural language the theater of cruelty was intended to
employ.

Actor and Spectator: The Affective Relationship

In direct opposition to the Western tradition of theatrical realism, Artaud
rejected characterization as a significant function of performance. In doing
so, he was not merely opposing the Stanislavskian notion of character, which
Appia, Craig, Meyerhold, and Copeau had done before him. By reimagin-
ing the function of the actor, he went further than any had done to propose
a notion of the actor as the provocateur (shaman or therapist) in an encounter
with the spectator designed to precipitate a catharsis as material as that
induced by homeopathy. What distinguishes Artaud's concept of total theater from that of his contemporaries was this unique notion of its affectivity.

> The theater is the only place in the world and the last collective means
> we still have of reaching the organism directly and . . . by physical means
> which it cannot resist. If music has an effect on snakes, it is not because
> of the spiritual notions it offers them, but because snakes are long,
> because they lie coiled on the ground, because their bodies touch the
> ground at almost every point; and the musical vibrations which are com-
> municated to the ground reach their bodies like a very subtle and pro-
> found massage; well, I propose that we treat the spectators like snakes
> that are being charmed, and that we lead them by way of the organism
> to the subtlest notions. . . . This is why in the "theater of cruelty" the
> spectator is in the middle and the spectacle surrounds him.[12]

This is one of the clearest and most extreme defenses of the efficacy of
performance as a live event. The image of theater as a personal and sensuous encounter between actor and spectator is a fundamental tenet of the
practitioners Eugenio Barba has grouped under the umbrella of third theater. By arguing for "no more masterpieces," Artaud sought to undermine
the dominance of a concept of dramatic performance first expounded by
Aristotle of a semiotic theater whose physical and sensuous elements are
externalizations of the germ of meaning encoded in a plot. In its place he
calls for a phenomenological notion of theater, whose essence resides in the
actualization of spectacle: "The objects, the props, even the scenery which
will appear on the stage will have to be understood in an immediate sense,

without transposition; they will have to be taken not for what they represent but for what they really are."[13]

The total artwork that Artaud proposed would not, as does the literary drama, employ its narrative and spectacular components, to communicate ideas and arguments. Its aim is not so much to communicate as to alter the consciousness of the spectator: "[We] must ask ourselves not whether it [this language of mise-en-scène] can state thoughts clearly but whether it can *make us think*, whether it can lead the mind to assume profound attitudes which are effective from its own point of view."[14]

Artaud's reconception of the modernist notion of total theater contains two opposing tendencies. At the same time as he argued fiercely for a theater that gave equal value to sounds, light, music, gesture, words, movement, and physical objects, so did he paradoxically demand the stripping down of the modern stage to rid it of its meaningless appurtenances—its reduction to an empty space suitable for the corporeal realization of the essential gesture.[15] This empty space was to be the environment for a performance in which dramatic representation gave way to bodily presence— the encounter between actor and spectator in a pure action untainted by the absurdity of theatrical pretence. It was this absolute concentration on the psychic transaction achieved through the agency of stage spectacle that distinguished Artaud's theater project from those of his predecessors and contemporaries. This focus on the unique affectivity through which the body in performance transforms the actor-spectator relationship marks the point of origin of the third theater.

In "Art and Death" Artaud had written that "there is a mind in the flesh, a mind quick as lightning."[16] Western civilization had corrupted the individual consciousness by causing a split between mind and body. It was the task of the actor, by making manifest the intelligent body in performance, to recover the embodied consciousness of the spectator. Given the extent to which civilization had repressed the carnality of the individual intelligence, this task could not be achieved easily, which is why Artaud's descriptions of the theater of cruelty are replete with vivid evocations of screams, groans, violent actions, and shock effects. In "An Emotional Athleticism" Artaud wrote of the actor as "an athlete of the heart," suggesting that the performer should be prepared to suffer in the act of incarnating the spectacle of the "victim, signalling through the flames."[17] The performer would resemble a scapegoat or martyr whose sacrifice was an act of self-liberation that would free every spectator from the repression and self-alienation that is a condition of modern consciousness.

The Performer as Athlete of the Heart

Although Artaud's essay "An Emotional Athleticism" is couched in somewhat mystical language, and its prescriptions are not directly practicable in a
literal sense, it is a profoundly suggestive essay on the art of the performer
that articulates a number of ideas that have dominated much subsequent
debate about voice and body training. An ideal that motivates much modern praxis might be seen to derive from ideas expressed in the essay—the
performer's goal of achieving the kind of body-mind wholeness that is prior
to any split between thinking, feeling, and corporeal expression.[18]

The central image in the essay of an actor as "an athlete of the heart" has
some features in common with the behavioristic notion of the actor as
exemplified in Meyerhold's biomechanics. While Meyerhold and Artaud
both insisted on the psychophysical unity of the performer as moving being,
Artaud maintained a notion of spiritual/psychic identity as paradoxically
located in and transcending the purely material level of the performer's corporeal existence. Artaud could not have known of Stanislavski's later experiments in actor training and rehearsal techniques (which were being conducted contemporaneously with the writing of *The Theater and its Double*).
However, in viewing the body as a medium for emotional expression,
Artaud addressed problems that Stanislavski was attempting to resolve
through the method of physical actions. Stanislavski had accepted a behavioristic explanation of the emotions as a function of intentional action,
apparently not having the time or inclination to examine precisely the
mechanism by means of which feelings are communicated to the spectator
as a by-product of the actor/character's objectives in action.

While Stanislavski had moved away from a notion of acting as the
expression of the character's emotions, Artaud was always interested in the
affective function of the body in registering the performer's passion.[19] A
typically Neoplatonist dualism of corporeal function was inherent in
Artaud's conception of acting. Whereas the athlete employed the muscula-
ture of the body to perfect purely physical movements, the actor used the
body to express the movement of the passions. Artaud's conception of the
double was refunctioned to indicate how the body could operate as a
signifier of sensibility: "The actor is like a real physical athlete, but with this
surprising qualification, that he has an emotional organism which is analogous to the athlete's, which is parallel to it, which is like its double, although
it does not operate on the same level."[20]

In some respects, Artaud's notion of the actor's emotional expressivity
was strikingly similar to that of Laban's idea of the "inner content" of effort

actions: "The muscular movements of human effort are like the effigy of another identical effort, which in the movements of dramatic performance is localised at the same points. . . . All the sudden movements of boxing, wrestling, the hundred-yard dash, the high jump, have analogous organic foundations in the movement of the passions; they have the same physical points of support."[21]

Although Artaud was not inclined to attempt anything resembling a systematic elaboration of the function of human effort, his idea of breathing as the connecting link between voice, mind, and body was original and suggestive:

> With this further qualification, however, that the movement is reversed and that with respect to breathing, for example, whereas in the actor the body is supported by the breath, in the boxer, in the physical athlete, it is the breath that is supported by the body. This question of breathing is, in fact, primary; it is related inversely to the importance of the external movement. The more restrained and internalised the movement, the fuller and heavier the breathing, the more substantial and full of resonance. Whereas when the movement is sweeping, broad, and externalized, the corresponding breathing is characterised by short and labored puffs. It is certain that for every feeling, every movement of the mind, every leap of human emotion, there is a breath that belongs to it.[22]

In grappling with the relationship between what Laban called the "inner (dynamic) content" and spatial form of human movement, Artaud had an intuitive sense that the connecting term was breathing. In physiological terms it is undeniable that movement affects the rhythm and intensity of breathing. As breathing is intimately connected with bodily feelings, Artaud was in general terms quite correct to point to its significance. Characteristically, however, Artaud chose to adopt the ideas and terminology of the *Kabala* as a mystical explanation of the "rhythms that give the human heart its form and give the movements of the passions their sex."[23]

Taken metaphorically, the idea that every feeling has a corresponding breath is highly suggestive, though Artaud's language tended to reify every breath and state of feeling as though each were isolatable from the "maze of vibrations" that he later, more helpfully, suggested was the physiological reality of the soul. "I have had the idea of employing a knowledge of breathing not only in the actor's work but in his professional training. . . . It is obvious that if breathing accompanies effort, the mechanical production of the breath will generate in the working organism a corresponding qual-

ity of effort. The effort will have the color and rhythm of the artificially produced breath."[24] Much of Cicely Berry's work on releasing and discovering
the energy of a text involves the physical stimulation of breathing patterns
and concomitant rhythms of feeling by movement, a method of working
that could be derived from Artaud's essay. Similarly Artaud's intuitive sense
of the way in which human feeling could be visualized in terms of "the
rhythm of the passions" is redolent of Laban's scale of eight effort actions.[25]

A powerful metaphor current among voice and speech teachers today
shaped the argument of Artaud's whole essay—that of breath as the life force
that activated the expressive potential of the actor as it animated her body:
"the breath rekindles life, it inflames its very substance."[26] Artaud explained
how the actor, by altering the rhythm of breathing, could produce different
emotional states: "Thus, by means of the sharpened penetration of breathing, the actor probes the depths of his personality."[27] Artaud borrowed from
the *Kabala* the schema of three kinds of breath with their corresponding
qualities and "sexes." The male breath corresponded with exhalation and
was emotionally positive; the female breath corresponded with inhalation
and was emotionally negative. A balanced state of breath (presumably equal
stress on inhalation and exhalation) was androgynous and emotionally
neuter, evoking "precious states of suspension."[28]

Artaud referred to points of localization for different feelings, again
employing a highly suggestive idea that is current as a metaphor in much
contemporary performance praxis. His location of anger and aggression in
the solar plexus is an idea that has parallels in contemporary practice, many
teachers regarding the solar plexus as the center from which all feelings radiate toward the periphery of the body or, since it is the most obvious location of human sexuality and the reproductive function, the point of origin
for all vital motion. While the essay offers nothing like a systematic exposition of breathing and movement as sources of corporeal expression, its suggestive mysticism has exerted a continuing appeal on generations of practitioners who have sought to investigate the body as the unconscious source
of the performer's expressive potential.

Although by his own account Jerzy Grotowski did not discover the writings of Artaud until 1964, his work from the early 1960s onwards seems spir-
itually more akin to that of Artaud than to his earlier acknowledged men-
tors, Stanislavski and Meyerhold. It appears unlikely that the later
development of Grotowski's methods of actor training were not deeply
influenced by "An Emotional Athleticism." Artaud's writings also resonated
powerfully within the arena of mainstream teaching and practice, and his
work has been an inspiration for two schools of alternative practitioners.

Brook, Grotowski, and Barba have developed a third theater tradition from the matrix of his ideas and, within the postmodern phase of the tradition founded by Craig and Meyerhold, avant-garde performance artists have been influenced by his ideas about the phenomenological presence of the performer. A number of body artists perform a diverse range of real acts on stage that exemplify Artaud's notion of performance as an actual, irreversible event. Franco B cuts himself in order to bleed onstage. Karen Finlay challenged sexist constructions of women by performing parodic pornographic acts that allowed her to be assertive rather than the passive object of the male gaze. Orlan had cosmetic surgical operations (undertaken without anesthetic) recorded on video. Ron Athey performed masochistic self-mutilations in the context of an autobiographical performance that presented "his own suffering and mortality, without artifice."[29] Although the postmodern turn from *acting* to *performance* represents a logical development of ideas inherent in art movements such as futurism, dada, the Bauhaus, abstract expressionism, pop art, and the music of John Cage, it is most obviously signaled in the work of Artaud.

11. Jerzy Grotowski

Although in retrospect Grotowski's search for the authenticity of the performance act appears remarkably consistent, the paths he took in pursuing his aim were continually surprising, to both his followers and his detractors. In 1970, just when it seemed that he had invented a new form of theatrical performance, Grotowski turned his back on theater to undertake an investigation into the very nature and possibility of performance. From this point he was to exploit the art of acting as a tool for practical research into the condition of being human. During most of his working life (1970 until his death in 1999), he did not make theater productions at all, yet his impact on contemporary theater practitioners and his legend has grown rather than diminished with the years.

By the early 1990s, Grotowski's work could be divided into five phases, the end of one phase both foreshadowing and necessitating a transition to the next. He named these phases Theater of Productions (1957–69), Paratheater (1969–78), Theater of Sources (1976–82), Objective Drama (1983–86), and Art as Vehicle (from 1986). The work on Art as Vehicle continues through the activities of Thomas Richards and his colleagues at the Workcenter of Grotowski and Thomas Richards in Pontedera, Italy.

At times Grotowski presented himself as a direct descendant of Stanislavski, whose ideas he had studied alongside those of Meyerhold and Vakhtangov as a directing student in Kraców (1954–56), and during a scholarship year at GITIS (State Institution of Theater Art) in Moscow (1955). Although he recognized the work of all three as seminal influences, it was Stanislavski's method of physical actions that Grotowski came to regard as a model for his research on the performer. Stanislavski's later praxis was the basis of what became a new understanding of performance as *doing* or *action* as opposed to representation. The challenge of Grotowski is manifested in the question, "Is theater necessary?" Although he accomplished complex and deeply affecting productions and provoked astonishing performances from the actors in his "poor theater," performance was a mode of exploration for Grotowski, rather than an end in itself. Grotowski employed the art of the performer in a quest to access and actualize what was fully human. Redefining the art of the performer in terms of openness rather than pretense, Grotowski demanded a complete "disarmament" of the human being, a dissolution of the usual social barriers:[1] "What does it mean not to hide oneself? Simply to be whole—'I am as I am'—then our experience and life are opening themselves. And every essential experience of our life is being realised through the fact that there is someone with us. . . . Where is my nativity—as brother?"[2]

According to Grotowski himself he was unacquainted with the writings of Artaud until 1964, yet his poor theater manifested itself in structures of ceremonial enactment that evoked Artaudian ideals of performance opposed to the realism of character associated with Stanislavski's approach. While approaching his craft from a perspective provided by the method of physical actions, Grotowski nevertheless achieved a concretization of aesthetic notions inherent in Artaud's writings on the theater of cruelty, giving precise form to the kind of relationship between spectator and actor envisaged by Artaud and specific content to Artaud's poetic evocations of theater as oneiric spectacle. With hindsight it appears that even Grotowski's movement beyond theater dating from 1970 was akin to Artaud's attempts to create the theater of cruelty—an unrealizable theater—as a way of using theater to destroy theatrical representation. In both, the demands of *performance* paradoxically make it necessary to go beyond theater.

All Grotowski's innovations in the period during which he characterized his experiments as poor theater involved an exploration of the confrontation between actor and spectator. The earlier phase of his experiments with mise-en-scène focused on the actor-spectator relationship within the space; the later phase of his work concentrated on the psychophysical process of the actor in the attempt to develop new forms of psychic connection with the spectator. Unlike many practitioners of the 1960s and 1970s, Grotowski saw that it was useless to create a derivative theater of cruelty by attempting to mimic the images conjured up in Artaud's writings through recycling his proposed scenic techniques. Nevertheless he was profoundly aware of Artaud's importance. In an article first published in 1967, Grotowski wrote:

We are entering the age of Artaud. The "theatre of cruelty" has been canonised i.e. made trivial, swapped for trinkets, tortured in various ways. . . . The paradox of Artaud lies in the fact that it is impossible to carry out his proposals. . . . Artaud left no concrete technique behind him. He left visions, metaphors. . . . an actor reaches the essence of his vocation whenever he commits an act of sincerity, when he unveils himself, opens and gives himself in an extreme, solemn gesture. . . . when this act accomplished through the theatre is *total* . . . it enables us to respond totally, that is, to begin to exist. This man gave us in his martyrdom, a shining proof of the theatre as therapy.[3]

Grotowski found the essence of the necessary theater demanded by Artaud to exist in the peculiar tension between anarchy (the authentic experience of the madman/martyr) and discipline. What Artaud had failed to realize in his own theatrical projects had been an aim of Grotowski's experiments from *Kordian* (1962) to *Dr Faustus* (1963), and it seems that his reading of Artaud encouraged him to be even more explicit in expressing his own understanding of this Artaudian vision in *The Constant Prince* (1965) and *Apocalypsis cum Figuris* (1968): "anarchy and chaos . . . should be linked to a sense of order, which he [Artaud] conceived in the mind, and not as a physical technique."[4] Artaud's dictum "Cruelty is rigour" signified for Grotowski the strict discipline of the performer's craft. It was balanced against the demand that "Actors should be like martyrs burnt alive, still signalling to us from their stakes," in order to create "a *conjunction of opposites* which gives birth to the total act."[5]

The early experiments in the creation of a poor theater focused on the use of the spatial relationship between performers and audience to effect a transformation of the spectator's consciousness. During the period when his company was based in Wroclaw and known as the Laboratory Theatre—beginning with the production of Marlowe's *Dr Faustus* (1963) and concluding with *Apocalypsis cum Figuris*—Grotowski and his actors devoted their research to the discovery of psychophysical methodologies that would redefine the psychic connection between actor and spectator. Even before he promulgated the concept of poor theater, Grotowski had begun to recognize the process of acting as a *via negativa,* a systematic elimination of superfluous layers of socially acquired behavioral mannerisms in the search for a radical form of self-revelation in which the actor's naked humanity radiated through the role prescribed by the written text of the play. The communion of actor and spectator at the most fundamental level of their humanity was for Grotowski the aim of theatrical performance. Character, narrative, and scenic structures were merely the catalysts through which this revelation of essential humanity might be accomplished.

One way of promoting the affective relationship between actor and spectator was to cast the audience in a specific role within the performance. Grotowski's production of Slowacki's *Kordian* represented his first attempt to use the experimental scenographic arrangements that he had been exploring for a few years as a means of assigning the audience a role in the performance. The production was set in a mental hospital (although only one scene in the play actually takes place there); the spectators become visitors who sit around the beds of the patients, unsure of whether the psychiatrists will pounce on them and treat them as patients. While there was no specific physical confrontation between performers and audience in *Akropolis* (1962), the audience was nevertheless assigned a role vis-à-vis the actors: the actors played the dead, while the audience were cast as the living. In *Dr Faustus,* the audience were guests at Faustus's last supper and were invited to sit at two long tables on the sides of the room. The scenographic arrangements for *The Constant Prince* suggested both a sports arena and an operating theater. The spectators overlooked the rectangular acting area as sadistic voyeurs, enjoying the physical and mental torture of the Christ-like hero as a cruel sport or a medical operation. In *Apocalypsis cum Figuris*, the spectators shared the same space as the actors, implying that the encounter between the Simpleton/Christ and his torturers was an incident that might occur at any moment in the journey of an individual spectator through life. Each spectator was free to accept or reject the role assigned to him by the structure of the mise-en-scène, but, however he chose, he would have been responsible for deciding the nature of the spectatorship—by *being there* either as a genuine witness or merely as a detached observer.

The Actor in the Poor Theater

Once Grotowski had clarified his aesthetic of poor theater as the opposite of the "kleptomaniac" principle of traditional Western theater (which operated through the acquisition of greater and more varied stylistic vocabularies and scenic technologies) the *via negativa* assumed a status within the sphere of acting, equivalent to the stripping-down that Grotowski and his scenographers were attempting with respect to misc-en-scène.[6] Poor theater was not, however, conceived as an aesthetic of decorative minimalism, as is the case with much contemporary avant-garde performance. Its aim was rather to destroy every obstacle that might hinder the most profound communication between performer and spectator.

The thoroughgoing empiricism that characterized Stanislavski's approach was for Grotowski paradigmatic in a number of respects. Firstly, Stanislavski's insistence that "the actor who wishes to be creative . . . [must] master a method" established the Western actor's obligation to work and train daily, in addition to performing. Second, Stanislavski's unsparing process of self-criticism and his ability to rethink his starting point time and again represented an inspiration to the methodical young performance researcher of the late 1950s and early 1960s, suggesting to Grotowski that the process of practical performance research might be more important than the creation of fixed performance texts. Stanislavski's emphasis on concrete and practical methods of training and preparation for performance as a bait for activating intangible psychological processes ultimately led Grotowski to formulate a notion of training in which specific work on somatic processes was inseparable from psychotherapeutic activity.

Elements of Stanislavski's method can be recognized in the essay "Methodical Exploration," but equally striking is the original way in which Grotowski transformed his source. According to Grotowski, the aims of a methodical investigation of acting were

> To stimulate a process of self-revelation, going back as far as the subconscious, yet canalizing this stimulus in order to obtain the required reaction.
>
> To be able to articulate this process, discipline it and convert it into signs. In concrete terms, this means to construct a score whose notes are tiny elements of contact, reactions to the stimuli of the outside world: what we call "give and take."
>
> To eliminate from the creative process the resistances and obstacles caused by one's own organism, both physical and psychic (the two forming a whole).[7]

Although Grotowski's poor theater has most often been presented as a new departure in both acting and scenography, his work in the 1960s in many respects represented not merely a brilliant demonstration of a new performance aesthetic, but also the most complete realization of ideals of performance variously formulated by Stanislavski, Copeau, and Artaud.[8] For Grotowski, as for each of these revolutionary figures, the development of new methodologies of performance was motivated by an insistence on the ethical purpose of theater-making. Unquestionably Grotowski's notion of acting training and practice as a spiritual quest for the reintegration of what in Western society is experienced as a mind-body split, originated in Stanislavski's ethics of performance. Stanislavski's later career as founder-teacher of the various Moscow Art Theater studios had provided the paradigm for the systematic investigation of the organic processes of acting. While Stanislavski himself insisted on an ethical foundation and purpose for a "life in art," it was Copeau who first conceived of the creative process of theater-making as in itself a quest for authentic existence.[9]

It is not clear how detailed Grotowski's knowledge of Copeau's work was in the 1960s; however, there are striking parallels between Copeau's *tréteau nu* and the poor theater.[10] When Peter Brook encountered the work of Grotowski in 1966 the aesthetic of Copeau was alive in Brook's consciousness as a British inheritor of the work of the director and teacher, Michel Saint-Denis.[11] Brook's empty space owed much to Copeau, but it also, consciously or not, echoed Artaud's and Grotowski's radical attempts to eliminate the superfluous elements that prevented the achievement of the total act of performance.

Mistrust of *cabotinage* is common to Copeau, Grotowski and Brook, although all three proved adept at the use of highly theatrical devices of acting and mise-en-scène at various stages of their careers. Indeed, Grotowski's idea of the facial mask, and his emphasis on gymnastic skills in body training and on the primacy of a physical performance score as a vehicle for the psychic encounter between actor and spectator, reveal how he had synthesized the later praxis of Stanislavski with the methodology of performance composition developed by Meyerhold through biomechanics: "In the theatre of which I speak, the result of the actor's work must have a quality of artificiality, but in order for this to be achieved in a dynamic and suggestive way, a certain internal engagement of the actor is necessary. . . . The physical action must be founded on and rest on the actor's personal, intimate associations, on his psychic batteries, his internal accumulators."[12]

By engineering a confrontation of the organic impulses of the performer's psyche with the artificially constructed mask imposed by the role as agent within a prescribed narrative Grotowski's performance methodology exploited the opposition between Stanislavski's biologism and Meyerhold's artificial approach to the actor as psychophysical agent: "[The] more we become absorbed in what is hidden inside us, in the excess, in the exposure, in the self-penetration, the more rigid must be the external discipline; that is to say the form, the artificiality, the ideogram, the sign. Here lies the whole principle of expressiveness."[13]

The notion of acting in the poor theater was founded on the dialectical tension between social forms and the organic impulses of the actor as subject. Grotowski's theater from *Kordian* to *Apocalypsis cum Figuris* reconstitutes in performance a confrontation between the vitality of living process and the morbidity of outmoded forms. Out of the conflict between dead habits and the vital impulses generated within the body of each spectator through the performance is born an authentic consciousness of personhood that must always involve confrontation with those aspects of the stories (myths) through which social regulation (dis)figures our humanity. Mythic archetypes are inscribed in memory and in collective consciousness as narrative patterns, whether or not they have ceased to pulse with creative energy.[14]

The French director Roger Planchon observed that Grotowski's means were already his ends, implying that he had devised a process of training and performance informed by the creative aims of the actual theater works he made.[15] The act of performance was for Grotowski a human experiment in which myths were tested in a crucible of human experience, in order to precipitate live energy from the compound of living and dead matter. Narrative components would, as enacted, have a different effect on each spectator, as indeed they would already have had on each performer during the rehearsal process. Far more sophisticated in his comprehension of myth than Artaud, Grotowski conceived every performance as an event structured to provoke a deeply personal response from each spectator, drawing on the private associations that the enactment of the story evoked in his individual consciousness.

Theatrical performance would no longer aim to manipulate all spectators to share a communal experience; no spectator would be required to repress his individual reactions in order to participate fully in the event. The performance was a dialectical process in which the conflict of individual encounters with the material created a complex of individual and shared experiences. Grotowski was sensitive to the multiplicity of perspectives through which reception might occur. Respect for the authenticity of every individual spectator's experience prevented the eradication of difference or otherness during the various interactions between performers and spectators. In this model of theater, performance was not simply a re-creation of communal myths. That would inevitably demand of the spectator a surrendering of self to the collective consciousness. Acting precipitated a performance that was a process of testing and deconstructing fundamental cultural paradigms, manifest not only within the psyches of the actor and the individual spectator but also as a dialogue among them.[16] Performance actualized the attempt of the group to achieve a lost wholeness of being. Using the masks of characters in action, actors exposed those features of inherited myths as paradigmatic narratives that still held a psychic charge for them, in order to offer spectators the opportunity of experiencing their own organic life within the forms of vitality channeled through performance.

Some accounts of Grotowski's presence in training sessions portray him as a guru with power to transform actors through a mystical ability to penetrate the deepest recesses of their psychosomatic life. More pragmatically oriented accounts of his speech and body training by observers such as Eugenio Barba stress both his psychological acuity and his absolute determination to push the performers beyond their physical limits. Barba's description of the quantum leap made by the great Ryszard Cieslak in his work with Grotowski on *The Constant Prince* is eloquent testimony to the unique relationship between the two men during the year-long process of creating the performance:

> When I left Grotowski's theatre, in 1964, Ryszard Cieslak was a good actor. He wanted to be an intellectual. It was as if his body, full of life, was encumbered by a huge brain, as if he was trapped in a two dimensional reality. I saw him again two years later, when he presented *The Constant Prince* in Oslo. From the moment the performance began, it was as if all my memories, the categories on which I depended, had been swept away and I saw another being, I saw a man who had found his fullness, his destiny, his vulnerability. That brain which before had been like a jelly blurring his actions, now imbued his whole body with phosphorescent cells. The power of a hurricane.[17]

What Barba noticed as a particular feature of the transformation was the body-mind integration that Cieslak had achieved. Whereas before *The Constant Prince* the actor's desire to be an intellectual had prevented him from achieving complete potency as an intelligent being/actor, by 1966 the actor's *intelligence* radiated through his *physicality*.

Grotowski's exploration of techniques that could release Cieslak's psychophysical potency as a unique instrument of expression appear to have been stimulated by his reading of Artaud.[18] Building upon his knowledge of Meyerhold's biomechanics and its transformation in Stanislavski's method of physical actions, he was particularly responsive to the ideas formulated in "Un Athletisme Affectif" regarding the relationship between bodily action and psychical process:

> [There] is an authentic parallelism between the efforts of a man who works with his body (e.g., picking up a heavy object) and the psychic processes (e.g., receiving a blow, retaliating). He [Artaud] knew that the body possesses a centre that decides the reactions of the athlete, and those of the actor who wants to reproduce psychic efforts through his body.

But if one analyses his principles from a practical point of view, one discovers that they lead to stereotypes: a particular type of movement to exteriorize a particular type of emotion. In the end this leads to clichés.[19]

In many respects, Grotowski may be seen to have invented a systematic method for the concrete realization of Artaud's ideal of the affective athlete. The orientation of Grotowski's actor training—the use of different breathing patterns to provoke various psychophysical reactions and the unique work that he did with actors to help them discover and activate resonators in different parts of the body—seem to have been a direct response to this essay, although the logic of Grotowski's own discoveries would inevitably have led him to Artaud. Grotowski was wary of interpreting Artaud's evocative words on the use of breathing literally: "Artaud represents a fruitful starting point for research and an aesthetic point of view. When he asks the actor to study his breathing, to exploit the different elements of respiration in his acting, he is offering him the chance of widening his possibilities, of acting which is inarticulate (inspiration, expiration, etc.). This is a very fertile aesthetic proposition. It is not a technique."[20]

Training for Performance: The *Via Negativa*

Even during the first phase of his own investigation into actor training between 1959 and 1962, Grotowski was skeptical of pure technique. Technical work was never to be separated from expressive work, just as psychic processes were always to interpenetrate physical activity. To this end, physical exercises aimed at warming up the actor at the start of the session or at loosening up muscles and enhancing the flexibility of the spine were to be justified by individual actors through the assignment of precise images based on personal associations. The aim of physical work was to eliminate the body's resistances, to make it capable of responding immediately and spontaneously to any stimulus: "The exercise is correctly executed only if the body does not oppose any resistance during the realization of the image in question. The body should therefore appear weightless, as malleable as plasticine to the impulses, as hard as steel when acting as a support, capable even of conquering the law of gravity."[21]

Exercises aimed always to make the actor wholly transparent as a psychophysical instrument. This approach has parallels with Saint-Denis's notion that expressive training should be integrated with technical training. There are also echoes of Craig's image of actor as Über-marionette, although Grotowski's strategy for enabling the actor to achieve perfect expressivity involves an organic psychophysical process as opposed to the mechanical instrumentality of Craig's imagining.

Working very closely with his small group of actors at the Laboratory Theater, Grotowski explored techniques of meditation and physical training designed to undo the "psychic penetration" of the individual actor by culturally determined forces that express themselves through every person as a consequence of socialization. The investigation by his actors of various unconnected methodologies to stimulate mind–body interpenetration was intended to constitute the first stage in a concrete exploration of the *via negativa*. Some of the exercises were derived from Asian and Oriental martial arts and meditative practices such as judo rituals and Hatha yoga, whereas others were based on Western systems of practice, such as Delsarte's hieroglyphic system of fixed facial and gestural positions and Dalcroze's eurythmics. In experimenting with alternative methods of training, Grotowski was seeking not to increase the actor's repertoire of techniques, but to discover ways of freeing him from unconscious habits, the artifice of whose conventions was obscured by centuries of tradition. Any alien technique or style of performance that might distance the actor from the naturalized grammar and vocabulary of performance that constituted a norm adhered to by the Western performer would aid in the elimination of the actor's "bag of tricks"—the obstacles to true expression.[22]

During this phase of his investigations, Grotowski discovered that the actor's work with the teacher in training and the director in rehearsal involved more than the teaching and learning of how to do something (a preexisting set of physical and histrionic skills), as was the practice with most traditional forms of professional theater. Instead, it demanded an intensely personal involvement of actor with director or teacher that was mirrored at a later stage of performance in the relationship between actor and spectator. The director had the responsibility of leading the actor on a journey of self-actualization and self-discovery. The director imparted no new techniques to the actor, but functioned as both catalyst of and witness to the psychophysical process in which the actor systematically rid himself of the physical, intellectual, and psychic blocks that prevented him from achieving the total act of self-revelation that for Grotowski is the end of acting. The task of the teacher or director was to assist the actor to "resign from not doing"—to help him surrender himself to the psychophysical demands of the role in an organic process of accommodation rather than in a conscious method of technical characterization.

Since the process of creating a performance score is as much a journey of discovery for the director as it is for the actor, Grotowski began to conceive of the actor's training not as a system of exercises designed to achieve a pre-scribed aim, but as a psychophysical process provoked by the director that resulted in a creative excavation of the actor's self. This meant that each actor had to adapt given exercises to help eliminate his own individual impediments to creativity. Technique could not be learned and applied *in general*.[23] The example of Grotowski's intensely personal work with per-formers at various stages of his career (Zbigniew Cynkutis, Ryszard Cieslak, Maud Robart, and Thomas Richards) provides a model of the process of the actor's self-actualization, a process not repeatable as a merely technical sys-tem of skills training. The performer discovers what he has to express in the act of creating the performance. The process of creation is a path to self-realization that in itself constitutes the actor's training. While some basic exercises to achieve body-mind mastery remain a constant aspect of the actor's repertoire of preparatory strategies, these do not in themselves con-stitute a training system. While the actors of the Laboratory Theater (and later the performers of Art as Vehicle) maintained their strength, focus of energy, and flexibility by means of the regular performance of sequences of bodily exercises, Grotowski was at pains to emphasize that it was in the unique relationship with the director-teacher that the actor discovered him-self as a performer. The director is the primary witness in Grotowski's the-ater, and the definition of the self as a fully human being is a function of the collaboration between performer and witness, or in the later phases of his work, among coparticipants.

Corporal and Plastic Exercises

Yoga provided a model of the kind of attitude that training exercises were designed to promote; but whereas yoga promoted an inward focus, Gro-towski conceived sequences of corporal exercises that would enhance the actor's sensitivity to the environment, and to other people. Warm-up exer-cises involved walking, running, and jumping. Exercises for the muscles and spine included the well-known "cat" sequence, in which the movements of a cat waking up, stretching and moving about in different ways promoted muscular control and spinal flexibility at the same time as they tested neu-romuscular coordination by demanding that the performer always be in a state of catlike readiness to react to stimuli. Headstands adapted from Hatha yoga positions were designed to explore ways of altering breathing patterns, heartbeat, and the relationship between stillness and motion.

Exercises modeled on birds in flight aimed to develop the ability to move through the air in different ways; these were combined with different types of leaps and somersaults and were intended to assist the investigation of the body's acrobatic potential, and to create a sensitivity to rhythm and dance, but they were all to be justified with personal motivations. In addition to exercising the feet, there were mime exercises concentrating on the hands and legs, and, intriguingly, "studies in acting on any theme, performed while walking and running."[24] It is significant that Grotowski integrated traditional acting study with purely physical activity. By doing so he was ensuring that acting did not become a purely emotional or psychological activity for the performer, but was focused in the body through accompanying physical activity even when that activity had, in terms of realistic representation, no connection with the internal emotional logic of the acting. This kind of exercise activated the unconscious processes and allowed the performer spontaneously to construct scenarios charged with psychic potency on the basis of preexistent vocabularies of movement.

Under the heading of plastic exercises, Grotowski grouped elementary exercises derived from "Dalcroze and other classical European methods."[25] Not as physically demanding as the corporal exercises, these *plastiques* involved sequences of movement emanating outwards from the spine toward the periphery of the body. The emphasis here was on precision and flow, the movement sequences being relatively detailed. These were initially intended to lead toward exercises in composition and were mainly based on opposite movements produced simultaneously in different parts of the body or of opposing gestural/mental attitudes expressed through different parts of the body. They would develop the actor's neuromuscular coordination, enhancing sensitivity, flexibility, and spontaneity of response. If the performer could achieve a free flow of the body, uninterrupted by the intervention of the conscious mind, a body memory would develop, automatically regulating the spontaneous performance of certain actions. As always, the desired end was the achievement of a kind of organicity in performance, a body-mind integration that allowed action to become a natural flow of psychophysical energy through a body free of blockages. In later phases of his work, Grotowski stressed the importance of motivating the performance of any physical exercise so that it was never merely a mechanical movement but a meaningful human action. Grotowski's determination to integrate expressive and technical training was clearly manifested in the "games with one's own body" in which one part of the body was opposed emotionally to the other so that the left side of the body was made to "jealously watch" the kinetic grace and beauty of the right side, "expressing in its movements its feelings of resentment and hate."[26]

The exercises in composition represented a strategy by which the actor could explore connections between the kinesthetic form of movement and codes of kinesic signification. By way of example, Grotowski cited "the formation of gesticulatory ideograms as in ancient and medieval theatre."[27] He did not conceive the relationship between kinesic signifier and its signified as unchanging (as, for example, in Peking opera, whose conventions ascribe fixed signifier-signified relationships, so that a flower is always denoted by a specific gesture). Animals and plants were common images that performers were required to represent. One of the body images commonly explored by Grotowski's actors was a newborn baby, and work on different kinds of gait was also a feature of these exercises in composition. One highly suggestive exercise involves the actor giving expression to a particular emotional impulse through a discrete part of the body: for example, the shoulder cries or the foot laughs.[28]

At the end of a talk at a theater school in Brussels in 1966, Grotowski summed up the essential features of his own voice and body training method:

> Imprint on your memory: the *body* must work first. Afterwards comes the *voice*.
>
> If you start on something, you must be fully engaged in it. You must give yourself one hundred per cent, your whole body, your whole mind and all its possible, individual, most intimate associations. During a rehearsal an actor may reach a climax that he will work on. He keeps the same gestures and the same positions but never again reaches the same intimate climax. *The peak of a climax can never be rehearsed. You must only exercise the preparatory stages of the process that leads to the heights of that climax. A climax cannot be reached without practice. The climax itself can never be reproduced.*
>
> In all you do you must keep in mind that there are no fixed rules, no stereotypes. The essential thing is that everything must come from and through the body. First and foremost, there must be a physical reaction to everything that affects us. Before reacting with the voice, you must first react with the body. If you think, you must think with your body. However, it is better not to think but to act, to take risks. When I tell you not to think, I mean with the head. Of course you must think, but with the body, logically, with precision and responsibility. You must think with the whole body, by means of actions. Don't think of the result, and certainly not of how beautiful the result may be.[29]

Grotowski stressed that his attitude toward training and the terms he used to explain it were the result of his own investigation into acting. Every practitioner should find his own individual approach to training rather than attempting slavishly to imitate Grotowski's as a ready-made technique.

Impact on Mainstream Training

Grotowski's speech at the theater school represents a lucid distillation of the kind of wisdom about performance to which the intelligent professional actor working in Britain today would fully subscribe. Possibly Grotowski's praxis has had an influence that permeated the mainstream theater through cross-pollination with the tradition inaugurated by Michel Saint-Denis. The earliest information about Grotowski's praxis in Britain was through his impact on Peter Brook. Whether their work was actually informed by a knowledge of Grotowski's practices, whether they absorbed such ideas through coming into contact with Peter Brook, or whether the parallel in teaching practices can be attributed to the zeitgeist, there is little doubt that the approaches of the three most influential British voice teachers of the last fifty years—Cicely Berry, Kristen Linklater, and their younger contemporary, Patsy Rodenburg—are in some respects strikingly similar to that of Grotowski.[30] Linklater and Rodenburg speak and write in a somewhat mystical way of the power of breath as a life force, whereas Berry's more consciously political approach to theater makes her wary of any methods that savor of mysticism. However, the work of all three certainly represents a break with the earlier tradition of voice and speech for the performer, which typically stressed the development of a special technique of voice production, somewhat akin to that of the opera singer, in order to achieve a standard stage voice, capable of projecting into the farthest reaches of a West End or Broadway theater.[31]

In opposition to this approach, Berry was the first to emphasize the unique quality of every individual actor's speech habits, and advocated the enhancement of the individual's vocal personality, rather than its eradication and replacement by a standard vocal personality for the stage. In this respect she was certainly responsive to Peter Brook's ideas; it is likely that they were both responding as much to Grotowski, who Brook had invited to London in 1966 to conduct some laboratory work in preparation for the RSC's production of *US,* as acting on their own instincts for change. In his approach to training the actor as a psychophysical whole, Grotowski's ideas are consonant with those of both Laban and Michael Chekhov. Although it is unlikely that Grotowski knew anything of Laban's system of effort actions, and Laban was dead before Grotowski had begun his mature work as a director and teacher, he may have learned something of Chekhov's work, or he may have developed kinesthetic training along parallel lines, by synthesizing Stanislavski's later work on physical actions and Meyerhold's biomechanics in a manner akin to Vakhtangov.

Two of Grotowski's ideas about training have also found echoes in a great deal of contemporary acting practice. Eugenio Barba's Odin Teatret has adopted Grotowski's idea that while training as part of a group, the actor transforms standard training methods into his own uniquely personal exercises, which are a product of his own private associations. It has also had some impact on mainstream theater training. The idea inevitably leads to the complementary view that physical exercises must always involve what Grotowski calls "give and take"—that they must not become solo studies in which the performer develops virtuoso technical abilities but that they should be determined and structured by the spontaneous contact with others that characterizes the type of improvisation that constitutes everyday behavior. In this way, the principle of give-and-take ensures that exercises are never devoid of human significance, but are an integral part of the actualization of relationships (even if purely imagined) within the group. Although in later years Grotowski was somewhat critical of the arbitrary use of improvisation as a technique of theatrical creation, this notion of give-and-take is implicit in the widespread theory and practice of theater games and improvisations.[32]

Beyond Theater: Performance as Research Method

Paratheater and Theater of Sources

Some words are dead, even though we are still using them. Among such words are: show, spectacle, theatre, audience, etc. But what is alive? Adventure and meeting . . . what do we need? First of all, a place and *our own kind*. . . . I should not be alone, then—we should not be alone. . . . What is possible together? Holiday.[33]

Grotowski's startling decision at the height of his public success to cease making theater productions can be viewed in retrospect as a logical stage in his search for the essence of human being that had begun with his redefinition of the actor's function. Although his direct influence on theater may have diminished in later years, his legendary status among scholars, theorists, and experimental practitioners was, if anything, enhanced by the transformation of his project from theater-making into paratheater, in which performance became a research tool that would be employed to continue "the quest for what is the most essential in life."[34] The structures of theater were dissolved to permit an equal collaboration among participants, so that freer and more spontaneous investigations of the nature of human relationship might take place in a context of "meeting" rather than theatrical performance. The notion of meeting had been inherent in the form of *Apocalypsis cum Figuris;* the paratheatrical activities can be seen to be a natural development of that work. Between 1970 and 1975, the activities were confined to a specially selected circle of participants led by the members of the Laboratory Theatre. While the forms of interaction were carefully planned, they were more open, allowing all to participate, rather than maintaining the division into actors and witnesses. Although totally consonant with Grotowski's existential project, the "road to active culture" represented by the years of paratheatrical activity from 1970 to 1979, involved less emphasis on the notion of performance or acting than at any other phase. According to Leszek Kolodziejczyk, Paratheater "meant a break with mediation through playing a role."[35]

The aim was to harness human creativity, to break down the masks of social role-play in an effort to actualize the full potential of the participants. The various events that constituted Paratheater were the most open and least structured performative activities of Grotowski's career. A notice in the lobby during performances of *Apocalypsis* in 1975, read, "Acting ambition is not required," clearly signaling that the wide range of happenings could not be evaluated according to any criterion of theater performance. They were encounters in a purely existential mode, confronting the participants with intense experiences of their presence in a natural environment (many events were planned to make striking use of outdoor locations such as forests and mountains) and provoking fresh awareness of the self in the presence of others. Accounts of various paratheatrical events regularly evoke the changed states of consciousness that were precipitated by the profoundly simple experiences most often shared in silence by participants. It was common for participants to experience an awakening to a new awareness of themselves and their sensuous relationship to the world. In their orientation, paratheatrical projects were a logical extension of the *via negativa,* participants having to discover an "internal passivity" that might permit them to *do* without *acting.* Creativity was developed through projects that demanded the overcoming of the routine attitudes and behavior conditioned by society with the aim of destroying resistance to one's natural impulses.

During the University of Research that was a part of the Theatre of Nations in Wroclaw in 1974, over eighteen hundred people from around the world participated in paratheatrical activities, some of which involved work in small, closed groups but which also involved twenty-one regular "beehives," sessions open to all who were prepared to participate actively. The comparatively large numbers of participants and the deliberate attempt to move away from theatrical representation meant that, while many of the paratheatrical activities transformed the lives of certain individuals, their "research" component was difficult to identify. By their very nature, the value of these events was not transferable to those who did not participate. While Paratheater had liberated the Laboratory Theatre (and other practitioners inspired by the project such as Brook and Barba) from the constrictions of formal theater, Grotowski's move in 1977 toward a Theater of Sources seems in retrospect to have been a dialectical development from the free form of the paratheatrical experiments. Supported by international funding foundations, he was able to gather a transcultural group of thirty-six individuals from milieus representing traditions with which Grotowski had some acquaintance, including African, Asiatic, American Indian, European, and Judaic. While each maintained a certain independence from Grotowski's research project, these expert practitioners nevertheless became a primary research resource in his quest to discover some ground of human performance that might constitute a "source of sources," a common human practice logically prior to cultural differentiation: "It is not a synthesis of techniques of sources that we are after. We search for sourcing techniques, those points that precede the differences. . . . what we search for in this Project are the sources of the techniques of sources, and these sources must be extremely unsophisticated. . . . it should be something given to the human being. . . . you can say that it's printed on one's genetic code."[36]

This was not a return to theater as such, but an attempt at a more rigorous investigation of primary modes of performance and their potentially transcultural significance. Although it involved a new strategy, it was intended to advance what had been consistent aims during the previous phases of Grotowski's project: "The Theatre of Sources will deal with the phenomenon of source techniques, archaic or nascent, that bring us back to the sources of life, to direct, so we say, primeval perception, to organic primary experience of life. Existence-presence. The theme will be original i.e. primary dramatic phenomenon seen in terms of human experience."[37]

The phase of Grotowski's work on Theater of Sources was interrupted by the imposition of martial law in Poland in 1981, whereupon he chose to leave Poland. His research during this period manifested itself in the Objective Drama project at the University of California, Irvine, between 1983 and

1992, although Grotowski himself was no longer continuously present after 1986.

From Objective Drama to Art as Vehicle

Just as the Theater of Sources had transformed the paratheatrical experiments that had foreshadowed it, so too did Objective Drama take the discoveries being made through Theater of Sources as the starting point for a new direction in practical research. No longer explicitly concerned to investigate precultural sources for performative behavior, Grotowski progressed to work that examined the objective effect of such forms of performance when transferred from their original ritual or religious context into a situation in which they became merely structures of action. From this phase he became particularly concerned with craft and the need for technical precision (as, for different reasons, he had been during the Theater of Productions): "We find ourselves face to the obligation to have competence. One should know how to dance and sing in a way that is organic and at the same time structured."[38] His speeches and writing from this period express impatience with dilettante approaches, and with improvisation as a method of discovering or creating performance forms.

> Group improvisation . . . First, one needs to see the banalities, the clichés which appear . . . to make "savages," to imitate trances, to overuse the arms and hands, to carry someone in a procession . . . to present one's own clichés of behaviour, social daily life behaviour as if they were naturalness. . . . we should begin by eliminating all these banalities plus several others. We should avoid stomping the feet on the floor, falling and creeping on the ground and making monsters. Block all these practices! . . . it will appear that contact is not possible if you are not capable of refusing contact.[39]

This phase of the research primarily involved a testing of archaic and surviving ancient modes of performance (movement, sound) in order to determine how they might still activate performers to channel complexes of feeling in ways that would today be regarded as aesthetic effects, but which actually predate the division of human existence into religion, art, and everyday behavior. In his proposal for funding from the Rockefeller Foundation, Grotowski listed one of his aims as the discovery of a type of performance in which "poetry is not separated from the song, the song is not separated from the dance, the dance is not separated from the acting."[40]

In an essay written in 1985, Grotowski invests special significance in the Greek word *organon* and the Sanskrit *yantra*. By analogy with architecture, these refer to both the performing body and the performance space as instruments in tune with external and internal forces. They allow a precise balance between the focusing of environmental factors and the expression of the human: "from the standpoint of the circulation of energy, the yantras (organons) are instruments which are really potent."[41] One of the chief tests that Grotowski set the performers during this work was the performance of what he called "a kind of individual ethnodrama."[42] This was an old song that the performer had to find, one that was significant within the domestic history of his family but also alive with specific meaning within the cultural tradition framing both the performer and his family. Work on the song became for the individual performer a kind of excavation of the formation of selfhood from familial and cultural roots, the research consisting of a process whereby the individual excavated more and more of his previously hidden identity by embodying in performance what is live for him in the old song. Grotowski spoke somewhat elliptically of the process whereby the potentiality "codified" in the song as a totality of "movement, action, rhythm" is discovered and embodied as a pattern of action that accompanies its vocalization. He compared the piecing together of "physical actions" to the process of montage in film, evoking a process in which actions are pared down to their essence so that the organic wholeness of the performance contained within the song's musical and vocal structure is revealed, while all extraneous interpolations are edited out. The artistic problem of who is the singer of the song prompted Grotowski to a discourse on how our ancestors are alive in us through cultural traditions that *speak* to us if we can let them: "You are not a vagabond, you come from somewhere, from some country, from some place, from some landscape. . . . It is you two hundred, three hundred, four hundred or one thousand years ago, but it is you . . . so, if you refind this you are someone's son. If you do not . . . you are cut off, sterile, barren. . . . It's not a matter of playing the role of someone you are not. So in all this work one goes always more toward the beginning."[43]

The anthropological question of human origin that Grotowski raises in concluding his discourse is approached almost mystically. This is surely a keynote that resounds throughout Grotowski's career, though here more insistently, as an underlying eschatology.

Having been invited in 1986 to establish a Workcenter sponsored by the Centro per la Sperimentazione e la Ricerca Teatrale in Pontedera, Italy, Grotowski initiated what was to be the final phase of his work, Art as Vehicle, in which he developed further some of the work on songs and the

Motions exercises from the Objective Drama phase. James Slowiak, who had led much of the work in Irvine, was for a few years a leader of some aspects of the practical research at the Workcenter, which accepted performers from a wide variety of cultural backgrounds for periods of a year or two as apprentices. Central to this work was Thomas Richards, the American student who had already become a creative heir to Grotowski, and the Italian Mario Biagini, who also became a leader of the work. The dedication of all the participants continues to be inspiring; they work eight or more hours a day, six days a week. Until 1993, participants were divided into two teams. The one led by Thomas Richards worked downstairs, and concentrated on actualizing the performative forms implicit in songs of the African and Afro-Caribbean tradition, while Maud Robart led work on Haitian songs and others that derived from Egyptian and Middle Eastern culture while reconstructing the corporal and plastic exercises from the Laboratory Theatre. The work of Richards and Grotowski crystallized in the form of *Downstairs Action* around 1990. The core of the work on singing was to identify the precise patterns of vibration in performance that would have a transformative effect on the consciousness of the performer. Re-creating the melody (as in modern Western musical performance) was not sufficient. The songs were explored in such a way as to activate vibratory patterns that produced an experience of body-mind wholeness, the organicity that was the psychophysical essence of what Grotowski named "Performer."

A sequence of exercises called Motions, originally elaborated during the Objective Drama phase and later employed at the Workcenter, remains a fundamental method of "tuning" the performer and promoting organicity in the approach to action. From the observer's viewpoint, Motions is a fairly straightforward sequence of movements, repeated with some variations a number of times. The sequences are always repeated in a set order with the body oriented first to the front, then diagonally to one side, then directly to that side, then to the back, and so on for a period of approximately forty minutes. The emphasis is not on technical virtuosity, although Motions is physically fairly demanding. The movements are slow, requiring very good balance and control, their fluidity, precision, and regular rhythm supporting what is an extraordinary feat of mental concentration, as performers' eyes are focused on specific points of orientation while they attempt to remain visually aware of the panorama of their visual field. The combination of physical and mental attention promotes the body-mind integration that is essential in all Grotowski's work, and affords practice of a simple psychophysical process that must underpin more complex interactions between psychic and somatic life.

Grotowski's Legacy: The Significance of Art as Vehicle

Almost by definition, Grotowski's working life presents paradoxical difficulties to the practitioner who wishes to learn from his performance research. While the power and intensity of some of his poor theater productions can be comprehended if not actually *experienced* through the filmed records of them, the only traces that remain of his twenty-nine years of post-theatrical research are his few short programmatic essays, accounts of his work by participants and fellow workers, and theoretical essays by theater historians and scholars. Grotowski himself was extremely sensitive to the danger of oversimplifying and betraying the authenticity of his practice by promulgating technical exercises through handbooks. He chose instead to exert an influence through his close work with colleagues in situations whose intimacy helped to maintain the authenticity of the human presence that was the core feature of his praxis. Despite the scholarly attention that has been paid to every aspect of his work, the findings of the post-theatrical research are inscribed in the consciousness of the participants in that work, and are not easily communicable to outsiders. His legend threatens to obscure the nature of his achievement, and most attempts to disseminate his "ideas" generalize them in such a way that they begin to resemble the clichés he devoted himself to destroying.

From the standpoint of the professional theater worker in the largely commercial systems that operate around the world today, Grotowski's way of disseminating his research findings might seem manipulative and obscurantist. In 1988, the critic and director Charles Marowitz offered what might be considered a salutary warning of the dangers of being an uncritical disciple. After praising the power of the Laboratory Theatre's performances of the late 1960s, Marowitz subjected Grotowski's later research methods to a scathing attack:

> In public, Grotowski's preferred atmosphere is cowed silence. His method of conducting a seminar is to allow brief, usually leading questions from which he can launch into long-winded, circuitous replies which, because they brook no interruption, allow contradictions and fallacies to go unchallenged. . . . It was not that members of his audience were resisting his ideas so much as trying to get him to justify the theories he had been expounding. This he never did, nor ever felt the need to do so. The real significance lay in the fact that they were hidden findings. . . . What is the relationship between your ideas and the living

theatre as we know it in our daily practice? . . . None! . . . what practical value does your work or your thinking have for the living theater in whose name both are being espoused? The answer again is None![44]

There is certainly a danger of responding too literally to Grotowski's utterances, which are often paradoxical and obscure. At times it seems that they need to be interpreted as poetic texts signposting his own spiritual progress. At others they make sense only if one refers to specific examples of his practice. "The proof of the pudding," Brecht was fond of saying, "is in the eating." Or conversely as Grotowski expressed it, "Knowledge is a matter of doing."[45] In his words: "*Performer,* with a capital letter, is a man of action. He is not somebody who plays another. He is a doer, a priest, a warrior: he is outside aesthetic genres. Ritual is performance, an accomplished action, an act. Degenerated ritual is a show. I don't look to discover something new but something forgotten. Something so old that all distinctions between aesthetic genres are no longer of any use. I am a *teacher of Performer.*"

Through the work with Thomas Richards on Art as Vehicle, Grotowski appeared to reposition himself as director and researcher so that he himself became an "ancestor" within what has been continued as a living tradition of work. Fulfilling the vocation of father-teacher in the process of transmission of ancient practices, Grotowski arrived at a stage where Richards himself assumed the role in relation to other apprentices, so that the tradition would continue. In the essay "Performer," Grotowski wrote somewhat cryptically of the double consciousness that this "Performer" needs to develop with the aid of a teacher. This capacity to see and do at the same time is nourished by being "passive in action and active in seeing. . . . *Performer* must develop not an organism-mass, an organism of muscles, athletic, but an organism-channel through which the energies circulate, the energies transform, the subtle is touched."[46]

The present form of *Action,* Grotowski's last work with Thomas Richards, has remained more or less unchanged since 1995. Its regular repetition, the form of its transmission, and the way in which it is witnessed reinforce its status as a contemporary ritual rather than a theater performance. Early in the millennium Thomas Richards and Mario Biagini began to work with a group of Singaporean actors on a "bridge" project, a production called *One Breath Left* that makes use of some elements of *Action* (in particular the vibratory singing). This work is, however, distinct from *Action,* which continues to be performed and witnessed as an aspect of the

Ryszard Cieslak in Grotowski's legendary production of *The Constant Prince,* 1966.
Courtesy of the Archive of the Grotowski Center, Wroclaw.

working life at the Workcenter.[47] In simple terms, its regular performance
can be understood as a ritual of human wholeness. *Action* is not a representation, although it is dense with signification. In Grotowski's words, "*Performer* knows how to link body impulses to the song. (The stream of life
should be articulated in forms.) The witnesses then enter into states of
intensity because, so to say, they feel presence."[48]

   The experience of witnessing *Action* at the Workcenter in Pontedera in
2001 was enough to convince me that the event Grotowski and Richards
have created is a distillation of all the experiments Grotowski had been making since the days of the Theater Laboratory. Although functioning not as
theater but in the quasi–ritualistic context of Art as Vehicle the structure of
Action more closely resembles a theater performance than any of Grotowski's post-theatrical activities and in my view vindicates much of the
writing by and on Grotowski since 1970. Grotowski's insistence that *Action*
be viewed outside the context of the professional theater system seems wise.
Its power to activate the spontaneous projection of one's deepest feelings

derives from the fact that one approaches it not in the spirit of a theater spectacle but as the sharing of the participants' ritual—a distillation of the love of life/work of its performers. The patent dedication of Thomas Richards, Mario Biagini, and their apprentice colleagues indicates that they are sharing with us an action performed in honor of the sacred joy of the life process. Grotowski's lifetime of practical research into performance was itself a demonstration that the doing is the meaning.

12. From Personal Encounter to Cultural Exchange: The Theaters of Peter Brook

Having by the early 1960s achieved enormous success in both commercial and mainstream art theaters, Peter Brook embarked on a voyage of discovery that has made him the most famous of alternative practitioners currently working in the theater. Although his approach to rehearsal is in many respects innovative, Brook's approach to training is not original. To say this is not to deny the power and significance of his productions. Indeed, he has been more consistently successful than any other contemporary practitioner in achieving performances that have thrilled audiences through their exploitation of an astonishing variety of forms and styles. But although he has been consistent in espousing a conscious eclecticism of styles and techniques of performance, he has tended to work with actors who have received extensive training in one or other tradition of world theater, so his initial work with actors could more properly be regarded as preparation for a particular process of creative discovery, rather than training as such. Like Stanislavski and Grotowski, he regards the cultivation of an appropriate ethos for creative work as more important than any specific form of technical accomplishment, but unlike them he has not become more interested in investigating the nature of acting than in presenting finished productions for theater audiences. After each phase of his concentrated experimental work, Brook has continued to make productions. These have employed a wide variety of styles, and addressed a great range of subjects. Although always sensitive to the problems of acting that arise as part of the process of every production he has made, Brook appears to have operated pragmatically as a director, rather than systematically as a researcher.[1]

Every one of his productions has aimed to ensure a fresh experience by questioning or undermining the conventions of existing theatrical performance in such a way as to avoid eliciting habitual responses to clichéd modes of presentation. Rather than evolving a coherent acting praxis, Brook has been both thoroughly pragmatic and completely open in his continuing search for theatrical means for the achievement of new ends. Thus his working methods have embraced an eclectic blend of practices from the major performance traditions of Asia, the Orient, Africa, and the West, although since 1962 his method of working has been distinguished by a consciously Socratic attitude, which has enabled him to be ruthlessly selective in his search for appropriate techniques and styles of performance.

His main assumptions about acting derive from Copeau as mediated through the work in Britain of Michel Saint-Denis. Although he was constantly aware of the achievements of Stanislavski, Meyerhold, and Brecht, Brook's own work with actors has since the 1960s drawn on the games of improvisation around a written text first introduced as a rehearsal method by Copeau, rather than the methods of the other practitioners. Meyerhold and Brecht have certainly influenced his approach to the creation of mise-en-scène, but it was his awareness of the praxis of Artaud and Grotowski that provoked him to push his way of working with actors beyond its previous limits. During the RSC Theatre of Cruelty project in which he collaborated with Charles Marowitz in 1964, Brook came to identify the confrontation between the theaters of Brecht and Artaud—in many respects polar opposites—as crucial to the redefinition of contemporary performance. The production of *Marat/Sade* (1964) was intended to stage that confrontation.

Around this time, he became acquainted with the theater of Grotowski, who was giving concrete form to Brook's notion of a necessary theater. When in 1967, Brook invited Grotowski to conduct workshops in preparation for his production of *US,* he expressed his own more limited sense of what a performance can do for the spectator in his description of the impact of Grotowski on the RSC actors:

What did the work do?
It gave each actor a series of shocks.
The shock of confronting himself in the face of simple irrefutable challenges.
The shock of catching sight of his own evasions, tricks and clichés.
The shock of sensing something of his own vast and untapped resources.
The shock of being forced to question why he is an actor at all.

    The shock of being forced to recognise that such questions do exist and that—despite a long English tradition of avoiding seriousness in theatrical art—the time comes when they must be faced. And of finding that he wants to face them.[2]

From the early 1960s onwards, Brook used a vocabulary that drew on the ideas of both Copeau and Grotowski to project an image of a theater reduced to its essential features. He encapsulated this idea in the title of his influential first book—*The Empty Space*.[3] His desire to create an "immediate" theater, echoed the intention of both Copeau and Grotowski to strip actors of their reliance on clichéd acting conventions and to remove superfluous decoration of the scenic space in order that the minimal scenographic design might function, not as an illusionistic background to stage action, but as an integral component of the performance itself. If furniture was not absolutely necessary to promote the collaboration of actor and audience in experiencing the essence of the drama, then the stage space should be left bare. Brook, however, came to be increasingly aware of the various possibilities of simple if startlingly unconventional playing places and has been adept at exploiting them in astonishing ways.[4]

Brook's demand for a necessary theater did not however lead him completely to eschew the virtuoso manipulations of mise-en-scène that had characterized his work in the 1940s and 1950s. In acknowledging the difference between Grotowski's theatrical aims and his own in 1967, Brook identified his own aim of achieving the liveness and richness of an "Elizabethan" relationship between actors and audience: "But the life of our theatre is in every way different from . . . [Grotowski's]. He runs a laboratory. He needs an audience occasionally, in small numbers. His tradition is Catholic—or anti-Catholic. . . . Our aim is not a new Mass, but a new Elizabethan relationship—linking the private and the public, the intimate and the crowded, the secret and the open, the vulgar and the magical."[5]

Shakespeare as Challenge and Model

Brook's experiments in the 1960s were framed by two Shakespeare productions—*King Lear* (1962) and *A Midsummer Night's Dream* (1970). While his production of the tragedy may be seen to inaugurate a phase of work directed toward the achievement of a "holy" theater, which aimed at confronting the cruelty of human existence, the comedy provoked him to realize what he had called "rough" theater—a popular theater capable of both manifesting and celebrating the power of the imagination to transcend human suffering. The Artaudian ideal of performance as a unique transaction between performer and spectator, akin to a religious ceremony, inspired Brook's series of experimental productions in the 1960s—*Marat/Sade, US* (1966), *The Tempest* (1968), and *Oedipus* (1968).

Shakespeare's plays served as Brook's model of the kind of drama that could achieve his desired integration of holy and rough theater:

> For a play to seem like life, there must be a constant movement that goes back and forth between the social and the personal view; in other words, between the intimate and the general. For instance, Chekhov's plays contain this movement. . . . There is also another movement. It alternates between the superficial aspects of life and its most secret ones. If this is also present, then the play takes on an infinitely richer texture. From the start, the cinema discovered the principle of changing perspectives, and audiences in every corner of the world accepted without difficulty the grammar of the long shot and the close-up. Shakespeare and the Elizabethans made a similar discovery. They used the interplay between everyday and heightened language, between poetry and prose, to change the psychological distance between the audience and the theme. The important thing is not the distance itself, but the constant in-and-out movement between various planes. . . . Shakespeare seems better in performance than anyone else because he gives us more, moment for moment, for our money. This is due to his genius, but also to his technique. The possibilities of free verse on an open stage enable him to cut the inessential detail and the irrelevant realistic action: in their place he could cram sounds and ideas, thoughts and images which make each moment into a stunning mobile.[6]

In order to achieve a modern approximation of the complex richness of Shakespeare's theater, Brook felt compelled to test Artaudian performance—in which the spectator is wholly submerged in the sensuous and emotional experience—against Brechtian distancing techniques, by means of which the social aspects of human behavior were exposed in a critical way: "Brecht's use of 'distance' has long been considered in opposition to Artaud's conception of theater as immediate and violent subjective experience. I have never believed this to be true. I believe that theatre, like life, is made up of the unbroken conflict between impressions and judgments."[7]

Brook's production of *King Lear* presented characters in a cool and balanced way: actors demonstrated their characters' motives rather than attempting to achieve emotional identification with them. At the same time, the bodily enactment of violence and suffering in the play possessed an intensity that called to mind Artaud's notion of cruelty. "We need to look to Shakespeare. . . . In Shakespeare there is epic theatre, social analysis, ritual cruelty, introspection. There is no synthesis, no complicity. They sit contradictorily, side by side, coexisting, unreconciled."[8]

Strategies for Playing Reality

How did Brook help his actors to achieve this Shakespearean complexity? While initially making the same assumptions as Copeau and Saint-Denis about how the language of the play should direct the actors, Brook's experience with Shakespeare led him to believe that their view of the process was too limiting:

> When I started work on Shakespeare, I did believe, to a limited extent, in the possibility of a classical word music, that each verse had a sound that was correct, with only moderate variations; then through direct experience I found that this was absolutely and totally untrue. The more musical the approach you bring to Shakespeare . . . the more you find that there is no way, except by sheer pedantry, that can fix a line's music. . . . In exactly the same way an actor who tries to set his performance is doing something anti-life. While he has to keep certain consistencies in what he's doing or it's just a chaotic performance, as he speaks it, each single line can reopen itself to a new music, made round these radiating points.[9]

The earlier speech-oriented approach to Shakespeare ran the risk of short-circuiting the process whereby actors come to grips with the human reality of the drama: Stanislavskian exercises might, Brook believed, help the actors to make the experience of the characters their own. This was certainly necessary, when working on a play whose subject matter was as violent and intense as *King Lear*. ("The whole problem of the theatre today," Brook had said in 1965, "is just this: how can we make plays dense in experience?")[10]

Equally, however, Brook wished to avoid the danger of ignoring the play's language and performing it in a naturalistic style, as was often the case with actors trained in Strasberg's Method techniques. What Brook was at this time groping toward was what David Williams identified in his analysis of *The Mahabharata* (1985) as "a consciously naive mixture of styles, traditions, races, and accents . . . a style of theatre characterised in truth by an absence of imposed unity of style."[11] Rejecting the notion of style as a unifying factor in performance (a key concept for Michel Saint-Denis), Brook formulated a production aesthetic in which differences in style were reflections of the different planes of reality on which a drama was operating:

> The distinction between the realistic play and the poetic one, between the naturalistic and the stylised is artificial and very old-fashioned. . . . Today we are beginning to see that Shakespeare forged a style in advance of any style anywhere, before or *since,* that enabled him, in a very compact space of time, by a superb and conscious use of varied means, to create a realistic image of life. . . . It can no longer be held for one second that such plays are "stylised," "formalised" or "romantic" as opposed to "realistic." . . . Eventually, we want to have actors who know with such certainty that there is no contradiction between the heightened and the real that they can slide effortlessly between the gears of verse and prose, following the modulations of the text.[12]

In the 1960s Brook consciously sought to mix the approaches of Stanislavski, Artaud, Brecht, and Meyerhold with that promoted in Britain by Michel Saint-Denis, in order to create a modern form of theater that might possess the qualities of a great performance of a Shakespeare play. Shakespeare has remained a challenge and an inspiration to Brook, whose achievements have alternated between epic performances and small-scale work.

Brook's decision to employ Marowitz as assistant director on the RSC *Lear* signaled his dissatisfaction with acting in contemporary British productions of Shakespeare. Marowitz's description of some of the work he did during rehearsals reveals Brook's desire to explore the new kinds of performance techniques exploited since the late 1950s by American avant-garde groups such as the Living Theater, as well as the legacy of Stanislavskian approaches of which British actors had only vague or generalized knowledge. Brook's response to the Living Theater's production of *The Connection* in 1960 was to formulate a set of reflections on the nature of acting at this time. These were uncannily prescient with respect to developments in film acting and to avant-garde experiments in physical theater that occurred in the late 1980s and the 1990s (especially the work of Jan Fabré and Pina Bausch in Belgium and Germany, as well as DV8 and Forced Entertainment in Britain):

> Julian Beck and Judith Malina's production of Jack Gelber's play *The Connection* in New York is fascinating because it represents one of the

few clear ways opening up for our theatre. . . . At first you cannot believe that the reaction against all the "lies" of theatre can be total. After all, in Pinter, in Wesker, in Delaney, there are new artifices to replace the old, even if they seem for the moment to be closer to the "truth." . . . But in *The Connection,* the tempo is the tempo of life itself. . . . *The Connection* . . . is a play about dope addicts. What we see is a roomful of junkies waiting for a fix. They are passing the time playing jazz, occasionally talking, mostly sitting. The actors who are portraying these characters have sunk themselves into a total, beyond Method, degree of saturated naturalism, so that they aren't acting, they are being. . . . it is the ultimate development of the utterly naturalistic theatre and yet we are completely "distanced" all through the evening. *The Connection* proves to me that the development of the tradition of naturalism will be toward an ever-greater focus on the person or the people, and an increasing ability to dispense with such props to hold our interest as story and dialogue. I think it shows that there is a super-naturalistic theatre ahead of us in which pure behaviour can exist in its own right, like pure movement in ballet, pure language in declamation etc. . . . Mustn't we relate this to the actor . . . in order to find the pattern of the theatre we need?[13]

In order to promote acting that could encompass the variety and clash of styles that Brook saw as necessary for his theater, actors had not merely to assimilate the techniques necessary to produce each style, but also the flexibility to switch suddenly from one to another. During the Theatre of Cruelty project, Marowitz devised improvisations designed to exercise the actor's ability to move suddenly from the portrayal of one level of reality to another. These improvisations challenged conventional notions of the relationship between content and form, dramaturgical meaning and playing style. By instructing the actor immediately and spontaneously to change an improvisation so that an initial subject is suddenly expressed in terms of a wholly different form, or so that stylistic aspects of the presentation remain the same while the content changes, Marowitz and Brook developed the actors' expressive capacities, enabling them to increase their vocabulary of performance modes.[14]

The sessions run by Marowitz drew on the techniques of Strasberg's Method and of the avant-garde attempts by the Living Theater to deconstruct and transcend it, being directly concerned with creating a type of acting that went beyond traditional styles, whether realistic or abstract, through which meanings could be communicated in physical and kinetic images without recourse to naturalistic characterization. In this respect, Brook transformed the game-playing, improvisatory techniques of Copeau and Michel Saint-Denis to produce an Artaudian vocabulary of gestures and sounds that was tested in *Marat/Sade, US, The Tempest,* and *Oedipus.* Many of the exercises devised at this time were similar to the postnaturalistic "sound-and-movement" exercises of Joe Chaikin, whose work with the newly formed Open Theatre in New York in the early 1960s emerged from the same matrix as that of Marowitz, and who became aware of the work of Grotowski at about the same time as Brook.[15] Marowitz described a number of the exercises used during work on the Theatre of Cruelty project. These included the disrupted set piece, text and subtext exercises, object associations, discontinuous improvisation, work on sounds and on contact, group interview, changing gears, and a series of variations on standard Method improvisations. He also devised a William Burroughs–like collage *Hamlet* as an extension of the discontinuity exercises: by removing the narrative frame, the actors were obliged to encounter the play as a structure of archetypal experiences, stripped of the conventional explanations supplied by the normal relationships between plot and character.

The exercises aimed to enhance the actor's ability to perform realistic scenes at a "mythic" level, without the naturalistic paraphernalia of sociological and psychological explanation and, conversely, to play more abstract and stylized drama with the density of experience that helped the actor to avoid the pitfalls of empty formalism. Most of the acting strategies Brook employed in the 1960s addressed the problem of how to express real emotions and experiences in non-naturalistic ways. Beginning by disrupting the surface realism of Method improvisations, Marowitz's exercises allowed the performers to deconstruct the forms of naturalistic representation. Commentators such as Albert Hunt have made the point that Brook's repeated attempts to create an Artaudian language of the theater that transcends specific languages and conventions were unnecessary and self-defeating: "'EyayeOoghn' and 'Eey-zoohz'? What were actors, directors, stage management, or the caretaker at the church hall to make of *that*? . . . What were the sounds to communicate that couldn't be communicated in straightforward dialogue? Some depths of sexual anguish previously unheard by man? Or woman? Describing . . . [another] exercise . . . Marowitz says that the sounds made by the actors . . . had the 'resonance of wounded animals; of prehistoric creatures being slain by atomic weapons.' For whom did the sounds have these resonances?"[16]

One might argue in defense of Brook and Marowitz that they were at least helping actors to free themselves of the restrictions of traditional British acting styles by forcing them to engage with the possibilities of vocal and

bodily expressiveness at the most fundamental level. It is true, however, that
Brook's rationalization of his practice has always been at its most pretentious
and least convincing in his attempts to justify his search for a prelogical and
universal language of theater. His stubborn refusal to accept the fact that
meaning in the theater is a function of linguistic and other theatrical codes,
is the most irrational aspect of his aesthetic credo. Brook's more recent pronouncements on his artistic aims have been more modest. Rather than
emphasizing the attempt to discover a "universal language of theatre," he
has stressed the need to liberate the communication between performers
and audience from existing clichés.

Marowitz's acting exercises provided the matrix from which Brook was
later to develop more complex rehearsal and preparation programs, but one
can discern in the pattern of different exercises three motifs that came to
dominate Brook's work with actors in the 1960s:[17]

1. Exercises designed to promote spontaneity and flexibility in responding immediately to changing stimuli. A typical example is the series of
   discontinuous improvisations in which one actor performing an
   action is joined by a succession of individual actors who perform
   actions that complicate the dramatic scenario, for example, workers
   digging up a road to lay a cable. At a certain point a new actor enters
   and performs an unrelated action to which the others must adapt as
   quickly as possible. The situations are repeatedly changed by the
   entrance of new performers, the fictional transformations testing the
   actors' ability to respond immediately to new imaginary situations.[18]
2. Improvisations and games to build a postnaturalistic performance
   vocabulary. Most of the exercises introduced by Marowitz aimed to
   interrogate and disrupt the automatic naturalism to which British and
   American actors revert in the playing of characters, irrespective of the
   style that the written text indicates. These included
   a. discontinuity exercises, in which the conventional emotional logic
      of naturalism is undermined through the contradictory emotional
      reactions demanded of a performer by means of the replaying, in
      rapid succession or simultaneously, of realistic scenes that were pre-
      viously devised;
   b. sound and movement similes, in which the performer must exter-
      nalize a highly emotional internal state using only a sound and a
      movement, thus preventing the expression from being naturalistic;
   c. conventional Method improvisations replayed using only essential
      words or nonverbal sounds, forcing the performer to break the

conventional association of psychological impulse and naturalistic form of expression;

d. speaking with paints, in which actors were required to convey their internal states in specific fictional situations by painting rather than acting them.

3. Work on sound and movement to enhance the actor's bodily/vocal expressiveness.

Most of these exercises were designed to produce the capacity Brook later called *transparency*—the ability to freely translate inner impulses into bodily form, bodily impulses into vocal sounds, and verbal cues into physical expression.[19]

Rehearsal as a Process of Discovery

In reaction against the dominant British tradition of acting as rhetorical interpretation of great literary drama, Brook wanted the performance of a play—particularly a great literary text such as *King Lear*—to have the impact of a personal confrontation between performers and spectators.[20] The Theatre of Cruelty project was Brook's first attempt to use rehearsal as a laboratory for the investigation of new forms of expression rather than as a way of arriving at an effectively finished interpretation of a dramatic text. He thus initiated himself and his actors into a process in which exploration became as important as the end result. Although from this moment on in his career, a major production would normally provide the culmination of the process of exploratory work that might last months or even years, he would seldom commit himself to creating a performance that was not the result of extensive experiment over a lengthy rehearsal period. This approach parallels the poor theater phase of Grotowski's work in that rehearsals took the form of research toward the discovery of new performance forms. It was not, however, until he moved to Paris that Brook was able to secure periods of rehearsal/laboratory time comparable to those of his eastern European counterparts.[21]

During rehearsals for *Lear,* Brook gave a brilliantly succinct definition of the function of rehearsals as "looking for meaning and then making it meaningful."[22] When working on a preexisting text, Brook's rehearsals were dedicated to the discovery of the central meaning of the play as well as the modes and conventions of performance that would allow the actors to release the potential of the text to engage the audience in the sharing of a fully human experience.

Not only did the Theatre of Cruelty project explore the theatrical dialectic of Artaudian versus Brechtian theater, it also revealed to Brook the possibilities of the kind of collaborative theater-making process envisaged by Craig, Meyerhold, and Copeau. Instead of starting with a complete play text, the performance was authored by the director, in collaboration with writers, actors, and scenographers who supplied the component parts of the unified artwork. In this case, Brook might start with a subject or problem he wished to explore, e.g., the Vietnam War, which was the subject of *US;* or a nondramatic literary work, e.g., *The Conference of the Birds* (1979), based on a twelfth-century Sufi poem of five thousand verses, *The Mahabharata,* taken from an ancient Sanskrit epic that is fifteen times the length of the Bible, or a drama whose form would be radically altered through adaptation. For a few months before formal rehearsals began, he would employ his improvisatory methods to explore both the intended subject matter and potential ways of expressing it. The two were closely connected. With few exceptions, Brook was to work in this way as author of a text for performance in the creation of all his subsequent productions.

During early rehearsals for *Lear,* Charles Marowitz noticed that Brook told individual actors "just enough to force an actor to reappraise his entire conception of a role but not enough to supply him with an alternative."[23] This is the key to Brook's consistent attitude to working with actors. "The crucial insights into any play will be found by the actors themselves."[24] So Brook's rehearsal method has not involved the systematic development of a unique set of psychophysical techniques for achieving certain creative ends, nor even a consistent search for a Grotowskian *via negativa.* Nevertheless he has made the rehearsal period a process in which the actors investigate the meaning of the material they are given at the same time as they discover forms through which it can be best expressed. In this way the actors enter into the collaborative process of making the performance: Brook's belief that "anybody's personal view of the [Shakespeare] play is bound to be less than the play itself," provided a rationale "for the process of group exploration, in which personal expression ceases to be an aim and we go toward shared discovery."[25] This ideal is very much in the tradition of Copeau, whose notion of a community of theater-makers living together in a rural environment and improvising their own folk dramas or performing classic plays is in many respects parallel to Brook's notion of collaborative work on Shakespeare.

Although there are many similarities with the methods of Grotowski, Brook has always remained far more vague about the ideology that motivates his own aesthetic practice. Insisting on his right to remain open to the discoveries that might be made through each new process of rehearsal/exploration, his attitude of Socratic ignorance ("I know only that I do not know") in the pursuit of wisdom through the trial-and-error methods of improvisational games, has at times infuriated critics and actors. Some, like Marowitz, have come to view Brook's reticence as a refusal to take responsibility for his political attitudes that leads to a confusion of genuine insight with meretricious theatrical effect:

> Brook has gradually become the purveyor of avant-garde clichés to the mass audience. *Oedipus* is thinly-disguised Open Theatre techniques, Grotowski-tactics and lifts from The Living Theatre. Plagiarism doesn't enter into it. All theatre-workers borrow from each other all the time. . . . But what in Grotowski or the Becks appears to be an inevitable expression of personally-arrived-at discoveries looks, in Brook, like elaborately camouflaged second-hand goods. . . . It's splendid but it doesn't quite fit. . . . In this way, Brook is the liaison between the true avant-garde and the bourgeois public and critics.[26]

Others have seen it as a directorial tactic designed to manipulate actors, designers, writers, and composers into thinking they are collaborating with him when in fact they are merely being used to work out Brook's own predetermined set of aesthetic problems.[27]

Whatever the extent of Brook's conscious manipulation of his actors in order to enable them to discover the form and meaning of the performance as a series of actively experienced insights, his characteristic approach to acting from the Theatre of Cruelty project to *A Midsummer Night's Dream* reflected the limitations endemic in a commercial theater system. In Britain, this affects even the subsidized theater. Brook himself, despite his huge international prestige as a director, was unable to secure more than a ten-week rehearsal period for a production.[28] Although his work with actors expressed his desire to revolutionize the form and quality of performance during this period, he was unable to achieve the working conditions that would allow the kind of radical redefinition of acting achieved by Stanislavski and Grotowski through years of working with the same group of performers. His concrete work on acting therefore involved strategies designed to enhance his actors' existing training, and to undermine and challenge their limitations and bad habits whenever necessary. The eclecticism of his rehearsal methods can be seen as pragmatic bricolage—a response to the requirements of the specific performance that he is creating at the time, although critics like Marowitz would claim this eclecticism as proof that he has nothing original to offer with respect to acting praxis. Whatever the case, Brook never separates laboratory work on acting from the overall problems of theatrical meaning, so his acting explorations are always tested in relation to experiments in scenography and dramaturgy, and eventually in the presence of an audience.[29]

A Midsummer Night's Dream can be seen as a culmination of Brook's theatrical experiments in the 1960s—a celebration of theater-making as process, of creativity as a way of life. In the production, play and game are imaginative responses to the harshness of experience (the wood). Both Brecht and Copeau had emphasized the gamelike nature of theater, at which Brook has since 1947 proved himself a supremely gifted player, while Stanislavski and Artaud had recognized the holiness of the act of performance as a sharing of profound existential truths. The production of the *Dream* was a "rough" celebration of the "holy." In Brook's words, "[The play] is a celebration of the theme of theatre: the play-within-the-play-within-the-play-within-the- play. One of its themes is theatre."[30] Brook's major productions after *A Midsummer Night's Dream* emphasized either the "rough" or the "holy," or both.

While the space was reduced to a white cube for Brook's *Dream,* the production was Meyerholdian in its thrilling use of stage effects as a component part of the actors' performances. Costumes made psychedelic splashes of color against the starkness of the cube. Puck appeared on stilts in certain sections of the play. The fairies descended in trapezes from above the stage, and actors appeared to fly onto the stage from trampolines concealed in the wings. But like the scenery in Meyerhold's constructivist productions, the set was a machine for acting that did not evoke locale or atmosphere in an illusionistic way. Brook has stated that "there are no secrets" in his theater.[31] The stage in *A Midsummer Night's Dream* was presented as a stage, a platform that would allow the physical virtuosity and the gamelike interactions of the actors to be exposed as tricks, not as an illusionistic space that concealed them. The same could be said of the equally spectacular *Mahabharata,* in which Chloe Obolensky's design in the found spaces of the different performances became an atmospheric background that revealed to the audience the scenic techniques through which the complex tales were being narrated. At a certain level, the scenography *was* the performance, since props, costumes, and space were all designed as instruments for the enactment of the narrative.[32]

Three Principles of Rehearsal

If in some ways the *Dream* was Brook's triumphant demonstration of the bricolage approach that had made him Britain's most famous theater direc-

Peter Brook's *The Mahabharata* at the Bouffes-du-Nord, Paris, 1985. Photo by Gilles Abegg.

tor, it was also the last production he was to undertake under the makeshift circumstances that forced him to work without adequate conditions for serious research. Despite the limitations of the commercially oriented system in which Brook worked during the 1960s, three principles of rehearsal emerged from his production experience and from his exposure to the praxis of Grotowski:

1. Research and improvisations to enable the actor's personal confrontation with the core experience of the play. From *Lear* onwards, Brook came increasingly to require that the actor find a way of relating the experience of the play to her own life experience. As part of the actors' work on the *Marat/Sade,* they visited an insane asylum to observe the behavior of mad people in preparation for their characterization as inmates of the asylum of Charenton. Brook encouraged the actors to "'dig out the madman' from themselves" and to construct their performances on the basis of what they had discovered inside themselves.[33] Brook's demand that each actor personally confront the subject of the play led to the direct collaboration of actors in

creating material for the production of *US,* so that the actor's investigation of her own experience within the perspective supplied by the subject of the drama became a regular feature of Brook's rehearsal process.[34] Brook's working practice involved a concrete attempt to actualize Stanislavski's belief that life was the best drama school.

2. The structuring of the work process itself to promote each actor's active engagement with the core experience embodied in the material of the performance. The production of *Lear* was apparently the first occasion on which Brook sought to make the rehearsal process itself a model of the experience represented by the play. *Orghast at Persepolis* may have been Brook's first total application of this principle. The actors were required to learn a new language called "orghast" especially invented for the representation of the mythic material by the poet Ted Hughes. The actual transportation of actors from Paris and an international festival audience to a quarry outside the Iranian capital of Persepolis in 1971 rendered literal a theme that had motivated his work for almost a decade. For the actors, the process of learning orghast was the first stage of the journey of enlightenment that the performance aimed to achieve. Their actual journey was a concrete realization of the voyage of discovery that they had made in the process of rehearsal. The three-month journey to North Africa in 1973 was an extension of the *Orghast* experiment. The interweaving of the imaginary experience of the fictional drama with the actual process of theater-making was a radical application of Copeau's idea of play as educative principle.[35]

3. The creation of a genuine ensemble. In casting performers for the Theatre of Cruelty season, Brook was aware of the need to assemble a group that would not be merely a collection of talented individuals but would constitute a creative ensemble capable of being open enough to risk self-exposure and of being genuinely collaborative in the exchange and sharing of experience and wisdom. Every one of his productions after 1963 was at one level an experiment in creating the working conditions conducive to the particular project in hand.[36] The longer-than-normal rehearsal periods required for each of these productions meant that his actors were obliged to cooperate for longer periods, and the specific demands of the material forced them to take greater risks. One of the factors that prompted Brook to establish La Centre International de Recherche Théâtrale (CIRT, later changed to CICT for *Création* rather than *Recherche*) in Paris in 1971 was his recognition that without the continuity guaranteed by an ensemble of regular creative collaborators, it was impossible to do the

necessary practical research to promote the performances he desired. In addition to working and (while on tour) living together as a group, the members of Brook's CICT committed themselves wholly to Brook's artistic aims; some of them (e.g., Bruce Myers, Yoshi Oida, Natasha Parry) have worked with him on projects spanning a period of more than two decades. The establishment of the CIRT in 1971 afforded Brook the opportunity to exploit a rich mix of cultural and ethnic identities for the production of new types of performance. At present the work of the ensemble is characterized by the intercultural exchange and eclectic range of performance skills and wisdom, rather than by the innovation of a homogenous form of transcultural training or an original performance style.

Over the last three decades, two exercises have been regularly employed by Brook to promote a sense of ensemble—the mirror exercise and working with sticks. In Brook's words: "The mirror exercise is an exercise by which two actors begin to work in harmony. Then four, then six, then eight, and then twelve, until the whole group is working in harmony. This is a basis of working, the product of an actual series of exercises of many different sorts by which the group works very freely together."[37] Pairs of actors must perform the same actions, the one mirroring the other without either leading the other. It requires intense concentration and eye contact and develops kinesthetic sensitivity and empathy between actors that begins in the body.

Brook's visit to a Chinese circus prompted his attempt to utilize some of its dazzling effects in his *Dream.* In preparation for his subsequent production, *Orghast,* he first asked actors to work with bamboo sticks, creating exercises based on Oriental methods of training that aimed to focus Brook's earlier voice and body work through small props that became an objectified extension of the performer's own body. "Holding the sticks, the group tapped out rhythms, formed bizarre mazes. . . . The actors used the sticks to contact each other, to elicit non-verbal responses, to measure their relationship to space."[38] The existence of CICT provided the time and the means to experiment with performance techniques in order to explore the theater-making process itself, without the immediate pressure of having to achieve results. The exercises with sticks do more than merely transform the actors into a working ensemble. According to Brook,

The essential purpose of the [stick] exercises is to create—it takes years— an actor so organically related within himself that he can think with his body to the point where the exercises actually take place by themselves. It is thought and action as one, like a conductor or the brush-strokes of a painter. In t'ai chi to do the exercise was to be it. And if the actor can produce the state of one, sensitive, responding whole, and many of the actors have, he will have developed and heightened his own natural creativity.[39]

Perhaps Brook's fundamental notion of acting is summed up in the above statement that succinctly suggests that the actor's task is to recover on behalf of the audience a primordial wholeness of being ("transparency") that Brook believes to have been lost as a consequence of the increasing logocentrism of modern (especially Western) cultures.[40] To discover the origins of this lost wholeness, it began to seem necessary for Brook to extend his research into performance not merely by incorporating performers from a wide range of cultures into his ensemble, but by undertaking actual journeys to the places where traces of such live culture might still exist.[41]

A Universal Language of Theater

Brook's production of the *Dream* had identified the play's problematic as a questioning of the nature of theater. The establishment of the CIRT enabled him to inaugurate a new phase of his investigations that aimed to find answers to questions he had formulated in a program note to the Round House *Tempest* in 1968: "What is a theatre? What is a play? What is an actor? What is a spectator? What is the relation between them all? What conditions serve this relationship best?"[42]

A number of critics had noticed the way in which the acting in the *Dream* had been marked by a joyous openness toward the audience, actors playing directly to and with them in an anti-illusionistic manner and shaking hands with them on their final exit. After Brook's numerous experiments in evolving a theater language that would enable the audience to engage fully in the performance event, the spectators' sheer delight at the end of performances of the *Dream* appeared as a fitting testimony to the power of such theater to communicate at the most fundamental level. However the challenge of having to maintain the freshness of such a performance on more than five hundred occasions was an impossible one. The next phase of Brook's theatrical experiments might be seen as a response to the paradox of a Western theatrical system that demands that a successful production be repeated over a number of years, resulting in an inevitable diminution of its power and spontaneity. The proper way to explore the questions Brook had posed during the Round House *Tempest* was to move beyond the confines of bourgeois theater and to test performances in the presence of a wide variety of actual audiences. The relationship with the audience thus became a central focus of investigation, actors being asked to show work in unlikely environments and to an extraordinarily wide cross-section of people, including workers, children, political activists, delinquents, regular metropolitan theater audiences around the world, and, eventually, inhabitants of a number of remote African villages.

Brook's reasons for wanting to understand the dynamic of the theater event emerge in his reply to a question by the journalist John Heilpern about the value of the exchange of songs improvised by the company and a group of African villagers who had invited them to a funeral ceremony: "One doesn't, in the theatre, create things for a museum or a shop, but for the moment, in a totally expendable way. And there [in an African village], an instance of that sort of theatre, of one which makes something just for that moment, actually happened. You ask: what did we leave? I think the true question is: what was shared?"[43]

One of Brook's most controversial projects, and a topic on which he appears to have made contradictory pronouncements, was his search to discover the essential features of theatrical communication that might operate in any context: "Our work is based on the fact that some of the deepest aspects of human experience can reveal themselves through the sounds and movements of the human body in a way that strikes an identical chord in any observer, whatever his cultural and racial conditioning."[44]

The hope of identifying a universal language of theatrical communication inspired a series of immensely ambitious projects, including *Orghast* in Iran (1971), the journey through an African desert (1972–73), and a trip across the United States from California via Colorado, Minnesota, and Connecticut to Brooklyn (1972) that culminated in *The Conference of the Birds* and later motivated the creation of *The Ik* (1975–76), and, more indirectly, *The Mahabharata*.

In some respects Brook's attempt to identify the sources of theatrical communication anticipated the work of Eugenio Barba in investigating the preexpressive level of performance, which Barba believes to be logically prior to specific forms of cultural expression. It also foreshadowed Grotowski's attempts in the early 1980s to identify the "source of sources" in order to employ the simplest forms of performance that precede cultural differentiation. Brook's project was probably inspired by Grotowski's move from the theater of productions to paratheater in the attempt to generate creativity by stimulating participants to rediscover their lost harmony with the elemental dramas of lived experience. With characteristically showman-like flair, Brook conducted his experiments in a comparative blaze of inter-national publicity and demonstrated his findings in the form of spectacular productions for prestigious audiences. It is doubtful whether the insights produced by Brook's various theatrical experiments contributed substan-tively to a systematic study of performance, but they did popularize a phase of practical research into the fundamental methodologies of theatrical per-formance that Barba has called theater anthropology, and they stimulated the subsequent growth of what the American academic and practitioner Richard Schechner has labeled performance studies—a discipline that brings the methods of anthropology to bear on performance activities from cul-tures around the world.

Brook's investigation of the possibilities of a universal language of the theater may in fact have turned out to be no more than his preparation for the creation of astonishingly inventive productions. The journeys to Iran, Africa, and America did have the consequence of initiating a fertile period of performance in which Brook elaborated an intercultural language of ensemble theater characterized by its simplicity and openness. One of the persistent aims of Marowitz's exercises during the Theatre of Cruelty season was the innovation of non-naturalistic languages of theatrical expression. Joseph Chaikin's "inside-outside" improvisations, in which performers employed sounds and movements to evoke at one moment the external form of an event and at another its inner dynamic as an experience, aimed to stimulate the free flow from external reality to interior state and vice versa. Brook has subsequently developed and transformed such "inside-outside" exercises to make this a central theme in his work to enhance the actor's transparency:

During preparatory work for *The Ik,* actors studied photographs in order to mimic postures of Ik tribespeople in precise detail before attempting to inhabit the psychophysical attitude of these alien bodies. In preparation for *The Man Who,* the company observed and imitated the symptoms of partic-ular neurological disorders with clinical accuracy, attempting to access states of mind through physical behavior. In other contexts, Brook has proceeded from the inside outward, providing actors with external theatrical symbols such as masks or precise patterns of language or gesture as conduits for the channeling of powerful expressive impulses. Whatever the starting point, Brook regards the relationship of inner impulse and outer expression as a central problematic of acting: "The true actor recognises that real freedom occurs at the moment when what comes from the outside and what is brought from within make a perfect blending."[45]

Intercultural Performance

By the mid-1980s Brook had become accustomed to having his search for a universal language of theater dismissed as philosophically naive and politically incorrect. The gist of the philosophical argument against his idea of performance as a transcultural means of communication was that theatrical conventions function as language systems enabling members of a culture to communicate with one another in ways that parallel linguistic communication. To deny this, it is claimed, is to misunderstand the nature of communication. In addition, Brook's equation of the primordial essence of theatrical communication with the orality of African cultures was seen as a patronizingly Rousseauistic idealization of African tribal performance. Politically, the objections to Brook's work in third world countries ranged from disgust at the contradiction between the allegedly decadent formalism of *Orghast* and the undisguised repressiveness of the regime that sponsored it, to accusations of neocolonialism in the exploitation of poor villagers as tryout audiences for material ultimately intended for consumption by privileged groups of bourgeois Western theatergoers.[46] In the 1960s and 1970s, Brook was something of a mythmaker, valorizing the uncompromising nature of his work process by means of a series of mystical-sounding explanations of its significance. In response to criticism of his philosophical aims he has since the early 1980s justified his working methods in more pragmatic terms, while at the same time pursuing an even more ambitious program in the preparation of his twelve-hour epic *The Mahabharata*.

Already in 1968 when he was planning the production of what became the Roundhouse *Tempest* at the Théâtre des Nations, Brook had conceived of a production with a multicultural group. It is likely that his frustration at the limitations of the British theater system encouraged him to grab this new opportunity of extending the vocabulary of performance conventions that he would have at his disposal. Having made determined efforts to overcome the limitations of the British tradition in productions from *Lear* onward, he now decided to explore the aesthetic possibilities of harnessing a multicultural mixture of styles and techniques in pursuit of the rich simplicity of acting he desired. Although Brook's absorption of an astonishingly eclectic range of performance techniques and styles from traditional theaters of Asia, Africa, the Orient, and the Western avant-garde laid him open to accusations that he was engaged in a simplistic syncretism that purported to

demonstrate the viability of a universal theatrical language, David Williams
claims that Brook's aim was otherwise:

> With his international group, Brook never intended to synthesise differ-
> ent world theatre techniques into a sort of "dramatic esperanto." He did
> not want his actors to exchange their individual "*trucs,*" although the
> group has inevitably borrowed methods of approach to the opening and
> preparation of the actor from the individual cultures represented. . . .
> The microcosm of the group combined a range of colours, sizes and
> skills as rich as that of a commedia dell' arte troupe; in its diversity, it
> would mirror the real world. It was hoped that creativity would be born
> from the setting up of a "difficult friction" so that "each one's culture
> slightly eroded the other's until something more natural and human
> appeared."[47]

The notion of intercultural performance that has been fashionable in
Western theater circles for the last twenty years seems to have been anticipated by Brook's work at the CIRT in the 1970s. The practice of performance exchange that Barba has named *barter* appears to have begun spontaneously during Brook's travels in North Africa and was certainly a crucial
aspect of the group's encounter with El Teatro Campesino in California in
1973.[48] The artistic strategy of *The Mahabharata* afforded Western audiences
not only the *verfremdungseffekt* of having their inherited aesthetic assumptions
challenged by the strangeness of a classic Asian text with its many layers of
cultural accretion, but also the shock of its being performed in a nontradi-
tional way by a multicultural group of actors who made no attempt at
achieving a unified style of playing.

According to Brook, the purpose of working with an international group
of performers was not to blur their individual differences, but to enhance
the sense of each performer's unique identity:

> To become true to himself he had to shed the superficial traits which in
> every country are seized upon and cultivated to make national dance
> groups and propagate national culture. Repeatedly we saw that a new
> truth emerges only when certain stereotypes are broken. . . . The Japa-
> nese becomes more Japanese, the African more African, until one reaches
> a level where forms aren't fixed; a new situation appears which allows
> people from different origins a new act of creation. They can create
> together and what they create takes on another colour.[49]

The Mahabharata was a triumphant success on the international avant-garde theater circuit, being presented between 1985 and 1989 in a variety of extraordinary environments at the Avignon Festival, in Paris at the Centre's Théâtre aux Bouffes du Nord, in Zurich, Los Angeles, Brooklyn, Glasgow, Australia, and Japan before being made into a film for television in 1990. The production was the subject of some highly publicized criticism that leveled charges of neocolonialist cultural appropriation.[50]

Brook's high profile has caused him to be attacked for exemplifying tendencies in avant-garde theater that are a result of his position as a major Western practitioner. It is probably true to say that Brook's version (the text itself is by his regular collaborator, Jean-Claude-Carrière) of *The Mahabharata* is ignorant of and insensitive to the complex intertextuality of philosophical ideas and social realities that define its unique status as a Hindu text. In performing it in a creolized fashion, Brook may be justly accused of having made a trendy Western performance that consciously and unconsciously misses the point of the original, creating a palatable distortion of Asian culture acceptable to Western viewers. It is equally true, however, that the history of every art form involves cultural appropriations that in various ways reflect and refract the changing structures of influence and power in the world, so that a dominant culture will inevitably be in a better position to appropriate for its own ends the cultures of less powerful groups.[51] Brook certainly did not set out to create an exotically Asian mode of performance, though he did exploit his habitual method of bricolage in mixing the conventions and styles contributed by his multicultural cast. In managing to respect the different performance traditions of actors from an extremely wide range of cultural backgrounds, while exploring the possibility of creating something new, he has certainly been one of the first to confront the aesthetic challenge posed by the development of an increasingly globalized world culture.[52]

The achievement of such productions as *The Ik, The Conference of the Birds, The Mahabharata, The Tempest* (1990), *The Man Who* (1993), *Hamlet* (2000), and *Le Costume* (2001) has been dependent upon Brook's intercultural explorations in the field of acting. What has he achieved with respect to the development of a modern approach to acting? He has wrestled with the difficulty of creating modes of acting that are not divorced from the real life they purport to represent. While not advancing a coherent methodology for performance, he has doggedly maintained a typical attitude while exploiting a surprisingly eclectic range of techniques of training and rehearsal. This has been well expressed by the actor Vittorio Mezzogiorno, who played Arjuna in *The Mahabharata:*

Brook wants everything to come from the actor, he must find it himself. He doesn't want to impose anything on him, and particularly not a culture that doesn't belong to him. The actors [of *The Mahabharata*] incorporated and assimilated impressions of the Indian world: we had to find whatever resonances it created within our own cultures, our own temperaments and sensations. . . . Brook has an extraordinary way of existing and of allowing us to exist. We created everything on our own, but he controlled every aspect in a concealed way, like a puppeteer. . . . the actors were not supposed to execute certain prescribed things so much as to participate with their whole being in the creation of something. The actor's performance comes from what he is in himself.[53]

13. Performance as Cultural Exchange: Eugenio Barba and Theater Anthropology

Eugenio Barba was largely responsible for publicizing the early work of Grotowski's Laboratory Theatre in Europe and North America. His own work since the early 1970s has stimulated debate about the relationship between the performance aesthetics of different cultures, and his cross-cultural investigations of methods of training and theater-making have provoked contemporary Western theater practitioners to reconsider the values and limitations of their own traditional approaches to acting. If the productions of Odin Teatret have not themselves achieved a status comparable with the legendary productions of Grotowski's Laboratory Theatre or the later work of Peter Brook, Barba's experiments in performance training and methods of performance composition have complemented the work of these two innovators in transforming our notion of what constitutes performance. Barba's development of theater anthropology as a field of practical research represents a step toward the formulation of transcultural principles that might comprehend performance practices around the world.

Between 1961 and 1964 Barba not only worked as a research assistant in Grotowski's Theater of Thirteen Rows in Opole, but he also publicized the work of the Polish Theatre Laboratory by writing articles with Ludwig Flaszen and the first book on its work,[1] and in 1968 editing Grotowski's creative testament, *Towards a Poor Theater*. Grotowski himself acknowledged Barba as a true disciple. In terms of form and creative methodology Barba's work since 1965 with his group Odin Teatret has been profoundly influenced by that of Grotowski. His practice has paralleled Grotowski in either initiating or reflecting a number of major shifts that have occurred within the field of performance since the 1960s, although the changes in orientation of Barba's performance work have never provoked him to move outside the sphere of theater altogether, as Grotowski did, and the Odin Teatret has until the present day continued to make productions, many of which have been directed by Barba himself.

Performing as Process: A New Culture of the Actor

Barba's identification of the third theater as a distinct grouping of practitioners was the first explicit recognition that a new paradigm had by the 1970s emerged in the field of performance. The third theater is so named to distinguish it from both the institutionalized theater (first theater) and the avant-garde (second theater): "The third theatre lives on the fringes, often outside or on the outskirts of the centers and capitals of culture. It is a theatre created by people who define themselves as actors, directors, theatre workers, although they have seldom undergone a traditional theatrical education and therefore are not recognised as professionals. . . . But they are not amateurs. Their entire day is filled with theatrical experience, sometimes by what they call training, or by the preparation of performances for which they must fight to find an audience."[2]

The third theater replaces the performance as product with performing as *process*.[3] In Barba's words, the third theater is dedicated not to the creation of performances that generate meaning but to discovering "an autonomous meaning for the action of doing theatre."[4] In their different ways, both Stanislavski and Copeau had already explored the possibility of a new kind of performance culture. In order to investigate the art of acting itself, Stanislavski established a succession of studios that operated in tandem with the regular rehearsal and production schedule of the Moscow Art Theater. Copeau's move away from the Vieux-Colombier to found a company and school in rural Burgundy was a parallel attempt to establish an institution that might foster exploration of the fundamental principles of theatrical art while remaining involved in the process of creating performances. Grotowski's transformation of his Theatre of Thirteen Rows into the Polish Theatre Laboratory reinforced the trend to investigate what Barba has called "the secret art of the performer" rather than to concentrate exclusively on making theater. Grotowski's move "beyond theater" in 1970 confirmed the significance of this project.

Barba's exposure to kathakali training during his visit in 1963 to the major kathakali academy, the Kalamandalam at Cheruthuruthy, provoked his realization that the essential difference between the Asian and the Western performer was the ability of the Asian performer "to live as an actor without living for performances."[5] This notion of living as an actor rather than for performances motivates all the groups that belong to the third theater—a loose and independent collection of "floating islands" that do not attempt to define themselves in relation to the official theater culture. Whereas the avant-garde exists within the established theater system by defining its artistic approach in opposition to the conventions of the institutional theater, third theater is a network of groups that aim to exist independently of the theater establishment, building bridges with one another and creating a culture of performance that has reference to the actor rather than the theater architect, scenographer, or playwright. Among the groups that Barba has identified as sharing the aims of the third theater are the Living Theater, Joseph Chaikin's Open Theater, the Bread and Puppet Theater, the Polish group Gardzienice, the Peruvian group Cuatrotablas, and the Mexican group La Rueca.

Barba could be said to have responded to Grotowski's move away from theater by taking performance outside the theater system, and building a culture based on the exploration of the relationships between different groups of practitioners, and between performers and new communities of spectators. Barba often speaks of "building bridges," a metaphor suggestive of the significance he invests in the idea of *relationships* as definitive of performance. Grotowski had come to conceive the *transaction* between the actor and the spectator as more important than its signification. Influenced by his mentor, Barba began to view the creation of a relationship between performer and spectator as the true function of performance. More important than the semantic content of the theatrical communication is the recognition of the performer's self that occurs as the consequence of an honest confrontation with *otherness*.

Barba would not claim that his methods of performance composition and performer training are entirely original. The significance of his work is its original attempt at a systematically transcultural survey of Eastern and Western performance praxis in the hope of finding a set of principles that govern the art of the performer, irrespective of the different ideological and cultural inscriptions that are the results of specific historical and social contexts.

Theater as Anthropology

Barba's peculiar history has undoubtedly shaped his approach to performance. Born in Brindisi in 1936, he grew up in Gallipolli in the south of Italy. He settled in Norway, where he worked as a welder and sailor from 1954. He spent some time on a kibbutz and obtained a master's degree in literature at Oslo University before leaving Norway to attend theater school in Warsaw. After a few months he gave up his studies to join Grotowski's theater in Opole where, apart from a short interruption in order to study kathakali training in Kerala in 1963, Barba served what he regarded as an apprenticeship with Grotowski until 1964, when he returned to Oslo to establish Odin Teatret. In 1966, he and two of the original Odin actors moved to Holstebro in Denmark, where they set up the Scandinavian Theatre Laboratory for the Art of the Actor. While three actors from the Holstebro group, Else Marie Laukvik, Torgeir Wethal, and Iben Nagel Rasmussen, have remained with the company, Odin Teatret has been joined by performers from countries with a wide variety of linguistic and cultural backgrounds, including Denmark, Sweden, Italy, the United States, Canada, Britain, Germany, Spain, and Argentina. Although actors who join the company are required to learn Danish, Barba himself, who speaks Norwegian (and can therefore understand Danish), does not actually speak Danish. His position as an outsider in an adopted culture, running a cosmopolitan theater group that spends much of the year touring internationally, could hardly fail to affect his attitude toward performance:

> Personally, I think my motor is my choice to be an emigrant, my indifference to national ties. The only territory into which I sink my roots is the "country of speed," that tangible and inscrutable dimension which is myself as presence, as a unity of soul-body-spirit, perceptible to others through their five senses. For me the theatre is the ephemeral bridge which in "elected" contexts links me to another: to the actor, to the spectator. It is the interweaving of one solitude with another by means of an activity which obliges a total concentration of my entire physical and mental nature. The theatre is the fortress on the mountain, visible and impregnable, which permits me to be sociable while following the way of refusal.[6]

For Barba, theatrical creation is not only a form of cultural resistance but constitutes a type of anthropology. By isolating itself from the surrounding sociopolitical context of the dominant culture, a third theater group empowers itself to achieve a distance from the immediate issues of the day in order to observe and process them in a much more complex way. Thus the performances generated by the group are the result of a process whereby the "body-soul-spirit" of each actor is able to effect a profound transformation of the raw material presented by social reality. Third theater affords the performer a kind of double perspective, enabling him to *process* social life as an anthropologist might, while at the same time experiencing it. Thus the third theater avoids being merely agit-prop. The discipline of training and a unique dramaturgical method enable the actor to avoid the danger of directly translating real experience into theater, which in agit-prop performances, according to Barba, usually results in banal forms of pseudojournalism.

Migration and Barter: From Personal Encounter to Cultural Exchange

In a development of the Artaudian notion of theater as a form of personal encounter between actor and spectator, Grotowski widened the parameters of performance to investigate forms of performance across a range of sources that antedate cultural differentiation, thereby broadening the scope of practical performance research to include nontheatrical contexts of performance. Brook's search for a universal language of theater led him to explore the relationship between performer and spectator in a wide variety of cultural contexts. Barba goes one step further. His definition of the actor-spectator relationship transforms performance into a form of cultural exchange. He has achieved this transformation by means of two pragmatic strategies—the publicizing of Odin's work through a continuous series of "migrations" (including trips to festivals, and journeys to many parts of the world to share performances and exchange knowledge with other third theater groups), and by the establishment in 1979 of the International School of Theatre Anthropology (ISTA).

Between 1965 and 1973, Barba's productions were performed for limited audiences consisting of no more than seventy spectators in indoor spaces. He first used the term *barter* in 1974 to describe a practice that was to become a regular feature of the Odin's touring program. During Odin Teatret's trip to Sardinia in January 1974, their production of *My Father's House* was presented in a wide variety of places and situations with no existing tradition of theater. The show was performed in town and village squares, with spectators standing at the periphery of the playing area. The success of these performances led to an invitation by the Italian Research Council to undertake a project in the underdeveloped area of Carpignano in southern Italy. In this context Barba developed the concept of barter as a form of cultural exchange. Just as the anthropological orientation of the Odin Teatret promotes its study of theater cultures around the world, so does the group offer itself to be studied in turn by the practitioners and spectators with whom it makes contact on its various migrations.

[The] object of study for this anthropological study is also the group itself. By placing itself in different situations, the theatre group explores its own identity. The daily work—training and the work with performance—changes in a situation where the theatre group becomes the study object of the population of a small town: the object of curiosity and interest. . . . Or, as was the case with the barter, the group has made it possible for two different cultural entities to study and experience each other. As a theatre group, Odin Teatret is transnational and has no actual national identity. . . . [It] is a nomad theatre, a journeying theatre, like the wandering performers of other times. . . . its identity derives from a particular professionalism and a particular craft which the group has been continuously able to profile in relationship to other cultures and theatre traditions.[7]

The notion of barter directly affected productions Barba made between 1974 and 1978, all of which were intended for large audiences and were maintained in the Odin's repertoire. The aim in this phase of the group's work was not so much to experiment with new forms of theatrical expression, as to explore the possibility of new kinds of exchange between actors and spectators in a wide variety of cultural contexts. More or less simultaneously with Peter Brook's journeys to Africa and North America to test performances before a range of different audiences, Barba was investigating the nature of the relationship between performer and spectator. The barter was not a one-sided communication by actors for spectators, but provided an opportunity for genuine exchange between the host culture and the visitors: "A man cannot meet another man if not *through something;* from this comes the paradox of the utility of apparently useless things. . . . A barter consists of a 'payment in kind'; it is the culmination of a process of relationship-building between two groups—a theatre and a community—which exchange their 'cultures.' The theatre group presents itself through its own training, open air activities, ways of improvising, performances, and the host community responds with its own dances, music, songs, oral literature, even religious ceremonies."[8]

Unlike Brook, Barba did not seek to discover any kind of "universal language" that would enable theatrical performances to make sense irrespective of cultural differences. The barter is an exchange of performances that creates a situation in which sharing can take place and differences can be recognized. Barter became for Barba an emblem of the third theater's refusal to commodify theater as an aesthetic or commercial *product.* The first performance presented as a barter was *The Book of Dances,* a collection of dances based on the Odin actors' training. Since 1974 a number of productions have been devised and presented with the intention of creating barters. *The Book of Dances,* (1974), *Johann Sebastian Bach* (1974), *Anabasis* (1977), and *The Million* (1978) have combined popular and folk dance from around the world, circus clowning, music, songs, commedia dell'arte, street parades, stilt walking, and cabaret, which often reflect the idea of the journey and of the group's transcultural identity in a carnivalesque mode of performance that engages very openly with its spectators and provokes them into offering some kind of performance by way of barter.

Productions made to initiate barters tended to have a looser, more improvisational quality than Odin's "indoor" productions. Because these shows are often performed as street theater, the actors had to develop the skills of the popular entertainer—circus performer or clown—in order to acquire the ability to control noisy crowds in town squares and to exploit the serendipitous possibilities of "found" spaces rather than the carefully planned scenographic effects available in conventional theater spaces. The aim of ISTA is to promote the transcultural study of the performer's art. By organizing festivals and conferences in various international locations, ISTA enables meetings to occur between groups of practitioners and theater scholars from around the world, thus extending Barba's earlier investigations into theater anthropology by establishing a genuine possibility of exchange between the researchers and the groups being researched and by varying the relationship between observed and observers through the location of meetings in many different countries.

Barba's observation of performance cultures from around the world led him to reject the traditional distinction, based merely on geographical location, between Eastern and Western, performers. Instead, he distinguishes between North Pole and South Pole performers. The North Pole performer bases his craft on the presentation of highly codified forms, transmitted by means of rigid training regimes based on the principle of strict repetition, such as Noh theater, classical ballet, kathakali, Peking opera, and Kabuki. The techniques of the South Pole performer are characterized by repertoires of posture and gesture modeled on social behavior, and involve a freer approach to training that emphasizes the value of innovation, spontaneity, and personal engagement in the creation of the performance score, such as Stanislavski's method of physical actions, Michael Chekhov's psychological gesture, the corporal mime taught by Etienne Decroux, and Grotowski's training system.

Training the Dilated Body

Barba initially adopted the training methods of Grotowski's Polish Theatre Laboratory, insisting that somatic training rather than any method of psychological introspection was the key to developing the actor's sensibility. The early work of the Odin Teatret involved a strict concentration on voice and plastic exercises based on those of Grotowski. In July 1966, Grotowski and Ryszard Cieslak were invited to Holstebro to conduct workshops with the members of Odin Teatret. Barba's approach began to change at about the time that Grotowski indicated in 1970 that he was no longer interested in making theater performances. From the beginning Barba had followed Grotowski in rejecting the notion that performance training involves the acquisition of technical skills. In the words of Torgeir Wethal, one of the founding members of Odin Teatret, the "purpose of the training has not been the acquisition of skills for later use in performance. The purpose of the training has been to help the actor to break down his conditioned reflexes, to help him to work on his own daily movement patterns and to overcome his learned fatigue limits. Our training was also intended to lead the actor to an understanding of the elemental rules of physical expression."[9]

This represents a version of Grotowski's via negativa. In Barba's view, the actor's training is his way of life, "a process of self-definition, a process of self-discipline which manifests itself indissolubly through physical reactions."[10] The actor does not train in order to learn to do something, but in order to achieve the body-mind presence that is the prerequisite of performance. This is what Barba refers to as the dilated body. By means of training the performer effects a transformation of the ordinary actions of daily life into "scenic behavior," an "extra-daily" form of action that provides the substratum of a performance. From the performer's point of view Barba does not make a distinction between dance, mime, and theater. In this respect, his approach reflects concepts elaborated earlier by Dalcroze, Appia, Craig, Meyerhold, and Lecoq, and expresses an attitude shared by a large number of contemporary experimental performance groups dedicated to creating physical theater, dance-theater, live or performance art, music theater, or devised theater. Rejecting the primacy of psychologically realistic characterization, he requires the actor to concentrate on the physiological manifestation of psychophysical intentions. To find the body's extra-daily techniques, the performer does not study psychology but creates a network of external stimuli that provoke physical actions.[11]

The Pre-expressive and Expressive Levels of Performance

Odin Teatret's exploration of methods of training and techniques of performance in a wide range of cultures led Barba to posit the idea of the pre-expressive—a level of performance practice that entails systems of body-mind organization logically prior to the cultivation of culturally determined techniques of performance.[12] The preexpressive represents for Barba an actor's "technique of techniques," an underlying level of preparedness for

The Odin Teatret's production of *Anabasis* in Peru, 1978. Photo by Tony D'Urso, courtesy of Odin Teatret.

performance common to all performers, irrespective of the way that their own cultural identities have determined the particular expressive character of their individual art forms. The pre-expressive is the fundamental level of performance culture; at this level, the daily behavior of the ordinary social body is transformed into the scenic behavior of the dilated body—the body in performance, existing as aesthetic object and agent.

> The performer's various techniques can be conscious and codified or unconscious but implicit in the use and repetition of a theatre practice. Trans-cultural analysis shows that it is possible to single out recurring principles from among these techniques. These principles, when applied to certain physiological factors—weight, balance, the use of the spinal column and the eyes—produce physical, pre-expressive tensions. These new tensions generate an extra-daily energy quality which renders the body theatrically "decided," "alive," "believable," thereby enabling the performer's "presence" or scenic *bios* to attract the spectator's attention *before* any message is transmitted.[13]

The concept of the pre-expressive has been a source of some controversy among performance theorists and practitioners, many of whom believe Barba to be ignoring the ideological basis or culturally specific nature of different performance aesthetics in a manner reminiscent of Brook's attempt to discover a universal language of theater. Barba is clear on two points:

1. The pre-expressive dimension of performance pertains to the structural features of body-mind organisation that are the precondition for the semiological function of communication.
2. The pre-expressive, although it cannot in the material context of a performance be properly separated from the culturally determined levels of expression, is a useful and coherent concept, enabling practitioners and analysts to isolate and observe those features of a performer's technique that do not in themselves express any meaning, but which nevertheless construct his behavior as *performance* rather than as merely *being* or *doing*.[14]

In performance, the pre-expressive is subsumed by the overall expression of meaning. The pre-expressive may therefore be invisible to the spectator, although it is of prime importance to the performer. Spectators see results; performers are involved in "the logic of the process."[15] What the spectator of a performance sees is the integration of pre-expressive and expressive levels of performance, the intention and meaning of action that incorporates a range of feelings and thoughts. A phenomenology of performance (as opposed to theater semiology) would reveal the operation of the pre-expressive as a phase of the creative process dedicated to the modeling of energy.

Barba's concept of the pre-expressive and the debates about its validity represent an important issue in acting theory. If a universal level of performer readiness is identifiable across cultures, then it is possible to devise a basic training system applicable to actors anywhere in the world. At present, training is rendered problematic by the large number of approaches that are taught to students as bibles of technique. Each method in fact constitutes a significant phase in the artistic formation of the student, who may, after having been molded by his training, realize that his technique expresses an aesthetic that encodes a singular view of the world. The point may be clearly demonstrated with reference to ballet training. Once the particular "deformation" of the body intended by ballet training has been achieved, the dancer's kinesthetic potential is formed, and he will be unable to perform a jazz dance with the requisite looseness, force, and variety of rhythmic punctuation. The precision of line, flow, and regularity of tempo that has been inculcated by his training render his body virtually unable to dance in any other way. He will bring the particular aesthetic qualities that have formed his cultivated "movement personality" to whatever dance form he is required to perform.

The possibility of training performer readiness at a pre-expressive level affords the performer the potential freedom to choose expressive techniques at a later stage of training. Barba's emphasis on the relativity of different performance cultures further implies the possibility of a more flexible actor, with a repertoire of different performance vocabularies. Whether such a training regime is achievable or indeed desirable has yet to be explored. Nevertheless, cross-cultural or intercultural experiments in performance training are being undertaken by exponents of Suzuki and butoh and by many actors who study an eclectic range of performance specialisms.

Scenic Bios: The Energy of Performance

While regarded as a key to the Odin Teatret's approach to performance composition and training, Barba's notion of energy is problematically formulated. One of the problems that has undermined the development of acting praxis is the tendency toward an arbitrary eclecticism, resulting in a failure by practitioners to approach problems of practice with a full understanding of the innovatory solutions proposed by earlier practitioners.[16] Barba's idea that energy implies both physical and mental impulses is equivalent to Rudolf Laban's concept of *effort,* yet Barba, although aware of Laban's movement analysis, does not acknowledge the usefulness of Laban's systematic conceptualization of the artistic manifestation of energy as effort. In referring to energy as thought, Barba echoes an aspect of Laban's conceptual system without comprehending its underlying logic.

Although the body is not normally conscious of the flow of energy, Barba observed that it can become conscious of it. The first task of the performer in training is to break the automatic flow of the body's energy made habitual in the process of conditioning through which the typical body culture of the society is formed. The scenic *bios* of the dilated body is achieved by modeling energy in a series of equivalent extra-daily forms:[17]

> The actor must undo this inculcated behaviour pattern and 'the natural connections' between impulse and expression. To a certain degree, this is a question of a deformation and denial of the actor's way of being and character, followed by a reconstruction of behaviour forms in a new way.
> . . . Training leads to a new form of behaviour and a new way of being

present. . . . Actions are tension-filled, even immobility is dynamic and not static because it is maintained by forces established in opposing directions which means that dramatic potential is present.[18]

The opposition between being and consciousness in Western thought indicates a perceived difference between the flow of energy in the body and the person's awareness of this flow. In training, the actor learns to produce a "rhythmic oscillation between existence and thought."[19] The three "rules" that Barba extrapolates from a wide range of performance cultures in various parts of the world entail strategies for modeling the body's natural flow of energy to produce the extra-daily forms of scenic behavior.

According to Barba, daily body techniques usually function to ensure maximal effectiveness in the execution of action for a minimal expenditure of energy.[20] On the other hand, extra-daily techniques are characterized by a wasteful or "luxury" expenditure of energy in the creation of scenic behavior.[21] Barba also distinguishes extra-daily techniques from virtuosity. Extra-daily techniques maintain a dialectical relationship between the social body and the dilated body of the performer, whereas the virtuoso cultivates extraordinary physical skills—a wholly "other" body—in order to amaze the spectator rather than to make the body's expressive form apprehensible.

The codified performance forms typical of North Pole performers are founded upon techniques designed to effect a perpetual alteration of balance in preference to the "natural" balance achieved in daily behavior. By maintaining a permanently unstable balance, the performer establishes tensions in the body that increase the expenditure of energy required not to lose balance, and creates scenic life in a way that can be kinesthetically experienced by the spectator.

Opposition

The principle of opposition is based on daily techniques for the accumulation and release of energy, as in the preparation for any physical activity requiring energy. If one wishes to jump, one first bends the knees slightly in a movement in the opposite direction that suggests the gathering or accumulation of energy as a precondition for its sudden release. This impulse to act is what Barba refers to as *sats:* "In the language of our work it indicates, among other things, the moment in which one is ready to act, the instant which precedes the action, when all the energy is already there, ready to intervene, but as if suspended."[22]

According to Barba, energy moves rhythmically in waves. The play of opposition is an alternation between the peaks and troughs of the waves. To create "the body-in-life," the performer must reveal to the spectator his body's experience of the tensions between opposing forces. Japanese Noh actors exemplify the way performers can withhold and accumulate energy in order to maximize and draw attention to the contrast between the accumulation of energy and its release. Noh and Kabuki exploit the tension of forces signified in the term *hippari hai*. The deformation of the daily techniques for using energy by resisting or retarding its release make the effort of releasing it visible. Meyerhold's "pre-acting" and the opposition in Balinese theater between *keras* (strong, hard, vigorous) and *manis* (delicate, soft, tender) are other ways of focusing the spectator's attention on the quality of energy in the performance of action.

"Consistent Inconsistency" and the Virtue of Omission

The principle of consistent inconsistency, although difficult to grasp, is a necessary concept. Without it, the performer would have difficulty in giving precise form to the performance composition. By this term, Barba seeks to indicate the quality of energy determined by the peculiar economy of theatrical representation. The word that is conventionally applied to the results of this modeling process is stylization, but this is a misleading term, since it fails to suggest the activities of concentration, framing, and abstraction through which a performer constructs an aesthetic montage of actions from the deformation of elements of daily activity.[23] The transformation from everyday activity involves a disruption of the functional cause–effect logic of daily impulse and action, even though the scenic behavior may reveal its form. For the performer to achieve an effective form of representation he must perform the chosen actions in a manner that, although inconsistent with their execution in daily life, possesses internal coherence as scenic behavior. To achieve such coherence, the performer simplifies the daily activity by omitting those details that are not essential to its shape as action. In order to achieve greater intensity of scenic life, the performer may scale down the amount of space required to execute the action in a process Barba calls *absorption*.

All this may seem like an overly complicated and excessive codification of the performer's art. In fact it derives from an experience which is common to performers from many different traditions: the compression, into restricted movements, of the same physical energies necessary to accomplish a much larger and heavier action. Engaging the whole body to light a cigarette, for example, as if the match was as heavy as a large stone, or as if it was incandescent, leaving the mouth slightly open with the same force needed to bite something hard. This process, which composes a small action as if it was much larger, conceals the energy and makes the performer's entire body come alive, even when immobile.[24]

In promoting the spectator's interpretation of scenic behavior, the three "rules" of energy entail a notion Barba calls *equivalence*. This involves the spectator's recognition of the metaphoric or metonymic relationship between the daily action and the equivalent form in which it is recomposed and re-presented through the extra-daily technique. In Barba's words, "It is a fundamental principle of the theatre: on stage, the action must be real, but it is not important that it be realistic."[25] The automatism involved in the daily use of the body must be disrupted in preparing for performance in order to create the possibility of expression or representation. According to Barba the transformation of the performer's body accomplished according to the three rules of energy does not "stylize" it but instead removes its daily aspect. The presentation of purely spontaneous behavior condemns the body "to resemble itself, to present and represent only itself."[26] Training creates the "decided body." The extra-daily techniques shape the performer's bios in such a way that he does not have to decide to act but that "he is decided." This paradox is Barba's way of explaining how training renders the performer's body expressive, thus avoiding the self-division that occurs when a performer consciously decides to express something.

Energy as Thought

Barba's conception of performance composition as a modeling of energy obviates the Cartesian mind-body split that has proved so problematic in conceptions of acting since Diderot. In the twentieth century, Stanislavski arrived dialectically at the notion of mind-body unity in acting by inventing the method of physical actions as a dialectical synthesis of his earlier methods of work that had separated the psycho-technique (work on the actor's states of consciousness) from physical technique (work on the actor's body). For Barba as for Rudolf Laban, energy is the psychophysical manifestation of intelligent being.[27] It is the rhythm of thought. In explaining his concept of energy as a factor in performance, Barba approvingly quotes Jouvet's dictum, "The actor thinks by means of a tension of energy."[28] Barba habitually uses two Norwegian words—*kraft* and *sats*—to analyze what happens when the actions of his performers are effective. *Kraft* can be translated as force or power, while *sats* is equivalent to impulse, preparation, or readiness. The performer's *sats* is both mental intention and physical readiness to act. One can conceive of the intention to act either psychologically as motivation (in Stanislavskian terminology) or physiologically as stimulus-response reflexes (in Meyerhold's vocabulary of biomechanics). It makes no difference how the performer justifies the actions, so long as they are articulated in aesthetic forms that enable the spectator to respond to them kinesthetically. In this way they become material for an interpretation determined by the signifying contexts of the performance.

Temperatures of Energy: Anima/Animus

Even though the spectator's interpretation of the action is not identical to that of the performer, the performer's use of energy shapes the spectator's response to his thought processes. Although energy is a process rather than a substance—a *how* rather than a *what*—Barba believes that in shaping a performance, it is useful for the performer to think of energy as though it were a substance. This permits the performer to articulate action as though he were manipulating an object, and permits him to invest it with what Barba refers to as *temperature,* existing along a continuum from strong or vigorous (*Animus*) at one pole, to soft and delicate (*Anima*) at the opposite pole.[29] Although Barba somewhat disingenuously insists that these terms should not be confused with either cultural stereotypes of gender or Jungian archetypes, much of his reflection on the temperature or intensity of energy in scenic behavior does depend on values associated with the terms *masculine* and *feminine* across a wide range of cultures. Barba believes that the dilated body of the performer is neither masculine nor feminine, and can therefore represent either male or female: "This 'art-body'—and thus, 'non-natural body'—is neither male nor female *in and of itself.* On the stage, it has the sex it has decided to represent. The performer's task is to discover the individual propensities of her or his own energy and to protect its uniqueness."[30]

Barba describes the early days of artistic apprenticeship as a time when some potentialities are eliminated as the student performer makes choices that allow him to focus his exploration of his own energy more deeply. The task of teacher and student is to accomplish a suitable selection from the individual student's complete repertoire of possibilities without ignoring potentially fruitful areas of future development: "Some choices, apparently 'natural,' turn out to be a prison. When the male student adapts himself from the beginning exclusively to male roles, and the female student exclusively to female roles, he or she undermines the exploration of her/his own energy on the pre-expressive level."[31]

Barba argues against limiting the individual performer's use of energy according to stereotypes of gender. The performer's approach should be "hermaphroditic" at the pre-expressive level in order to permit him to exploit the full range of *temperatures* from strength to softness. At the expressive levels, the presentation of gender is determined by cultural codes, and varies greatly according to historical period and cultural location: for example, boy actors played women in the English Renaissance theater; in Kabuki, the *onnagata* is a male who only plays female roles; the principal boy in nineteenth- and twentieth-century English pantomime is played by a female performer; in modern naturalistic theater there is an agreement between the gender of the character and that of the actor.

Barba's reflections on the relationship between the performer's biologically given body and the virtual body ("art-body") that is the source of his identity in performance provide a useful frame of analysis for the performer and spectator. Actor training begins by transforming the person of a student into that of a performer, with expressive possibilities that tap energies that are prior to an individual's normal sociocultural conditioning. This undoing of inherited and acquired habits of being is a key theme in the training of any performer. Barba's comparative study of the way energy is conceived and utilized as a principle of composition in a wide range of North and South Pole performance traditions reveals a recurrence of certain features across a range of cultures. While each is identifiable in the peculiar terms of its own culture, such common features nevertheless suggest the existence at the pre-expressive level of common aesthetic problems in performance cultures as diverse as butoh, Stanislavskian acting, Noh, Peking opera, Craig's approach to the actor as Über-marionette, Balinese theater, Decroux's mime, Meyerhold's system of biomechanics, Chinese Kung-Fu, Pina Bausch's dance theater, and Michael Chekhov's technique of the psychological gesture.[32]

Barba's politically admirable commitment to respecting the integrity of each culture's expressive forms does, however, have the disadvantage of perpetuating the eclectic range of modern approaches to acting, without holding out the possibility of a synthesis of the various techniques and attitudes. When he moves beyond the level of the pre-expressive, Barba offers no coherent approach, other than a loose collection of illuminating insights into specific aesthetic problems. Although members of Odin Teatret regularly give compelling demonstrations of the techniques each of them has developed over the years as a personal training regime, Odin's eclectic use of performance forms and training methods from other cultures promotes useful reflection on transcultural issues in performance without itself providing a model of a new method of making theater.

The Performance Score and the Spectator's Meaning

Odin Teatret adopted Grotowski's idea that the physical form of the performance could be fixed as a performance score that might be infinitely repeatable. It has become a fundamental principle of their dramaturgical process. Even on the rare occasions when their performances were derived from a written drama (e.g., *Ornitofilene* by Jens Bjornboe, and *Ferai* by Peter Seeberg) the composition of the performance score was never a straightforward attempt to realize the writer's conception of a potential performance, but evolved in a complex process of collaboration between Barba and the actors. As in Grotowski's theater, the score was the outcome of an encounter between the writer, the actors, and the director. It was a design of physical action that fixed the performance from one night to the next.

Barba further elaborated Grotowski's process of building the score from the personal encounter of actor and role. The first phase of composition involves the improvisation by individual actors of personal material that is then fixed as segments of the performance score. However, in contrast to Grotowski's working method, performers do not necessarily divulge the private memories and images that motivate these segments. As director, Barba takes responsibility for designing the montage of actions without knowing the precise inner justifications of each actor's performance text. In memorizing the actions of his individual score, the actors give precise physical form to a process that may have been motivated by a complex set of mental associations. Once memorized, the physical score can be reproduced over and over again to produce the same effects, without necessarily invoking the mental states from which it originates.[33]

Barba's method of composing an overall mise-en-scène from the individual scores of the performers is informed by Grotowski's method of "scenic polemics" in which different elements are counterpointed, for example, text and physical action, music and lighting, voice and gesture. Working through a principle of contrast and juxtaposition, Barba develops his own performance texts through the montage of actors' scores, written text, and scenographic elements. His rejection of linear narrative and emphasis on the physical shape of the actors' scores rather than on their inner (psychological) content provokes the spectator to project his own images and experiences onto the signs of the performance, giving him an active role in creating its meaning.

Barba emphasizes that once the performer's body has properly absorbed the score, its kinesthetic form may be animated in different ways over a period of time, according to the infinite variety of attitudes that a performer may bring to it. Barba uses the Japanese term *kata* to explain how the shape of a performance score can stimulate an ideoplastic process in which meaning is renewed through repetition:

> Experience teaches us that if a performer learns to execute a *kata* which is for her/him a precise but empty score, repeating it over and over again, then s/he will succeed in personalising it, discovering or renewing its meaning. An empty score does not in fact exist. Ideoplastic precision, the sensation which passes through the body of the performer who has mastered a precise pattern, makes it possible, with time, to extract a meaning from what seemed to be pure form. . . . From the point of view of the individual [Kabuki] performer, to learn to represent a *kata* is a process which is closely connected to the search for his own personal and artistic individuality.[34]

In Kabuki, as in many forms of North Pole performance, the apprentice performer first learns to reproduce the score slavishly, copying all the nuances of interpretation inscribed by his predecessors; once the performance of the score has become second nature, he is free to vary the nuances of interpretation according to his own artistic personality, and eventually to invent his own score.

New Attitudes to Training

A Self-Sustaining Discipline

Barba recognized in the attitude of Stanislavski and Copeau a tendency that became increasingly noticeable in many theater groups throughout the twentieth century. In the nineteenth century, actors trained to acquire a repertoire of specific presentational skills that were actually used in certain stage performances, for example, dancing, fencing, singing, tumbling, or they rehearsed in preparation for actual performances. Much training in the twentieth century was concerned with developing the discipline characteristic of a professional ethos or with transforming the actor's sensibility, so that exercises were performed to enhance the actor's sensitivity, power of concentration and imagination. At a certain point in their careers, many performers continue with a regime of exercises, not to learn anything new, but simply to maintain their identity as performers. This is what Barba calls "the drift of the exercises," and it is a typical feature of groups that could be said to belong to the third theater. Grotowski's "art as vehicle" may in some respects represent a "drift of the exercises" but it does not involve a divorce between training and theater-making, because it is the artwork itself, rather than a program of exercises, that is continuously being performed as a psychophysical discipline.

Repetition, Improvisation, and the Shift to Individual Training

Odin Teatret's work has certainly reflected the "drift of the exercises," but the approach to training and the function of the exercises has been in a continuous process of change throughout the group's existence. In the earliest phase of the Odin Teatret's existence, the training involved a combination of vocal and plastic exercises with a strong emphasis on technical and acrobatic perfection, and individual performer's improvisations. It was the actors' responsibility to motivate the plastic exercises, so that they never involved the mere mechanical repetition of set movements. Conversely, the improvisations were always somehow expressed in space, so that the actors were learning to create and memorize relationships between impulse and expression (mental images and physical forms) from the start of their training. The actors might keep the personal content of the improvisations private by exploiting a principle of transference in which an action that in reality would be performed in one part of the body, was transferred to another. What was important was to maintain the temperature and quality of energy that characterized the original action, rather than to illustrate it by imitation. As the group began to make different kinds of performances, the focus of the training varied. Barba seems always to have been sensitive to the needs of individual performers, and was keen to use exercises to explore a range of aesthetic problems, so he provoked the exploration of a unique artistic vocabulary for every production by varying the content and aim of training exercises in contrast with the previous phase of work.

> After each production, it is important to return to zero. . . . In contrast to *Ornitofilene,* which was very dynamic, rich in imagery and full of light *Kaspariana* was dark and slow, like slow motion. It began in the dark and ended in the dark. And the actors had a completely different way of moving. We made a conscious choice to work with slow-motion training. We also had an inner motivation while we worked, an inner motor, which coloured our actions. *Ornitofilene* was composed of more coolly planned action patterns interspersed with some "hot" scenes, that is, scenes which were emotionally stronger for the actors. *Kaspariana* was a completely "hot" production. In our terminology, we differentiate

between "hot" scenes, in which the actions are influenced by an inner narrative, a stream of images, like a movie, and "cold" scenes, which are purely technical movement forms without personal motivation.[35]

By continually changing the focus of the training, Barba has prevented the performers from lapsing into clichés and ensured that the training process itself is consistently challenging and creative. Barba himself conducted all the training sessions for the first twelve years of the group's existence, after which the actors began to take on responsibility for the training. During the 1970s Barba moved away from the idea of group training, in which the whole company learns and repeats the same set of exercises, toward a looser and more flexible approach to training. This involves individual performers simultaneously working individually in the same room, improvising and devising variants on the original sets of exercises, and eventually inventing and mastering their own exercises to provide sequences of scenic behavior that might eventually become raw material for a performance. In this way individual actors gradually learn to take responsibility for their own artistic development, and to monitor their own training needs in relation to the demands of the work they are making.

Cross-Cultural Practice and the Spectator's Ethnocentrism

Barba's aim of investigating the fundamental principles of the pre-expressive was clearly signaled by the founding of ISTA. Like Grotowski's work in the 1960s, his construction of performances was an aspect of his research into acting, rather than a purely artistic project. Barba's unique contribution to performance praxis has been to promote recognition of the possibility of dialectical relationships in the fields of performer training and performance composition from different cultures in many parts of the world. His attempt to conduct a transcultural study of the nature and techniques of performance has made possible the identification of a culture of the performer and consequently supports the comparative study of key issues in performance practice. Until Barba these were treated as largely subjective matters of preference on the part of individual performers, who chose their aesthetic vocabulary arbitrarily. Barba has maintained a determination to comprehend the widest possible range of performance techniques and forms in a transcultural framework.

It is too early to attempt a definitive evaluation of the significance of Barba's contribution to contemporary performance practice. My view is that his own research as a new type of practically engaged performance ethnologist is more interesting than his creative work. While the training demonstrations I have observed by Barba and members of the Odin Teatret have persuaded me of the sophistication of their training methods as well as their sound pragmatic approach to the development of appropriate craft skills, I have found some of the group's later performances to be whimsical and obscure—beautifully crafted but lacking the urgency that might make them compulsive viewing. The productions have increasingly appeared to illustrate Barba's concepts of performance rather than to express any complex or passionate response to being alive.

In Barba's terms, my reaction may miss the point. By conducting a comparative survey of the culture of the performer, Barba has drawn attention to the bias involved in Western critics' preoccupation with results rather than creative processes. This tendency to analyze and evaluate finished performances as products, rather than to examine the processes that determine their creation, he has called the "spectator's ethno-centrism." Theater anthropology is itself an analytical approach to exploring the dialectic of sameness and difference that relates cultures from around the world. By means of such comparative analysis it is possible to recognize those issues of performance aesthetics that transcend the differences between one culture and another. It is a truism to say that the global economy has begun to bring alien cultures closer together. Barba's insistence on the need to consider Western traditions of performance practice within the wider context of "world" theater certainly chimes with initiatives in the field of Performance Studies to survey performance across the whole range of world cultures and to examine performative phenomena beyond the confines of conventional theater. Although some of his concepts and categorizations may be problematic, the continuing project of theater anthropology has made a significant impact on many who make performances as well as on those who analyze them. The third theater now comprises a distinct group of experimental artists and companies who regard themselves as theater-makers rather than merely actors and who consider the exploration of new approaches to performance composition to be inseparable from methods of training.

Conclusion

How may one characterize acting in contemporary Western theater? Two opposing tendencies in culture determine the state of acting in the new millennium. On the one hand, there is a movement toward the effacement of the cultural distinctions that make the theater of one country different from that of another—a phenomenon one might classify as globalization. On the other hand, there is a growing awareness of the cultural differences that make the performance forms of each country unique, and a tendency to cultivate—at times at the risk of fetishizing—the specificity of alien theatrical forms. Most young English-speaking actors tend to strive for careers in Hollywood films or American-style television drama series, because these are not merely pervasive in Western culture but rewarding in career terms.

Mainstream acting styles and techniques adapt themselves to the demands of the entertainment industry they serve, although, as the potent influence of Lee Strasberg's Method has shown, a new approach to acting can itself create a new dramaturgical paradigm. There is a reciprocal relationship between new ideas and new forms of expression. At moments when a society changes, there is a need for new aesthetic forms and for corresponding techniques through which to express these forms as a new culture. In modern democratic societies a diversity of subcultures or countercultures contests the hegemonic status of the dominant culture. This is why mainstream performance modes exist in tension with alternative approaches. Understandably, then, theatrical performance around the world today reflects a proliferation of naturalistic forms and techniques of acting—and this is so even in those countries whose indigenous performance traditions bear no resemblance to Western notions of theatrical realism. Notwithstanding the fact that a large number of avant-garde and alternative performance styles and techniques simultaneously persist in the majority of cultures manifesting forms that interrogate and subvert naturalism, it remains the dominant convention of acting on film, television, and in the theater.

The assumption that acting is an integrated body-mind function remains fundamental to most systems of performer training today—naturalistic or not. This is a view held in common by Stanislavski, Meyerhold, and Copeau, notwithstanding the many other differences in their aesthetic attitudes. A majority of contemporary approaches to training integrates Asian and Occidental practices as means of activating the neurological connection between the mental and corporeal aspects of the human organism. The persistence of an ethics of body-mind training in classical Oriental and Asian traditions provides holistic models for contemporary practitioners in the West, where the increasing pressures of commercialism and the demand for novelty tend to make the preservation of unbroken traditions rare.

Student actors today are usually trained in conservatories or university graduate programs according to one or another scheme or system. Many such institutions in Western countries are themselves in crisis. Most of their programs were created more than forty years ago, usually with the aim of producing actors for a specific type of theater but, increasingly, young actors are attracted to both the aesthetic possibilities and the lucrative rewards of film and television work. There is thus a growing gap between the techniques of performance taught at drama conservatories and the styles of acting that students themselves admire and imitate. Students are encouraged by each teacher they encounter to believe that theirs is the sole authentic way of preparing for all types of performance. The rapid commercialization of actor training since the 1960s has induced a crisis for students, who are now confronted by a bewildering range of different—and sometimes opposed—training methods and approaches, each claiming to be the sole authentic way of preparing for any type of performance. (Can it be possible to train an actor to perform Brecht's plays effectively using wholly Stanislavskian techniques? Or to play a role in a Spielberg film using an approach derived from Meyerhold?)

Versions of Method Acting

Mainstream acting generally involves the direct imitation of actual behavior as appropriate to contemporary film and television drama. This straightforward technique of mimicry is often combined with the use of introspective methods of characterization. Increasingly, actors seem to acquire such techniques on the job. The comparative lack of esteem that training commands among Western theater professionals produces actor-technicians who conceive of their craft entirely pragmatically rather than as an artistic vocation. In an international context, the most powerful ideal of acting is that which can be seen in the most well-crafted Hollywood films—a kind of post-

Stanislavskian realism of characterization that effaces the difference between actor and character. This kind of acting is now typical of performances in mainstream theater, film, and television drama, and in turn affects the dramaturgical approach of contemporary playwrights. Broadly speaking, American film acting in this respect still reflects the influence of Strasberg's habitual emphasis on spontaneous expression and on the pathology of feelings. From the late 1940s film actors such as Montgomery Clift, Marlon Brando, Rod Steiger, Julie Harris, Shelley Winters, and James Dean perfected techniques to express the generic emotionalism of film melodrama—think of Elia Kazan's *Streetcar Named Desire* and *Splendor in the Grass,* Vincente Minnelli's *The Bad and the Beautiful,* Fred Zinnemann's *From Here to Eternity,* or Nicholas Ray's *Rebel without a Cause.* Such films demanded that actors produce the kind of volatility, spontaneity, and intimacy typical of the introspective acting style taught by Strasberg. Not every actor who perfected an acting style of such psychological intensity was schooled in Strasberg's Method: actors such as Kirk Douglas, Judy Garland, Burt Lancaster, and others produced performances of radiant intensity without any Method training.

The Method, however, created a powerful model for Hollywood film acting at its most prestigious, establishing a performance culture that privileges all the features of acting that Strasberg's teaching aimed to cultivate. Method-trained Hollywood stars such as Al Pacino, Robert De Niro, and Dustin Hoffman serve as role models for aspiring actors, valorizing the aesthetic and the techniques that typify the Method. The persistent aim of utilizing introspective and psychoanalytic methods to articulate intense states of emotion through precisely detailed behavior is part of Strasberg's legacy. At its most effective such acting transcends conventional naturalism to represent an interior landscape of the psyche that was also a goal of expressionist performance. Hollywood film noir incorporated both cinematographic and acting techniques from German expressionist cinema so that the modern conventions of Hollywood filmmaking involve an aesthetic tension between expressionism and the older techniques of naturalism originally derived from the nineteenth-century stage.

In his analysis of Anna Karina's acting in Jean-Luc Godard's *Pierrot le Fou* (1966), the film critic David Thomson identified a language of modern film acting that matches the effect of Strasberg's techniques: "There's less impression of the character being presented to us than of a meeting with a stranger in which one notices the physical actions of behaviour without having any idea what sort of character lies behind them. When we look at Anna Karina we see not an intended meaning but an alert personality. . . .

The most effective actors and actresses in the cinema are those who can achieve such a degree of external relaxation while being filmed that the camera records their nature without defining it."[1]

This is precisely the kind of acting Strasberg's Method was designed to produce. Following Vakhtangov's suggestions about *justifying* the character's behavior in preference to Stanislavski's method of motivating it according to the play's "logic of actions," Strasbergian acting emphasizes the indefinable mystery of the actor's presence rather than the meaning of the character. Such film acting offers an existentialist rather than a naturalistic representation. Strasberg's emphasis on spontaneity and fidelity to the discontinuities of moment-to-moment experience implies recognition of the unconscious determinants of behavior. The film director Michelangelo Antonioni believed it was better for the actor *not* to share the director's understanding of the artistic intention of a shot or scene in a film: "The film actor need not understand, but simply be. . . . the film actor should work not on the psychological level, but on the imaginative one. And the imagination reveals itself spontaneously. . . . It is not possible to have a real collaboration between actor and director. They work on two different levels. . . . I prefer to get results by a hidden method; that is, to study in the actor certain of his innate qualities of whose existence he is himself unaware. . . . the actor is one of the elements of the image itself."[2]

Antonioni suggests that the film director should tap into the actor's unconscious in order to elicit a performance as spontaneous and irrational as real behavior. In a sense the aim of the Method was to enable actors to allow their psyches to be exploited in this way as the raw material of performance. The kind of behavioral authenticity that transcends conventional naturalism can be manifest in theater as well as film. There are forms of avant-garde theater in which acting seems to have reached degree zero. The Happenings of the 1960s and the many subsequent attempts to blur the boundaries between theater and everyday life have in some respects made the categories of acting and behavior interchangeable.[3] Performance becomes a game of quoting real behavior. This may be advantageous for film and television drama, but it has had a deleterious effect on those types of theater that utilize traditional theatrical and mimetic skills to reveal, demonstrate, or (re)present the significance of human action.[4]

A Cool Style

As one would expect, Hollywood acting is in a constant process of change. The younger generation of contemporary American film actors appears to have been influenced by methods of working in television. Surface behavior is emphasized rather than depth psychology, a reflection of the emphasis postmodern culture places on style and image and of its skeptical attitude to "naive realism." Many young actors in the early 2000s gained their initial professional experience working in television. Actors such as Will Smith, Jennifer Aniston, George Clooney, Brad Pitt, David Duchovny, Courtney Cox-Arquette, Sarah Jessica Parker, and Matthew Perry produce self-aware, casual, ironic performances. Faces are deliberately inexpressive, reflecting the social mask of indifference or irony that signals postmodern identity. Acting is *cool*. Moments of intense feeling are characterized by alternations of carefully signified *masking* with violent physical outbursts, in contradistinction to the histrionic revelations of intense psychological states that typified film acting from the 1950s to the 1970s.

To some extent this new style of Hollywood acting is similar to the generic style of modern British acting that has been developing since the 1960s. In British culture, the attitude of ironic detachment from one's own feelings stems from the Edwardian social code of middle-class good manners that insisted that it was vulgar to show one's true feelings in public. The stiff-upper-lip approach to the presentation of emotions typified naturalistic acting on the British stage, in the cinema, and on television throughout the twentieth century. Changes in style were more a consequence of changing fashions of speech and social behavior than any radical change in artistic convention or performance techniques. In the hands of virtuoso actors such as Edith Evans, Ralph Richardson, John Gielgud, Peggy Ashcroft, Judi Dench, Derek Jacobi, Ian Holm, Maggie Smith, Ian McKellen, and Michael Gambon, such emotional reticence in performance can paradoxically produce immensely powerful emotional effects through carefully placed pauses and momentary glimpses of subtextual feeling.

This kind of acting has been employed by writers like Rattigan, Coward, Pinter, and Osborne to express the rage and the pain experienced by individuals as a consequence of a culture whose oppressive social demands tend to encourage psychological denial. Concomitant with this emotionally reticent acting is, typically, the British actor's skill in articulating the nuances of social interaction. Clearly the most powerful imperialist nation of the early twentieth century with its rigidly hierarchical class system was bound to create a theatrical culture highly sensitive to social status and class difference. The history of twentieth-century British drama has mirrored the gradual disintegration of the empire and its social hierarchy. From the subversive comedies of the Irish Oscar Wilde, via Noel Coward's ambivalent representation of the new meritocracy and Rattigan's exposure of the miseries of the postwar middle classes, to the working-class attack on empire by the angry young writers, the overtly Marxist drama of the 1970s, and the oppositional gay and feminist theater of the 1980s and 1990s, the theater has continuously been redefining social and cultural identities within post-imperial Britain.

Although the teaching of Michel Saint-Denis created a new theatrical ethos that broadened the range of British stage acting between the 1940s and the 1960s, the British actor's traditional skills of irony and understatement remain the stock-in-trade of television and film acting. Television (in Britain a much more important industry in economic terms than film) has had a huge impact on theater acting, so much so that critics since the 1960s have repeatedly complained that young actors do not possess the vocal skills to act Shakespeare on stage. The youth culture of the Swinging Sixties introduced the kind of "laid-back" classless style of social behavior into British pop music, film, television, and theater. Paradoxically, as British behavior has become more volatile and social mores less bound by middle-class norms of propriety, acting styles have grafted the colloquial images of popular culture onto the middle-class reticence of pre-1960s acting. Although there are differences between the younger generation of contemporary British actors and their American counterparts, these are not as noticeable as they were in the 1950s. This might be viewed as an effect of the postmodern tendency to efface differences between the local and the global.

Alternative Performance(s)

At the opposite end of the spectrum, forms of performance that have come to be classified as physical or visual theater derive their technical methods and stylistic vocabularies from the total theaters of Appia, Meyerhold, Craig, Reinhardt, and Artaud. In the contemporary avant-garde tradition, the idea of the actor as scenographic instrument has animated the work of such great practitioners as Tadeusz Kantor and Robert Wilson, who have conceived the performer's role as akin to that of Craig's Über-marionette ("the actor plus fire minus egoism"). The nature of Kantor's productions is grotesque and painterly, its sophisticated interplay of the actor's masklike faces, emotive vocal jabberings, and stiff bodies with life-size mannequins and strange mechanical contraptions resembling nothing so much as a travesty of Craig's theater by Meyerhold. The kaleidoscope of visual images is ritualized both by the incessant repetition of various motifs and by the accompanying thunderous music as though Kantor, himself an onstage witness, is relentlessly forced to replay the film of his own relationship to the inexorable march of history. Wilson's work is technologically very complex. Lighting plays a major part in the sculpting of the performer's slow and dancelike movements in a gradually changing spatial field. Many of his works are entitled operas, indicating the importance of music in scenographically dominated performances that seem to utilize Appia's notions of music-drama to create painterly and sculptural events whose lengthy duration calls into question the relationship between the time and space of performance.

Live Art, Physical Theater, and Devised Performance

Both Kantor and Wilson trained as visual artists, and their significant use of music suggests that music is as central to their conceptions as painting and sculpture. Robert Lepage's use of lighting, music, and scenic technology is subtle and complicated, although the performers' vocabulary is drawn from contemporary realist drama. While the aura of the live performer is essential to the work of all three, the actor is a part of the visual and aural field, no more important than other elements of scenography and often appearing as moving sculpture or dancer within the work. Many of the performers appearing in such work receive no specific training, but learn how to serve the vision of their auteur-director by working with him on a regular basis. Training as a dancer or mime, however, is a prerequisite for performers who work in the postmodern dance theater of Pina Bausch, William Forsythe, DV8, or the physical theater of Lindsay Kemp, Steven Berkoff, Jan Fabré, or Frantic Assembly. The hugely popular Cirque du Soleil draws upon the traditions and training of conventional circus to create wonderful spectacles that integrate highly poetic scenography with acrobatics, clowning, music, and dance to create a magical form of total theater.

Jerzy Grotowski, Peter Brook, Cicely Berry, Jacques Lecoq, and Anne Bogart have all understood that the nature of the performer's techniques are functionally related to performance composition. Acting training makes no sense without a notion of what you desire to express. In order to create new performance forms the actor needs to develop correspondingly new techniques. In the twentieth-century theater, the principle of the ensemble motivated forms of artistic practice that allowed actors to hone their craft while they collaborated in creating new performances. Much devised and physical theater depends on the interplay of performers who create the performance in rehearsal, rather than work from a written text. Dramaturgical, choreographic, and scenographic forms are often combined to create a type of *Gesamtkunstwerk* (total artwork) that exemplifies Wagner's principle of theater as an art form combining elements of all other art forms.

Influential as it was in introducing radical notions of alternative performance to the United States, the work of American experimental theater groups in the 1960s has had little lasting effect in the field of mainstream American actor training. The Living Theatre, The Bread and Puppet Theater, and the Open Theatre constituted a tradition of performance reflecting the leftist libertarian political movements that had become invisible by the 1980s. The anti-Stanislavskian bias of their work and the fashion for non-naturalistic dramaturgy created by absurdist theater and the performance art movement certainly contributed to the development of a strong avant-garde tradition of American performance. Mainstream acting and performer training in the American theater, cinema, and television nonetheless remains dedicated to sustaining the forms of film and television naturalism, on one hand, and Broadway musical theater on the other. Where commercial theater forms do involve non-naturalistic styles and methods of performance, their approach is a technologically updated version of nineteenth-century traditions of performance. The enormous commercial success of the musical theater in New York and London, with the global networks of production and marketing that proliferated in the 1980s, has meant that large numbers of performers are training for a career in musicals like *Les Misérables* or *The Lion King*. While such productions are often very sophisticated in scenographic terms, rehearsal and training methods that underpin the staging of such shows usually involve a pre–Stanislavskian attitude to the cultivation of virtuoso physical and vocal skills.

While major dramatists like Maria Irene Fornes, Edward Albee, and Sam Shepard write non-naturalistic texts, and David Mamet inveighs against Stanislavskian methods of rehearsal, the common vocabulary of nonmusical performance in the contemporary American theater is largely derived from one or other version of Stanislavski.[5] Since Joseph Chaikin's Open Theatre ceased to mount productions in the mid-1970s, the most high-profile attempts to challenge the hegemony of this acting tradition has been the work of the Wooster Group and that of acclaimed director and teacher Anne Bogart. Her *Viewpoints* method of rehearsal and training represents a challenge to the pervasive Stanislavskian and Strasbergian approaches to training in the United States, offering actors the opportunity to equip themselves for the collaborative process of modern theater-making. Contemporary directorial approaches demand that the actor be able to function both intellectually and physically in the devising of performances that utilize the typical skills of dancers or mime artists. In enabling the actor to employ such skills as part of the imaginative process of devising performance, Bogart's system continues the tradition of performance composition initiated by Appia, Craig, and Meyerhold in the early twentieth century.

The principle of improvisation and games in performance composition and performer training is widespread among alternative practitioners. Parallel with the philosophical notion that meaning is produced in a series of language games, Copeau's original idea is today most obviously manifest in theater created by three generations of performers trained by Jacques Lecoq.[6] The insistence of Lecoq on the centrality of movement (as opposed to dance) training and his exposure of students to the full range of dramatic "territories" has meant that Lecoq-trained theater-makers have applied Copeau's methodology of play to create the kind of improvisatory theater envisaged by Craig and Meyerhold. Ariane Mnouchkine's work with her legendary Théâtre du Soleil was influenced by the teaching of Lecoq, and his approach has stimulated the growth of a wide range of groups working in this field. These have included the Austrian company Mummenschantz; British groups, such as Steven Berkoff's London Theatre Group, Footsbarn (latterly in France), the Moving Picture Mime Show, and the Clod Ensemble; French companies like the Théâtre de la Jacquerie and the Bouvier/Obadia group; and the Théâtre de la Jeune Lune in Minneapolis. The most famous company to have been created by ex-students of Lecoq is the Theatre de Complicité, unquestionably the most successful alternative theater group to have emerged in Britain during the last three decades.

Parallel to such groups are improvisational groups who draw on the teachings of Viola Spolin (Second City, based in Chicago, Paul Sills's Story Theatre) or Keith Johnstone (Theatre Machine, originally British, now based in Canada; Improbable Theatre, based in Britain). Popular on television and stage in Europe and the United States for the past two decades are improvisation competitions (e.g., *Whose Line Is It Anyway?*) in which teams of improvisers respond on the spot to lines or situations, playing out improvised comic dramas for the amusement of a studio audience. This is an entertainment format invented by Keith Johnstone, whose Theatre Machine has toured the world performing such off-the-cuff improvisations. He has since pioneered the *Life Game* format in which performers act out scenes from the life of a well-known personality who feeds them bits of her biography during the course of the performance. Less concerned with innovations in performance style or physical theater than that of the Lecoq-based companies, these groups are interested in exploring character and situation as an alternative tradition of improvised performance that is a modern equivalent to the commedia dell'arte: the performer's skill at improvising is the source of the spectator's pleasure. Although their location within a commercialized theater system prevents such performances from constituting the kind of community theater intended by Les Copiaux in the 1920s, they do utilize the same skills of storytelling, mime, and clowning that animated Copeau's group.

The Brechtian Influence

Brecht's conception of epic and dialectical theater as exemplified by the legendary performances of the Berliner Ensemble made an enormous impact on a number of theater companies, directors, writers, and performers from the 1950s to the 1970s, offering a model of what consciously political performance could be. With the rise of the New Right in Europe and the United States in the late-1970s, much of the overtly left-wing theater of the period disappeared, partly as a consequence of the withdrawal of state subsidy. Experimental playwrights and directors had, however, absorbed Brecht's aesthetic ideas, so that they began to permeate the vocabulary and inform the practice of a great deal of oppositional and avant-garde practice. Companies like the Wooster Group, Mabou Mines, and Goat Island (United States) and Gloria, Kneehigh, and Forced Entertainment (Britain) have employed an eclectic range of experimental methods and techniques in devising their own work. Although not primarily dedicated to political theater, their productions demonstrate a postmodern awareness of Brechtian approaches to the deconstruction and collaging of existing texts for the purpose of initiating an intertextual play of meaning. Such post-Brechtian groups combine an understanding of the possibilities of improvisation and game playing with a facility for scenographic and musical composition. Many directors, playwrights, and actors whose work is in the vanguard of new theater have absorbed the significance of Brecht's strategy of revising old stories and plays, and adapting or reframing old narratives or plays to create new work.

In 1964, Peter Brook wrote that contemporary theater was developing as a product of the confrontation between Brechtian and Artaudian theater. In his production of Peter Weiss's *Marat/Sade*, Brook counterpointed an Artaudian mode of presentation against a Brechtian. He therefore managed to find the appropriate performance modes to effect a grotesque juxtaposition of Sade's metaphysics of desire against Marat's rationalist ethics of revolution. A number of Heiner Müller's texts *(Hamletmachine, Quartet, Medea-Material)* imply a mode of performance that is both Artaudian in its visceral imagery of nihilistic despair and Brechtian in its deconstruction of classic texts. Many types of progressive theater in the new millennium are being created through the confrontation or dialogue between a Stanislavskian and a Brechtian form. In *Top Girls,* Caryl Churchill and the director Max Stafford-Clarke moved the action effortlessly from an opening scene of surrealist comedy to a few scenes of Stanislavskian realism, interspersed with detached and witty episodes that expose the economic system determining social relationships and personal destinies. By inverting the chronological order of the two final scenes, Churchill achieved a Brechtian framing device that made it possible for the spectator to question the powerfully naturalistic impact of the last scene. The concrete engagement of characters in fictional moments of "reality" is thus framed by more detached presentation of political arguments. In this way the audience's response is split between moments of empathy with the powerful feelings presented, and moments of objective judgment and comic self-awareness.

A majority of feminist and gay practitioners since the 1970s have made creative use of Brecht's ideas to unmask patriarchal forms and the norms they represent, and to propose new models of culture and society.[7] Thus Brechtian acting is fairly pervasive in alternative traditions of performance, and Brecht's methods are often employed to deconstruct the values enshrined in popular or conventional performance forms, challenging conservative values by subverting the forms that encode them. A brilliant example of such a strategy is Tony Kushner's *Angels in America* (1993) in which the camp framing devices and the epic narrative exposition deliberately clash with the soap opera saga of ordinary lives to produce a radical interrogation of the politics of sexuality in contemporary American society. The actors are required to switch from an extremely intense style of televisual naturalism to the camp performance mode of drag cabaret. Thus the play confronts mainstream American culture with the gay sensibility, expressing the conflict of mentalities through a dialogue of performance forms. Writers such as Tony Kushner, Caryl Churchill, Mark Ravenhill, and Timberlake Wertenbaker employ forms of Brechtian praxis in writing performances that challenge the political status quo, while the continually developing practice of Augusto Boal offers opportunities for direct political intervention to theater-makers who wish to change themselves and transform society. Boal's ideas are being absorbed and developed by practitioners in the fields of theater education, social work, and psychotherapy.

British playwright, director, and performer Steven Berkoff deliberately yokes a pseudo-Shakespearean expressionism that involves a style of intense vocal and mime performance, with a clown-style burlesque of East London argot. The clash of opposing styles is comic and grotesque, and functions like a Brechtian distancing device. Actors working in such productions must be *au fait* with Stanislavskian, expressionistic, and Brechtian techniques, and understand their different aesthetic implications. This kind of neo-Brecht-ian eclecticism is not a *fusion* of styles but a *confrontation* of one style with another, allowing the values inherent within each style to be critiqued by the other. It has become necessary for the progressive actor to be well versed in the ideas and performance strategies of Bertolt Brecht, even though these are not fully assimilated within the mainstream of European and North American theater.

Globalism and Its Discontents

Occasionally, acting schools such as East 15 in Britain teach Brechtian techniques alongside those of Stanislavski and Laban or Lecoq. In Britain and the United States, the teaching of Brechtian praxis usually occurs within university theater and drama departments. These departments are often receptive to alternative forms of theater and sympathetic to fully theorized notions of practice. Professional conservatories and acting schools, on the other hand, tend to be more prescriptive in their approach to practice. Although more rigorous in their emphasis on the acquisition of vocal and physical techniques, they are more conservative with regard to interrogative approaches to experimental praxis. Their success is founded on equipping actors for the theater as it exists; commercial factors make it difficult for them to breed actors determined to change the nature of theater. Even such a progressive school as the École Internationale de Théâtre Jacques Lecoq in Paris does not offer a comparative approach to performer training but presents the most up-to-date version of a syllabus that derives its ethos and methodological principles from Jacques Copeau. The Lecoq school does, however, insist that its students master the complete range of Western dramatic "territories" (styles) in order to enhance their flexibility as theater-makers

The majority of British drama schools currently base their curricula on versions of Michel Saint-Denis's scheme, often including a few token Stanislavski courses.[8] North American actor training is still dominated by one or another Stanislavskian approach, but there are a few whose programs are structured according to the principles of Michel Saint-Denis.[9] Although the majority of conservatories now regard it as standard practice to teach the method of analysis through actions and events (some also teach Stanislavski's more radical method of active analysis as rehearsal method), variants of Stanislavski's approach are taught by followers of Strasberg, Stella Adler, Robert Lewis, Sanford Meisner, and Uta Hagen.[10] Some American institutions combine the teaching of Stanislavski's principles with the improvisation games of Viola Spolin, aiming to balance the seriousness of his approach to character in action with the spirit of play.

Aesthetic Confrontation as Principle of Composition

The great Russian director Lev Dodin, who runs the Maly theater, works with actors trained in a Stanislavskian method but blends the psychological realism of character with strikingly stylized scenographic and musical effects to produce elaborate mise-en-scènes in a manner akin to Vakhtangov's "fantastic realism." Peter Brook blends acting styles and theatrical conventions from many cultures without imposing a limiting conception of stylistic unity on his productions. Brook is such a brilliant editor that his productions invariably achieve artistic coherence, even as they draw on a multiplicity of perspectives and styles. In her professional career, the competent modern actor will ideally possess a range of alternative techniques in order to create work in a variety of styles and for a range of different purposes.

The conscious stylistic eclecticism characterizing much postmodern performance was anticipated by the work of Meyerhold and Brecht. Self-reflexivity and a dialectic of aesthetic confrontation appear as distinctive qualities of performance early in the new millennium. The deliberate diversity of aesthetic models, the apparently perverse yoking of performance styles and techniques drawn from different cultures and the ironic opposition in contemporary theater of form and content, high art and pop culture, reflect an awareness of social and cultural diversity attendant on the disintegration of the European and North American colonial enterprises. Changing attitudes toward Africa, Asia, and the Orient have resulted in a new respect for the ancient arts of these regions, and an interest in creating a dialogue between Western and non-Western forms.

The work of Ariane Mnouchkine exhibits this dialectic of aesthetic confrontation, through its deliberate eclecticism in the yoking of Western and Asian or Oriental performance forms. Having founded the Théâtre du Soleil in Paris in 1964, she began to apply a range of popular performance modes such as clowning, acrobatics, mime, song, and masked performance to such complex naturalistic plays as Gorky's *The Petit Bourgeois* and Arnold Wesker's *The Kitchen*. The course she followed at the Lecoq school enhanced her own ability to devise physical performances, and her production of *A Midsummer Night's Dream* employed dancers from the Béjart company as Oberon and Titania. Mnouchkine achieved international fame as a director with her collectively devised production *1789*. The production combined a popular appeal via the radical simplicity of clowning and improvisation inherited from Copeau with a Meyerholdian self-consciousness in the grotesque use of theatricality as an ironic counterpoint to verbal text. As a left-wing practitioner, Mnouchkine appears to have been indebted in this production and others to Brecht, although she herself has tended to stress the impact of Meyerhold and Copeau as influences.

Mnouchkine's study of Oriental theater in the 1960s provided the starting point for the development of an eclectic vocabulary of non-Western theater forms employed to create her famous cycle of Shakespeare productions (*Richard II, Henry IV,* 1 and 2, *Henry V, Twelfth Night,* and *Love's Labour's Lost*) between 1981 and 1984. The cultural forms of feudal Japan provided a frame through which the feudal culture of *Richard II* was viewed. The stylized vocal and gestural repertoire of the Japanese theater promoted a nonrealistic style that allowed the narrative sweep of Shakespeare's play to be comprehended without contamination by the pseudo-naturalistic clichés that tend to accumulate in Western productions. *Twelfth Night* drew its costumes from India, although its performance blended styles from various performance cultures. Mnouchkine's acclaimed production of Aeschylus's *Oresteia (Les Atrides)* in the 1990s again employed a clash between conventional stylistic expectations and exotic modes of representation in order to surprise the spectator into the fresh apprehension of a classic Western drama. She has continued to combine conventions drawn from an eclectic range of Western and non-Western performance modes, including puppetry, in the production of both contemporary plays and classic texts.

Intercultural and Cross-Cultural Practice

The most progressive practitioners have for some time been seriously engaged in the study of non-Western performance techniques and ideas. Barba and Brook have taught Western practitioners to discover and define their own artistic identity by learning to view their own craft within a comparative framework that includes alien artistic cultures. Asian, African, and Oriental practitioners have long had to learn to deal with the potentially negative effects of colonialism on their own indigenous cultures. Now many of them are finding ways to appropriate the techniques and attitudes of major Western practitioners in order to ensure that the maintenance of their own classical traditions does not simply result in the preservation of ossified and anachronistic feudal cultures. There is, however, a serious danger that the "mix and match" approach typical of consumer capitalism at the start of the twenty-first century will result in a new kind of globalization, with certain forms and techniques of performance being dislocated from their original cultural contexts and becoming fetishized—the latest fads in international theater. The increasing festivalization of theater, while it allows smaller groups to be seen on the international circuit, has the disadvantage of divorcing performances from their sociopolitical contexts. This process of aestheticization can render productions and performance techniques from other cultures both exotic and devoid of meaning.[11]

In the 1980s the theater practitioner and scholar Richard Schechner and the anthropologist Victor Turner began to use the term *performance studies* to identify a discipline that might analyze any possible manifestation of human performance, ranging from the ceremonies and rites of primitive tribes to theater as an art form, and including modes of performance in everyday life (e.g., the conduct of a court case, a teacher giving a lesson, the behavior of young people at a nightclub), sports matches, popular entertainments such as rock concerts, games played by adults and children, and so forth.[12] While Schechner's aim was to transform the academic discipline of theater studies through his anthropological research project, rather than to engage directly with approaches to Western theater training, he exerted an influence on discourse about theatrical performance at the same time as Eugenio Barba's rather different notion of theater anthropology began to provoke thinking about the possible existence of transcultural universals of theatrical performance and performer training. During this period the cross-cultural creative practices of major Western directors such as Peter Brook, Peter Sellars, Robert Wilson, and Ariane Mnouchkine began to be labeled intercultural. Interculturalism became a new category employed by academic scholars to account for cultural exchanges and fusions in the field of performance. During the 1990s the notion of intercultural performance became fashionable among Western practitioners, but though exerting influence on performance practice this ubiquitous term has also become extremely problematic. In political terms, interculturalism does not distinguish which culture is dominant in the exchange or fusion, and thus has the effect of promoting a number of traditionally colonialist practices. It may also obscure the very real possibility of exchanges among subcultures ("intraculturalism"), and the term *interculturalism* is at times a misleading way of classifying phenomena that might more accurately be understood in terms of translation or cross-cultural exchange.

Possibly the most pervasive intercultural practice in modern dance theater is that of butoh, created in 1959 by the Japanese practitioners Tatsumi Hijikata and Kazuo Ohno. Hijikata had trained in Europe and was inspired by German experimental dance and by his reading of Artaud, De Sade, and Genet to approach some aspects of traditional Japanese theater in the spirit of such transgressive Western aesthetic attitudes. Hijikata and Ohno created a radical dance theater that defied the taboos of a conservative society, resisting purely aesthetic ideals in the struggle for a completely authentic mode of personal expression. Whereas conventional dance is composed of steps consciously imposed upon the body, butoh is an expression that is created from the need of the performer's body to move, from the body's openness and sensitivity to the forces of the natural world. Rather than dancing, the performer "is danced." Since the early 1980s, butoh has become a creative inspiration to dancers in many parts of the world. It is a radical practice that deliberately resists being packaged as a new style of performance but which offers an ongoing challenge to theater-makers who share its aim of seeking to transcend the formal limitations of existing dance conventions rather than merely imitating its original forms.

Since the beginning of the twentieth century, Western practitioners have drawn inspiration from Asian and Oriental performance and have borrowed ideas and techniques from other cultures to enrich their own. Over the last thirty years, such activity has become less naive and more conscious of the cultural negotiations that become necessary in the exchange of cultural forms and their inherent techniques of production. While yoga, t'ai chi, judo, and kung fu have all become part of an international repertoire of exercises aimed at achieving relaxation and physical fitness in daily life, Western performers and teachers have since the 1970s become increasingly fascinated by the rigorous training regimes that underpin such classical performance traditions as Indian Kathak and Japanese Noh, and have made detailed studies of their techniques in order to learn lessons for their own practice.

A movement training system that has made some impact on performer training in the United States today is that invented by the Japanese director Tadashi Suzuki. Paradoxically, Suzuki's own approach derives from an intercultural perspective in the sense that his own observation of the impact of Noh performances in France inspired him to create a modern Japanese theater capable of communicating the power of Shakespeare, Chekhov, and the ancient Greek drama to a Japanese audience. In seeking initially to develop the skills of his own company, Suzuki distilled a number of key principles from classical Noh and Kabuki training, but his technique also reveals some affinities with European ballet and Indian kathakali dance: "The main purpose of my method is to uncover and bring to the surface the physically perceptive sensibility which actors had originally, before the theatre acquired its various codified performance styles, and to heighten their innate expressive abilities."[13]

Suzuki's project has similarities with Barba's search for the preexpressive, although his approach goes further in attempting to integrate modern peo-

ple into a shared sensibility, "beyond all differences in race and nationality."
It is as though Grotowski's notion of the sources of performance prior to
cultural differentiation has become the goal of a new intercultural mode of
performance training.

Today Suzuki's movement techniques form part of the curriculum of a
number of actor training programs in the United States.[14] Although its rel-
evance to American forms of performance has been questioned, adherents
of the Suzuki approach believe that the intense concentration of energy in
the lower body achieved through squatting, walking, and stamping on bent
knees enables the actor to achieve an extraordinary presence, a focused
energy that makes stillness theatrically meaningful. Suzuki suggests that the
performance traditions of premodern Japanese theater represent a model
reliant on the animal energy of the performer. In his view, the modern theater dilutes the impact of the live performer's presence because it is mediated in so many ways through technology: Suzuki aims to "restore the
wholeness of the human body in the theatrical context" not by merely
reproducing the techniques of the traditional theaters but by exploiting the
essential impulse behind such techniques in a new approach that transcends
the dismembered forms of contemporary performance. Suzuki's concentration on the feet is intended to ground the performer in the earth, providing
a modern equivalent to ancient ways of maintaining contact with supernatural forces below the ground. Some directors believe that Suzuki training
enables actors to achieve the kind of control and focus in the body that
allows them to be expressive in a range of theatrical conventions.

The Gardzienice Centre for Theatre Practices founded in 1975 by
Wlodzimierz Staniewski in Poland is devoted to making theater that relates
directly to a rural environment, drawing on indigenous local traditions of
performance (especially singing) to create performances that challenge the
domination of urban culture. Their training is rigorous but is always relevant to the artistic aims of the project on which they are engaged.
Influenced by his experience of Grotowski's para-theater in the early 1970s,
Staniewski's group works with local communities in eastern Poland to
research and rediscover the roots of a theater of voice and gesture that reintegrates the body of the actor within the natural environment. Gardzienice
rejects the sophisticated artifice of modern stage and media technology in
favor of performances that promote an ecological harmony with the
rhythms of rural life.

Many alternative forms of performance are motivated by the desire to
experiment with new actor-spectator relationships in order to combat the
dominance of television and film as mass entertainment media. By explor-

ing new spatial and architectural configurations, theater-makers aim to create new psychological relationships between actor and spectator that
emphasize the modality of performance as a live form. In foregrounding the
spectator's responsibility for creating the performance, such experimental
work challenges the passive habits of film and television viewing, in an
effort to demonstrate the uniqueness of performance as a live event. Theatrical performance has been exploited in various ways to interrupt the flow
of everyday life and startle spectators into recognition of the performative
basis of social existence. The use of digital technology, video, and film to
extend the vocabulary of live performance offers contemporary performers
a range of possible ways of representing the incremental increase in the
mediatization of modern life as it creates new possibilities for the interaction
between human and nonhuman instruments of expression.

The effective domination of the global economy by consumer capitalism
makes a significant impact on the arts. A majority of Western actors today
are obliged to be pragmatic in pursuing the type of training that will most
effectively serve the needs of the entertainment industry.

While American actors are still most influenced by the versions of
Stanislavskian training popularized in the United States since the 1930s,
British actors tend to be more skeptical of systematic approaches and are
more sympathetic to the trial-and-error spirit of play and improvisation initiated by Copeau. The commercial values of the mass entertainment industry do, however, threaten to undermine the advances made in twentieth-
century acting praxis by privileging technical specialization at the expense of
the performer's creativity. Ironically, the postmodern menu of training possibilities may on occasions encourage a consumerist approach that privileges
eccentric and esoteric modes of training, unconnected with the forms of
expression they should serve. There is a danger that the economic advan-
tages possessed by certain societies is promoting a new colonial culture that
threatens to efface local differences and absorb all performance traditions in
a kind of consumer-friendly "world" theater that has nothing to say to the
spectator except "Buy me!"[15]

Performance has the power to interrogate and humanize people on the
basis of both common experience and difference. The challenge for acting
in the twenty-first century is to ensure that cross-cultural exchange and
fusion will enrich the diversity of traditions from around the world and produce new forms that both express and challenge the changes in culture and
society that are transforming the way we live.

Notes

Introduction

1. A recent controversy concerned the question of whether the work of British and American voice teachers to free the actor's voice is grounded in a neo-Romantic illusion that the body can "naturally" be free in a society fractured by inequalities with respect to class, gender, race, sexuality, etc. See Sarah Werner, "Performing Shakespeare: Voice Training and the Feminist Viewpoint," *New Theatre Quarterly* 47 (August 1996): 249–58, and "Shakespeare, Feminism and Voice: Responses to Sarah Werner," *New Theatre Quarterly* 49 (February 1997): 48–52.

2. Eugenio Barba has devoted much of his research into discovering the universals of performance, which he believes are prior to culturally determined performance styles: he refers to this level of performance as the *pre-expressive*.

3. Copeau proposed an ideal neutrality of personality through which the actor should endeavor to avoid the "intrusive" marks of her temperament in becoming a flexible expressive instrument; Craig's notion of the Über-marionette ("the actor plus fire minus egoism") was a parallel idea.

4. Laurence Olivier is typical of British actors in opposing these two approaches: in an interview in *Great Acting,* ed. Hal Burton (London: BBC Publications, 1967), he claimed to work from the "outside in," emphasizing a physical technique of characterization through voice and movement rather than an "inner" technique of psychological preparation for inhabiting the role.

5. Stanislavski himself claimed that his rehearsal and training methods were applicable to all forms of theater, although many critics believe that the naturalistic principles inherent in his system resulted in repeated failure to create a convincing production of a Shakespeare play.

6. The ideal of fidelity to the playwright's conception as inscribed in the text underpins the approaches to acting of Stanislavski, Copeau, and Michel Saint-Denis; Craig and Meyerhold, on the other hand, insist on the director's right to compose the play through the invention of a mise-en-scène that accompanies, illustrates, and even comments on the writer's text.

7. This is the central issue of Saint-Denis's book *Theatre: The Rediscovery of Style* (New York: Theatre Arts Books, 1960); Meyerhold provides an alternative approach to the question of style.

8. Craig insisted that the actor was merely one of an ensemble of scenic elements. See "The Actor and the Über-marionette" in Edward Gordon Craig, *On the Art of the Theatre* (London: Heinemann, 1968).

Chapter 1

1. Johann Wolfgang von Goethe, "Rules for Actors," trans. Arthur Woehl, *Quarterly Journal of Speech Education* 8, no. 3 (1927): 247.

2. The principle of decorum was the cornerstone of Renaissance theories of rhetoric.

3. From Toby Cole and Helen Krich Chinoy, eds., *Actors on Acting* (New York: Crown, 1970), 272–75; rule numbers have been omitted.

4. George Henry Lewes, *On Actors and the Art of Acting* (New York: Grove, 1957), 91.

5. Émile Zola, *Naturalism in the Theatre,* trans. Albert Bermel, in *The Theory of the Modern Stage,* ed. Eric Bentley (London: Penguin, 1968), 367.

6. In the twentieth century, Gordon Craig, Stanislavski, Copeau, Strasberg, and others made direct reference to issues identified by Diderot.

7. From Cole and Chinoy, *Actors on Acting,* 165.

8. Denis Diderot, *The Paradox of Acting,* trans. Walter Herries Pollock (London: Chatto and Windus, 1883), 60. In the twentieth century, Gordon Craig was famously to concur with this view; see chapter 4.

9. Ibid., 69.

10. Quoted in Joseph Roach, *The Player's Passion* (Ann Arbor: University of Michigan Press, 1993), 139.

11. Ibid., 161.

12. Ibid., 181.

13. Lewes, *On Actors,* 96.

14. William Archer, *Masks or Faces? A Study in the Psychology of Acting* (London: Longmans, Green, 1880), 210.

15. Cole and Chinoy, *Actors on Acting,* 328, 329.

16. The notion that the great playwright implicitly *directs* the actor is one that motivates the practice of Stanislavski, Copeau, and their many important followers.

17. Cole and Chinoy, *Actors on Acting,* 327, 328.

18. "Betterton," quoted by Harold Newcomb Hillebrand, *Edmund Kean* (New York: Columbia University Press, 1933), 369.

19. See George Taylor, *Players and Performances in the Victorian Theatre* (Manchester: Manchester University Press, 1989), 34–37, for an account of Edmund Kean's acting and its influence.

20. Quoted in Taylor, *Players and Performances,* 38.

21. Quoted in ibid., 43.

22. See ibid., 43–50; 119–33; Michael Booth, *English Melodrama* (London: Harold Jenkins, 1965), 190–210; Martin Meisel, *Realizations: Narrative, Pictorial, and Theatrical Arts in Nineteenth Century England* (Princeton: Princeton University Press, 1983), 38–57.

23. In the early twentieth century, Ferdinand de Saussure revealed the arbitrariness of the connection between the signifier (the physical sensation) and the signified (that which was represented) in all forms of representation. Theater semiologists later identified codes governing the signifier-signified relationship in theatrical performance.

24. Roach, *The Player's Passion,* 182.

25. Quoted in Roach, *The Player's Passion,* 183.

26. Lewes, *On Actors,* 94.

27. Lewes, *On Actors,* 93, 94.

28. Quoted in Roach, *The Player's Passion,* 158.

29. Quoted in Cole and Chinoy, *Actors on Acting,* 357.

30. Quoted in Norman Marshall, *The Producer and the Play* (London: Davis-Poynter, 1975), 12.

31. Taylor, *Players and Performances,* 21.

32. Quoted in Clifford Leech and T. W. Craik, eds., *Revels History of Drama in English,* 8 vols. (London: Methuen, 1975), 6:130.

33. Accounts of Duse's acting and the criteria used to praise it suggest that her approach was essentially not different in kind from great stage actresses over the last fifty years, such as Laurette Taylor, Peggy Ashcroft, Madeleine Renaud, Dorothy Tutin, Judi Dench, and Vanessa Redgrave.

34. Quoted in Cole and Chinoy, *Actors on Acting,* 465.

35. *Memoirs and Artistic Studies of Adelaide Ristori,* trans. G. Mantellini (New York: Doubleday, Page, 1907), 164, 165.

36. Leech and Craik, *Revels History of Drama,* 7:82.

37. Émile Zola, *Naturalism on the Stage,* trans. Samuel Draper, in *Playwrights on Playwriting,* ed. Toby Cole (New York: Hill and Wang, 1961), 6.

38. Bentley, *Theory of Modern Stage,* 361.

39. Cole and Chinoy, *Actors on Acting,* 212, 213.

40. For a discussion of Antoine's views on acting, see Jean Chothia, *André Antoine* (Cambridge: Cambridge University Press, 1991), 33–37.

41. Cole and Chinoy, *Actors on Acting,* 213.

Chapter 2

1. Stanislavski's understanding of the terms *naturalism* and *realism* was somewhat eccentric. In his view, the Moscow Art Theater's productions of Chekhov's plays were not naturalistic but realistic, representing a poetic distillation of naturalism that was concerned not merely with reproducing the material surfaces of social reality, but with revealing the essential truths of human behavior. Clearly, this is a view that ignores the actual articulation of these categories within the historical development of nineteenth-century European aesthetics. In fact, Stanislavski's understanding of the "essential truths of human behavior" harks back to prenaturalistic Romantic aesthetics.

2. Jean Benedetti, *Stanislavski: A Biography* (London: Methuen, 1990), 125.

3. This aspect of his work on training the actor anticipates the ideas of Copeau and influenced such practitioners as Viola Spolin (see chap. 6).

4. Constantin Stanislavski, *My Life in Art* (Harmondsworth: Penguin, 1967), 63–64.

5. *Sobranie Sochinenii,* vol. 5, p. 90, quoted in Benedetti, *Stanislavski,* 32.

6. Stanislavski, *My Life in Art,* 423–25.

7. Meyerhold in his essay "The Naturalistic Theatre and the Theatre of Mood" (written in 1906), although critical of the naturalistic aesthetic that he believed MAT had developed under the influence of the Saxe-Meiningen Players, had drawn attention to a nonnaturalistic tendency that was in tension with the MAT's predominantly naturalistic approach to Chekhov. See *Meyerhold on Theatre,* ed. and trans. Edward Braun (London: Methuen, 1978), 23–34.

8. Nikolai M. Gorchakov, *Stanislavski Directs* (New York: Limelight Editions, 1985), 143.

9. Stanislavski, *My Life in Art,* 430.

10. Stanislavski himself never used the Freudian term *unconscious*. When referring to psychophysical processes that were not directed by the conscious mind, he used the term *subconscious*.

11. The *method of physical actions* is the subject of his fourth, unfinished book, *Creating a Role,* first published in English in 1961.

12. Eighteenth-century notions of sensibility and nineteenth-century ideas about the feelings predate Stanislavski's idea of a psycho-technique, but no one had explored the possibility of creating a method to enable the optimum functioning of these faculties in the act of performance.

13. The concepts of inner and outer tempo-rhythm were elaborated in Constantin Stanislavski, *Building a Character,* trans. Elizabeth Reynolds Hapgood (London: Methuen, 1968), 183–248.

14. Gorchakov, *Stanislavski Directs,* 96, 97.

15. The standard English translations of Stanislavski's writings employ the term *objective;* Sharon Marie Carnicke has recently proposed *problem* as a more precise rendering of Stanislavski's concept.

16. Stanislavski referred to *units of action* as *bits;* in the United States they came to be known as *beats.*

17. Vasily Toporkov, *Stanislavski in Rehearsal,* trans. Christine Edwards (New York: Theatre Arts Books, 1979), 157.

18. Stanislavski's pre-Freudian concept of the subconscious did not prevent him from recognizing the function of levels of the imagination and body-wisdom that Freud believed were repressed during the process of oedipalization into what he named the unconscious.

19. Although very different as a structured system of rehearsal from Copeau's looser approach, the way in which the method of physical actions utilizes improvisation parallels the use made of games and improvisations by Copeau in discovering the gestic structure of a dramatic text. Both approaches address the problem of integrating mind and body in the psychophysical performance process.

20. See Philip Auslander's discussion of Stanislavski's notion of the actor's self in Phillip B. Zarrilli, ed., *Acting (Re)Considered* (London: Routledge, 1995), 60–63.

21. Constantin Stanislavski, *Creating a Role,* trans. Elizabeth Reynolds Hapgood (New York: Theatre Arts Books, 1961), 209.

22. For a detailed comparison between Stanislavski's understanding of the human mind and that of Freud, see Erica Munk, ed., *Stanislavski and America* (Greenwich, Conn.: Fawcett, 1966).

23. Mel Gordon, *The Stanislavski Technique* (New York: Applause, 1987), 85.

24. See chapter 8 for a full consideration of the use of play and game as methods of training and rehearsal.

25. This was certainly the view of some members of the Group Theatre when he lectured to them in 1935. While greatly impressed by his acting they were, in some respects, confused by his explanation of his praxis.

26. Quoted in Gordon, *The Stanislavski Technique,* 130, 131.

27. Ibid., 134.

28. Chekhov derived the association of movements of the head, chest and feet with the faculties of thought, feeling and will from Rudolf Steiner's *eurythmy.*

29. Michael Chekhov, *On the Technique of Acting* (New York: Harper, 1991), 3.

30. Ibid., 5.

31. Ibid., 36.

32. Ibid., 37.

33. Laban was investigating the kinetic qualities of movement in industry during the 1930s, developing the theory of effort first articulated in Rudolf Laban and F. C. Lawrence, *Effort* (London: Macdonald and Evans, 1947). (See chapter 7.) By coincidence, Laban was invited to teach at Dartington Hall by Kurt Jooss in 1939, so it is possible that Chekhov was aware of his theories.

34. Chekhov, *Technique of Acting*, 39.

35. Laban did not separate *actions* from *qualities:* by defining action as a precise technical term in his system, he showed how the correct performance of a particular *effort action* entailed certain dynamic qualities. See chapter 7 for a discussion of Laban's theory of effort.

36. Chekhov, *Technique of Acting*, 41.

37. Ibid., 43.

38. Ibid., 52.

39. Ibid., 64.

40. Ibid.

41. Ibid., 65.

42. Ibid., 95.

43. Ibid., 96.

44. Ibid., 98.

45. There appear to be similarities on this point between Michael Chekhov's approach to psychophysical testing of character in action and Copeau's *play* with text, voice, and gesture. Both are trial-and-error methods of achieving the psychophysical embodiment of action inherent in the patterns of speech supplied by the written text, and anticipate methods employed by Jacques Lecoq, whose work is in a direct line of descent from Copeau, but also employs techniques derived from his commedia dell'arte training.

46. Lecture notes of Boleslavsky, organized and translated by Michael Barroy, manuscript, 1923, reprinted in Cole and Chinoy, *Actors on Acting*, 511.

47. Ibid., 512.

48. Richard Boleslavsky, *Acting: The First Six Lessons* (New York: Theatre Arts Books, 1933), 84.

49. Ibid., 92.

50. Paul Gray, "From Russia to America: A Critical Chronology," in Munk, *Stanislavski and America*, 150.

51. Ibid., 156.

52. Quoted in Christine Edwards, ed., *The Stanislavski Heritage* (New York: New York University Press, 1965), 425.

53. Quoted by Paul Gray, "From Russia to America: A Critical Chronology," in Munk, *Stanislavski and America*, 159.

54. Scene study still constitutes an important aspect of the typical American curriculum of actor training. It is far less common as a teaching strategy in British training institutions.

55. The notes were reprinted in Toby Cole, ed., *Acting: A Handbook of the*

Stanislavski Method (New York: Crown, 1947), 116–24, which has an introduction by Strasberg.

56. Craig was also very much preoccupied with this paradox. See chapter 4.

57. Lee Strasberg, *Strasberg at the Actors Studio,* ed. Robert H. Hethmon (New York: Viking, 1965), 74.

58. Ibid., 75.

59. Strasberg's way of expressing the problem appears in some respects to anticipate Grotowski's concept of the "via negativa" (see chap. 10).

60. Vakhtangov, in Cole, *Acting,* 116, 117.

61. Ibid., 118, 119.

62. Ibid., 119, 120.

63. See Boleslavsky, *Acting,* 92.

64. "Working with Live Material," an interview with Lee Strasberg by Richard Schechner, in Munk, *Stanislavski and America,* 186.

65. Strasberg's ideas are based on the assumption of the duality of "inner" experience and "outer" expression, which he derived from early Stanislavski.

66. Strasberg, "Working with Live Material," 197.

67. Ibid., 193.

68. Similar training exercises involving observation and mimicry of animal behavior were employed by Michel Saint-Denis and Jacques Lecoq.

69. Charles Marowitz, *The Method as Means* (London: Herbert Jenkins, 1961), 45, 46.

70. See "The Moment Itself," interview with Richard Schechner and Theodore Hoffmann in Munk, *Stanislavski and America,* 201–9.

71. Ibid., 203.

72. Ibid., 202.

73. Ibid., 228, 229.

74. Ibid., 235–37.

75. Ibid., 231, 232.

76. See "Would You *Please* Talk to Those People?" interview with Richard Schechner in Munk, *Stanislavski and America,* 228–42.

77. Paul Gray, *The Reality of Doing,* in Munk, *Stanislavski and America,* 215, 216.

78. Ibid., 217.

79. See Stella Adler, *The Technique of Acting* (Toronto: Bantam, 1988).

80. See Sharon Marie Carnicke, *Stanislavski in Focus* (London: Harwood, 1998), 107–23.

81. Stanislavski derived some of his ideas on emotion memory and the psychophysical basis of acting from the theories of William James and Ivan Pavlov.

Chapter 3

1. Copeau's proposed approach to the actor, although it had something in common with that of Appia, differed in many respects from those of Craig and Meyerhold. (See chap. 5).

2. Angelo Philip Bertocci, *From Symbolism to Baudelaire* (Carbondale: Southern Illinois University Press, 1964), 77.

3. Maurice Maeterlinck, *The Treasure of the Humble,* trans. Alfred Sutro, in *Playwrights on Playwriting,* ed. Toby Cole (New York: Hill and Wang, 1961), 33–34.

4. Independently and with no detailed knowledge of the other's work until after 1905, Appia in Switzerland and Craig in England developed strikingly parallel notions of staging that could be said to derive from the scenic implications of symbolism and expressionism. Both men later acknowledged the similarities and differences in their respective approaches to theater art.

5. Note the parallel here with Michael Chekhov's use of *eurythmy*.

6. Adolphe Appia, quoted in Lee Simonson, *The Stage is Set* (New York: Theatre Arts Books, 1963), 353.

7. Ibid., 358.

8. E. T. Kirby, ed., introduction to *Total Theatre* (New York: Dutton, 1969), xxi–xxii.

9. Adolphe Appia, "L'Origine et Les Debuts de la Gymnastique Rhythmique," in Kirby, *Total Theatre,* 25.

10. See Clark M. Rogers, "Appia's Theory of Acting: Eurythmics for the Stage," in Kirby, *Total Theatre,* 25.

11. Adolphe Appia, *Music and the Art of the Theatre,* trans. R. W. Corrigan and M. D. Dirks (Coral Gables, Fla.: University of Miami Press, 1962), 13.

12. Ibid, 36.

13. In the 1920s and 1930s, Rudolf Laban began to develop theories of expressive movement more sophisticated than those of Dalcroze, yet equally founded on the notion of artistic expression as "natural" to the human body. His *Tanztheater,* later elaborated by his students Kurt Jooss and Sigurd Leder, was a manifestation of this aesthetic philosophy that utilized expressionist conventions to create a new type of dramatic dance (see chapter 7 for a discussion of Laban's influence on British actor training).

14. Craig, "Re-arrangements," in *Craig on Theatre,* ed. J. Michael Walton (London: Methuen, 1983), 39.

15. Ibid.

16. Craig, "The Actor and the Über-Marionette," in Edward Gordon Craig, *On the Art of the Theatre* (London: Heinemann, 1968), 55–58.

17. Stanislavski's attempts to fuse the organic reality of the actor's emotional life with the artificial elements of literary and scenographic material are in direct opposition to Craig's conception of the unified artwork.

18. Modern notions of the performance score (elaborated by Grotowski and Barba from Stanislavski's method of physical actions) do acknowledge the necessity to fix the physical form of the performance in order to focus and control the feelings it evokes in both performer and spectator. Craig, in fact, offers a very extreme notion of what has come to be known as the performance score.

19. Craig, *Craig on Theatre,* 61.

20. Craig, "The Artists of the Theatre of the Future," *Craig on Theatre,* 79.

21. Ibid.

22. Ibid.

23. Craig, "Henry Irving," in *Craig on Theatre,* 77.

24. Craig; "Stanislavski's System," in *Craig on Theatre,* 89.

25. Ibid, 89.

26. "The Art of the Theatre, The Second Dialogue," in Craig, *On the Art of the Theatre,* 240.

27. Quoted in Denis Bablet, *The Theatre of Edward Gordon Craig* (London: Eyre Methuen, 1981), 164.

28. Craig, "Stanislavski's System," in *Craig on Theatre*, 90, 91.

29. Craig, *The Theatre Advancing* (Boston: Little, Brown, 1919), 19.

30. Craig, "The Perishable Theatre," in *Craig on Theatre*, 17.

31. See Edward Braun, ed. and trans., *Meyerhold on Theatre* (London: Eyre Methuen, 1969), 18, 112.

32. See Meyerhold, "The Naturalistic Theatre and the Theatre of Mood," in *Meyerhold on Theatre*, 23–34.

33. From Meyerhold's journal, *The Love of Three Oranges*, in *Meyerhold on Theatre*, 147.

34. Ibid., 148.

35. Ibid., 51–52.

36. Ibid., 81.

37. Ibid., 81–82.

38. Ibid., 85.

39. Ibid., 82.

40. This is an idea that derives from the French actor Constant Coquelin. See Cole and Chinoy, *Actors on Acting*, 190–202.

41. See Edward Braun, *Meyerhold: A Revolution in Theatre* (London: Methuen, 1995), 71–72.

42. Meyerhold, "The Fairground Booth" (1912), in *Meyerhold on Theatre*, 141.

43. Braun, *Meyerhold*, 74.

44. "The New Theatre Foreshadowed by Literature" (1907), in *Meyerhold on Theatre*, 38.

45. Ibid., 126.

46. Valentina Vergina, cited in *Meyerhold on Theatre*, 70.

47. "The Stylised Theatre" (1907), in *Meyerhold on Theatre*, 63.

48. This point was made by Chekhov in his criticism of aspects of Stanislavski's productions of his plays. See Edward Braun, *The Director and the Stage* (London: Eyre Methuen, 1982), 59–76.

49. Quoted in Braun, *Meyerhold*, 125–26.

50. See *Meyerhold on Theatre*, 153–56.

51. Ibid., 152.

52. Quoted in Braun, *Meyerhold*, 74.

53. *Meyerhold on Theatre*, 129.

54. Ibid.

55. Meyerhold, "Biomechanics," in *Meyerhold on Theatre*, 197.

56. Ibid., 198.

57. Marjorie L. Hoover explains the derivation of the term in *Meyerhold: The Art of Conscious Theater* (Amherst: University of Massachusetts Press, 1974), 297: "Biomechanics, in its original meaning, is that subdivision of physiology concerned with the motions of animals and humans. Applying the data of anatomy, physiology, and theoretical mechanics, it weighs the rationality and economy of movements in order to perfect them."

58. *Meyerhold on Theatre*, 199.

59. Ibid.

60. Ibid.

61. Igor Ilinsky, "Biomechanics," in Cole and Chinoy, *Actors on Acting,* 504.

62. Although they did not meet often until the 1930s, Stanislavski and Meyerhold preserved a relationship of mutual respect, openly disagreeing in their views on theater but each maintaining a high opinion of the other's abilities.

63. *Meyerhold on Theatre,* 201.

64. Ibid., 198.

65. Alma Law and Mel Gordon, *Meyerhold, Eisenstein, and Biomechanics: Actor Training in Revolutionary Russia* (Jefferson, N.C.: McFarland, 1996), 103–5.

66. Ibid., 150.

67. Ibid., 99.

68. This remains a fundamental principle of stage movement.

69. Jerzy Grotowski and Joseph Chaikin have placed significant emphasis on the relationship of voice and movement, as has voice teacher Cicely Berry.

70. Ilinsky, in Cole and Chinoy, *Actors on Acting,* 505.

71. From a lecture by Meyerhold, in *Meyerhold on Theatre,* 200.

72. Meyerhold in conversation with Harold Clurman (1935), quoted in *Meyerhold on Theatre,* 202.

73. On its introduction in 1922, Ippolit Sokolov, an opponent of Meyerhold, criticized biomechanics on a number of counts, including what he perceived as a contradiction between its physiological aims as an acting training system and its theatrical use as a kinesthetic vocabulary. See Law and Gordon, *Meyerhold, Eisenstein, and Biomechanics,* 144–48.

74. See ibid., 173–76, 183–85.

75. Ibid., 252, 253.

76. *Meyerhold on Theatre,* 206.

77. For Bogart's approach to combating theatrical and dramaturgical stereotypes see Anne Bogart, *A Director Prepares* (New York: Routledge, 2001), 91–111.

78. From Eelka Lampe, "The Paradox of the Circle: Anne Bogart's Creative Encounter with East Asian Performance Traditions," in *Anne Bogart: Viewpoints,* ed. Michael Bigelow Dixon and Joel A. Smith (Lyme, N.H.: Smith and Kraus, 1995), 157.

79. Tina Landau, "Source-Work, the Viewpoints, and Composition: What Are They?" in Dixon and Smith, *Anne Bogart,* 20.

80. Meyerhold had pointed out that Stanislavski's approach to acting was based on the assumption that the spectator feels what the actor/character was feeling, while he himself had realized that this was not the case, and that the performer's job was not to feel but to affect the spectator's feelings.

81. Landau, "Source-Work," 26–28.

82. See Bogart, *A Director Prepares,* 17, for her explanation of how her performers benefit from experiencing the very different training systems of Suzuki and Viewpoints.

83. See ibid., 18.

84. Lampe, in Dixon and Smith, *Anne Bogart,* 159.

85. From an unpublished interview with Anne Bogart by Porter Anderson, quoted in Dixon and Smith, *Anne Bogart,* 125.

Chapter 4

1. John Gielgud, Laurence Olivier, Peggy Ashcroft, George Devine, Michael

Redgrave, and Alec Guinness were among the important British actors who were influenced by Saint-Denis.

2. Saint-Denis's example and teaching inspired George Devine to establish the English Stage Company at the Royal Court Theatre in 1956. Saint-Denis's impact on Peter Hall and his years as an artistic director of Hall's newly established Royal Shakespeare Company are a reminder of the pervasive nature of his influence on non-commercial theater in England.

3. Jacques Copeau, *Copeau: Texts on Theatre,* ed. John Rudlin and Norman H. Paul (New York: Routledge, 1990), 27.

4. In 1887 Antoine's productions of Zola's adaptation of *Jacques Damour* and Metenier's *En Famille* at his newly established Théâtre Libre had astonished the Parisian theater world with their stark naturalism, inaugurating a tradition of naturalistic productions as well as the establishment of a series of small, independent art theaters around Europe.

5. Copeau, *Texts on Theatre,* 27.

6. Kenneth MacGowan and Robert Edmond Jones, *Continental Stagecraft* (New York: Classic, 1922), 172.

7. Michel Saint-Denis, *Training for the Theatre* (London: Heinemann, 1982), 27.

8. In this respect, Copeau's view of the actor-audience relationship is entirely consonant with that of Brecht.

9. Copeau, *Texts on Theatre,* 87, 88.

10. Ibid., 89.

11. Ibid, 81.

12. Ibid., 11.

13. Ibid., 24.

14. Ibid., 25.

15. Ibid., 25.

16. In theorizing the practice of biomechanics, Meyerhold, whose concept of performance emphasized the conscious construction of meaning through the manipulation of the machinery of theater, did nevertheless revert to an organicist image of the "whole person." His behaviorist model views the body/mind as a biological machine whose neurological reflexes provide the physiological means of stimulating emotions.

17. At its most extreme, the Nazi image of the perfect Aryan male as depicted in the films of Leni Riefenstahl illustrates the way in which ideology may be expressed at the level of body culture.

18. Both Stanislavski and Copeau were confusing means and ends, or form and content. Logically, there is no reason why the means of expression should agree with that which is being expressed. The actor is merely the vehicle (signifier) employed to signify character; naturalistic acting is a theatrical effect that has no intrinsic truth-value.

19. Quoted in Copeau, *Texts on Theatre,* 57.

20. Copeau, *Souvenirs de Vieux-Colombier,* quoted in Maurice Kurtz, *Jacques Copeau: Biography of a Theater* (Carbondale: Southern Illinois University Press, 1999), 35.

21. At the end of the nineteenth century, the prevalent idea was that movement and gesture were an accompaniment to speech, rather than an inevitable aspect of it, and English actors were often complimented for acting "between the lines," as though this were a special achievement.

22. Copeau, *Texts on Theatre,* 40.

23. Ibid.

24. Ibid., 43.

25. Ibid., 43.

26. Ibid., 50.

27. There are striking parallels between this idea of surrendering one's identity to the character of the mask and Grotowski's *via negativa*. See Jerzy Grotowski, *Towards a Poor Theatre* (New York: Simon and Schuster, 1968), 17 and 133.

28. Saint-Denis, *Training for the Theatre*, 33.

29. Quoted in John Rudlin, *Jacques Copeau* (Cambridge: Cambridge University Press, 1986), 49.

30. Copeau, *Texts on Theatre*, 49.

31. Ibid., 57.

32. Copeau's interest in eurythmics as a system of musical-kinesthetic training for actors is comparable with that of Michael Chekhov, and in some respects anticipates the use of Laban's effort system as a means of developing the actor's physical expressiveness.

33. From the notebook "L'École du Vieux-Colombier," quoted in Copeau, *Texts on Theatre*, 95.

34. Copeau, *Texts on Theatre*, 61.

35. Ibid.

36. Ibid, 63.

37. Eugenio Barba identifies such training as preparation for the pre-expressive dimension of performance.

38. Letter from Dalcroze to Copeau, October 1, 1921, quoted in Copeau, *Texts on Theatre*, 66.

39. From "Adolphe Appia et l'art de la scène (16 Avril)," quoted in Copeau, *Texts on Theatre*, 99.

40. Ibid., 99, 100.

41. MacGowan and Jones, *Continental Stagecraft*, 99.

42. Harold Clurman, quoted in Kurtz, *Jacques Copeau*, 90.

43. From a letter by Jouvet written January 31, 1916, quoted in Copeau, *Texts on Theatre*, 227.

44. From *Le Théâtre Populaire*, quoted in Copeau, *Texts on Theatre*, 178.

45. Robert H. Hethmon, ed., *Strasberg at the Actors Studio* (New York: Viking, 1965), reprinted in Cole and Chinoy, *Actors on Acting*, 624.

46. Copeau, *Texts on Theatre*, 72.

47. Ibid., 77.

48. Ibid., 73.

49. Ibid., 77.

50. Saint-Denis's work also had some impact in the United States and Canada through his involvement as co-director of the Juilliard School in New York, and as artistic advisor to the new National School of Dramatic Art in Montreal.

Chapter 5

1. Robert Speaight, *William Poel and the Elizabethan Revival* (London: Society for Theatre Research, 1954), 90.

2. Robert Speaight, *Shakespeare on the Stage* (London: William Collins, 1973), 136.

3. *Saturday Review,* July 31, 1909, cited in Speaight, *William Poel and the Elizabethan Revival,* 63.

4. *Saturday Review,* July 16, 1927, cited in Speaight, *William Poel and the Elizabethan Revival,* 90, 91.

5. *Saturday Review,* September 28, 1912, cited in Speaight, *William Poel and the Elizabethan Revival,* 91.

6. See chapter 4.

7. Introduction to acting edition of *A Midsummer Night's Dream,* 1914, cited in Speaight, *Shakespeare on the Stage,* 141.

8. Harley Granville Barker, *Prefaces to Shakespeare, First Series* (London: Sidgwick and Jackson, 1951), xxiv.

9. Ibid., 27.

10. Saint-Denis, *Training for the Theatre,* 13.

11. Ibid., 42.

12. Ibid., 42, 43.

13. Ibid., 32.

14. Marius Goring, in a letter to Maud Allen, cited Irving Wardle, *The Theatres of George Devine* (London: Eyre Methuen, 1979), 56.

15. Saint-Denis, *Training for the Theatre,* 47.

16. Ibid., 48.

17. Ibid., 83.

18. Ibid., 82.

19. Ibid., 84.

20. Ibid., 84, 85.

21. Ibid, 85.

22. Ibid., 103.

23. Laban's work on effort actions in my view affords the most coherent model for a bodily training in expressivity. For an exposition of Laban's ideas about the use of effort in acting, see chapter 6 and Rudolf Laban, *The Mastery of Movement* (London: Macdonald and Evans, 1950), or Jean Newlove, *Laban for Actors and Dancers* (London: Nick Hern, 1993).

24. Saint-Denis, *Training for the Theatre,* 104.

25. Cf. Meyerhold, Michael Chekhov, Laban, and Eugenio Barba on parallel conceptions of the kinetic center of the performer's body.

26. Wilfred Barlow, *The Alexander Principle* (London: Victor Gollancz, 1990), 194.

27. Saint-Denis, *Training for the Theatre,* 109.

28. Ibid., 114, 115.

29. Ibid., 116.

30. Ibid., 124.

31. Ibid., 128.

32. Such a notion of play was parallel to the development by psychologists between the 1930s and 1960s of the idea of play as a tool for learning, applied first in the field of Drama-in-Education and, later, by Theatre-in-Education companies.

33. Saint-Denis, *Training for the Theatre,* 153.

34. Copeau's aesthetic aim was slightly different from that of Stanislavski, who stressed that, although the actor might find the components of the character's emotions

and actions from her own experience and observation, she should entirely disguise her own personality underneath the external features of the role.

35. Saint-Denis, *Training for the Theatre,* 159.

36. In a rather different context, Lee Strasberg employed animal improvisations to help actors with physical aspects of characterization; see chapter 2.

37. Saint-Denis, *Training for the Theatre,* 164.

38. Ibid., 170.

39. The idea that the actor should not merely exploit the normal faculties of social role-play on stage also preoccupied Edward Gordon Craig, who insisted in "The Actor and the Über-Marionette" (1907) that the human actor is unable to control spontaneous facial and bodily movement with sufficient precision for acting to be an art.

40. Saint-Denis, *Training for the Theatre,* 46.

41. Ibid., 189.

42. Ibid, 190.

43. This is not to deny the significant way in which Brechtian notions of dramaturgy have continued to animate much theater writing from the 1980s to the present—particularly in the sphere of feminist and gay writing.

44. At his school in London, Phillipe Gaulier teaches a mode of practice derived from Copeau via Lecoq.

Chapter 6

1. These actors were not all themselves from an upper-middle-class background, but as actors they were obliged to imitate the speech and manners of this class.

2. Saint-Denis, *Theatre: The Rediscovery of Style.*

3. John Barton, *Playing Shakespeare* (London: Methuen, 1984), 3.

4. Ibid., 3.

5. Ibid., 6, 7.

6. Ibid., 168.

7. Ibid., 7.

8. F. R. Leavis was for many years tutor at Downing College, Cambridge, and with I. A. Richards was responsible for revolutionizing methods of literary criticism in Britain.

9. Barton, *Playing Shakespeare,* 8, 9.

10. Ibid., 15.

11. Ibid., 20.

12. Ibid., 180.

13. The essay was later expanded into a short book.

14. John Russell Brown, "Free Shakespeare," in *Shakespeare Survey* 50 (1971): 131.

15. Cicely Berry, *The Actor and His Text* (London: Harrop, 1987).

16. Cicely Berry, *Voice and the Actor* (London: Virgin Books, 1989), 76.

17. Ibid., 16, 17.

18. Berry's approach to the blocks that prevent the actor from being fully expressive is reminiscent of Grotowski's *via negativa.* She would certainly have been aware of his work with Peter Brook's Theatre of Cruelty group in 1964. The aim of training to remove barriers to self-expression is, of course, central to the work of Lee Strasberg (see chap. 2).

19. This is the opposite of the view held by Eugenio Barba, who believes that acting entails a *deformation* of the everyday functions of speech and movement.

20. Berry, *The Actor and His Text,* 24.

21. Ibid, 115.

22. Ibid, 229, 230.

23. Ibid, 21.

24. All drama schools in Britain and France devote time to movement study. Most teachers employ an eclectic range of approaches to physical training, drawing on a combination of techniques, those of F. Mathias Alexander, Moshe Feldenkrais, and Jacques Lecoq being the most popular. Yat Malmgren at the Drama Centre in London was unique in having developed and utilized the ideas of Laban in teaching movement to actors. For a discussion of Malmgren's use of Laban, see Vladimir Mirodan, "'The Way of Transformation' (The Laban-Malmgren System of Dramatic Character Analysis)," Ph.D. diss., University of London, 1997, 192–93.

25. Joan Littlewood, *Joan's Book* (London: Minerva, 1995).

26. The Laban Centre based in Deptford, London, is now a major center for training in all aspects of modern dance.

27. Dalcroze's eurythmics could in some respects be seen as a precursor to Laban's systems of eukinetics and choreutics, and they both reject the nineteenth-century theories, such as Delsarte's, that produced taxonomies detailing the alleged relationship between movements and corresponding feelings. Whereas Laban's ideas about the effort qualities and spatial forms of movement were based on scrupulous empirical observation, many of Dalcroze's ideas about the harmonious relationship between movements, sounds, and colors were pure speculation.

28. Cf. the organicist approach whereby Cicely Berry regards the breath in speech as a fundamental "life" principle. In this respect, both Berry and Laban are opposed to the attitude common to both Craig and Barba.

29. Rudolf Laban and F. C. Lawrence, *Effort* (London: Macdonald and Evans, 1947), xi.

30. Rudolf Laban, *The Mastery of Movement* (London: Macdonald and Evans, 1960), 13.

31. There are clear parallels with the approach of Michael Chekhov, although Chekhov's approach was the result of his own personal experience as an actor rather than the systematic observation of movement that led Laban to formulate his system.

32. Laban, *Mastery of Movement,* 8.

33. Ibid., 91.

34. Ibid., 95.

35. Cicely Berry's exercises use movement to provoke a lively and flexible range of speech attitudes, representing an untheorized use of what Laban would identify as complete and incomplete effort actions.

36. Laban, *Mastery of Movement,* 110.

37. Ibid., 127, 128.

38. Delsarte and earlier nineteenth-century analysts of movement attempted to codify the relationship between the physical form of a facial expression, posture, or gesture and its emotional effect.

39. Rudolf Laban, *Modern Educational Dance* (London: Macdonald and Evans, 1963).

40. Ibid., 25.

41. Ibid., 44.

42. Under the artistic directorship of Mark Rylance, directors are nominated "masters of the play," and there is a particular emphasis on speech work as a preparation for performing the plays of Shakespeare and his contemporaries in the outdoor conditions of an Elizabethan public playhouse. Notwithstanding the emphasis on the exploration of texts by actors, a production at the Globe is unmistakably the expression of its director's interpretation of the play, often involving experiments with all-female and all-male (adult) casts.

Chapter 7

1. Viola Spolin, *Improvisation for the Theatre* (Evanston, Ill.: Northwestern University Press, 1983), ix.

2. Parallels between Spolin's ideas and Jean Piaget's theories of learning have been noted: see ibid., viii.

3. Neva L. Boyd, quoted in ibid., 5.

4. Spolin, *Improvisation for the Theatre,* 4.

5. Ibid., 16, 17.

6. Ibid., 26.

7. In other respects, of course, Brecht's approach is very different from that advocated by Johnstone. The Brechtian actor is conscious of herself and the artistic choices that she makes in the performance from moment to moment in order to show that she might have made other choices. The notion of creativity as a natural or organic process is the opposite of Brecht's idea that the performance is a construct, consciously designed to demonstrate a point of view about the world. Brecht wished his actors to demonstrate their ideas concretely because as a Marxist he believed in the material basis of reality and was skeptical of abstract theories that had no connection with the material world.

8. C. D. Lau, trans., *Tao te Ching,* quoted in Keith Johnstone, *Impro: Improvisation and the Theatre* (London: Eyre Methuen, 1981), 20.

9. Johnstone, *Impro,* 43.

10. Ibid., 38, 39.

11. Ibid., 97.

12. Ibid., 105.

13. Ibid., 111.

14. Ibid., 118.

15. The recent productions of Phelim McDermott and Julian Crouch with their Improbable Theatre are clearly influenced by Johnstone's methods of generating narrative.

16. Clive Barker, *Theatre Games: A New Approach to Drama Training* (London: Eyre Methuen, 1977).

17. Pioneers in these movements include Peter Slade, Brian Way, and Dorothy Heathcote.

18. Patsy Rodenburg and Kristen Linklater have developed their own versions of Berry's approach; the work of all three continues to be promulgated by voice teachers in drama schools and theater companies in Britain, e.g., Barbara Berkerry and Julia Wilson-Dixon.

19. The idea that play is essential to the child's learning process was most famously

formulated by Jean Piaget in *Play, Dreams and Imitation in Childhood,* trans. F. M. Hodgson and C. Gattegno (New York: W. W. Norton, 1962).

20. It was Littlewood who introduced him to the work of Laban.

21. Barker, *Theatre Games,* 50.

22. Ibid., 29.

23. Ibid., 30.

24. Ibid., 51.

25. This is reminiscent of Stanislavski's method of physical actions in which the actor's body learns through a psychophysical process of improvising the action of the play over a long period of time to execute every physical action with its appropriate intention.

26. Barker, *Theatre Games,* 44.

27. Ibid., 46.

28. Ibid., 57.

29. Ibid., 69.

30. Roger Callois, *Man, Play and Games* (London: Thames and Hudson, 1962).

31. Barker, *Theatre Games,* 88, 89.

32. Ibid., 89, 90.

33. See chapters 5 and 6 on Michel Saint-Denis and Cicely Berry.

34. Barker, *Theatre Games,* 110.

35. Ibid., 124.

36. This explanation of the way in which game playing and improvisation help actors to maintain the kinesthetic spontaneity of a dramatic interaction constitutes a coherent rationalization of the method of physical actions, in many respects restating Stanislavski's ideas in terms of movement theory.

37. It is this problem that, among others, Stanislavski's method of physical actions was intended to address.

38. He does note Joan Littlewood's success by means of this approach, but notes that she only used it for short sections of scenes, and often had the prompter feed the actual words of the text to the actor a half a line before it was needed.

39. Erving Goffman, *The Presentation of Self in Everyday Life* (Harmondsworth: Penguin, 1959), and *Frame Analysis* (Harmondsworth: Penguin, 1974).

40. Barker's term "non-existent languages" refers to *grummelot,* as used by Saint-Denis (see chapter 6).

41. Chris Johnston's *House of Games: Making Theatre from Everyday Life* (London: Nick Hern, 1998) is the latest book to develop a performance practice based on ideas drawn from Spolin, Keith Johnstone, and Barker.

42. In North America, the praxis of Anne Bogart occupies a position equivalent to that of Lecoq in Europe.

43. He came into direct contact with the praxis of Copeau through his encounters with Jean-Louis Barrault, Marie-Hélène and Jean Daste, and Claude Martin (a pupil of Dullin). In Italy, his work was influenced by collaborations with Amleto Sartori (the great commedia dell'arte mask-maker), Carlo Ludovici (a famous Venetian Arlecchino), Giorgio Strehler and Dario Fo.

44. The psychophysical approach of Michael Chekhov has a similar appeal for actors; like Lecoq's it is a suggestive but less scientific system of analyzing movement than that of Laban.

45. Jacques Lecoq, *The Moving Body,* trans. David Bradby (London: Methuen, 2000), 15.

46. Ibid., 29.

47. See Richard Schechner, *Between Theatre and Anthropology* (Philadelphia: University of Pennsylvania Press, 1994), 35–116, for discussion of his concept of restored behavior.

48. Again, Lecoq reveals his kinship with Copeau's anti-Stanislavskian viewpoint.

49. See chapter 4, especially with reference to the *noble mask.*

50. Lecoq, *The Moving Body,* 20.

51. Ibid., 38.

52. Ibid., 46.

53. Ibid., 22.

Chapter 8

1. *Brecht on Theatre,* ed. John Willett (London: Methuen, 1964), 7.

2. Bertolt Brecht, "A Little Private Tuition for my Friend Max Gorelik," in *Brecht on Theatre,* 160.

3. Ibid., 173.

4. Brecht's first play, *Baal,* contains songs for which he himself composed tunes; in imitation of Wedekind, he would sing them to his own guitar accompaniment.

5. *Brecht on Theatre,* 3, 4.

6. Ibid., 7.

7. Ibid., 3.

8. In Ronald Hayman, *Brecht: A Biography* (London: Weidenfeld and Nicholson, 1983), 49.

9. Quoted in Margaret Eddershaw, *Performing Brecht* (London: Routledge, 1996), 10.

10. *Brecht on Theatre,* 224.

11. Bertolt Brecht, *Journals* (London: Methuen, 1979), 140.

12. The word Brecht came to use for such physical demonstration was *Gestus.*

13. *Brecht on Theatre,* 56.

14. Ibid., 68.

15. Ibid., 162.

16. Bertolt Brecht, "A Letter to an Actor," in *Brecht on Theatre,* 233.

17. *Brecht on Theatre,* 161.

18. Ibid., 114.

19. Ibid., 36.

20. Ibid., 38.

21. Ibid., 55.

22. Ibid., 55.

23. Ibid., 26.

24. Ibid., 133.

25. The usual English translation, *alienation* (A-effect), has misleading connotations. There is, of course, a logical reason for connecting *Verfremdung* with *Entfremdung* (the Marxian notion of alienation), in that Brecht is attempting to create a Marxist aesthetic device (alienation in the sense of making-strange) in order to expose to the spectator her own alienation *(Entfremdung)* as an effect of capitalism.

26. *Verfremdung* is a translation of *priem ostrannenie*, first used by Victor Shlovsky, a leading literary theorist of the Russian formalist school. Brecht may have heard the term during his Moscow visit in 1935.

27. *Brecht on Theatre*, 11.

28. Ibid., 341.

29. Ibid., 91, 92.

30. Ibid., 93.

31. Ibid., 95.

32. In this respect, Brechtian theater can be seen to differ from that of Meyerhold, who also aimed to produce effects of defamiliarization in performance but who achieved these by conscious stylization. Brecht's theater, unlike that of Meyerhold, can be seen to aim for a broad realism.

33. *Brecht on Theatre*, 96.

34. Ibid., 97.

35. Traditional types of comic acting have seldom functioned by requiring either actor or spectator to empathize with the character, but comic acting has historically been treated as a lesser—because usually popular—art.

36. *Brecht on Theatre*, 122.

37. Ibid.

38. Ibid., 138.

39. Ibid.

40. Ibid.

41. Ibid., 129.

42. Brecht's approach here is directly comparable with that of Meyerhold: both refunction the traditional skills of earlier forms of "theatrical theater" (commedia dell' arte, nineteenth-century melodrama, circus clowning, etc.) to permit the performer to address the audience directly.

43. *Brecht on Theatre*, 198.

44. Ibid., 165.

45. Bertolt Brecht, *The Messingkauf Dialogues,* trans. John Willett (London: Methuen, 1965), 85, 86.

46. *Brecht on Theatre*, 202, 203.

47. Ibid., 282.

48. Ibid., 277.

49. Ibid., 238.

50. Brecht, "Notes on Stanislavsky," *Tulane Drama Review* 9, no. 2 (1964): 160.

51. *Brecht on Theatre*, 237.

52. Ibid.

53. Ibid., 162.

54. This was, indeed still is, a characteristic feature of both naturalistic and expressionistic theater and film. It was also the end to which the techniques of Artaud's theater of cruelty were directed.

55. *Brecht on Theatre*, 248, 249.

56. Brecht, *The Messingkauf Dialogues,* 87.

57. *Brecht on Theatre*, 79.

58. Hayman, *Brecht*, 374.

59. Brecht, *Helene Weigel*, in Bentley, *Theory of Modern Stage*, 105.

60. *Brecht on Theatre,* 28.
61. Ibid.
62. Ibid., 59.
63. Bentley, *Theory of Modern Stage,* 107.
64. Ibid., 108.
65. Quoted J. Rouse, "Brecht and the Contradictory Actor," *Theatre Journal* 36, no. 1 (1982): 36.
66. *Brecht on Theatre,* 243.
67. Ibid., 244.
68. Ibid., 245.
69. See Elin Diamond, *Unmaking Mimesis* (London: Routledge, 1997), 43–103.

Chapter 9

1. See Mady Schutzman and Jan Cohen-Cruz, eds., *Playing Boal* (London: Routledge, 1994).
2. Augusto Boal, *Theater of the Oppressed,* trans. Charles A. McBride and Maria-Odilia Leal McBride (London: Pluto Press, 1979), 172.
3. Ibid., 139.
4. Boal follows Brecht in portraying Aristotle as the representative of a theater of empathy that reinforces the conservative values of the ruling class. In Boal's scheme, Aristotle's *Poetics* presents a "coercive" system of tragedy, which manipulates spectators into a passive acceptance of the status quo.
5. Boal, *Theater of the Oppressed,* 122
6. For a detailed analysis of the arguments in *The Theatre of the Oppressed,* see Jane Milling and Graham Ley, *Modern Theories of Performance* (New York: Palgrave, 2001), 143–71.
7. Perhaps the most wide-ranging critical exposition of this theme is undertaken in *The Decision,* one of a series of *Lehrstücke* collected in Brecht, *Plays 3,* ed. John Willett (London: Methuen, 1997). Azdak, the judge in *The Caucasian Chalk Circle,* is typical of the corrupt individual whose personal identity has been formed by the ideology of capitalism, yet whose intelligence nevertheless directs him to bend the unfair laws, in order to exact an approximation of socialist justice within the context of a capitalist society.
8. Schutzman and Cohen-Cruz, *Playing Boal,* 131.
9. See chapter 13 on Peter Brook's mirror exercise, which bears some resemblance to the hypnosis exercise described by Boal.
10. Boal, *Theater of the Oppressed,* 134.
11. Ibid., 142.
12. Quoted by Daniel Feldhendler in Schutzman and Cohen-Cruz, *Playing Boal,* 99.
13. Augusto Boal, *The Rainbow of Desire* (London: Routledge, 1995), 13.

Chapter 10

1. Artaud's radical conception of theater motivated the experiments of the Living Theater, Joseph Chaikin's Open Theater, Peter Brook and Charles Marowitz's Theater of Cruelty season, and Grotowski's poor theater. In some respects Artaud's writing also influenced the Bread and Puppet Theater, the Happenings of the performance artists in the United States in the 1960s, Richard Foreman's Ontological-Hysterical Theatre, the development of butoh by Hijikata and others, American performance artists such as

Chris Burden and Vito Acconci, the Japanese writer and director Terayama, American feminist performers such as Carolee Schneeman, Yvonne Rainer, Linda Montano, and Yoko Ono, and the playwrights Jean Genet and Fernando Arrabal, among others.

2. Among the current generation of practitioners whose practice is in some respects inspired by Artaud are body artists such as Ron Athey, Eleanor Antin, Bob Flanagan, Franco B, Orlan, and Kate Bornstein and feminist performers such as Suzanne Lacey, Annie Sprinkle, and Karen Finlay.

3. Antonin Artaud, "On the Alfred Jarry Theater," in *Selected Writings*, ed. Susan Sontag (New York: Farrar, Straus and Giroux, 1976), 156–57.

4. See Jacques Derrida, *Writing and Difference*, trans. Alan Bass (Chicago: University of Chicago Press, 1978).

5. From letter to Dr. Paulhan, January 25, 1936, quoted in *Artaud on Theatre*, ed. Claude Schumacher (London: Methuen, 1989), 87.

6. Indeed, the Artaud-inspired Living Theatre did use the essay "Theatre and the Plague" in the 1960s as the basis for one of its performances.

7. Artaud, "Mise-en-scène and Metaphysics," in *Selected Writings*, 231–39.

8. Artaud, "On the Balinese Theater," in *Selected Writings*, 215, 216.

9. Ibid., 218–20.

10. Artaud, "Oriental Theater and Western Theater," in *Selected Writings*, 269, 270.

11. Similarly, those who witnessed the attempt at rehabilitating Artaud after the war, when he made his public appearance at the Vieux-Colombier theater in 1947, after being released from his incarceration in the asylum at Rodez, claim this event to have been his most authentic realization of the theater of cruelty.

12. "The Theater of Cruelty (First Manifesto)," in *Selected Writings*, 257, 258.

13. "Manifesto for a Theater That Failed," in *Selected Writings*, 160.

14. "Oriental Theater and Western Theater," in *Selected Writings*, 268.

15. The drama of Beckett can in this respect be viewed as Artaudian, as can the poor theater of Grotowski, the work of Peter Brook after 1970, and the work of Barba's Odin Teatret.

16. Artaud, *Selected Writings*, xlix.

17. Ibid., 259.

18. Grotowski's work on corporeal training is indebted to ideas and attitudes expressed in "An Emotional Athleticism," while movement teachers such as Laban and voice teachers such as Cicely Berry, Kristin Linklater, and Patsy Rodenburg develop approaches to the relationship between body and voice in training and performance that, deliberately or not, echo Artaud's ideas.

19. In this respect, Artaud returned to an early-nineteenth-century Romantic conception of the aim of theatrical performance.

20. Artaud, *Selected Writings*, 259, 260.

21. Ibid., 260.

22. Ibid.

23. Ibid.

24. Ibid., 262.

25. See chapter 6 for a discussion of Cicely Berry and Laban.

26. Artaud, *Selected Writings*, 263.

27. Ibid.

28. Ibid.

29. Quoted in William Harris, "Demonised and Struggling with his Demons," *New York Times,* October 23, 1994, H31.

Chapter 11

1. There are obvious parallels here with Copeau's aversion to *cabotinage* and Stanislavski's demand for truth. The ethical demand for total honesty from the actor underlies a number of twentieth-century conceptions of acting, representing a leitmotif in the modern history of performance.

2. From *Holiday,* in *The Grotowski Sourcebook,* ed. Richard Schechner and Lisa Wolford (London: Routledge, 2001), 222–25.

3. Jerzy Grotowski, "He Wasn't Entirely Himself," in *Towards a Poor Theatre* (New York: Simon and Schuster, 1968), 117–25.

4. Ibid., 125.

5. Ibid.

6. The theaters of Reinhardt, Meyerhold, and Piscator might be viewed as typical of the principle of "artistic kleptomania" that Grotowski rejected.

7. Grotowski, *Towards a Poor Theatre,* 128; Grotowski's designation of these aims by letters *a, b,* and *c* has been omitted from the quotation.

8. Whatever specific knowledge Grotowski possessed of Copeau's praxis would most probably have been the result of his study of Étiénne Decroux, a famous student of Copeau.

9. Copeau's retreat to the country to devise improvised performances and to produce plays with religious themes, e.g., medieval drama, represented a radical return to the earth, where it was assumed it would be possible to create new spiritual communities, better able to live morally healthy lives, away from the corrupting sophistication of the cities.

10. Grotowski's small community of actors, dedicating their entire working lives to practical research into acting rather than merely to rehearsing and presenting shows to the largest possible audiences, is reminiscent of Copeau's attempts between the two world wars to create a rural community of actors working as an ensemble to realize his quasi-religious ideal of theater.

11. Grotowski went to London at Brook's invitation in August 1966 to run workshops with RSC actors in preparation for Brook's *US.*

12. Jerzy Grotowski, *Mozliwosc teatru,* Opole, Materialy warsztatowe Teatru 13 Rzedow, February 1962, quoted in Eugenio Barba, *The Paper Canoe* (London: Routledge, 1995), 114.

13. Barba, *The Paper Canoe,* 115.

14. Again, Grotowski's model of theater as an archaeology of the living impulse appears in some respects to be a concrete actualization of Artaud's plan for a theater of cruelty that, by destroying the morbid forms of Western civilization, would animate the living humanity of the individual that society had repressed.

15. Roger Planchon, "Conversation avec Roger Planchon. Propos récueillis par E. Copfermann," quoted in Jennifer Kumiega, *The Theatre of Grotowski* (London: Methuen, 1987), 128.

16. Cf. Mikhail Bakhtin's notion of the dialogical structure of narrative.

17. Kumiega, *The Theatre of Grotowski,* 81–82.

18. By his own account, he did not have specific knowledge of Artaud's work until

1964, when he demonstrated some of his own working practices for the benefit of RSC actors preparing Brook's "Theatre of Cruelty" season that year. Between 1964 and 1966 he was working with Cieslak on *The Constant Prince* (as discussed by Barba, above); in 1967, he published his essay on Artaud, "He Wasn't Entirely Himself."

19. Grotowski, *Towards a Poor Theatre*, 206.

20. Ibid.

21. Ibid., 135.

22. This "bag of tricks" was what Copeau referred to disparagingly as *cabotinage*, and what Meyerhold regarded as the primary resource of the actor.

23. Cicely Berry makes the same point in *The Actor and His Text*. She would have known about Grotowski's work at the time of his workshops for Peter Brook during rehearsals for *US* (1966) in London. Her approach suggests she had absorbed certain of Grotowski's ideas. The mid-1960s was a moment when acting teachers in Britain reoriented their work, transforming the universalist methods of teaching standard techniques into a pragmatic, holistic, and personal approach that treated every actor as an individual.

24. Grotowski, *Towards a Poor Theatre*, 139.

25. Ibid.

26. Ibid., 141.

27. Ibid., 142.

28. Although not identical with Michael Chekhov's work on actions, gestures, and qualities, these exercises in many respects resemble those designed by Chekhov to make every part of the body expressive.

29. Grotowski, *Towards a Poor Theatre*, 204.

30. Kristen Linklater has for a number of years been based in New York.

31. The approach is exemplified by Clifford Turner's *Voice and Speech for the Theatre*, which advocates and illustrates the system of intercostal diaphragmatic or rib-reserve breathing as a way of producing the extra power and resonance required to produce a beautiful and audible voice. A modification of the singer's technique, this method was encouraged by Saint-Denis, who employed singing teachers to teach voice at his theater schools in England.

32. Clearly, Viola Spolin and Keith Johnstone did not derive their praxis from Grotowski, although there are, in spite of the vast difference in aesthetic aims, striking parallels with aspects of their practice. Clive Barker's notion in *Theatre Games* that all technical exercises should take the form of games echoes Grotowski's "give and take."

33. Grotowski, *Holiday*, 215.

34. Ibid.

35. Leszek Kolodziejczyk, *On the Road to Active Culture*, 1978, in Schechner and Wolford, *The Grotowski Sourcebook*, 97–98.

36. Grotowski, *Theatre of Sources*, in Schechner and Wolford, *The Grotowski Sourcebook*, 261.

37. Grotowski, "The Art of the Beginner," in Schechner and Wolford, *The Grotowski Sourcebook*, 214.

38. Grotowski, "Tu Es Fils De Quelqu'un," in Schechner and Wolford, *The Grotowski Sourcebook*, 296.

39. Ibid.

40. Quoted in Schechner and Wolford, *The Grotowski Sourcebook*, 289.

41. Grotowski, "Tu Es Fils De Quelqu'un," 301.

42. Ibid., 302.

43. Ibid., 304.

44. Charles Marowitz, "Grotowski in Irvine: Breaking the Silence," in Schechner and Wolford, *The Grotowski Sourcebook,* 353, 354.

45. Grotowski, "Performer," in Schechner and Wolford, *The Grotowski Sourcebook,* 376.

46. Ibid., 378.

47. They are currently developing a new *Action,* but it remains to be seen whether or not this will assume the ritual status of the work elaborated under the guidance of Grotowski himself.

48. Ibid., 377.

Chapter 12

1. Although he claims at times to have made discoveries as a researcher, Brook has not communicated these in terms of a systematic discourse; this in no way undermines the success of the productions or the value of his explorations as a personal method of achieving them.

2. From the preface to Grotowski, *Towards a Poor Theatre,* 13.

3. Peter Brook, *The Empty Space* (Harmondsworth: Penguin, 1968).

4. One of the reasons that Brook refused to perform *The Mahabharata* in London was that no space comparable to Glasgow's Tramway could be made available for the production.

5. Grotowski, *Towards a Poor Theatre,* 14.

6. Peter Brook, "Peter Weiss's Kick," reprinted in *The Shifting Point* (London: Methuen, 1987), 45–47.

7. Ibid, 47.

8. Peter Brook, "Manifesto for the Sixties," in *The Shifting Point,* 54, 55.

9. Peter Brook, "Points of Radiance," in *The Shifting Point,* 94.

10. Peter Brook, "Peter Weiss's Kick," in *The Shifting Point,* 47.

11. David Williams, "Peter Brook's 'Great Poem of the World,'" in *Peter Brook: A Theatrical Casebook,* ed. David Williams (London: Methuen, 1992), 355.

12. Peter Brook, "What is a Shakespeare?" in *The Shifting Point,* 84, 85.

13. Peter Brook, "The Beck Connection," in *The Shifting Point,* 25–30.

14. There are parallels here with Eugenio Barba's eclectic method of adopting training exercises and techniques from across a wide range of cultures in order to sensitize his performers to the expressive possibilities of a variety of performance cultures.

15. Chaikin was later to be invited by Brook to work with actors during preparations for *US* and *Oedipus.*

16. Albert Hunt and Geoffrey Reeves, *Peter Brook* (Cambridge: Cambridge University Press, 1995), 73, 74.

17. Many of these exercises had become part of the repertoire of teachers at British drama schools by the end of the 1960s.

18. This was an exercise commonly used by Joseph Chaikin's Open Theater.

19. Many of Marowitz's sound-and-movement exercises are identical to those used by Joseph Chaikin; see Robert Pasolli, *A Book on the Open Theatre* (New York: Avon, 1970), 4–8.

20. This, of course, had been the ambition of all the great modern directors, from Stanislavski to Grotowski, although it was in practice often the case that productions— particularly productions of the classics—offered readings rather than happenings.

21. Brook's RSC *Antony and Cleopatra* (1978) is one example of a production that was not prepared over at least a number of months, but it was rehearsed for eight weeks—almost double the normal rehearsal period for a Shakespeare production at the RSC.

22. Charles Marowitz, "The Lear Log," in Williams, *Peter Brook,* 9.

23. Ibid.

24. Ibid.

25. Brook, "What is a Shakespeare?" 78, 79.

26. Charles Marowitz, review of *Oedipus* in *The Village Voice,* reprinted in Williams, *Peter Brook,* 124.

27. For a critical view of the contradictions evident in Brook's approach to actors in *US,* see Hunt and Reeves, *Peter Brook,* 112–20.

28. The Theatre of Cruelty showings were the result of eight weeks of exploration subsidized by Peter Hall from RSC funds and a Gulbenkian grant. *US* had a twelve-week rehearsal period, but that included the devising/writing of the show with the actors.

29. In this respect his later work has embodied Craig's theatrical ideals.

30. Quoted in Hunt and Reeves, *Peter Brook,* 150.

31. The title of one of his books on theater is *There Are No Secrets: Thoughts on Acting and Theatre* (London: Methuen, 1993).

32. In this respect, Brook has been as much influenced by Brecht's insistence that the actor should "show the showing" as he has been by the brilliant example of Meyerhold's techniques of histrionic and scenic defamiliarization.

33. J. C. Trewin, in Williams, *Peter Brook,* 64.

34. This particular aspect of Brook's rehearsal method had been central to Stanislavski's method of characterization, but Brook is less conservative with respect to the actor's function as a co-creator of the performance, insisting on the actor's responsibility to open herself fully to the existential questions posed by the fictional material.

35. During rehearsals for *The Ik,* actors playing Ik tribespeople built and inhabited an Ik stockade and enacted a great deal of material from Colin Turnbull's book about the tribe that never became part of the theatrical presentation.

36. The fact that many actors found the experience of working with Brook on particular productions difficult or profoundly unsettling suggests that his rejection of outmoded conventions and his insistence on untried forms of creative exploration often throws the performers back on their most basic human resources.

37. Hunt and Reeves, *Peter Brook,* 139.

38. Ibid., 154.

39. Ibid., 155.

40. Peter Brook, *Threads of Time: A Memoir* (London: Methuen, 1998), 224.

41. Brook's various journeys of discovery were contemporaneous with Grotowski's move beyond theater and with the beginning of Barba's many "migrations."

42. Hunt and Reeves, *Peter Brook,* 141.

43. Ibid., 184.

44. Ibid., 185.

45. Brook, *There are No Secrets,* 69.

46. Ernst Wendt in *Theater Heute,* quoted in Hunt and Reeves, *Peter Brook,* 171.

47. Williams, *Peter Brook,* 170.

48. See the accounts of the group's encounters with various African tribes in John Heilpern, *The Conference of the Birds* (Harmondsworth: Penguin, 1979), and of their work with El Teatro Campesino in Hunt and Reeves, *Peter Brook,* 195–96.

49. Peter Brook, quoted in Williams, *Peter Brook,* 171.

50. Essays critical of Brook's "orientalism" include Rustom Barucha's "Peter Brook's *Mahabharata:* A View from India," in *Theatre and the World* (New Delhi: Manohar, 1990), 94–120; and Gautam Dasgupta, "*The Mahabharata:* Peter Brook's 'Orientalism,'" in Bonnie Marranca and Gautam Dasgupta, *Interculturalism and Performance: Writings from PAJ* (New York: PAJ Publications, 1991), 75–81.

51. I do not believe that Brook's idea of adapting texts from other cultures or making performances with multicultural groups of actors is inherently immoral or politically suspect. He cannot be held responsible for the naïveté and hypocrisy of some practitioners who justify their cultural appropriations as interculturalism, ignoring the inequalities that that label may mask. Brook himself has never used the term.

52. Whereas Barba has invented the discipline of theater anthropology to achieve a transcultural understanding of comparative performance cultures, Brook has in effect been testing certain transcultural possibilities in practice.

53. Williams, *Peter Brook,* 375, 376.

Chapter 13

1. Eugenio Barba, *Alla Ricerca del Teatro Perduto* (Padua: Marsilio, 1965).

2. Eugenio Barba, *Beyond the Floating Islands* (New York: Performing Arts Journal, 1986), 193.

3. This idea is parallel to that implicit in Grotowski's post-theatrical notion of the value of performance as a research process.

4. Eugenio Barba, "The Third Theatre: The Legacy from Us to Ourselves," *New Theatre Quarterly* 8, no. 29 (1992): 7.

5. Barba, *Beyond the Floating Islands,* 246.

6. Eugenio Barba, "The Way of Refusal: The Theatre's Body-in-Life," *New Theatre Quarterly* 4, no. 16 (1988): 298.

7. Erik Axe Christofferson, *The Actor's Way* (London: Routledge, 1993), 192, 193.

8. Ferdinando Taviani, "The Odin Story," in Barba, *Beyond the Floating Islands,* 267.

9. Christofferson, *The Actor's Way,* 48.

10. Barba, *Beyond the Floating Islands,* 56.

11. Barba, *The Paper Canoe,* 35.

12. Although somewhat differently framed, Barba's concept of the pre-expressive resembles Grotowski's notion of sources. Grotowski speaks somewhat mystically about origins of performance before the stage of cultural "differentiation," whereas Barba looks synchronically across performance cultures for a transcultural phenomenon of performer-readiness.

13. Barba, *The Paper Canoe,* 9.

14. Barba has in a sense demonstrated the existence in certain traditions of performance (which he would call North Pole traditions) of Craig's desired control on the part

of the creative artist over the medium of her body. Barba's dilated body is the social body transformed into the material of performance art; Irving was the one South Pole performer whose "dilated body" was in Craig's opinion adequately formed for its expressive purpose. Barba's distinction between North and South Pole performers helps to explain why it is more likely that Craig would have found his ideal Über-marionette formed by the training that is a prerequisite of the highly conscious and codified performance traditions of the East. Indeed, without ever having studied non-Western theater forms systematically, Craig's own intuitions did lead him to refer to forms of Oriental theater in formulating his own ideas of performance. (See chap. 4.)

15. Barba, *The Paper Canoe,* 107.

16. In Britain, this arbitrary eclecticism is commonly manifested in the ignorance of practitioners: what they regard as a wholly intuitive approach is in fact characteristic of the dominant British tradition deriving from Copeau and inculcated through the work of Michel Saint-Denis.

17. In this respect, Barba differs from Laban, who although aware of the different function of effort in daily and extra-daily contexts, nevertheless analyzed the effort component of instrumental and artistic movement on the same grid. Laban's notion of the modeling of energy starts from the pre-expressive level and, in my view, is rather more coherent.

18. Christofferson, *The Actor's Way,* 79, 80.

19. Ibid., 79.

20. This idea directly parallels Laban's conception of the economical performance of effort actions. It may well be a deliberate echo of Meyerhold's aim that biomechanics would train the performer to achieve the most economical expenditure of energy.

21. Although in *The Paper Canoe* Barba refers to Laban's system of movement notation, he seems unaware of the full significance of Laban's system of effort actions, and of the relationship Laban traces between the dynamic quality of effort and its spatial forms. (See chap. 6.)

22. Ibid., 40.

23. This idea recapitulates some of the thoughts of Craig and Meyerhold on the abstraction from real behavior that forms a necessary precondition for performance as art.

24. Barba, *The Paper Canoe,* 29.

25. Ibid., 32.

26. Ibid.

27. There are clear parallels between Barba and Laban on this point, although Barba's reflections lack the coherence of Laban's conceptualization of the scale of effort actions. (See chap. 6.)

28. Quoted in Barba, *The Paper Canoe,* 52.

29. Again, cf. Laban's concept of effort, chapter 6.

30. Barba, *The Paper Canoe,* 62.

31. Ibid., 63.

32. As a South Pole practitioner, Michael Chekhov's treatment of the way energy is paradoxically manifested in both mental and physical aspects is clearly parallel to that of many North Pole traditions. Chekhov's ideas serve in Barba's view to demonstrate the common problems faced at the pre-expressive level by practitioners in both North and South Pole traditions.

33. This postmodern approach to the performer's relationship to the mise-en-scène

was not shared by Grotowski, who insisted that the actor should re-experience the original associations that created the score, even though they may differ from the meaning as perceived by the audience.

34. Barba, *The Paper Canoe,* 133.

35. Else Marie Laukvik, interviewed in Christofferson, *The Actor's Way,* 33.

Conclusion

1. David Thomson, *Movie Man,* cited in Ronald Hayman, *Techniques of Acting* (London: Methuen, 1969), 133.

2. Michelangelo Antonioni, interview in *Film Culture* 22–23 (1961), cited in Hayman, *Techniques of Acting,* 135.

3. Peter Brook's comments on the performance of Jack Gelber's *The Connection* in 1960 correctly identify the tradition of acting as behavior. (See chap. 12.)

4. This is precisely the reason why Jacques Lecoq and Anne Bogart have elaborated training programs that stress the physical and theatrical basis of performance composition.

5. See David Mamet, *True and False: Heresy and Common Sense in Acting* (London: Faber and Faber, 1998). Mamet's real target is Strasberg's Method, which he wrongly attributes to Stanislavski.

6. The idea that language generates meaning by means of a series of games was first promulgated by the philosopher Ludwig Wittgenstein.

7. See Elin Diamond, *Unmaking Mimesis* (London: Routledge, 1997).

8. These include RADA (Royal Academy of Dramatic Art), Central School of Speech and Drama, Guildhall School of Music and Drama, Webber-Douglas Academy, LAMDA (London Academy of Music and Dramatic Art), Mountview Theatre School, and the Bristol Old Vic Theatre School. The Drama Centre and East 15 are exceptions, teaching syllabi based on aspects of the praxis of Stanislavski and Laban.

9. The most notable is the Juilliard School in New York.

10. Uta Hagen continued to teach at her own studio in New York until her death in 2004, and there are Actors Studios in New York and Los Angeles, and Lee Strasberg Institutes in various parts of the Western world.

11. To a certain extent, I believe this has happened with the techniques of Tadashi Suzuki, whose strict training regime has become fashionable among alternative practitioners in Britain and the United States, where it is often taught as a preparation for the kind of performance that has virtually no use for its techniques.

12. Schechner is known both as a theater scholar and the director who founded the Performance Garage in New York and created a number of experiments in environmental theater in the late 1960s and 1970s.

13. Tadashi Suzuki, "Culture is the Body," in Marranca and Dasgupta, *Interculturalism and Performance,* 241.

14. Among the institutions that offer Suzuki training as part of their program are the American Conservatory Theater in San Francisco, the School of Drama at the University of Washington, Seattle, and Anne Bogart's SITI, a summer program based at Skidmore College, Saratoga, New York.

15. An example of such cultural colonialism is Disney's *The Lion King,* which makes stunning use of music and dance traditions from South Africa, as well as puppets from a variety of non-Western cultures to sell the rather simplistic cartoon that is its core content.

Select Bibliography

Adler, Stella. *The Technique of Acting*. Toronto: Bantam, 1988.

Alexander, F. Mathias. *The Resurrection of the Body*. Ed. Edward Maisel. Boston: Shambhala, 1969.

Appia, Adolphe. *Essays, Scenarios and Drawings*. Trans. Walter Volbach. Ann Arbor, Mich.: UMI Research Press, 1989.

Artaud, Antonin. *Selected Writings*. Ed. Susan Sontag. Trans. Helen Weaver. Berkeley and Los Angeles: University of California Press, 1976.

———. *The Theatre and its Double*. Trans. Victor Corti. London: Calder and Boyars, 1970.

Auslander, Philip. *From Acting to Performance*. London: Routledge, 1997.

Bablet, Denis. *The Theatre of Edward Gordon Craig*. Trans. Daphne Woodward. London: Eyre Methuen, 1981.

Barba, Eugenio. *Beyond the Floating Islands*. New York: Performing Arts Journal Publications, 1986.

———. *The Floating Islands*. Holstebro, Denmark: Odin Teatret Forlag, 1979.

———. *The Paper Canoe*. London: Routledge, 1995.

Barba, Eugenio, and Nicola Savarese. *A Dictionary of Theatre Anthropology*. London: Routledge, 1992.

Barber, Stephen. *Antonin Artaud: Blows and Bombs*. London: Faber and Faber, 1993.

Barlow, Wilfred. *The Alexander Principle*. London: Victor Gollancz, 1973.

Bartram, Graham, and Anthony Waine, eds. *Brecht in Perspective*. London: Longman, 1982.

Barucha, Rustom. *Theatre and the World*. London: Routledge, 1993.

Beacham, Richard. *Adolphe Appia: Artist and Visionary of the Modern Theatre*. London: Harwood Academic Publishers, Gordon and Breach, 1994.

———. *Adolphe Appia: Texts on Theatre*. London: Routledge, 1993.

Benedetti, Jean. *Stanislavski: A Biography*. London: Methuen, 1990.

———. *Stanislavski: The System. An Introduction*. London: Methuen, 1981.

———. *Stanislavski and the Actor*. London: Methuen, 1998.

Benjamin, Walter. *Understanding Brecht*. Trans. Anna Bostock. London: New Left Books, 1974.

Berry, Cicely. *The Actor and His Text*. London: Harrop, 1987.

———. *Voice and the Actor*. London: Virgin Books, 1989.

Billington, Michael. *The Modern Actor*. London: Hamish Hamilton, 1973.

Black, Lendley. *Mikhail Chekhov as Actor, Director and Teacher*. Ann Arbor, MI: UMI Research Press, 1987.

Blumenthal, Eileen. *Joseph Chaikin*. Cambridge: Cambridge University Press, 1982.

Boal, Augusto. *Games for Actors and Non-Actors*. London: Routledge, 1992.

———. *Legislative Theatre: Using Performance to Make Laws*. London: Routledge, 1990.

———. *The Rainbow of Desire*. London: Routledge, 1995.

———. *Theatre of the Oppressed*. London: Pluto Press, 1979.

Bogart, Anne. *A Director Prepares: Seven Essays on Art and Theatre*. London: Routledge, 2001.

Boleslavsky, Richard. *Acting: The First Six Lessons*. New York: Theatre Arts Books, 1933.

Bradby, David, and David Williams. *Director's Theatre*. Basingstoke: Macmillan, 1988.

Braun, Edward. *The Director and the Stage*. London: Methuen, 1982.

———. *Meyerhold: A Revolution in Theatre*. London: Methuen, 1995.

Brecht, Bertolt. *Brecht on Theatre*. Ed. John Willett. London: Methuen, 1964.

———. *The Messingkauf Dialogues*. Trans. John Willett. London: Eyre Methuen, 1965.

Brestoff, Richard. *The Great Acting Teachers and Their Methods*. Lyme, N.H.: Smith and Kraus, 1995.

Brook, Peter. *The Empty Space*. Harmondsworth: Penguin, 1968.

———. *The Shifting Point*. London: Methuen, 1987.

———. *There Are No Secrets: Thoughts on Acting and Theatre*. London: Methuen, 1993.

———. *Threads of Time: A Memoir*. London: Methuen, 1998.

Callow, Simon. *Being an Actor*. London: Methuen, 1984.

Carlson, Marvin. *Performance: A Critical Introduction*. London: Routledge, 1996.

Carnicke, Sharon Marie. *Stanislavsky in Focus*. London: Harwood Academic Publishers, Gordon and Breach, 1998.

Chaikin, Joseph. *The Presence of the Actor*. New York: Athenaeum, 1972.

Chekhov, Michael. *On the Technique of Acting*. New York: Harper Perennial, 1991.

———. *To the Actor*. New York: Barnes and Noble, 1985.

Christoffersen, Eric Axe. *The Actor's Way*. London: Routledge, 1993.

Clurman, Harold. *The Fervent Years: The Group Theatre and the Thirties*. New York: Alfred A. Knopf, 1950.

Cole, Toby, ed. *Acting: A Handbook of the Stanislavski Method*. New York: Crown, 1947.

Cole, Toby, and Helen Krich Chinoy, eds. *Actors on Acting: The Theories, Techniques and Practices of the World's Great Actors, Told in Their Own Words*. New York: Crown, 1970.

———, eds. *Directors on Directing: A Source Book of the Modern Theatre*. New York: Bobbs-Merrill, 1963.

Copeau, Jacques. *Texts on Theatre*. Ed. and trans. John Rudlin and Norman H. Paul. London: Routledge, 1990.

Counsell, Colin. *Signs of Performance: An Introduction to Twentieth Century Theatre*. London: Routledge, 1996.

Craig, Edward Gordon. *On the Art of the Theatre*. London: Heinemann Educational Books, 1968.

Decroux, Étienne. *Words on Mime*. Trans. Mark Piper. Pomona, Calif.: Mime Journal, 1985.

Diamond, Elin. *Unmaking Mimesis*. London: Routledge, 1997.

Dixon, Michael Bigelow, and Joel A. Smith, eds. *Anne Bogart: Viewpoints*. Lyme, N.H.: Smith and Kraus, 1995.

Easty, Edward Dwight. *On Method Acting*. New York: Ivy Books, 1981.

Eddershaw, Margaret. *Performing Brecht: Fifty Years of British Performances*. London: Routledge, 1996.

Edwards, Christine. *The Stanislavski Heritage*. New York: New York University Press, 1965.

Esslin, Martin. *Artaud*. London: Fontana, 1976.

Feldenkrais, Moshe. *Awareness Through Movement*. Harmondsworth: Penguin, 1980.

Frost, Anthony, and Ralph Yarrow. *Improvisation in Drama*. Basingstoke: Macmillan, 1990.

Fuegi, John. *Bertolt Brecht: Chaos According to Plan*. Cambridge: Cambridge University Press, 1987.

Garfield, David. *A Player's Passion: The Story of the Actors Studio*. New York: Macmillan, 1980.

Gaskill, William. *A Sense of Direction: Life at the Royal Court*. London: Faber and Faber, 1988.

Goldberg, RoseLee. *Performance Art: From Futurism to the Present*. London: Thames and Hudson, 1988.

Goorney, Howard. *The Theatre Workshop Story*. London: Methuen, 1981.

Gorchakov, Nikolai. *Stanislavski Directs*. Trans. Miriam Goldina. New York: Funk and Wagnall, 1954.

Gordon, Mel. *The Stanislavski Technique: Russia*. New York: Applause, 1987.

Grotowski, Jerzy. *Towards a Poor Theatre*. New York: Simon and Schuster, 1968.

Hagen, Uta, with Haskell Frankel. *Respect for Acting*. New York: Macmillan, 1973.

Hayman, Ronald. *Artaud and After*. Oxford: Oxford University Press, 1977.

———. *Techniques of Acting*. London: Methuen, 1969.

Heilpern, John. *Conference of the Birds*. Harmondsworth: Penguin, 1979.

Hirsch, Foster. *A Method to Their Madness: The History of the Actors Studio*. New York: Norton, 1984.

Hodge, Alison, ed. *Twentieth Century Actor Training*. London: Routledge, 2000.

Hodgson, John. *Mastering Movement: The Life and Work of Rudolf Laban*. London: Methuen, 2001.

Hoover, Marjorie. *Meyerhold: The Art of Conscious Theater*. Amherst: University of Massachusetts Press, 1974.

Hornby, Richard. *The End of Acting: A Radical View*. New York: Applause, 1992.

Hunt, Albert, and Geoffrey Reeves. *Peter Brook*. Cambridge: Cambridge University Press, 1995.

Innes, Christopher. *Avant-Garde Theatre, 1892–1992*. London: Routledge, 1993.

———. *Edward Gordon Craig*. Cambridge: Cambridge University Press, 1983.

Kirby, E. T., ed. *Total Theatre*. New York: Dutton, 1969.

Krasner, David, ed. *Method Acting Reconsidered: Theory, Practice, Future*. Basingstoke: Macmillan, 2000.

Kumiega, Jennifer. *The Theatre of Grotowski*. London: Methuen, 1985.

Kurtz, Maurice. *Jacques Copeau: Biography of a Theater*. Carbondale: Southern Illinois University Press, 1999.

Laban, Rudolf. *The Mastery of Movement*. London: MacDonald and Evans, 1960.

———. *Modern Educational Dance*. London: MacDonald and Evans, 1975.

Laban, Rudolf, and F. C. Lawrence. *Effort*. London: MacDonald and Evans, 1947.

Law, Alma, and Mel Gordon. *Meyerhold, Eisenstein and Biomechanics*. Jefferson, N.C.: McFarland, 1996.

Leach, Robert. *Vsevolod Meyerhold*. Cambridge: Cambridge University Press, 1989.

Lecoq, Jacques. *The Moving Body*. Trans. David Bradby. London: Methuen, 2000.

Leiter, Samuel L. *From Stanislavsky to Barrault: Representative Directors of the European Stage*. New York: Greenwood Press, 1991.

Lewes, George Henry. *On Actors and the Art of Acting*. New York: Grove Press, 1966.

Lewis, Robert. *Method—or Madness*. New York: Samuel French, 1958.

Littlewood, Joan. *Joan's Book*. London: Minerva, 1995.

Mamet, David. *True and False: Heresy and Common Sense for the Actor*. London: Faber and Faber, 1998.

Marowitz, Charles. *The Act of Being*. London: Secker and Warburg, 1978.

Marowitz, Charles, and Simon Trussler, eds. *Theatre at Work*. London: Methuen, 1967.

Meisner, Sanford, and Dennis Longwell. *Sanford Meisner on Acting*. New York: Vintage, 1987.

Meyerhold, Vsevolod. *Meyerhold on Theatre*. Ed. and trans. Edward Braun. London: Eyre Methuen, 1969.

Milling, Jane, and Graham Ley. *Modern Theories of Performance*. Basingstoke and New York: Palgrave, 2001.

Mitter, Shomit. *Systems of Rehearsal*. London: Routledge.

Moore, Sonia. *Training an Actor: The Stanislavski System in Class*. Harmondsworth: Penguin, 1979.

Munk, Erika, ed. *Stanislavski and America*. New York: Hill and Wang, 1965.

Newlove, Jean. *Laban for Actors and Dancers*. London: Nick Hern, 1993.

Oida, Yoshi, with Lorna Marshall. *An Actor Adrift*. London: Methuen, 1992.

Pasolli, Robert. *A Book on the Open Theatre*. New York: Avon, 1970.

Pavis, Patrice, ed. *The Intercultural Performance Reader*. London: Routledge, 1996.

Richards, Thomas. *At Work with Grotowski on Physical Actions*. London: Routledge, 1995.

———. *The Edge-Point of Performance*. Pontedera, Italy: Documentation Series of the Workcenter of Jerzy Grotowski, 1997.

Roach, Joseph. *The Player's Passion: Studies in the Science of Acting*. Ann Arbor: University of Michigan Press, 1993.

Rodenburg, Patsy. *The Actor Speaks: Voice and the Performer*. London: Methuen, 1998.

Rudlin, John. *Jacques Copeau*. Cambridge: Cambridge University Press, 1986.

Rudnitsky, Konstantin. *Meyerhold the Director*. Ann Arbor, Mich.: Ardis, 1981.

Saint-Denis, Michel. *Theatre: The Rediscovery of Style*. London: Heinemann, 1960.

———. *Training for the Theatre*. London: Heinemann, 1982.

Schechner, Richard. *Essays in Performance Theory, 1970–1976*. New York: Drama Book Specialists, 1977.

Schechner, Richard, and Lisa Wolford, eds. *The Grotowski Sourcebook*. London: Routledge, 1997.

Schmidt, Paul, ed. *Meyerhold at Work*. Austin: University of Texas Press, 1980.

Schutzman, Mady, and Jan Cohen-Cruz, eds. *Playing Boal: Theatre, Therapy, Activism*. London: Routledge, 1994.

Sellin, Eric. *The Dramatic Concepts of Antonin Artaud*. Chicago: University of Chicago Press, 1968.

Smith, A. C. H. *Orghast at Persepolis*. London: Eyre Methuen, 1972.

Stanislavski, Constantin. *An Actor Prepares*. Trans. Elizabeth Reynolds Hapgood. London: Methuen, 1980.

————. *Building a Character*. Trans. Elizabeth Reynolds Hapgood. London: Methuen, 1968.

————. *Creating a Role*. Trans. Elizabeth Reynolds Hapgood, London: Methuen, 1961.

————. *My Life in Art*. Trans. J. J. Robbins. Harmondsworth: Penguin, 1967.

Strasberg, Lee. *A Dream of Passion: The Development of the Method*. Boston: Little, Brown, 1987.

————. *Strasberg at the Actors Studio: Tape-Recorded Sessions*. Ed. R. Hethmon. New York: Theatre Communications Group, 1965.

Suzuki, Tadashi. *The Way of Acting: The Theatre Writings of Tadashi Suzuki*. New York: Theatre Communications Group, 1986.

Taylor, George. *Players and Performances in the Victorian Theatre*. Manchester: Manchester University Press, 1989.

Temkine, Raymonde. *Grotowski*. Trans. Alex Szoygi. New York: Avon, 1972.

Thomson, Peter, and Glenda Sacks, eds. *The Cambridge Companion to Brecht*. Cambridge: Cambridge University Press, 1994.

Toporkov, Vasili. *Stanislavski in Rehearsal: The Final Years*. Trans. Christine Edwards. New York: Theatre Arts Books, 1979.

Trewin, John C. *Peter Brook: A Biography*. London: Macdonald, 1971.

Tytell, John. *The Living Theatre: Art, Exile and Outrage*. London: Methuen, 1997.

van Gyseghem, Andre. *Theatre in Soviet Russia*. London: Faber and Faber, 1943.

Vineberg, Steven. *Method Actors: Three Generations of an American Acting Style*. New York: Schirmer, 1991.

Wardle, Irving. *The Theatres of George Devine*. London: Eyre Methuen, 1979.

Watson, Ian. *Towards a Third Theatre: Eugenio Barba and the Odin Teatret*. London: Routledge, 1995.

Whitton, David. *Stage Directors in Modern France*. Manchester: Manchester University Press, 1987.

Willett, John. *The Theatre of Erwin Piscator*. London: Methuen, 1986.

Williams, David, ed. *Peter Brook: A Theatrical Casebook*. London: Methuen, 1992.

Worrall, Nick. *The Moscow Art Theatre*. London: Routledge, 1996.

Wright, Elizabeth. *Postmodern Brecht: A Re-Presentation*. London: Routledge, 1989.

Zarrilli, Philip. *Acting (Re)Considered, Theories and Practices*. London: Routledge, 1995.

Index